Trials of Engagement

Diplomatic Studies

Series Editor

Jan Melissen

Netherlands Institute of International Relations 'Clingendael'

VOLUME 6

Trials of Engagement

The Future of US Public Diplomacy

Edited by
Ali Fisher and Scott Lucas

MARTINUS
NIJHOFF
PUBLISHERS

LEIDEN • BOSTON
2011

This book is printed on acid-free paper.

Library of Congress Cataloging-in-Publication Data

Trials of engagement : the future of US public diplomacy / edited by Ali Fisher and Scott Lucas.
p. cm. -- (Diplomatic studies, ISSN 1872-8863 ; v.6)
Includes index.
ISBN 978-90-04-17940-0 (hardcover : alk. paper) 1. United States--Relations. I. Fisher, Ali. II. Lucas, Scott.
JZ1480.T75 2011
327.73--dc22

2010041928

ISSN 1872-8863
ISBN 978 90 04 17940 0

CONTENTS

LIST OF CONTRIBUTORS

NAREN CHITTY A.M. is Foundation Chair in International Communication at Macquarie University, Sydney, Australia. He was awarded the Order of Australia in 2009 "for services to education, particularly in the field of international communication as a researcher and an academic and to a range of professional associations". He was a public diplomat in Washington D.C. during the Reagan Administration.

DARYL COPELAND is an analyst, author and educator specializing in foreign policy, global issues, diplomacy and public management. As a Canadian diplomat and executive from 1981-2009, he served abroad in Thailand, Ethiopia, New Zealand and Malaysia, and his first book, Guerrilla Diplomacy: Rethinking International Relations (Lynne Rienner Publishers) was released in 2009 (see www.guerrilladiplomacy.com). Mr. Copeland is a peer reviewer for *Canadian Foreign Policy,* the *International Journal,* and *The Hague Journal of Diplomacy,* and a member of the Editorial Board of the journal *Place Branding and Public Diplomacy.*

NICHOLAS J. CULL is professor of Public Diplomacy at the University of Southern California in Los Angeles, where he directs the Masters Degree in Public Diplomacy. He has written widely on the history and practice of public diplomacy and his publications include The Cold War and the United States Information Agency: American propaganda and public diplomacy, 1945-1989 (Cambridge, 2008) which has recently appeared in paperback. He is president of the International Association for Media and History.

ALI FISHER has been Director of Mappa Mundi Consulting since 2008, where he works as an independent public diplomacy strategist and researcher. He specializes in providing insight to enhance organizational strategy and evaluation through network analysis. He regularly advises governments, charities, companies, and NGO on best practice for online engagement, collaboration and network building. Ali recently wrote a chapter on the use of social media following the

Iranian election in Yahya R. Kamalipour, Media, Power, and Politics in the Digital Age; The 2009 Presidential Election Uprising in Iran (Rowman & Littlefield, November, 2010) and edited The Playbook; Case Studies of Engagement with Nick Cull. He is honorary research fellow in the School of Clinical and Experimental Medicine at the University of Birmingham where he also completed his PhD in the Department of American Studies.

Elizabeth Fox has written several books and articles on the development of Latin American broadcasting systems, including: Latin Politics Global Media, (co-editor) Austin: University of Texas Press, 2002, From Tango to Telenovela: a History of Broadcasting in the Americas, London: John Libbey, 1997; "History of Latin American Broadcasting," Cambridge History of Latin America, Cambridge University Press: New York, 1995; Media and Politics in Latin America: the Struggle for Democracy, London: SAGE, 1988 She is an Adjunct Professor at the School of International Service at American University. She currently works for the U.S. Agency for International Development in Washington DC. "The views expressed in this article are those of the author and do not necessarily represent those of the U.S. Government."

Eytan Gilboa is Professor of Communication and International Relations and Director of the Center for International Communication at Bar-Ilan University in Israel. He is also a Visiting Professor of Public Diplomacy at the University of Southern California. He has written several books and numerous works on international communication, public diplomacy and American-Israeli relations. He has served as a consultant to the Ministries of Foreign Affairs and Defense.

John Robert Kelley is an assistant professor at the School of International Service, American University. He received his PhD in International Relations from the London School of Economics. He has been an active participant in the establishment of a research program in public diplomacy; in 2007 he was selected to be a postdoctoral fellow in public diplomacy at the Center for International Studies, University of Southern California. His recent publications on the subject include a contribution to The Routledge Handbook of Public Diplomacy (edited by Nancy Snow and Philip M. Taylor), and articles in Diplomacy & Statecraft, Orbis and The Hague Journal of Diplomacy.

LINA KHATIB is a Program Manager at the Center on Democracy, Development, and the Rule of Law at Stanford University, where she manages the Program on Good Governance and Political Reform in the Arab World. Her research interests focus on the intersections between media and politics in the Middle East.

SCOTT LUCAS is Professor of American Studies at the University of Birmingham, United Kingdom, and the creator of EAWorldView. He is the author/editor of nine books and more than 50 major articles on US and British foreign policy from 1945 to the present.

DAVID RYAN works in the School of History and is Associate Dean, The Graduate School, University College Cork, Ireland. He is the author and editor of numerous books and articles including US-Sandinista Diplomatic Relations (1995), US Foreign Policy in World History (2000), The United States and Europe (2003), and Frustrated Empire (2007). He is the co-editor of The United States and Decolonization (2000), Vietnam in Iraq (2007), and America and Iraq (2009). He is currently completing a book on US Collective Memory and Intervention since 1969.

GILES SCOTT-SMITH is a senior researcher with the Roosevelt Study Center and Associate Professor in International Relations at the Roosevelt Academy, both in Middelburg, the Netherlands. At the beginning of 2009 he was appointed the Ernst van der Beugel Chair in the Diplomatic History of Transatlantic Relations since WW II at Leiden University. His research covers the role of non-state actors and public diplomacy in the maintenance of inter-state (particularly transatlantic) relations, and their contribution to the ideological 'battle of ideas' during the Cold War and beyond. His publications include Networks of Empire: The U.S. State Department's Foreign Leader Program in the Netherlands, France, and Britain 1950–70 (Peter Lang 2008), The Politics of Apolitical Culture: The Congress for Cultural Freedom, the CIA, and Post-war American Hegemony (Routledge 2002), and numerous articles in journals such as British Journal of Politics and International Relations, Cold War History, Revue Francaise d'Etudes Americaines, and the Annals of the American Academy of Political and Social Science.

Biljana Scott was trained as a linguist (BA in Chinese, M.Phil and D.Phil in Linguistics, University of Oxford). She is a Senior Lecturer in Political Language and Public Diplomacy at DiploFoundation (Geneva and Malta), and a Faculty Lecturer in Chinese Linguistics at the University of Oxford. All her research interests, both professional and personal, concern the way in which language influences the way we think about the world and act upon it. They include political rhetoric, public speaking, public diplomacy, photography and poetry. Dr Scott runs workshops on Language and Diplomacy for a variety of clients: senior EU officials (DG Relex Diplomatic training programme), Ministries of Foreign Affairs and Diplomatic Academies worldwide, Universities and the private sector. Topics covered include: Building Relationships; Handling Disagreement; Understanding the Unsaid; Constructive Ambiguity; Standing Firm; and the Language of Negotiation and Persuasion.

Bevan Sewell is a Lecturer in American History at the University of Nottingham. He has published articles in Diplomatic History and the English Historical Review, and is presently working on a study of US economic policy towards Latin America.

Nachman Shai is a Member of the Israeli Parliament. He received his PhD in public communication from Bar-Ilan University. He held senior positions including spokesperson for Israel's UN delegation, the Embassy in Washington, DC, the Minister of Defense, and the Israel Defense Forces. He also served as Director General of the Ministry of Science, the Army Radio and the Second Television and Radio Authority.

Phil Taylor is Professor of International Communications in the Institute of Communications Studies at the University of Leeds. His many publications include 'Munitions of the Mind: a history of propaganda from the ancient world to the present day' (3rd edition 2003); 'Global Communications, International Affairs and the Media since 1945' (1997), 'British Propaganda in the 20th Century: Selling Democracy' (1999), 'Shooting the Messenger: the political impact of war reporting' (co-authored with Paul Moorcraft, Potomac, 2008) and the Routledge Handbook of Public Diplomacy (co-edited with Nancy Snow, 2008). His latest publication is as contributing author to 'Pockets of Resistance: British news media, war and theory in the 2003 invasion of Iraq' (Piers Robinson, Peter Goddard, Kate Parry, Craig Murray, 2010).

R.S. ZAHARNA is an Associate Professor in the School of Communication, American University in Washington, DC. She specializes in intercultural and international strategic communication, with an emphasis on culture and communication in the Arab and Islamic regions and relational approaches in public diplomacy, and is author of Battles to Bridges: US Strategic Communication and Public Diplomacy after 9/11. In addition to her writings on public diplomacy, she has repeatedly testified before the US Congress and has addressed diplomatic, military and corporate officials on cross-cultural communication and public diplomacy, including the United Nations, World Bank, USAID, and NATO. She holds an undergraduate degree from Georgetown University and a doctorate from Columbia University.

INTRODUCTION

Ali Fisher and Scott Lucas

In the first instance, public diplomacy is a practice conducted by those seeking to influence the behaviour of communities overseas. Whether or not those pursuing theoretical concepts ever agree if public diplomacy, or a "New Public Diplomacy" is an academic discipline in its own right, individuals and organisations will continue to exploit the forms of influence available through its deployment.[1]

The desire to have influence is not new, of course. Public diplomacy received general recognition and significant scholarly attention during the Cold War, and that attention was renewed after 11 September 2001. Public diplomacy is now recognised as "one of the most salient political communication issues in the 21st century".[2] However, the focus of this collection is the emergence of a new dimension in Public Diplomacy; the movement away from audiences as passive objects experiencing Public Diplomacy (or non-kinetic military operations) to cooperation with active, autonomous participants capable of involvement in a complex global "network society".

Gone are the imagined herds of potential followers with hearts and minds only capable of being won over to your side or that of the enemy. The public diplomacy of the 21st century will rest on a view of these communities as "participants" and potential collaborators with whom to cooperate and co-create. This approach recognises networks of connections between communities, highlighted by mathematicians and sociologists in the small world experiments.[3] The proliferation of numerous forms of digital media accelerate the imperative and

---

[1] See, Philip Seib. *Toward a New Public Diplomacy: Redirecting U.S. Foreign Policy* (2009) & Jan Melissen, *The New Public Diplomacy* (2006).

[2] Snow / Taylor, Routledge Public Diplomacy Handbook, (2009) p. ix.

[3] Travers, Jeffrey & Stanley Milgram. 1969. "An Experimental Study of the Small World Problem." Sociometry, Vol. 32, No. 4, pp. 425–443.

For limitations of this study see:

Judith S Kleinfeld, "The Small World Problem", *Society*, January / February 2002.

Schnettler, Sebastian. 2009. "A structured overview of 50 years of small-world research" Social Networks, 31(3), pp. 165–178.

potential for genuine cooperation with communities, rather than the dominant approach in the 20th Century which subjected audiences to competitive assertions of identity, policy, and soft power.

This is the foreign policy equivalent of the shift from ecosphere to ecosphere; the future of public diplomacy is not "competing to see who can have the biggest 'I', the most entitled self".[4] It is to find effective ways of working collaboratively for collective benefit within the ecosphere of the network society. As Admiral Mike Mullen, US Chairman of the Joint Chiefs of Staff has stated, "No one nation can meet the challenges of an interconnected world acting alone."[5]

Writing about the social construction of leadership, Keith Grint has used Rittell and Webber's typology of "Tame" and "Wicked" problems to argue, "A *Tame Problem* may be complicated but is resolvable through unilinear acts because there is a point where the problem is resolved." In contrast;

> A *Wicked Problem* is complex, rather than just complicated, it is often intractable, there is no unilinear solution, moreover, there is no "stopping" point, it is novel, any apparent "solution" often generates other "problems", and there is no "right" or "wrong" answer, but there are better or worse alternatives.[6]

Many Foreign Policy challenges with which public diplomacy is engaged closely resemble *wicked* problems. And, as Grint posits, "The leader's role with a Wicked Problem is to ask the right *questions* rather than provide the right *answers* because the answers may not be self-evident and will require a collaborative process to make any kind of progress."

For public diplomacy, this entails collective decisions and collaborative processes rather than assertions that one country leads and others should follow. This collection identifies the limitations of current public diplomacy and offers perspectives on the benefit that could be achieved by a collaborative approach.

---

[4] Aaron Elliot, Thoughts, 2003.
http://www.aelliott.com/pdf/thoughts/egosphere.pdf

[5] Admiral Mike Mullen, chairman of the Joint Chiefs of Staff *Kansas State University, Manhattan, Kansas Wednesday, March 03, 2010.*

[6] Keith Grint, "Problems, problems, problems: The social construction of "leadership", *Human Relations*, 2005, vol, 58, pp. 1467–1494.

How Did We Get Here? (I Know We're not in Kansas)

The shift toward a genuinely new Public diplomacy is much more than the references to "engagement" which appear, for example, in the Djerejian, Princeton Project on National Security, and CSIS "Smart Power" reports.[7] Equally, this approach does not recognise a false distinction between "engagement" and "influence". Unless practitioners abolish the identification of priority regions or groups and put equal effort into acting with every individual globally, public diplomacy will *always* be about influence. It is the type of influence and the approach deployed to achieve it which distinguishes one form of public diplomacy from another.

In a 2008 article, Eytan Gilboa has illustrated and critiqued public diplomacy's constantly-evolving definitions, practice, and theoretical concepts,[8] the majority of which are egocentric with their focus on informing others and promoting understanding. Some have expanded these conceptions. In the opening of his collection *The New Public Diplomacy*, Jan Melissen proposed that public diplomacy was "the relationship between diplomats and the foreign publics with which they work". More recently, Nick Cull has focused on "an international actor's attempt to manage the international environment through engagement with a foreign public", broadening the number of actors and potential methods.[9] However, even if conceived as a two-way street, many past and present interpretations of public diplomacy identify discrete actors projecting messages back and forth. This ignores or marginalises a future public diplomacy marked by organisations cooperating and collaborating to achieve shared goals and influence.

Beyond the evolving theoretical debates, there are struggles over the numerous labels and definitions within the field of influence—propaganda, soft power, cultural diplomacy and public diplomacy—

---

[7] Edward Djerejian, *Changing Minds Winning Peace; A new strategic direction for U.S. Public Diplomacy in the Arab & Muslim World*, Report submitted to the Committee on Appropriations US House of Representatives, October 2003.

G. John Ikenberry and Anne-Marie Slaughter, *Forging a World of Liberty Under Law, U.S. National Security In The 21st Century*, Final Report of The Princeton Project on National Security, September 2006

Craig Cohen, Joseph Nye and Richard Armitage, *A Smarter, More Secure America*, Report of the CSIS Commission on Smart Power, November 2007.

[8] Eytan Gilboa, "Searching for a Theory of Public Diplomacy", *The ANNALS of the American Academy of Political and Social Science* 2008; 616; See particularly pp. 55–58.

[9] Cull, Nicholas. *Public Diplomacy: Lessons from the Past*. LA 2007, p. 6.

each with multiple definitions, interpretations, and particular meaning for the user. For example, the *Auswärtige Amt* (German Foreign Office) employed numerous labels before resorting to the English "Public Diplomacy".[10] Equally, the strained distinction and shifting line between cultural relations and public diplomacy in the UK owes much to the competing priorities of government funding and an appearance of independence.[11]

Within these debates, one of the greatest tensions is whether it is an exclusive or inclusive definition, a definition which seeks to assert ownership over the territory or one recognising and embracing the contribution and collaboration of multiple actors from numerous fields. In this context there are those who assert narrowly that public diplomacy acts "as an agent of government", and work conducted independently from government should be thought of as a separate concept.[12] In contrast, Nancy Snow and Philip Taylor take an inclusive approach:

> The new social groups involved in public diplomacy's articulation and formulation have made the topic of public diplomacy (and its negative, pejorative corollary: propaganda) recognizable and meaningful to a varied and vast arena of publics,[13]

This argument for the broader understanding of public diplomacy with multiple actors and stakeholders is reinforced by the White Oak Recommendations for US public diplomacy and the *Survey of Current Proposals and Recommendations* produced by RAND.[14] Rather than isolate public diplomacy in a narrowly defined government silo, these broader perspectives embed the discipline in the complex, contemporary understandings of network society.

---

[10] Fisher / Bröckerhoff, Options for Influence, (2008) p. 3.

[11] See Lord Carter of Coles Public Diplomacy Review, December 2005 http://www.fco.gov.uk/resources/en/pdf/public-diplomacy-review and Wilton Review 2002, executive summary avaible as Annex to Carter Report.

[12] See Wilton Review 2002 Martin Rose and Nick Wadham Smith, *Mutuality, trust and cultural relations* (Counterpoint: 2004) p. 5 http://www.counterpoint-online.org/download/156/Mutualit_Report.pdf

[13] Snow / Taylor, Public Diplomacy Handbook p. xi.

[14] White Oak Recommendations, *MountainRunner*, (emphasis added) http://mountainrunner.us/files/whiteoak/The_White_Oak_Recommendations_on_Public_Diplomacy.pdf

Specifically, recommendations from The Defense Science Board's Center for Global Engagement, CSIS, and Brookings Institution. See Christopher Paul, *Whither Strategic Communication? A Survey of Current Proposals and Recommendations*, (RAND: 2009) p. 10–12 http://www.rand.org/pubs/occasional_papers/2009/RAND_OP250.pdf

Managing a Collection of Silos

Conceiving public diplomacy in these broader terms within the complex networks of the 21st Century creates challenges for government departments and other organisations seeking to create a coherent interface between them, their domestic stakeholders, and communities in other countries. In response, some have recommended a bureaucratic approach, looking to establish an authority to encourage, cajole, or coerce the different departmental or institutional silos into an array encouraging—even if grudgingly—cooperation.[15]

This approach leans toward the imposition of a new organisational structure, managing through an organogram and seeking to control "authority" rather than engaging with the flow of influence. Others seek to develop a domestic alliance around a consistent narrative which they would then articulate and demonstrate to the rest of the world. While both approaches embrace the diversity of actors and stakeholders, they also reinforce a particularly centralised, egocentric endeavour.

Public diplomacy is more than centralised methods of telling others about yourself, enacted through optimistically neat organisational charts. One step forward in the White Oak Recommendations, was to "promote better foreign understanding of American values, policies and goals, and better inform the US policy-making process".[16] This argument was mirrored when the first Obama-era Under Secretary of State, Judith McHale, dropped the Bush era references to "war" and "extremism". Instead she declared, "We have to listen more and lecture less." Yet, in the end, McHale still exalted American "leadership", not

[15] Some comment on bureaucratic challenges are considered in;

Nick Cull, "Public diplomacy: seven lessons for its future from its past" in *Engagement: Public Diplomacy in a globalised world* (Foreign and Commonwealth Office, 2008 http://www.fco.gov.uk/en/about-the-fco/publications/publications/pd-publication/7-lessons.

Bruce Gregory, "Public Diplomacy and Strategic Communication: Cultures, Firewalls, and Imported Norms" Presentation at the American Political Science Association Conference on International Communication and Conflict, August 31, 2005 http://www8.georgetown.edu/cct/apsa/papers/gregory.pdf

Matthew Armstrong, "Operationalizing Public Diplomacy", in Snow / Taylor, *Public Diplomacy Handbook*, pp. 63–71.

[16] White Oak Recommendations, *MountainRunner*, http://mountainrunner.us/files/whiteoak/The_White_Oak_Recommendations_on_Public_Diplomacy.pdf

only as a guide for others but as the essential centre of anyone's and everyone's interests and activities:

> We have to learn how people in other countries and cultures listen to us. We need to understand their interests and aspirations, and use our leadership to provide them with information and services they value. If we do this right, we can forge relationships that become part of their daily lives. They may come to see their relationship with us, the United States of America, our government, and our greatest asset of all – the American people – as essential to their ability to achieve progress and prosperity, and fulfil their dreams of a brighter future.[17]

While this acknowledges the interests of others, it also maintains the view of an "audience" which can be made to understand. the common mantra "the more you know us, the more you like us" might travel well at home, but has real limitations when interacting with communities overseas. Aspiration to relationships while proclaiming leadership creates an asymmetry in objectives, limiting public diplomacy.

Managing the environment, "leading a relationship", asserting a global role, and "winning" others to your cause stems from concepts of control and fails to recognise and respect communities of "the other" as autonomous agents. Although President Obama's Inauguration speech, visit to Ankara, and speech in Cairo were steps toward "engagement" in comparison to his predecessor's approach, they were not examples of fully-fledged, mutual cooperation. In the 21st century public diplomacy operations cannot extend an open hand for a relationship, only to expect the "other" to follow meekly on your terms. To do so is to fail to seek their genuine involvement; as a result the extended open hand turns out to be a slap in the face.

The Movement to the Network in Public Diplomacy

Public diplomacy is the attempt to influence or change behaviour.[18] This means the focus has to be on the outcome, not the message,

[17] Judith McHale, Public Diplomacy: Renewing America's Engagement With the People of the World, DIPNOTE http://blogs.state.gov/index.php/entires/public_diplomacy/.

[18] David Ronfeldt and John Arquilla "The promise of noöpolitik" *First Monday,* volume 12, number 8 (August 2007), http://firstmonday.org/issues/issue12_8/ronfeldt/index.html.

understanding, or perception.[19] The attempt to influence does not have to be limited to targeting passive objects only capable of experiencing public diplomacy.[20] Within a network society, public diplomacy is less and less concerned with asserting an identity or soft power, presented ex-cathedra. Kathy Fitzpatrick's work on relationship building strategies, and technological developments most clearly seen through social networking platforms, significantly shifts the emphasis away from small numbers of producers and high numbers of receivers to a more balanced approach which recognises the agency and autonomy of others while valuing their answers to important questions.

This shift to collaboration, though applicable in the physical world, is most prominent through the development of "Public Diplomacy 2.0".[21] The emphasis on interaction through digital media has become increasingly important as the barriers of entry into the business of influence through these means are lowered. However, this is not merely a question of using the latest gadgets in vogue, such as Twitter, Facebook, or YouTube, as new conduits through which to push the message.[22] Instead the potential lies in the ability to work

---

Behaviour in this sense is understood to mean both taking action and choosing not to act in a specific situation as convincing people not to do something may be a policy goal as much as convincing them to do something.

[19] See for example *Changing Perceptions; Review of Public Diplomacy (Wilton Review)*, 22nd March 2002. http://www.fco.gov.uk/Files/kfile/PDWiltonReview_March2002.pdf

Equally the mission statement for DG Relex of the European Commission states: "The Directorate-General for External Relations contributes to the formulation by the *Commissioner for External Relations*, together with her colleagues of an effective and coherent external relations policy for the European Union, so as to enable the EU to assert its identity on the international scene". http://ec.europa.eu/dgs/external_relations/general/mission_en.htm

[20] Doug McKenzie-Mohr & William Smith, *Fostering Sustainable Behaviour: An Introduction to Community-based Social Marketing*, (New Society Publishers 2000).

Everett Rogers, *Diffusion of Innovations*, (Free Press: 2005).

Rogers et al. "Complex Adaptive Systems and the Diffusion of Innovations", *The Innovation Journal: The Public Sector Innovation Journal*, Volume 10(3).

[21] James Glassman, "Public Diplomacy 2.0", speaking at the New America Foundation, 12 December 2008 http://www.newamerica.net/events/2008/public_diplomacy_2_0 also see Evan Potter, "Web 2.0 and the new public diplomacy: impact and opportunities', in *Engagement: Public Diplomacy in a Globalised World.*

[22] In December 2008 Colleen Graffy, the Deputy Assistant Secretary of State for Public Affairs wrote an opinion piece for *The Washington Post*: "To keep our public diplomacy relevant today, we have to reach out and connect with people on their terms, whether we use blogs or texts – or tweets." ["A Tweet in Foggy Bottom", *The Washington Post*, 24 December 2008, p. A11] This prompted an exchange on the State Department's use of social media in public diplomacy in Scott Lucas, "That US State Department

through participatory and collaborative methods to influence behaviour.[23]

One possibility, considered by academics and practitioners alike, is changing mindsets from competitive expressions of identity to searches for the means of sustainable behaviour change based on intrinsic motivation and collective action.[24] David Rothkopf argues that this altered mindset recognises the "tectonic shifts that are transforming the very nature of global society".[25]

> The realpolitik of the new era is cyberpolitik, in which the actors are no longer just states, and raw power can be countered or fortified by information power. The mighty will continue to prevail, but the sources, instruments and measures of that might are dramatically changed.[26]

The future of public diplomacy is in the continuation of this shift, not through finding different ways to prevail but moving from hard power through soft power to a collaborative approach.

To apply this to policy, public diplomats have to recognise they are members of complex networks and identify their position within those networks. To do this effectively, an organisation conducting public diplomacy has to go further than a centralised and egocentric view of projection or even a shift towards the understanding of its sphere of influence. The nature of the network is constantly shifting as

---

Twitter-Diplomacy in Action", *Enduring America*, 4 January 2009, http://enduringamerica.com/2009/01/04/that-us-state-department-twitter-diplomacy-in-action/, Colleen Graffy, "US State Department Twitter-Diplomacy: Colleen Graffy Responds", 5 January 2009, http://enduringamerica.com/2009/01/05/us-state-department-twitter-diplomacy-colleen-graffy-responds/, and related comments; "To Tweet or not to tweet; What is the Question?" *Wandren PD* http://wandrenpd.com/2009/01/15/to-tweet-or-not-to-tweet-what-is-the-question/.

[23] Amelia Arsenault, "Public Diplomacy 2.0," Chapter 7 in Philip Seib, ed., Toward a New Public Diplomacy: Redirecting U.S. Foreign Policy (Palgrave Macmillan, 2009), 135–153.

[24] Edward L. Deci and Richard M. Ryan, "Self-Determination Theory: A Macrotheory of Human Motivation, Development, and Health", *Canadian Psychology* 2008, Vol. 49, No. 3, 182–185.

[25] David J. Rothkopf, 1998. Cyberpolitik: The Changing Nature of Power in the Information Age, *Journal of International Affairs*, volume 51, number 2 (Spring), p. 325.

[26] David J. Rothkopf, 1998. Cyberpolitik: The Changing Nature of Power in the Information Age, *Journal of International Affairs*, volume 51, number 2 (Spring), p. 326.

Also see Shaun Riordan, "Reforming Foreign Services for the Twenty-First Century" *The Hague Journal of Diplomacy*, Volume 2, Number 2, September 2007, pp. 161–173.

the relationships which comprise that network are reformed by a process of ongoing dynamic negotiation. In essence the organisation does not "own" a sphere of influence but engages in a network of influence comprised of multi-vector links between numerous nodes.[27]

Early steps in collective practice have been developed through EUNIC, which has demonstrated its role through initiatives such as the "Night of EU Cultural Institutes" organised in Croatia, "The Network Effect" in Moscow and "Who is afraid of Mobility" organised by the EUNIC Brussels cluster.[28] Attempts by the European Commission and NATO to conduct public diplomacy have been ongoing trials in collective action, while the academic conception of the movement to collective action has been highlighted by RS Zaharna, Geoffrey Cowan, and Amelia Arsenault.[29] Recent work has started to move public diplomacy from monologue through dialogue to co-operation, as in RS Zaharna's Associative Public Diplomacy or Open Source methodology.[30]

To sustain these approaches, the future of public diplomacy will have to go beyond Joseph Nye's conceptualisation of soft power, "getting others to want the same outcomes as you want [by] understanding how they are hearing your messages and fine-tuning it accordingly".[31] Real engagement will be a process of genuine involvement, rather than a more attractive sounding method of trying to garner followers.

Yet it is here that both the theory and practice of public diplomacy collide, rather than co-exist, with contemporary foreign policy: do

---

[27] Lavrov, S. (2006). Diplomacy Today: Subject and Method. *International Affairs: A Russian Journal of World Politics*, 1–10.

[28] Night of EU Cultural Institutes, *The Playbook; Case-studies of Engagement.* http://the-playbook.com/2009/02/23/night-of-eu-cultural-institutes-croatia/ for other examples see www.the-playbook.com

[29] RS Zaharna, "Information and Relational Communication Frameworks of Strategic Public Diplomacy," in N. Snow and P.M. Taylor (eds.) *The Public Diplomacy Handbook* (Routledge, 2008).

Geoffrey Cowan and Amelia Arsenault, "Moving from Monologue to Dialogue to Collaboration: The Three Layers of Public Diplomacy" *The ANNALS of the American Academy of Political and Social Science*, Vol. 616, No. 1, 10–30 (2008).

[30] RS Zaharna, "The Soft Power Differential: Network Communication & Mass Communication in Public Diplomacy," *The Hague Journal of Diplomacy*, 2 (2007), pp. 213–228.

Ali Fisher, "Music for the Jilted Generation: Open-Source Public Diplomacy". *The Hague Journal of Diplomacy* **3**(2):129–152.

[31] Joseph Nye, *Soft Power: The means to Success in World Politics*, (Public Affairs: New York) 2004 p. 111.

Governments and other agencies conceive of public diplomacy as a vehicle which is not just for one-way persuasion? Do they consider public diplomacy as a means to receive perspectives which shape existing policy or for an interchange permitting different, though compatible, outcomes? Can public diplomats on the ground be given sufficient freedom to negotiate networks when staying "on message" or using the corporate monotone will not work?[32]

The 2006 Princeton Project on National Security ostensibly sought an alternative to the Bushian unipolar approach, "We need to reassure other nations about our global role and win their support to tackle common problems."[33] However, it interrogated neither the interaction leading to the identification of "common problems" nor the methods of public diplomacy to ensure communal support. The current movement from "soft power" to "smart power" moves public diplomacy away from potential cooperation to fusing persuasion with coercion. A centralised view of "our" role remains, which undervalues other actors. Complex problems require collaboration rather than a "leader" asserting they have the correct answer.

The Princeton report simply wrapped up public diplomacy within soft power, "the power to attract", and in turn fused that with hard power, "the power to coerce".[34] The outcome of "A Grand Concert of Democracies" envisaged division—a reprise of George W. Bush's us versus them formulation—rather than unity or an engagement based on recognition, and it subsumed further complexities. If a country or community engaged by public diplomacy proved unsatisfactory in its policies, institutions, or values, would the Concert of Democracies, with its predominance in hard power, pursue "liberal intervention"? And what of the tension within, namely that some political/military/economic allies might prove to be far from democratic?[35]

The tensions are still present because the Princeton model of power continues to reduce/empty/negate political space and marginalise genuinely negotiated collective action, privileging the power imposed by a dominant participant. Far from challenging that reduction or

---

[32] Rick Levine, Christopher Locke, Doc Searls, and David Weinberger, *The Cluetrain Manifesto*, Perseus Books 2000.

[33] Princeton Project on National Security (co-directors, G. John Ikenberry and Anne-Marie Slaughter, "A World of Liberty Forged Under Freedom", http://www.princeton.edu/~ppns/report/FinalReport.pdf, p. 7.

[34] Princeton Project, p. 13.

[35] Princeton Project, p. 25.

negation, approaches to public diplomacy reinforce it by focusing on "leadership"—in this case, American leadership—misunderstanding or even precluding collective action.[36] When President Obama emphasises the need for American leadership, there are clear echoes of Joseph Nye's argument the US is "bound to lead" with the implied expectation that others are bound to follow.

To realise the true power of dispersed networks and collaboration, as Daniel Kimmage has argued, an international actor must give up the assertive methodology of the traditional diplomat to enable the credible voices the space to speak.[37] Doing so offers the recognition, suggested by Nick Cull, that "sometimes the most credible voice in public diplomacy is not one's own".[38]

We contend that this conception of "influence" must not be limited to a concern with how the actions of an audience of "others" can be moulded to fulfil "our" objectives. The public diplomacy of tomorrow must not merely foster subservient participation; it has to support a space for discourse and collective action on complex problems, which have multiple potential outcomes and effects.

US Public Diplomacy Today

Constructing the argument for a public diplomacy of tomorrow, the first section of the collection draws insight from the public diplomacy of today. The intention is to interrogate the current status quo, not by looking for a new gadget for the public diplomacy tool box but by identifying the limitations to current approaches to the field. These challenges inform the second part of the collection, identifying approaches, concepts and skills in the development of the public diplomacy of tomorrow.

Among the challenges identified for contemporary public diplomacy is that of avoiding isolation, either of one section of a public diplomacy organisation from another or the state officials from a diversification of digital media providing countless forms of information.

---

[36] See the critique of Paul Cammack, "Smart Power and US Leadership: A Critique of Joseph Nye", *49th Parallel* (Autumn 2008), http://www.49thparallel.bham.ac.uk/back/issue22/1_Cammack.pdf

[37] "Considering online networks" *Wandren PD*, http://wandrenpd.com/2008/05/12/19considering-online-networks/

[38] Cull, "Public diplomacy: seven lessons for its future", Lesson 5.

Philip Taylor highlights this difficulty, accompanied by the naïve optimism of many practitioners hoping information can be controlled or keep secret. Taylor posits a structure through which a State can organise its Strategic Communication and public diplomacy through which to (re)connect and overcome the isolation felt by some foreign ministries.

The attempt to manage the difficulties which bureaucracies face in contemporary public diplomacy is also analysed by Eytan Gilboa and Nachman Shai, as they consider the demand of achieving a degree of coordination in a fragmented system. The study of both centralised approaches and systems embracing higher levels of public participation concludes with an analysis of the dichotomy between information-based initiatives and those based on greater levels of engagement. Whatever language policymakers use to describe their approach, the position of the public diplomat within the policymaking structure highlights whether the role is primarily an advocate for a predetermined policy or an advisor that provides perspectives during the policymaking process.

If public diplomacy organisations can organise in a manner which overcomes some of the current bureaucratic challenges, the task which the organization is intended to achieve also faces obstacles. The US currently faces the dilemma of rhetorically pursuing greater "engagement" while emphasising a preponderance of power and asserting American leadership. Most understandings of engagement conceive of it as a "two-way street", but the demands of predominance, as demonstrated by Scott Lucas, clog up the return lane, projecting the message down a "one-way avenue".

David Ryan expands this examination of rhetoric, highlighting the image of a Manichaean approach within communities outside the US. This does not suggest that other views were not present, but they are marginal to the thrust of social preference and performance. The language of division between us and them framed policy options and fundamentally limited the possibility for collaboration on any basis other than American terms, bolstering the unipolar approach highlighted by Scott Lucas.

An approach based on dominance and unilateral declaration of leadership means that any engagement or soft power will be based on co-optation rather than collaboration. The attempt to create a favourable international environment does not alter this approach but reinforces it, as a nation seeks to claim legitimacy while it shapes international rules in a way that promotes its interests and values—in the American case, liberal democratisation and a normative US-led world order. As Giles Scott-Smith argues, this perspective has great difficulty adjusting to a contested global environment more suited to collaborative strategies rather than the current strategies centred upon rapid reaction and dissemination of information.

The challenge is how to shift US public diplomacy, and diplomacy in general, away from realpolitik and towards the realities of 21st-century interdependence, even if US involvement remains a *sine qua non* for successful outcomes. To make this shift, public diplomacy has to overcome the distortion caused by pursuing goals driven by a desire to influence the domestic constituency. This can lead to the adoption of strategies which try to "move the needle" in a foreign population or, failing that, gain support within the domestic electorate. As Nick Cull argues, there is a need to recognise the challenges this can create and to maintain distinctions between different roles within a nation's public diplomacy. In particular, the public diplomat should avoid the desire to demonstrate successful advocacy within programmes framed in terms of exchange or listening.

The need for clarity of approach is also emphasised in Lina Khatib's critical assessment of the dynamics of success and failure of public diplomacy efforts in the Middle East. The challenges are highlighted through the public diplomacy of the United States, the state of Qatar, and Hizbullah, three actors who provide diverse yet complementary case studies. The attempt to use television to "define the legitimacy of the use of force" causes tension in both structural and cultural dimensions, particularly when this approach is pursued by national or state information services. Strategies orientated around information projection are less able to adapt to an evolving operational or political context. Similar challenges are identified by Elizabeth Fox as she analyses the attempt to align US public diplomacy aims with those of commercial initiatives in Latin America, particularly in broadcast media.

Continuing the consideration of public diplomacy in Latin America, Bevan Sewell demonstrates the challenges which faced US public diplomacy in recent years. The approach focusing on gaining compliance from others to pre-determined goals was largely unsuccessful, as US officials were never in a position where they could control the predominant dialogue of inter-American relations. This was largely due to the shared history between the US and the Latin American states, one characterised predominantly by instances of US intervention.

The Public Diplomacy of Tomorrow

Manuel Castels has argued the public sphere is the space for the communication of ideas and projects that emerge from society.[39] This supports a broad definition of public diplomacy in which collaboration rather than an attempt to co-opt or contradict would bring the benefit of a wide diversity of possible answers to global challenges.

Through the analysis of contemporary paradoxes in public diplomacy, Daryl Copeland identifies the need to engage in meaningful exchange. This points to an imperative for the future of public diplomacy to rely on personnel with the appropriate set of skills and empowered within their organisation to do so. The outcome is an escape from models of process-driven administration which dominate contemporary bureaucracy and leave the "administrative tail wagging the policy dog".

In addition to employing the right people, meaningful exchange will also rely on successfully identifying the right people with which to interact; "strategic stakeholder engagement". Building on Copeland's emphasis on personnel and skills, RS Zaharna demonstrates the key considerations for public diplomats as they identify with whom they should interact and the form of that interaction. This analysis demonstrates the chief concern of an initiative focused on networks, collaboration, and the building of relationships rather than information or image dissemination: the shift from planning a message *for* a particular audience to planning *with* a stakeholder.

The importance of stakeholder engagement is also emphasised by Biljana Scott who analyses how individuals conducting public diplomacy interact with stakeholders. She identifies that, if there is a single overriding accomplishment that all public diplomats should hone, it is language awareness. Specifically, they should pursue (1) a mastery of language and rhetoric, (2) an aptitude for narrative, both with regard to its creation and interpretation, and (3) a heightened awareness of the elements that contribute to allegiance, as well as an awareness of the influence of language and narrative on the positioning and repositioning of allegiance. These skills contribute significantly to the most valuable asset in public diplomacy—credibility.

---

[39] Manuel Castells, "The New Public Sphere: Global Civil Society, Communication Networks, and Global Governance", *Annals*, AAPSS, March 2008.

The future will be defined by an increasing number of stakeholders, public diplomats with the skills to identify them, and the behaviours or language to interact with these communities. In conjunction, public diplomacy will need to develop ways of conceptualising itself to embed the shift from an emphasis on assertive strategies and ego-sphere to participation in a network of influence. Naren Chitty takes an interdisciplinary approach to theorising how public diplomacy might be conducted, drawing particularly on the influence of Confucianism. Public diplomacy is no longer the preserve of the public sector, but a public project with the goal of a sustainable world politics focusing on a collective non-exclusionary security, based on principles of humanitarianism and reciprocity rather than the current US model of assertive leadership and predominance of power.

Working with these complementary perspectives on the future of public diplomacy, Ali Fisher focuses on the issue underlying the discussions: the understanding of power within the field. What public diplomats or scholars conceive of as "powerful" shapes their priorities for different elements in the field. The perception of a stakeholder's influence, the desire to claim leadership over an initiative, or the relationship with the domestic constituency are all underpinned by a particular understanding of power, from strategy and planning to resource allocation and evaluation. These understandings of power must be renegotiated if a genuinely collaborative public diplomacy is to emerge.

With these perspectives on the current state of public diplomacy and the trials in adopting an "engagement" strategy, this collection seeks to contribute to the debate on the future evolution of public diplomacy in theory and practice. It holds out the prospect that those engaged in public diplomacy will "go beyond simple messaging, towards dialogue and cooperation", not through differentiation of their initiatives nor through a simple assertion of "leadership" but "in collective effort to find solutions to the global challenges exemplified by climate change, violent extremism, or poverty".[40]

[40] Jim Murphy, "Foreword", Engagement: public diplomacy in a globalised world.

US PUBLIC DIPLOMACY TODAY

PUBLIC DIPLOMACY ON TRIAL?

Philip M. Taylor

Is it right to put public diplomacy on trial? After all, most of its advocates are genuine believers in the merits of its practice, whether as a lubricant to foreign policy, as a means of promoting international mutual understanding, as a trust-building exercise or, as I like to describe it, as propaganda for peace. While public diplomacy differs from propaganda – as it is popularly misunderstood[1] – by virtue of its mutuality and its reciprocity of intentions as well as gains, it remains a form of "national self-advertisement" or what some of its supporters now label as "nation branding".[2] Essentially, public diplomacy emphasises all that is best about a society to foreign audiences. Its historians look back to the Cold War and attribute some role to its practice in helping to convince the world, including in central and Eastern Europe, of the merits of democracy over communism as a better way of doing politics.

Unfortunately, democratic politicians were so confident that the promotion of western value systems had played a key role in defeating the "Evil Empire" that, once the Soviet Union collapsed in 1991, they no longer felt any priority was needed for public diplomacy activities like international educational exchanges and international broadcasting (or what the KGB called "the voices" as a collective nickname for the Voice of America, the BBC and others). The post-Cold War downsizing of American public diplomacy culminated in the closure of the United States Information Agency (USIA) in 1999. Public diplomacy may indeed have played some role in helping the west to "win" the Cold War, but its neglect in the decade that followed may equally have

---

[1] Propaganda is here defined in value-neutral terms as a planned process of communication which utilises available means (media) to promote thought and/or behaviour amongst target audiences that primarily benefits the source, either directly or indirectly. It does not exclude the possibility that the recipient may also benefit as well.

[2] In particular, see the work of Simon Anholt, editor of the journal *Place Branding and Public Diplomacy*, and the founder and author of three major global surveys, the *Anholt Nation Brands Index*, City Brands Index and State Brands Index of the reputations of places.

had something to do with 9/11. As a result, in the inter-war decade of 1991–2001, an information and explanation vacuum was created which allowed dangerous terrorist activists to spread their message of hate, virtually unchallenged.

It was the political machinations of the dying Clinton administration which did in the USIA, despite Joseph Nye's repeated calls in the 1990s for the greater deployment of soft power. Perhaps there was also a little arrogance because it was felt that the power and prestige of the sole surviving superpower in the world could, and would, now speak for itself. Hard power is difficult to explain amongst peace loving peoples, however. It is frightening, intimidating and menacing. If the United States saw itself as a force for good in the world, then its hard power would need to be cloaked by a bodyguard of soft power. However, despite its attempts to project military interventions in places like Somalia and Kosovo as humanitarian missions, mere rhetoric alone was not sufficient to convince the frightened, intimidated, or menaced that the USA was not in the business of coca-colonialism or McDomination. This was most evident in the anti-globalisation demonstrations of the 1990s where thinly disguised anti-Americanism was all too in evidence. Moreover, and much more dangerously, the resultant information and explanation void, especially in the first decade of the world wide web, was filled with all sorts of disinformation and misinformation, as the decade also saw the emergence of Al Qaeda as the most sophisticated terrorist propaganda organisation the world has ever seen.

Of what else can public diplomacy be accused? After 9/11, we heard much talk of new terrorist enemies from the "Arab street" and of their new alleged megaphone, Al Jazeera, dubbed the "Arab CNN". Both labels were nonsense. The 9/11 hijackers were from the traditional target audience of public diplomacy: highly-educated Muslims, potential leaders of tomorrow, and western-educated at research degree student level. Instead of choosing the path of internationalism, they chose instead to move and shake the twin towers of the World Trade Centre and the Pentagon. Fifteen of the nineteen were from Saudi Arabia, regarded as a strong ally of the USA. The hardly penniless Saudi leader of Al Qaeda, moreover, was flipped from being a proxy ally of the US in their joint covert operations against the Godless Soviets in Afghanistan during the 1980s to an outright enemy. Usama bin Laden watched with horror as American troops landed en mass in the Holy Kingdom of Mecca during Operation Desert Shield in the second half of 1990. At the very time when the US needed to explain its foreign policy in places like the Middle East and Somalia under a proclaimed New World Order, its voice was turning into a whisper while that of its jihadist opponents were exploiting new global information spaces like the world wide web and new regional media players like Al Jazeera. And all this was taking place against a backdrop of mounting US media disinterest in world affairs, as its principal media outlets reduced the number of their foreign correspondents and turned inwards to celebrate the triumph of liberal free market democratic capitalism.

International journalism underwent profound changes during the 1990s in terms of the technology available to bring news instantaneously from everywhere while, paradoxically, media organisations were reducing their commitment to foreign news reporting. This was particularly pronounced in the United States prior to 9/11. In 1998, it was claimed that only 2% of total American newspaper coverage was devoted to international news, compared to 10% in 1983.[3] Network television coverage similarly dropped from 45% of total broadcast output in the 1970s to 13.5% in 1995.[4] No *Time* magazine cover in 1997 was given over to a foreign affairs story (as compared to 11 in 1987) while that magazine's international news coverage followed *Newsweek* in a reduction to almost 10%.[5] Specialised foreign and defence correspondents all but disappeared in Britain and the United States, and those that survived found it harder and harder to secure a place for their stories.[6] Moreover, as one veteran reporter pointed out, "We depend for our front-line reporting on a generation of war reporters who, like the politicians, have no experience of soldiering."[7]

Indeed, the very fact that the question "Why do they hate us so much?" was even asked about the 9/11 terrorist attacks represents not

---

[3] David Shaw, "Foreign News Shrinks in Era of Globalization," *Los Angeles Times*, 27 September 2001.

[4] C. Moisey, "The Foreign News Flow in the Information Age," Joan Shorenstein Centre on the Press, Politics and Public Policy, Harvard University discussion paper D-23, November 1996.

[5] For further details, see J. Hoge, "Foreign News: Who Gives a Damn?" *Columbia Journalism Review*, (November–December 1997), 36, pp. 48–52.

G. Utley, "The Shrinking of Foreign News: From Broadcast to Narrowcast," *Foreign Affairs* (1997), 76:2, pp. 2–10; Jonathan Randal, "The decline, but not yet total fall, of foreign news in the US media," Joan Shorenstein Centre on the Press, Politics and Public Policy, Harvard University working paper, 2000, No. 2000-2.

[6] Shaw, "Foreign News Shrinks".

[7] Martin Bell, *Through the Gates of Fire* (Weidenfeld and Nicholson, 2003), p. 43.

only a serious failure of public diplomacy but also of domestic public affairs. The US had gone into its shell in a sort of post-Mogadishu recognition of New World Disorder. Even when it periodically came out that shell – in Bosnia (eventually!), Haiti, and Kosovo – the President was forced to explain to the American people on a map where such distant places actually were and, indeed, who were the new enemies. History may indeed judge that one of the root causes of 9/11 was the failure of American public diplomacy and that the subsequent response was equally a failure of public affairs in the afterglow of self-proclaimed victory in the Cold War.

Al Jazeera, founded in 1995 in Qatar, had revolutionised the concept of television broadcasting in the Middle East. Its little-noticed (in the West) innovation was to break the shackles of state-controlled media in the region by virtue of its promotion of bottom-up viewpoints; when it was "discovered" by the West in the aftermath of 9/11, it was shocking to realise that the global media were no longer American. Al Jazeera's employees resented the "Arab CNN" label not because the tag suggested an attempt to reclaim or recast the phenomenon through American lenses but because most of them had been trained by the BBC. Such training in the BBC's public service broadcasting tradition made it axiomatic that, if they covered one side of a dispute, they should "balance" off the argument with representations of the opposing side. Such a philosophy did not sit easily with the post-9/11 warnings of President George W. Bush that "you are either with us or against us" or that "there is no neutral ground in the War on Terror". These semantic frames were hardly conducive to the spirit of public diplomacy.

Yet, while the policy failure to sustain public diplomacy came in the 1990s, the real crime against the practice has been committed more recently. The day after 9/11, *Le Monde* famously printed the headline that "we are all Americans now". Today, the so-called GWOT ("global war on terror") – a phrase that we must no longer use – is in fact longer than US involvement in World War Two. Never before have levels of anti-Americanism and anti-Western sentiment been so high in the Arab and Islamic world. There is no need to dwell on how this has come about, from the initial use of the word "crusade" by the American President through to Guantanamo Bay and Abu Ghraib, but it should be obvious how the disastrous mistakes made in the first six years of the War on Terror have been disastrous from a public diplomacy point of view. Those mistakes have made the task of public diplomacy today even harder and its success more difficult and longer to achieve.

For all the renewed debate about public diplomacy and the struggle for hearts and minds in the GWOT, there remains a legacy of Cold War/soft power thinking in the "to know us is to love us" philosophy which drives the creation of Radio Sawa and Al Hurra TV or even Radio Farda. The 9/11 hijackers knew the West, including Florida strip joints, pretty well and drew a different conclusion. The 7/7 London bombers were home grown. Soft power may be about making yourself attractive so that others might want to be like you, but there are many extremist elements which do not want that. Al Qaeda propaganda skilfully exploits elements of Islamic culture and thought to explain that what is going on is in fact a clash of civilisations and that we are approaching the last battle in the thousand year crusade between Judeo-Christianity and Islam. They use the internet with skill, especially with their Islamic target audience, and they exploit the western media with terrorist acts that are mainly designed as propaganda of the deed.

Public diplomacy, of course, was designed as a means for governments to address foreign audiences directly, bypassing government and media filters. But herein lies another problem, especially on the internet, but also in our globalised, 24/7 digital news environment. Where is the line between the national and the international? The inability to grasp this post-Cold War, internet age conundrum underpins American debates about the 1948 Smith-Mundt Act[8] or about the revival of the USIA in new forms such as the Centre for Global Engagement[9] or Senator Sam Brownback's proposed National Centre for Strategic Communications. Largely absent from these debates is the role of journalism and public affairs. In democracies which parade freedom of the press as one of the cornerstones of liberty, no one seems prepared to grasp the nettle that a national media which thrives on bad news, including terrorist acts, may in fact be part of public diplomacy's overseas problem. Especially in the Islamic world, the negative

[8] One of the leading advocates of reform is Matt Armstrong, who runs the Mountainrunner blog website (http://mountainrunner.us), one of the best online sources for public diplomacy and related matters.

[9] *Center for US Global Engagement*, http://www.usglobalengagement.org/AbouttheCenter/tabid/678/Default.aspx (accessed 14 November 2008).

impression, of American or Western society generated by US media concentration on celebrity, crime, drugs, infidelity, and materialism hardly makes democracy as a way of life attractive, and certainly not something to be emulated. Familiarity can breed contempt.

When a nation declares "war" on terror, its warriors are called upon to fight and win. Consequently, prevailing ideas about the role of influence activities tend to play second fiddle to the kinetic business of actually fighting "the enemy". Since the emergence of Information Operations (IO) doctrine in the mid-1990s, largely on the basis of experience in the Balkans,[10] most NATO countries have recognised the significant impact which new communications technologies have had in revolutionising military affairs. They have yet to recognise, however, that utilising such technologies may actually be an alternative to war-fighting. As a result IO still remains a support tool – not an after-thought as it once was, but a "combat force multiplier" to lubricate the business of military activity, rather like the role of public diplomacy in lubricating foreign policy.

Within the military IO community, there have been ongoing fights about whether public affairs should be part of its influence activities in theatre either under the umbrella of IO or of what is now being called Strategic Communications and 'Global Engagement'. Those tasked with the job of dealing with the media often insist that they are not part of the influence business; rather their task is just to "hand out information". A somewhat disingenuous argument given that media views are formed on the basis of the news released by public affairs officials, this nonetheless reveals the ongoing tension which exists between those whose job is to retain media credibility and those officials who have to try and win hearts and minds abroad. These assumptions are a legacy of Cold War thinking which identifies different types of official communication into vertical pillars rather than as a seamless horizontal info-sphere in which a YouTube video uploaded from Ulan Bator may have more strategic significance than a New York Times editorial, and they belong more to the 20th century than the 21st. This is what makes the absence of any public affairs capability within Senator Brownback"s proposed bill to create a National Centre for Strategic Communications so odd. Perhaps the election of President

[10] Philip M. Taylor, "The Balkans Conflict and the Emergence of the Information Operations Doctrine" in Andrew Hammond (ed.), *The Balkans and the West: Constructing the European Other, 1945–2003* (Ashgate, 2004), pp. 184–198.

Obama will be sufficient to project a new image of the United States, a country having changed its tune concerning engagement with the rest of the world by means other than military action.

Yet new journalism, together with old media, will remain more of a problem than a solution. When survivors of the 7/7 bombings in London or guards executing Saddam Hussein in Baghdad take moving images on their mobile phones, who are the journalists? How does military preoccupation with Operational Security (OPSEC) or Force Protection sit in the era of Google Earth or military bloggers? Why is there still a distinction being made between tactical, operational, and strategic information in an era in which a PSYOP leaflet dropped on a mountain in Afghanistan can be scanned into a laptop computer and uploaded to the internet with a global audience? When the military talk of full spectrum dominance and the "strategic corporal", how can that be achieved in the age of the unregulated, chaotic internet and the "citizen journalist"? Why is there still a prevailing impression in military and diplomatic circles that it is still possible to keep information secret? Sooner or later (sooner in the 21st century), government secrets will be unearthed, as evidenced by the fact that information about the Office of Strategic Influence (OSI) was leaked from inside the Pentagon itself.

For all their talk of transparency and accountability, democratic governments still seem to operate on the basis of keeping information in rather than letting it flow out. In a "war" on terror, perhaps this is understandable, but it is a basis that stands diametrically opposed to that of terrorist adversaries. Terrorists know that what they do is 10% violence and 90% propaganda, whereas the Western, US-led response to 9/11 is 90% violence (war) and 10% propaganda (or "perception management" or "strategic communication"). Fear is, of course, their objective, and they do not have to play by the same rules as democratic governments and their diplomatic or military representatives. Hence their preferred information battlespace is the internet, an unregulated global info-environment in which a teenager in a bedroom on one side of the globe can communicate with audiences everywhere provided they are "wired". Meanwhile, the news-oriented mass media can report on propaganda-of-the-deed terrorist acts, generating the kind of fear and alarm that facilitates non-opposition of counter-terrorist strategies and the erosion of civil liberties. So while Western democracies and their mass media find themselves in the position of actually facilitating terrorist objectives, their public diplomacy activities struggle against the blurring of national and international information activities.

I would argue that one of the great advantages of public diplomacy – and even, within a military context, of psychological operations – is that it bypasses the commercial free media and addresses its audiences directly. Ten years ago, I published a book[11] which was severely criticised for arguing that governments needed to do more informational work because they could not, and nor should they, rely on the media to represent their positions and policies to the wider domestic and international audiences. I was criticised because this implied more trust in democratic governments to tell the truth than it did the media. Little did I think then that the *New York Times* would end up apologising for not asking the searching questions in the build-up to war in Iraq in 2003.

Some critics even pointed to my earlier work on propaganda which showed how democratic governments had manipulated the media into becoming lapdogs rather than watchdogs, especially in time of war. Today, I still believe that there is no inherent contradiction in this argument because I have always believed that democracies should conduct propaganda – defined in a value-neutral sense – for peace and that democratic governments cannot expect the commercial media to do this for them. What is now being called strategic communication does however need certain "rules", for in communications, credibility is everything if operations are to succeed. Lying, or even putting out misleading information, should be strictly out of bounds. To develop credibility as a source of accurate and reliable news and views, the material must be verifiable from different open sources. If this is achieved, any counter-propaganda, which must be done quickly before information being refuted takes root – is more likely to succeed.

Below is a strategic communications map which locates all government information activities within the context of each other. I have devised this map in order to clarify the current confusion which exists about government influence activities, even with the international information community. The former American Under Secretary of State for Public Affairs and Public Diplomacy, James Glassman, has even added to this confusion by claiming that strategic communications

[11] Philip M. Taylor, *Global Communications, International Affairs and the Media since 1945* (Routledge, 1997).

is a sub-set of public diplomacy.[12] For people with a little more experience in the field, the map represents more widely-held views.

The public diplomacy piece, the responsibility of Foreign Offices or State Departments where no central overseas information agency exists, is for simplicity's sake subdivided into cultural diplomacy and international broadcasting. Cultural diplomacy encompasses what John Brown calls "arts diplomacy" as well as international cultural and educational exchanges, language teaching and the establishment of libraries, both virtual and real. International broadcasting may be undertaken directly by governments (such as the American model which, through the Broadcasting Board of Governors, oversees the Voice of America and its "family" of specific target stations such as Radio and TV Marti, Radio Free Asia, Radio Sawa and Al Hurra TV and Radio Farda) or more indirectly through proxy agencies (such as the role of the BBC World Service within the British model). Cultural diplomacy is closest to Nye's concept of soft power, but it is essentially a long-term activity designed to promote all that is best about a society, its people and culture. It combats the negative impressions that are so often gleaned from a foreign reading of a national media. For example, US cultural diplomacy has to counter negative impressions of American values in the Islamic world gleaned from Hollywood movies that concentrate on violence, drugs, divorce and extra-marital relations.

[12] Bud Goodall, "Strategic Communication vs. Public Diplomacy vs. Dialogue," *COMOPS Journal,* http://comops.org/journal/2008/10/28/strategic-communication-vs-public-diplomacy-vs-dialogue (accessed 14 November 2008).

International broadcasting is more of a short-term, news and views based, approach. To ensure credibility, it needs a high degree of editorial independence from government control, an independence which often generates its own internal tensions, especially within the public service broadcasting tradition that balances opposing views. We shall return to its controversial dotted line on the map connecting it to psychological operations in due course.

The information operations component, the responsibility of Ministries or Departments of Defence, is also for simplicity subdivided into two components. The Computer Network Operations component essentially consists of the data protection of one's own military information systems (often through civilian backdoors), the exploitation of adversary systems, electronic warfare and deception. The other side of IO is broadly called human factors. It is the "people" side of the piece – human intelligence rather than signals intelligence – and the attempt to influence behaviour and thought in Information Age Warfare. It is here that psychological operations sits, alongside other influence activities such as civil-military co-operation (CIMIC). These attempts at influence, within a military context, are often simplistically dismissed as "propaganda", usually in support of a military mission. However, they are also about "hearts and minds" as pioneered by General Templer during the 1950s Malaya campaign with counterinsurgency methods that were only belatedly learned by US forces following the fall of Baghdad in 2003. However well or badly military communications or IO are conducted at the tactical and operational levels in a theatre of operations, they also have a strategic impact, especially in the age of the internet. While these operation can impact on the ability of public diplomacy to go about its business successfully, it is at the strategic – political or geo-political – level which sets the frame in which hearts and minds are more likely to be lost.

The third component of the map, Public Affairs, is responsible for ensuring that this does not happen. Although Public Affairs is sometimes labelled "spin", it is an essential part of modern democratic government in that it has a responsibility to inform the public, through the media, of why certain decisions have been made in the name of that public. Within a military context, giving out information to the media often runs contrary to the needs of operational security (OPSEC), but military public affairs is inevitably part of influence operations, despite its organisational separation from IO. This frequently creates tensions, with public affairs officials who maintain that their job is simply to hand out factual information in as timely a manner as is feasible within the constraints of OPSEC and with IO officials who recognise that the news that is released can shape the views that are formed as a result.

The strategic communications map can only really work if different components and subcomponents are joined up. But that may well be asking too much, given the size and the scale of the bureaucracies that have been created to deal with each of the activities. For example, sometimes it appears as if the Pentagon are more interested in fighting the State Department in Washington rather than Al Qaeda's skilful propaganda campaign in the Islamic world. Bureaucracies of this complexity are slow, reactive and at odds over where the line exists between the national and international. Never was this more apparent when the leaked information about the Office of Strategic Influence caused a media storm in March 2002. Deception – a time honoured military tool – within IO appeared to be seeping into the international public affairs realm, from which the US domestic media gleaned much of its foreign information following the indigenous decline of foreign news reporting. As a result, the credibility of *all* the different parts of the map was placed in severe jeopardy.

There is also a danger that international broadcasting activities may be interpreted as psychological operations. This is where the other dotted line on the map is controversial. Think of the target audiences for the American family of official radio stations. Radio Marti (Cuba) and Radio Free Asia (China, North Korea) look like ongoing legacies of the Cold War in so far as their communist targets are concerned, even though Radio Free Asia was launched by the Clinton Administration. It was reported in 2006 that Commando Solo, a converted Hercules EC130 which carries comprehensive TV and radio broadcasting capabilities and operated under the auspices of Fort Bragg's 4th Psychological Operations Group through the Pennsylvania National Guard, was actually relaying Radio Marti broadcasts into Cuba.[13] The George W. Bush Administration even beefed up its Persian-language service, creating Radio Farda in 2002 to broadcast into Iran.

---

[13] Council on Hemispheric Affairs Report, "Radio and TV Martí: Washington Guns after Castro at Any Cost", 29 March 2006, http://www.coha.org/NEW_PRESS_RELEASES/New_Press_Releases_2006/COHA%20Report/COHA_Report_06.03_Radio_TV_Marti.html (accessed 14 November 2008).

Many public diplomacy experts believe that international broadcasting needs to be a completely separate activity, for fear that it can be accused of psychological warfare against hostile regimes. But equally, it should not be forgotten that cultural diplomacy can also be accused by those on the receiving end as a new form of cultural imperialism. PSYOPS (renamed MISO in the US) within this context begins to look like "hard propaganda" with cultural diplomacy serving a "soft propaganda" role.

There is also no doubt that the job of Strategic Communications as a joined-up concept is even harder to achieve because the credibility of many politicians – whether it be over connections between 9/11 and Iraq or over weapons of mass destruction – is perhaps lower than it has ever been. A study of social psychology tells us that credibility is not like virginity; it can be regained. However, it needs different techniques and philosophies than those applied during the last great Cold War struggle for hearts and minds. The West is now dealing with a completely different kind of enemy and it should be doing more to explain what kind of people Westerners really are rather than telling Islamic target audiences what kind of people they should be. To do that, it needs to follow Sun Tsu"s advice that you should not only know the enemy; you should first come to know yourself – warts and all.

Supporters of public diplomacy agree that it is as much about listening than speaking, whether softly or not. However, there is a difference between listening and actually hearing what is being said. When a previous Undersecretary of State for Public Diplomacy, Karen Hughes, went on her infamous "Listening Tours" of the Middle East in 2005, she was shocked to discover that an audience of handpicked Saudi women displayed no interest in learning to drive. The cultural filters through which this revelation was processed saw a group of repressed women with no interest in Western modernity living in a medieval patriarchal society, when in fact closer scrutiny and cultural sensitivity would have revealed that most of the women in the audience had chauffeurs!

This type of dissonance has been repeated many times, from the initial label of the GWOT as "Operation Infinite Justice" to the publication of the Danish cartoons. This is not to suggest that this does not also happen in the Islamic world as well, where offence is often taken (or stirred up) when none is intended. One need only recall the case of the English teacher jailed in the Sudan for naming a teddy bear Mohammed, and some fanatics also take offence at the *Winnie the Pooh* by virtue of the presence of "Piglet". However, my concern here is with the Western projection. When a prospective US Vice-Presidential candidate whose view of Russia is determined by her view from her Alaskan bedroom window makes a joke about "lipstick on a pig" it is one thing. When a former US Undersecretary of State for Public Affairs at the Pentagon publishes a book with the very same title,[14] one can only despair that those in charge of improving America's image abroad clearly do not understand the harm which rhetoric at home can do abroad.

Perhaps this is the price of democracy which, as a result of its cherished individualism and freedoms, will always be its own worst enemy. Much western media do not exactly represent the best that Western societies have to offer. Whether it is the news media"s obsession with human interest stories and bad news, or the preoccupation of Western movies with "real bad Arabs"[15] a dialogue is needed with governmental public diplomacy because there is no longer a distinction between what is said at home and what is said to foreigners. In other words, governments must first restore their credibility at home before their public diplomacy abroad can succeed.

The first step towards doing this is to realise how, even before 9/11, the West – and America in particular – has become the enemy rather than a force for good in the world. Public diplomacy then needs a grand strategy which encapsulates a realistic and realisable end state to this – to this what? This "war"? You can't fight a war against an idea, at least not with tanks and bombs and missiles. That is why the West is losing the propaganda war and why it will continue to lose it, and indeed make it harder to win. The struggle needs to be defined in informational and educational terms. It needs to recognise that if it continues to be waged with hard power it will not be the "Long War" but the "Forever War". Terrorist enemies will continue to wage asymmetric warfare against the West in the global information battle-space, and unless they are engaged more effectively on that battle-space, in the domestic media as well in cyberspace where national boundaries have no real meaning, there will be no chance of victory – and the verdict of history will be guilty, as charged.

---

[14] Torie Clarke, *Lipstick on a Pig: Winning In the No-Spin Era by Someone Who Knows the Game* (Free Press, 2006).

[15] J. G. Shaheen, *Reel Bad Arabs: How Hollywood Vilifies a People* (Interlink Publishing Group, 2001).

REBUILDING PUBLIC DIPLOMACY: THE CASE OF ISRAEL

Eytan Gilboa and Nachman Shai

Introduction

Revolutionary changes in international relations and communication technologies have inspired state and non-state actors to initiate public diplomacy (PD) programs or to examine and adjust existing ones.[1] States face different challenges and have different needs. The big powers like the US, China and Russia receive substantial attention due to their standing and influence in the world. The middle powers like Australia, Canada and Norway are searching for a mission or a niche that would best serve their political and economic interests in the world. Small states, especially developing countries, seek attention and acknowledgement that they exist and have something to contribute. States and non-state actors engaged in war and conflict like Israel and the Palestinians, wish to gain support for their respective causes in international organizations and world public opinion.

States have been aware of the need to develop and adjust their PD programs to the challenges and opportunities of the information age. They have invested considerable resources in evaluation and creation of new initiatives. States that failed to cope with the challenges of the information age denied themselves a critical instrument of diplomacy and foreign policy. From both theoretical and practical perspectives it is vital to investigate how different actors have approached the need to evaluate and reform PD. A comparative analysis may yield a list of strategies which actors may adopt and modify according to their specific needs. A comparative analysis of reform strategies may also contribute observations and findings to the slowly emerging field of comparative PD.[2]

---

[1] Research for this work was supported by the Center on Public Diplomacy at the University of Southern California.

[2] Eytan Gilboa, "Searching for a Theory of Public Diplomacy," *The Annals of the American Academy of Political and Social Science* (2008), 616, pp. 55–77.

States have developed various approaches to evaluation, development and conduct of PD programs. They have established investigative committees, commissioned research, held hearings, consulted experts and even solicited views and ideas from the general public. States employed two basic approaches: a closed one that primarily is held in house and involves extensive consultations among officials responsible for PD with the help of outside experts; and an open one which involves the public in the evaluation process. Norway and Poland for example, employed the closed process, while Canada and Australia preferred the open approach.

Following the end of the Cold War, Norway was concerned with its diminishing visibility in world affairs, and in 2002 contracted the Foreign Policy Centre in London to produce a new PD strategy.[3] In 2002 and 2003, the plan was discussed in a series of seminars with selected representatives of several government and non-governmental agencies, journalists, scholars and businessmen. The results were released to the public in 2003.[4] In 2002, Poland launched a PD campaign designed to secure accession to the EU. The government developed a program for the promotion of Poland in the EU and instructed the ministers of foreign affairs, culture, economic affairs and education to implement it.[5] Just before the admission to the EU, Poland hired Wally Olins, Chairman of Suffron Brand Consultants, to brand Poland.[6]

Canada and Australia adopted a different approach to reforming their PD systems. They opened up the process for direct wide public participation in the process. In January 2003, the Canadian Department of Foreign Affairs and International Trade published a Dialogue Paper and invited the public to discuss major questions of diplomacy and PD. Many organizations and thousands of individuals responded

---

[3] Mark Leonard and Andrew Small, *Norwegian Public Diplomacy* (The Foreign Policy Centre, 2003).

[4] Jozef Bátora, "Public Diplomacy between Home and Abroad: Norway and Canada," *Hague Journal of Diplomacy* (2006), 1, pp. 71–72.

[5] Beata Ociepka and Marta Ryniejska, *Public Diplomacy and EU Enlargement: The Case of Poland* (Clingendael, Netherlands Institute of International Relations, Discussion Papers in Diplomacy, No. 99, 2005).

[6] Wally Olins, "Poland searches for its identity," *ThisIsMoney*, November 5, 2007. http://www.thisismoney.co.uk/saving-and-banking/polski/article.html?in_article_id=425992&in_page_id=53517 (accessed 19 November 2008). See also Jarosław *Szczepankiewicz*, "From Public Diplomacy to a Brand for Poland," *Yearbook of Polish Foreign Policy* 1 (2006), pp. 269–276.

on-line and many participated in town meetings and conferences. The results were presented to the public in a special report.[7] A parliamentary committee in Australia initiated a major study of PD and made many interesting and useful recommendations.[8] The committee opened up the process, invited heads and leaders of relevant organizations to submit papers, and held hearings.

These few cases may suggest that sates select approaches to reform based on their respective PD systems. Those of Norway and Poland were centralized and selective while those of Canada and Australia were more fragmented and inclusive, and both the processes of reforms and the conduct of PD may reflect the different societal composition of the states: more homogenic in the first two and more multicultural in the last two.

This chapter examines how Israel has attempted to reform its PD. More than any country, Israel needed a major overhaul of its PD.[9] In the last twenty years the Jewish state has faced enormous foreign policy and national security challenges.[10] The main threats evolved from a protracted low intensity conflict with the Palestinians and Iran's proxies in the Middle East: Hezbollah in Lebanon and Hamas in Gaza. Several dramatic events exposed serious weaknesses in Israeli PD including the first Palestinian Intifada (1987–1992), the failure of the Oslo peace process (1993–2000), the unilateral Israeli withdrawal from Lebanon (2000), the Second Palestinian Intifada (2000–2006), the infamous UN World Conference Against Racism held in Durban (2001), the Israeli unilateral disengagement from Gaza (2005) and the Second Lebanon War between Israel and Hezbollah (2006). All these events demonstrated that Israel was paying heavy political and diplomatic costs for the failure to effectively employ PD.

Successive Israeli governments have been aware of the need to rebuild Israel's PD. Leaders have called for major reforms but the awareness and the vigorous statements have never been translated into

---

[7] Canada, Department of Foreign Affairs and International Trade, *A Dialogue on Foreign Policy: Report to Canadians* (DFAIT, 2003).

[8] Australia, Senate. Senate Standing Committee on Foreign Affairs, Defence and Trade *Australia's Public Diplomacy: Building our Image* (Commonwealth of Australia August 2007).

[9] Eytan Gilboa, "Public Diplomacy: The Missing Component in Israel's Foreign Policy," *Israel Affairs* (2006). 12, pp. 715–747.

[10] Robert O. Freedman, ed., *Contemporary Israel: Domestic Politics, Foreign Policy, and Security Challenges* (Westview, 2008).

actions. Substantial public support and engagement in PD is required for successful expansion and utilization of PD. The Israeli public has strongly supported reforms in the PD system. The media often complained about the lack of effective PD, the public has been aware of this deficiency and several bodies such as the State Comptroller and the Knesset Committee on Defense and Foreign Affairs issued critical reports documenting the abysmal results and demanding major reforms. Yet, the government has never made a serious attempt to build an effective PD system and has never consulted the people and local civil society organs in the formulation and implementation of PD.

This chapter systematically examines Israeli attempts to change and adjust its PD to the challenges of both the information revolution and the low intensify conflict with the Palestinians and other regional enemies. It first maps governmental and extra-governmental agencies and organizations pursuing PD on behalf of Israel. It then examines various plans and actions to reform and rebuild the system. The findings reveal a highly fragmented and deficient system, and reforms attempts which failed due to bureaucratic and personal interests of politicians and officials. The last section presents an optimal model for Israel that with some modifications may be suitable for other countries, particularly those facing similar challenges and threats.

Governmental Public Diplomacy

Many organizations in Israel pursue public diplomacy, directly or indirectly, but the system has been fragmented and there has never been one authority for direction and coordination (see Figure 1). The military establishment, the Ministry of Defense (MOD), and the Israeli Defense Forces (IDF) have dominated Israel's defense and foreign affairs, and as the owners and practitioners of hard power have not appreciated the value of soft power and PD.

The Prime Minister Office's (PMO) is responsible for policy planning, formulation and implementation and has several bodies to accomplish these tasks. The most relevant offices for PD are those of the Spokesperson and the Foreign Communication Adviser, the Government Press Office (GPO), which provides services to foreign reporters stationed in Israel, and the National Security Council (NSC); however, the PMO is also responsible for the intelligence services

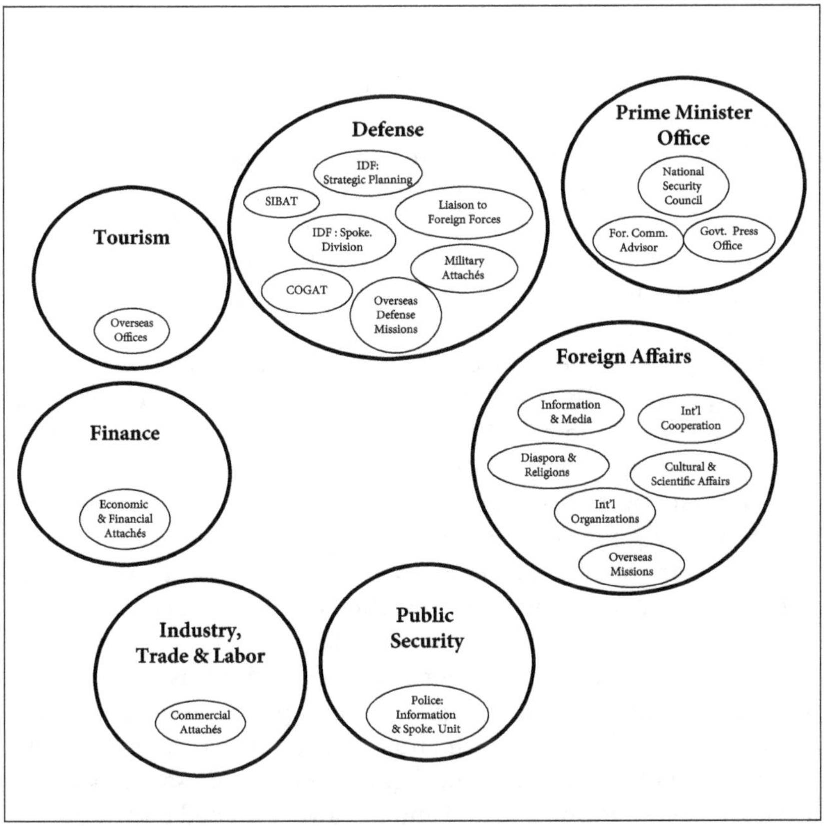

Figure 1: Clusters of Governmental PD.

including the domestic General Security Agency (GSA) and the Mossad, the institute for intelligence and special operations abroad.[11] In times of low intensity conflict, these organizations may provide useful information for PD or will be engaged in activity that bears directly on PD. GSA may provide information on terrorist activity and leaders of terrorist organizations which could justify a military operation against them, and the Mossad may be implicated in illegal or problematic activities abroad, as it did in recent years in Jordan, New Zealand and Switzerland.

[11] The Mossad operates like the American *Central Intelligence Agency* (CIA) and the British *Secret Intelligence Service* (MI6). It collects and processes *intelligence, combats terrorism*, and conducts *covert operations.*

In general, given the fragile structure of Israeli coalition governments, the PMO's media and communication officials are mostly concerned with the Prime Minister's political interests. Occasionally, they respond to crises or create opportunities for PD during official state visits abroad. The GPO's duties have been mostly confined to technical matters and has never been given a prominent role in the formulation and implementation of PD. The establishment in 1970 of a unit for communication with foreign reporters at the Foreign Ministry also eroded the GPO's standing in the PD system. The NSC was established in 1999 in order to improve the quality of policymaking and coordination among the different governmental units responsible for defense and foreign affairs. This body could have served as an excellent organ for planning and coordination of PD. From the outset however, it became clear that the NSC could nott accomplish its goals. The MOD and IDF, wanting to preserve their domination of the policymaking process, strongly opposed the Council and undermined its work.[12]

The Ministry of Foreign Affairs (MFA) could have been the natural centre for the development and practice of PD. Headed by Deputy Director Generals, several divisions and departments are employing a variety of PD instruments.[13] Information and Media is the principal division. It covers public affairs (publications, productions, and special projects), press relations, information and the Internet, and external relations (friendship societies, local government, and other links). The division however, is understaffed and has a very limited budget for PD activities, about $10 million per year. The other relevant divisions include Cultural and Scientific Affairs, International Cooperation (foreign aid), International Organizations and the UN, Diaspora and World Jewish Affairs, and Religious Affairs.

Although Israeli culture, literature, music, film, theatre, dance and plastic arts are highly popular around the world, the cultural division budget is extremely limited, and after recent budgetary cuts, MFA was forced the reduce the number of cultural attachés from 14 to 4.[14] Until

[12] Charles Freilich, "National Security Making in Israel," *Middle East Journal* (2006), 60, pp. 635–663.

[13] Israeli Ministry of Foreign Affairs, "Ministry of Foreign Affairs: Structure," http://www.mfa.gov.il/mfa/mfaarchive/2000_2009/2003/2/ministry%20of%20foreign%20affairs-%20structure (accessed 19 November 2008).

[14] Israeli Ministry of Foreign Affairs, "Culture; 60th Anniversary Edition," http://www.mfa.gov.il/MFA/Facts+About+Israel/Culture/CULTURE.htm (accessed 19 November 2008); Viva Press, "Israeli Arts and Entertainment Breaks through to the

the UN Durban Conference, the MFA ignored NGOs and concentrated on the UN and international organizations where Israel increasingly has faced hostile debates and one-sided severe condemnation and criticism. Since the Durban conference, however, the Division of International Organizations and the UN is devoting more attention and is allocating more resources to NGOs.

The Center for International Cooperation (*Mashav*) was established in 1958 and has trained over 250.000 students from the developing world, primarily from Africa.[15] Training and projects were designed to harness Israel's innovations and experience in agriculture, health, education, and science for helping developing countries to become more productive and meet their essential economic and social needs. Israeli aid to developing countries was more attractive than aid from big powers because the Jewish state was free of colonial past and imperial ambitions, and was viewed as less threatening to the sovereignty and independence of the recipient states.[16] Israel's long-term aid to Africa may have contributed to the relative favourable Israeli reputation in states such as the Ivory Coast, Kenya, Uganda, Ethiopia, and Ghana.[17] Israel, however, invests annually only $10 million in foreign aid. While several projects are done in cooperation with other countries, boosting the actual annual sum is larger, it is still very low in comparison with the OECD's recommended allocation of 0.7% of GNP to aid.

MOD and IDF have several departments and units that conduct PD directly or indirectly, including the IDF Spokesperson Division, the Planning Branch, the Home-front Command, the Foreign Defense Assistance and Defense Export Department, the Coordinator of Government Operations in the Territories, and the Liaison Unit to Foreign Forces. MOD operates three procurement missions in New York, Paris, and Berlin, which mainly deal with defence export

Big Time," Israel 21c, November 5, 2006, http://www.israel21c.org/bin/en.jsp?enZone=Culture&enDisplay=view&enPage=BlankPage&enDispWhat=object&enDispWho=Articles∩l1464 (accessed 19 November 2008).

[15] Israeli Ministry of Foreign Affairs, "Mashav," http://www.mfa.gov.il/mfa/mashav%20-%20international%20development/what%20is%20mashav/ (accessed 19 November 2008).

[16] David Harris and Itamar Rabinovich (eds.), *Israel and Africa* (The American Jewish Committee and Tel Aviv University, 2006).

[17] The Pew Global Attitudes Project, *Global Unease with Major World Powers* (The Pew Research Center, 2007), p. 55.

promotion and technological and industrial cooperation, while the IDF sends military attachés to Israeli embassies abroad.

The IDF Spokesperson Division is the largest spokesperson unit in Israel with more than 400 officers, civilians and soldiers and with a reserve unit of almost 1,200 soldiers and officers. Its mission is to report on IDF's accomplishments and activities to the Israeli and international public, to nurture public confidence in the IDF, and to serve as the IDF's primary professional authority on matters of public relations and distribution of information to the public. The IDF Spokesperson's Division performs a variety of functions, serving as the spokesperson for the IDF both at home and abroad, developing and implementing public relations (PR) policies, disseminating military related information to the public, instructing IDF personnel in matters pertaining to PR, and developing relationships with media outlets and accompanying them to military events.[18]

The IDF Planning Branch, a central body of the IDF General Staff, deals with strategic planning, building military forces and organizing them. Two of its units, Foreign Relations Division and the Liaison Unit to Foreign Forces are responsible for cooperation with foreign armed forces. The Foreign Relations Division is responsible for cooperation with foreign armed forces overseas and the deployment and direction of military attachés stationed in Israeli embassies, while the Liaison Unit to Foreign Forces is responsible for relations with various foreign forces stationed in the Middle East, particularly with peacekeeping units.

The Home Front Command and the Public Security Ministry, which includes the Police spokesperson unit, are relevant to PD because of the Palestinian and the Hezbollah attacks on Israeli civilians residing in towns and villages. In low-intensity conflict the boundaries between the home front and the military front are blurred. The Command instructs the public how to cope with conventional and non-conventional threats. Police routinely attempts to foil terrorist attacks, restore order when they happen and investigate who are the terrorists, how they carry out the attacks and who send them. Police is also relevant to PD because it routinely deals with sensitive PD issues including immigration, foreign labor and international crime.

---

[18] Israeli Defense Forces, "IDF Spokespersons Unit," http://dover.idf.il/IDF/English/units/branches/amatz/Spokesperson/default.htm (accessed 24 November 2008).

MOD's Foreign Defense Assistance and Defense Export Department (SIBAT) promotes marketing and sales of Israeli advanced defense systems, products and consultancy services.[19] SIBAT is relevant to PD because exporting weapons is a sensitive and sometimes controversial issue. The Coordinator of Government Operations in the Territories (COGAT) participates in the formation of policies towards civilians in Judea, Samaria and Gaza and implements them. The unit coordinates activities of government bureaus, the IDF, and the security establishments opposite the Palestinians in relevant civilian areas. COGAT also promotes humanitarian issues, infrastructure and economical projects.[20]

Several other Israeli ministries have representation and offices abroad and by definition are engaged in PD activities. They include the Ministry of Tourism which has offices in 15 countries, and the Ministry of Industry, Trade and Labor (MITL) which has commercial attachés in 21ccountries. The Ministry of Finance also employs financial attachés in several selected countries.

Extra-Governmental PD

Several public and private organizations in Israel and abroad conduct activities related directly or indirectly to PD. Many were created by concerned citizens, both Jews and non-Jews, who were frustrated with the Israeli government failures to address the information and communication challenges presented by the enemies of the Jewish state and their supporters around the world, primarily in the US and Europe. Several Jewish organizations added PD on behalf of Israel to their otherwise wide mission and activities. Others were created to confront a specific challenge in a specific country, such as the Academic Friends of Israel (AFI) created in the UK in 2002 to combat anti-Semitism in British universities and repeated attempts by the University and College Union (the union of British lecturers) to boycott Israeli scholars and academic institutions.[21]

---

[19] Israeli Ministry of Defense, "About SIBAT," http://www.sibat.mod.gov.il/SibatMain/sibat/about/overview.htm (accessed 24 November 2008).

[20] Israeli Defense Forces, "Coordinator of Government Operations in the Territories," http://dover.idf.il/IDF/English/units/other/coordinator/default.htm (accessed 24 November 2008).

[21] Menachem Kellner, "Resisting Falsehood and Protecting Integrity," *Babylon* (2007), 5, pp. 122–131; Stanley Waterman, "*True Exchanges or Thought Crime?*",

The extra-governmental network is also highly fragmented.[22] It includes organizations and groups that may be classified into five basic clusters: advocacy and lobbying, media relations, Diaspora PD, academic affairs and specific areas (see Figure 2). The principal advocacy organizations include the American-Israel Public Affairs Committee (AIPAC), the Israel Project (IP) and the Israel Advocacy Initiative (IAI) in the US; Britain-Israel Communications and Research Centre (BICOM) in the UK; I Like Israel Movement (ILI) in Germany; and The Australia/Israel and Jewish Affairs Council (AIJAC) in Australia. They mostly conduct lobby activity in local parliaments, disseminate information on Israel and the Middle East, and sponsor visits of politicians, journalists, scholars and opinion leaders in Israel.

Diaspora PD organizations include veteran institutions established even before the establishment of Israel to promote Jewish and Israeli

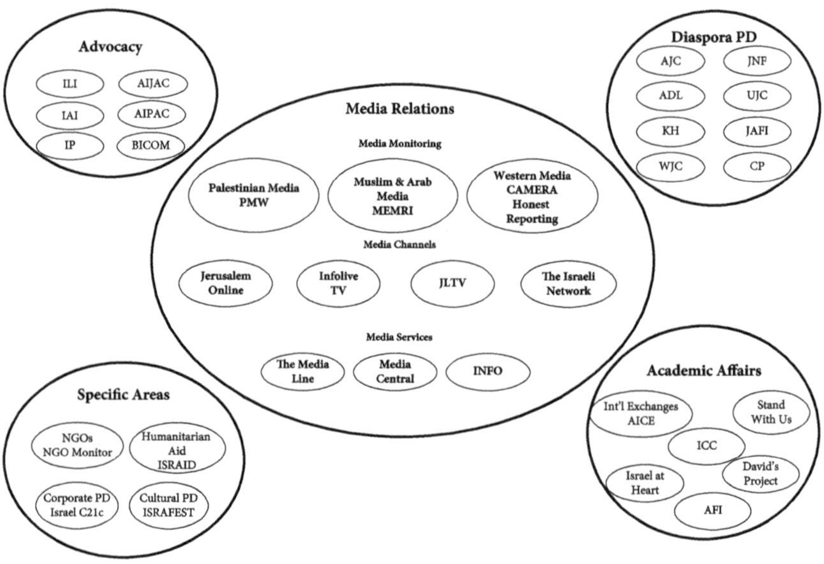

Figure 2: Clusters of Extra-Governmental PD.

Political Geography (2005), 24, pp. 998–1001; Ronnie Fraser, "The Academic Boycott of Israel: Why Britain?" in Manfred Gerstenfeld (ed.), *Academics against Israel and the Jews* (Jerusalem Center for Public Affairs, 2007), pp. 198–213.

[22] The term extra-governmental is used here because it is broader than the term NGOs which is now closely associated with organizations interested in global issues such as human rights, environmental protection, religion, and health.

causes. They include the Jewish Agency for Israel (JAFI), Keren Hayesod (KH), the Jewish National Fund (JNF) and the World Jewish Congress (WJC). Several American Jewish organizations added PD on behalf of Israel to their routine local or national community activities. They include the Conference of Presidents of Major Jewish American Organizations (CP), the United Jewish Communities (UJC), Anti-Defamation League (ADL), the American Jewish Committee (AJC) and the American Jewish Congress (AJCo).[23] Many of these organizations have offices in Israel established to gather and disseminate information and conduct local activities.

Supporters of Israel who felt that the Western media systematically distorts coverage of Israel and the Palestinian-Israeli conflict established organizations to monitor media outlets and correct factual mistakes and unfounded interpretations. Other organizations provide services to reporters covering Israel and the Middle East and operate independent media channels. Most of these organizations solicit and receive donations to carry out their activities. The Committee for Accuracy in Middle East Reporting in America (CAMERA) and Honest Reporting monitor media coverage of Israel and the Middle East in the Western media, primarily in the US and the UK. CAMERA also established REVISTA to monitor media published and broadcast in Spanish. BBC World Service enjoyed wide audiences and enormous credibility around the world, and therefore biased, inaccurate and misleading coverage could substantially damage the reputation of Israel. Following many complaints against the network, BBC Watch was established to monitor its coverage.[24]

The Middle East Media Research Institute (MEMRI) monitors Arab and Muslim media, The Palestinian Media Watch (PMW) monitors the Palestinian media. Media Central, Media Line and Israel Newsmakers Forum (INFO) provide services to foreign reporters stationed in Israel. The Israeli Network, American Jewish Life Television (JLTV), Infolive TV (a news service), and Jerusalem Online operate channels, broadcasting news and commentary on current affairs that are ignored by the mainstream media.

---

[23] David Singer and Lawrence Grossman (eds.), *American Jewish Year Book* (The American Jewish Committee, 2007).

[24] *BBC Watch*, www.bbcwatch.com (accessed 24 November 2008). See also Douglas Davis, "Hatred in the Air: The BBC, Israel and Antisemitism," in Paul Igansky and Barry Kosmin (eds.), *A New Antisemitism? Debating Judeophobia in the 21st Century* (Profile Books, 2003), pp. 130–147.

Several organizations deal with specific areas, such as academic affairs, NGOs, the UN, and corporate or business diplomacy. The radical left, Arab and Moslem organizations are increasingly conducting anti-Israeli and anti-Semitic campaigns primarily on American and European campuses.[25] These include lectures, workshops, exhibitions, festivals and demonstrations. Several organizations were created to monitor and combat these activities including StandWithUS, Israel on Campus Coalition (ICC) Israel at Heart, David's Project, and Campus Watch. The American-Israeli Cooperative Enterprise (AICE) supports exchanges of faculty members and students with American universitirs.

NGO Monitor exposes abuses, unfounded allegations and biased criticism leveled against Israel by local and international NGOs including Amnesty International, Human Rights Watch, Christian Aid and Oxfam International.[26] Israel21c conducts corporate or business diplomacy and promotes Israel's image through documentation of Israeli contributions to science and technology with emphasis on health, energy and the environment.[27] Based on Israeli experience and unique technology and instruments, IsraAID helps states and populations to cope with natural disasters. Cultural diplomacy consists of many activities such as annual festivals of Israeli films organized for example by the IsraFest Foundation and other organizations in key US cities and in other parts of the world.

Figure 2 shows that among the extra-governmental organizations, media relations attract attention and resources more than any other PD instrument. It also shows that much of the activity focuses on the US, where the standing of Israel among both the public and policy makers is highly positive. The contributions of all these many diverse organizations have never been assessed in any systematic way. AIPAC, for example, has been recently criticized by American politicians, officials and scholars who among other things blamed the advocacy organization and Israel for pushing the US to wage the war in Iraq. Most of the claims made by the critics have been discredited but the

---

[25] Gerstenfeld (ed.), *Academics against Israel and the Jews*.

[26] *NGO Monitor*, http://www.ngo-monitor.org/articles.php?type=about (accessed 24 November 2008. See Gerald Steinberg, "Soft Powers Play Hardball: NGOs Wage War against Israel," *Israel Affairs* (2006), 12, pp. 748–768.

[27] *Israel 21c*, http://www.israel21c.net/ (accessed 24 November 2008)

overall effects of the controversy on public opinion and policy aren't yet known.[28] Similarly, the effects of media monitoring are also not clear.[29]

Rivalries and Reform Attempts

Successive Israeli Governments recognized the need to reform the PD system. They conducted studies, established committees, held conferences and produced many reports. Most proposals however, were ignored and the few that were implemented didn't last long. The various proposals included the appointment of a minister or a deputy minister for information in the PM office, establishment of bodies such as a national information division at the PM Office, an intergovernmental coordinating body under the chairmanship of the Director General of the PM Office or a ministerial committee for information.

The drive for reforms stemmed from widespread feelings that Israel's PD is not working because of fragmentation and bureaucratic and personal fighting over authority, policy, information sharing and resources. Ministries, primarily the PM Office, Foreign Affairs and Defense, have often clashed over foreign policy and PD strategies. Clashes have occurred both at the highest ministerial levels as well as at lower levels, over structural and policy issues as well as on specific or relatively insignificant problems. Clashes have occurred inside ministries, among ministries, and between governmental agencies and extra-governmental organizations.

A few examples from the Second Intifada well illustrate the rivalries and their disastrous effects both on the conduct of PD and the attempts to reform the system. The Foreign Ministry often complained that MOD and the IDF did not provide or share critical information on military activity that has direct bearing on Israel's reputation and standing in the world. The same Ministry, however, completely ignored the GPO when, at the beginning of the intifada, it opened a communication center for foreign journalists. At the same time, PM Ehud Barak instructed his office to prepare and disseminate a "white paper" on the

---

28 Eytan Gilboa and Efraim Inbar (eds.), *US-Israeli Relations in a New Era: Issues and Challenges after 9/11* (Routledge, 2009).

29 Manfred Gerstenfeld and Ben Green, "Watching the Pro-Israeli Media Watchers," *Jewish Political Science Review* (2004), 16, pp. 1–27.

involvement of Arafat and the Palestinian Authority in terrorism. Foreign Minister Shlomo Ben-Ami opposed the strategy and refused to disseminate the book, claiming that Arafat was still a partner for negotiations. Nevertheless, the Prime Minister distributed the book to foreign visitors and organizations abroad, creating confusion at home and abroad about Israel's policy. After Operation "Defensive Shield" in Jenin, Barak's successor, Ariel Sharon, rejected a UN proposal to send an investigative committee, but Foreign Minister Shimon Peres endorsed it.[30] With Israel speaking in two opposite voices, it was unclear what was the policy and who was making it.

Several PMs attempted to reform the PD system but could not make any significant progress. Barak, for example, wanted to build a national information and communication division in his office, and in October 2000 he appointed Nachman Shai to "guide" and "coordinate" all Israeli communication and information activities. These functions were written into the appointment letter but were not sufficiently clear. Shai was also hindered by internal strife inside the Prime Minister's office between the Bureau Chief and the Chief of Staff and Security Adviser and by the reluctance of the different government agencies responsible for communication and PD to cooperate with him.

In August 2001, PM Sharon attempted to repair Israeli PD via the appointment of a minister dedicated the function. He asked Tzipi Livni, a minister without portfolio, to plan and coordinate PD strategies and programs. Livni concluded that effective guidance and coordination of PD requires the establishment of a central authority at the PM Office. She had no chance to implement her proposal, however, because Foreign Minister Peres and his senior staff did not want to lose their PD monopoly and undermined her initiatives. As Sharon did not want to confront Peres on this issue, Livni had no other choice but to resign from her PD assignment. Sharon then attempted to fill the position of Communication and Information Head in his office but the official appointed, Yossi Gal, a veteran diplomat from the Foreign Ministry, survived only two months.

Rivalries and reform attempts also occurred at lower levels of the national security and foreign policy establishment. The IDF became

---

[30] The UN and several human rights organizations conformed that 52 Palestinians were killed—all but three—were combatants. Israel lost 23 soldiers—several of whom were killed because they did not want to injure Palestinian civilians. See, for example, Human Rights Watch Report, "Jenin: IDF Military Operations," http://www.hrw.org/legacy/reports/2002/israel3/ (accessed 24 November 2008).

aware of the need to address PD and communication challenges, but units and officers pursued personal initiatives. For example, at the beginning of the Second Intifada, the Central Command (responsible for the West Bank) established a Center for Documentation and Communication, contending that IDF spokespersons were incapable of providing effective communication responses. The Center, however, was isolated from both the IDF Spokesperson unit and the Foreign Ministry. When a Palestinian boy, Mohammed al-Dora, died at the beginning of the Intifada in a war zone in Gaza, the IDF spoke in two voices. The General Staff hurriedly accepted responsibility for the death of al-Dora, while the Southern Command did not and vehemently denied media reports suggesting that Israeli soldiers deliberately killed the boy.[31]

Tensions also occurred between the government and extra-governmental organizations. For example, after Operation Defensive Shield, the Israel Project conducted a major advertising campaign against Palestinian terrorism. The Foreign Ministry criticized this campaign as hysterical, believing it damaged Israeli economic and tourisminterests.

More successful but limited reforms occurred at lower levels of the bureaucracy. For example, both the MFA and the IDF recognized the need to deal more effectively with the Arab media. The communication revolution in the Arab world, primarily the emerging of numerous regional and global Arab satellite television networks such as Al-Jazeera, required adjustments in the existing administrative structures. Hence, the Information and Media Division at the Foreign Ministry established a special unit for the Arab media, first within the Press Department and later as a separate independent department. In May 2004, the IDF Spokesperson Division also established a desk for the Arab media. These initiatives, however, were limited and could not

[31] The death of al-Dura inflamed the violence, became a symbol and an icon for the Palestinian fighting and substantially damaged Israel's image in the world. It is not clear, however, whether the boy was killed by Israeli bullets or Palestinian fire. The sole television reporting on the incident, by France 2, has been investigated and questioned, and the report's credibility is still being deliberated in French courts. See James Fallows, "Who Shot Mohammed al-Dura?", *The Atlantic Monthly*, June 2003, pp. 49–56; Stephanie Gutmann, *The Other War: Israelis, Palestinians and the Struggle for Media Supremacy* (Encounter Books, 2005), pp. 39–83; Nidra Poller, "Myth, Fact and the al-Dura Affair," *Commentary* (September 2005), 120, pp. 23–30; Philippe Karsenty, "We Need to Expose the Muhammad al-Dura Hoax," *Middle East Quarterly* (2008), 15, pp. 57–65.

meet the growing needs for sustained and well organized relations with the Arab media.

Attempts have also been made to reform specific PD instruments. The Brand Israel Group, a coalition of seven marketing and communications executives, has concluded that due to Israel's poor reputation abroad and PD failures, it needs a re-branding campaign. The work began when the advertising firm Young & Rubicam included Israel in its quarterly review of 13,000 brands. The survey found that Israel is well known but has little relevance for younger Americans, who only associate it with war.[32] Foreign Minister Tzipi Livni, who had been exposed to weaknesses in Israel's PD when she served as a minister at the PM Office, strongly supported the initiative. In 2005, the PM Office, the Foreign Ministry and the Ministry of Finance decided to authorize the Foreign Ministry to direct the branding project and allocated about $2.5 million for that purpose.

The Centralized Model: A PD Authority

The optimal model for Israeli PD must be centralized and sufficiently flexible to meet the needs of both peace and war. Officials and experts have suggested different administrative ways to accomplish this task. Often, however, these proposals reflected bureaucratic or personal interests. Foreign Ministry officials, for example, have always advocated a system with the Foreign Ministry at the center. One Prime Ministerial Bureau Chief suggested a new PD body and placed himself at the helm to increase his personal power at the PM Office. If the Foreign Ministry is a natural place to plan, coordinate and supervise PD, and although the National Security Council could also fulfil this function, the traditional weakness of these two bodies and their limited role in the making of Israel's foreign and defense policy means that the solution can only come with the establishment of new powerful PD authority at the Prime Minister's Office.

In 2001 and 2002, the Israeli State Comptroller examined the *Hasbara* (PD) system, including activities of the PMO, MFA, MOD and IDF, the Ministry for Public Security and Police, and the

[32] Gary Rosenblatt, "Marketing a New Image," *New York Jewish Week*, 21 January 2005; Nathaniel Popper, "Israel Aims To Improve Its Public Image Israel," *Forward*, 14 October 2005.

intelligence services.[33] The results were extremely critical. The report concluded that although the government recognized PD as one of the most important tools in the formulation and implementation of foreign policy, particularly during the Intifada, the system failed to prepare for and to deal with Arab and Palestinian information campaigns. The report attributed failure to the following factors: a lack of a "supreme head" and coordinator for the national PD effort; a lack of coordination among the ministries and agencies involved in PD; a lack of PD strategies and programs; and insufficient resources. The report defined "Arab propaganda" as a "strategic threat" and recommended an effective PD program with a clear and well-defined strategy, adequate administrative structure and resources, and most importantly, a "supreme head" that would manage and coordinate the national PD system.

In response to this critical report, the Cabinet in December 2003 established a committee to recommend measures for a major reform in Israel's PD, with Prime Minister Sharon appointing his Cabinet Secretary Yisrael Maimon as chair. The Committee was instructed to submit a report in 30 days, but the work lasted more than three-and-a-half years. An interim report was submitted in April 2006 for discussion and approval by the Cabinet, but the sudden eruption of the Second Lebanon war delayed the discussion. Moreover, the war was the occasion for a major Israeli PD failure,[34] and another committee of inquiry, the Vinograd Committee, established by the Cabinet to investigate the conduct and consequences of the war, criticized Israel's PD and made several recommendations for remedies.[35] Consequently, the Maimon Committee now had to consider the State Comptroller's report, the PD conducted during the war, and the recommendations of the Vinograd Committee.

The Maimon Committee eventually recommended establishing one central authority to guide and coordinate all the PD efforts under the leadership of a professional high ranking official. The official would be appointed by the Prime Minister, would report to him, would

---

[33] Office of the Israeli State Comptroller, "State Comptroller Annual Report," No. 53A, 7 October 2002, *Ma'rach Ha'ha'sbara*, pp. 9–23.

[34] Amos Harel and Avi Issacharoff, *34 Days: Israel, Hezbollah, and the War in Lebanon* (Palgrave, 2008).

[35] Anshel Pfeffer, "Analysis: Shattering Illusions," *Jerusalem Post*, 30 April 2007, http://www.jpost.com/servlet/Satellite?cid=1177591168908&pagename=JPost%2FJPArticle%2FShowFull (accessed 24 November 2008).

participate in Cabinet critical meetings on national security and foreign policy, and would have authority to guide ministers and senior officials.[36] On 8 July 2008, however, the Cabinet adopted only a diluted version of Maimon's proposal. It established a new national PD coordination unit at the Prime Minister's Office, but it downgraded its standing and that of its head. The unit would only "coordinate" and not "guide and coordinate". The head would be the Prime Minister's communication advisor who, given pressing national and political matters related to the Prime Minister, would have little time for PD.

This work builds on suggestions made by the State Comptroller and the Miamon Committee but offers a much more elaborate centralized PD model, built around a new authority at the Prime Minister's Office. This central authority would function over the next five to ten years, until PD is adequately immersed in the foreign policy and defense establishment; selection of the authority's head, the administrative structure and resources would meet the agency's principal functions of effective government-wide guidance and coordination. If possible and desirable, the authority may also coordinate PD activities among extra-governmental organizations.

Figure 3 describes the structure and components of a new PD system built around this authority. It consists of a head, public advisory council, several functional departments, an information and communication centre, and desks for short-term and long-term PD instruments.

It is possible to appoint a minister or a deputy minister at the Prime Minister's Office to lead the authority, but a professional director is preferable, as politicians are likely to inject political or personal interests into the working of the authority and are likely to battle with other ministers, especially those responsible for defense and foreign affairs. To increase the prestige and authority of the head, the holder of this position would be appointed by the PM and directly report to him. In addition, the head would receive the rank of Director General, the highest rank in the civil service, and would regularly participate in cabinet meetings on defense and foreign affairs.

The Public Advisory Council should include prominent representatives from various sectors including businessmen, industrialists,

---

[36] Itamar Eichner, "Government Secretary Calls for National PR Staff," *Ynet News*, May 24, 2007. http://www.ynetnews.com/articles/0,7340,L-3403839,00.html.

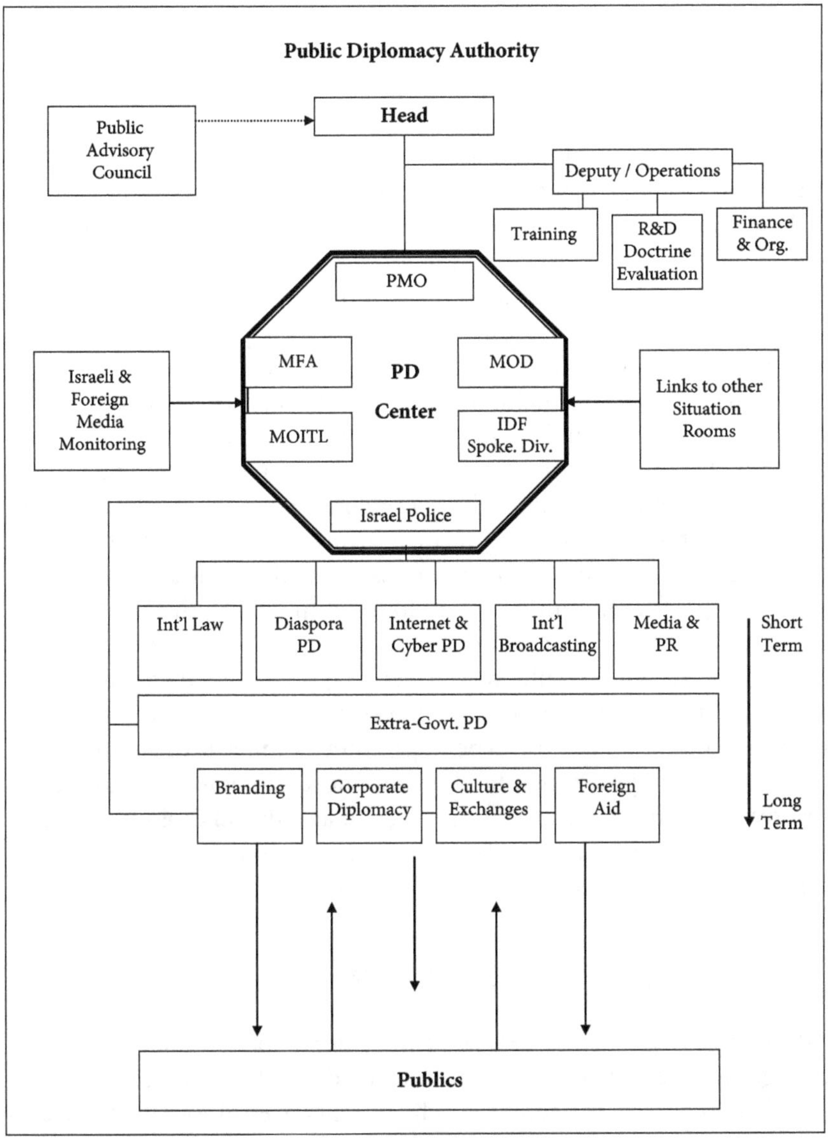

Figure 3: The Centralized Model.

authors, artists, musicians, scholars, publishers, journalists, and retired diplomats and military officers. It would meet at least once a year and provide both advice and networking. Council members would be appointed by the Prime Minister and approved by the Cabinet.

The proposed PD authority would have several functional departments, especially for research and development, doctrine, training, and evaluation. The research and development department would prepare the infrastructure and data needed to formulate PD strategies. It would also conduct thorough evaluation of activities and programs. The training department would train both the authority staff and officials working on PD both in the governmental and the extra-governmental sectors.

The communication and information centre would serve as the heart of the authority, guiding and coordinating existing and future activities. The centre would gather and process relevant information from various sources, including the media and all the governmental and extra-governmental organizations, and would initiate and employ effective listening methods. Based on information received from sources, the center would produce guidelines for all bodies working on specific short-term and long-term PD instruments, submitted them first to the head for approval, transmission, and coordination.

Working with relevant representatives of the PMO, the MFA, MOD, MITL, and Police, the authority would handle both short-term and long-term PD and would recommend appropriate instruments for specific situations and audiences. Several instruments such as media relations, public relations, cyber PD, international broadcasting, law fare, and extra-governmental PD are more suitable for short-term reactive and pro-active PD.[37] Others, such as cultural diplomacy, international exchanges, corporate or business diplomacy, branding, and foreign aid are more suitable for long-term PD.

Conclusions

Adjusting PD to the challenges of the information age and the rapid changes in international relations may be divided into three categories based on whether the required adjustments are minor or major and

[37] "Lawfare" refers to the use of international law in general and international legal institutions in particular as weapons of war and confrontation. Thus, it is also an instrument of public diplomacy. Israel's enemies have extensively used lawfare to damage the country's image and reputation. See, for example, Anne Herzberg, *NGO Lawfare: Exploitation of Courts in the Arab-Israeli Conflict* (NGO Monitor Monographs, 2008), http://www.ngo-monitor.org/data/images/File/lawfare-monograph.pdf (accessed 24 November 2008).

whether they deal with issues or fundamental structures. The three categories are revising, reforming and rebuilding. Revising refers to situations where the PD system works effectively and needs only minor adjustments in areas such as personnel, budgets and programs. Reforming refers to situations where parts of the system do not work properly or are outdated and more far-reaching structural changes are needed. Reforms may include creating new positions or offices, abolishing or moving offices. or altering hierarchies. Rebuilding may also include these activities, but it refers to systems that do not work and need substantial structural overhaul. Based on our typology, Israel's PD needs rebuilding.

Despite overwhelming security threats from immediate neighbors and more distant enemies, and despite the increasing importance of soft power and PD, Israel has not been able yet to overhaul its PD system. The country adopted the closed approach to reform, similar to the one used by states such as Norway and Poland, but so far the effort has been very limited and produced very little results. Many governmental and extra-governmental units and organizations are active in PD. Their contributions, however, are hampered by a lack of direction and coordination. As a result, the inadequate and highly fragmented system often fails to meet the challenges of modern PD and the low intensity conflict with the Palestinians and Hezbollah.

The main problem in the system is structural, and therefore the existing highly fragmented and ineffective model should be replaced by a centralized model based on a new PD authority which should be established at the Prime Minister's Office. The mere establishmen of the agency, however, would not be sufficient. In making critical decisions on national security and on war and peace, Israel must consider PD effects and ramifications. The proposed authority head should be present in cabinet meetings and add PD to the deliberation of options. Israel must also develop a coherent PD strategy and systematically apply it to organizations, instruments and evolving crises situations. The proposed authority should help to develop this strategy in cooperation with the Public Advisory Council and the relevant ministries and organizations inside and outside the government.

The authority should conduct an annual PD conference with all the relevant governmental and extra-governmental actors from Israel and abroad, to evaluate and discuss existing programs and activities and to consider new ones. The authority may initiate a dialogue with the Israeli public on PD, similar to that held in Canada and Australia.

The government has to substantially increase funding for PD and create a better balance between hard and soft power in Israel's foreign policy. A successful and functional PD system also requires constant monitoring and evaluations of programs and activities.

Different state and non-state actors have different PD needs, and they often have to adjust their strategies and programs to rapidly changing trends and circumstances. While we have focused on Israel, the approach suggested here may assist with the design and implementation of reforms in PD systems, primarily in cases of small states or middle powers facing serious international challenges.

ADVISOR NON GRATA:
THE DUELLING ROLES OF U.S. PUBLIC DIPLOMACY

John Robert Kelley

Introduction

More than forty years have passed since Edmund Gullion of the Fletcher School of Law and Diplomacy popularized the term "public diplomacy", sanitizing what had previously passed as "propaganda".[1] At the same time, the new term added shape and form to niche study of the intersection of policy, international communications, and diplomacy. It did not, however, prevent long and complicated discussions amongst public diplomacy scholars, who have yet to settle on a concise definition of what it is. There is much ground yet to be covered empirically. Should public diplomacy be domestically or internationally focused? What is the relationship between public diplomacy and propaganda?[2] And who can claim specialization in public diplomacy these days – official diplomats or a new class of actors from the global public domain?[3]

Without a concise definition on which most can agree, it may be a simpler task to interpret public diplomacy through its associated activities, thereby concentrating not on what it is but rather on the question of what its practitioners do (i.e. we know it when we see it). A few close observers have been bold enough to submit general categories of activity: (1) information management and distribution with an emphasis on short-term events or crises; (2) longer-term persuasion campaigns aiming to effect attitudinal change amongst a target population (sometimes referred to as "moving the needle"); and (3) building relationships,

---

[1] Nicholas J. Cull, *"Public Diplomacy" Before Gullion: The Evolution of a Phrase* (USC Center for Public Diplomacy, 2006).

[2] R.S. Zaharna, "From Propaganda to Public Diplomacy in the Information Age," in Yahya R. Kamalipour and Nancy Snow (eds.), *War, Media, and Propaganda* (Rowman & Littlefield, 2004).

[3] This echoes an observation by Hocking, who calls attention to diplomacy "by rather than of publics". [Brian Hocking, "Rethinking the 'New' Public Diplomacy," in Jan Melissen (ed.), *The New Public Diplomacy: Soft Power in International Relations* (Palgrave Macmillan, 2005), p. 32].

also over the long-term, to cultivate trust and mutual understanding between peoples (be they groups, organizations, nations, etc).[4]

If one accepts that this encompasses the vast majority of public diplomacy activities, then one may also discover two distinct but interrelated features with implications for the process and the practitioner respectively. In the first instance, there is a dichotomous relationship between communications activities on the one hand, and relationship-building, or what are now commonly called "engagement" activities, on the other. Communicators generate information either by relentless persuasion or the more nuanced pursuit of information/education by way of exchanges. Alternatively, engagement is less concerned with informing or persuading than understanding. This is why public relations scholars differentiate "one-way" (monologic) communications from "two-way" (dialogic) communications.[5]

Transferring this conception to the act of public diplomacy, the practitioner straddles two roles for which he is responsible. The pure communications components of persuasion and information underlie the activities of the advocate, who is charged with conveying a message, portraying an image, and acting as the mouthpiece for the generating party. In an engagement mode the practitioner's communication imperative is more indirect. Here, he instead assumes the part of an intermediary possessing information from interlocutors which he can then use to educate each one about the other.

Time is an essential factor for distinguishing between these two roles. When acting as advisors, public diplomacy practitioners are not unlike intelligence operatives or regional experts; they have access to privileged information that they use to inform the judgment of policymakers *at the point* of policy formulation. Conversely, practitioners acting as advocates become germane to the discussions of policymakers *after* decisionmaking has occurred. In light of the decision reached, advocates then develop a strategy for building foreign public support

---

[4] Joseph S. Nye, Jr., *Soft Power: The Means to Success in World Politics* (Public Affairs, 2004), pp. 107–110; Christopher Ross, "Public Diplomacy Comes of Age," *The Washington Quarterly* (Spring 2002), 25:2, pp. 77–82; Mark Leonard, *Public Diplomacy* (The Foreign Policy Centre, 2002), pp. 8–11.

[5] Carl Botan, "Ethics in Strategic Communication Campaigns: The Case for a New Approach to Public Relations," *The Journal of Business Communication* (1997), 34:2, pp. 188–202; James E. Grunig and Todd Hunt, *Managing Public Relations* (Holt, Rinehart and Winston: 1984).

for policy. Edward R. Murrow, the legendary American broadcaster and one-time lead figure for American public diplomacy as the director of the U.S. Information Agency (USIA), famously captured this distinction by placing advisors at the "takeoffs" or genesis of policy, with advocates often brought in at the moment of policy failure, the "crash landings".

To be fair, Murrow's dichotomy arose spontaneously from a moment of frustration. But scholars often return to this momentous occasion due to the way his metaphor effectively categorizes public diplomacy activities as divided. His impulse also reflected an inherent tension. For American practitioners it is a tension that has persisted since before Murrow's time at the USIA through the end of the Cold War and up to the present time. This paper attempts to trace this rather tumultuous history of a continuing duel between advocacy and advisory roles. In so doing, it revisits normative understanding of public diplomacy's principal roles and implies reconsideration of how they may be arranged to best serve in the contemporary international context.

Tension Between Public Diplomacy and Policy in the United States

Though disproportionately represented in scholarly literature, the American case is instructive for viewing the tension between public diplomacy and policy. Melissen, for one, highlights important precedents from the American model, including the necessary establishment of consistency between policy and public diplomacy aims, the importance of developing a long-term public diplomacy strategy with centrally coordinated policy, the recognition of the need for private sector involvement, and the unlocking of the "citizen diplomacy" potential of domestic civil society organizations operating overseas.[6] Opening the debate to new and updated applications of public diplomacy is more than just a reflection of its increasingly integral connection to policy *per se*; it recognizes the inescapable reality that the changing international context requires this consideration.

---

[6] Jan Melissen, "The New Public Diplomacy: Between Theory and Practice," in Melissen (ed.), *The New Public Diplomacy*, pp. 6–8.

US Public Diplomacy Organizations and Proximity to Policy: A Historical Perspective

The post-9/11 era of U.S. public diplomacy brings into sharp focus the ongoing conflict over the appropriate level of that diplomacy in relation to foreign policymaking and its inner workings. Because public diplomacy is multi-faceted by nature, a categorical solution is too simplistic. Advocates for cultural and educational exchange prefer considerable distance from policymakers to ward off charges of political tampering. International broadcasters demand independence to protect their journalistic integrity. In contrast, the Bureau of International Information Programs, which crafts and articulates policy advocacy messages for foreign audiences, is ideally situated close to the policymaking process so it can reconcile messages with policy intentions.

These were the principal observations of the Stanton Report, which sought to move exchanges to the USIA, spin off the Voice of America (VOA) under an independent, quasi-governmental board of directors, and relocate information and advisory programs within the Department of State so that they could be closer to policymaking centres.[7] These suggestions were never fully implemented and became moot in the aftermath of the 1999 merger between the USIA and the Department of State, which was motivated by a perceived need by some to integrate public diplomacy into basic policymaking institutions, not to mention a private settlement of disputes between President Clinton and Senator Jesse Helms.[8]

The subsequent trials stemming from the merger indicate that it did not settle the debate over public diplomacy's proximity to policy. Several recent studies on the subject have proposed creating a new

[7] Panel on International Information, Education and Cultural Relations (Frank Stanton, chairman), "International Information, Education and Cultural Relations: Recommendations for the Future," *CSIS Special Report Number Fifteen* (Center for Strategic and International Studies, 1975).

[8] Senator Olympia J. Snowe, Meeting of the U.S. Senate Foreign Relations Committee, *Congressional Record*, 31 July 1995, S10933; Edward Djerejian, *Report of the Advisory Group on Public Diplomacy for the Arab and Muslim World* (Government Printing Office, 2003), p. 6; Bill Clinton, *My Life* (Random House, 2004), p. 753: "I spent most of the month [April 1997] in an intense effort to convince the Senate to ratify the Chemical Weapons Convention: calling and meeting with members of Congress; agreeing with Jesse Helms to move the Arms Control and Disarmament Agency and the U.S. Information Agency into the State Department in return for his allowing a vote on the CWC, which he opposed…"

independent agency to oversee public diplomacy activities both to increase its influence and to raise its profile at the White House via presidential directive.[9] Meanwhile, international broadcasters grapple with the question of credibility exhibited in U.S. government-sponsored outlets and revisit the question of how strongly it should advocate views favourable to the White House.[10]

The question of the proximity of public diplomats to policymaking unearths a history of an insecure and highly-qualified arrangement that seldom achieved satisfaction amongst its participants. From the earliest days of the US Information Agency, the Eisenhower Administration, like the Truman administration before it, exhibited a keen interest in psychological warfare, bolstered by the president's experience in the use of propaganda to achieve political and military goals during the Second World War.[11] The "P factor", as Eisenhower called it, sought a close-knit relationship between public opinion and foreign policy, manifest in the extensive propaganda campaigns carried out abroad and domestically in cooperation with the Departments of State and Defense as well as the CIA.[12] However, the embrace of propagandistic tactics, demonstrated by the covert information programmes of the CIA, did not extend to all public diplomacy activities, and the newly-established USIA was kept at a distance from policymaking. The first director of the agency, Ted Streibert, did not have a personal relationship with Eisenhower and their correspondence was limited to monthly progress reports. [13]

The position of the USIA was further compromised by anti-communist investigations, led by Senator Joseph McCarthy, which alleged subversion in USIA's overseas libraries. Though unsubstantiated, the claims alone were a stigma that fractured the USIA's relationship with the fledgling National Security Council (NSC). One NSC official, upon being asked to share classified reports with the agency, replied he did

---

[9] See Susan B. Epstein and Lisa Mages, "Public Diplomacy: A Review of Past Recommendations," *CRS Report for Congress*, 2 September 2005. Of the ten reports proposing a Presidential Directive or reorganization of public diplomacy at the White House, seven also proposed a new independent agency.

[10] Sanford J. Ungar, "Pitch Imperfect?", *Foreign Affairs* (May/June 2005), 84:3; David S. Jackson et al. "His Master's Voice?", *Foreign Affairs* (July/August 2005), 84:4.

[11] Wilson P. Dizard, Jr., *Inventing Public Diplomacy: The Story of the U.S. Information Agency* (Lynne Rienner, 2004), p. 66.

[12] Kenneth Osgood, *Total Cold War: Eisenhower's Secret Propaganda Battle at Home and Abroad* (University Press of Kansas, 2006).

[13] Author's interview with Walter Roberts, 14 December 2006.

not trust USIA officials.[14] Successive administrations would establish their own arrangements determining how the USIA would liaise with the NSC, but they were always tenuous throughout the former agency's lifetime, and the policy relevance of the USIA was constantly called into question.

The Kennedy Administration's selection of CBS newsman Edward R. Murrow to be USIA director in early 1961 came with direct encouragement by the new president for Murrow to participate in policy discussions "when appropriate".[15] This included a seat for Murrow on the NSC. According to Walter Roberts, former associate director of the USIA, Edward Murrow was the only director in the history of the agency "to try to change foreign policy from an information point of view":

> Murrow dispatched now and then little memoranda to John F. Kennedy on little foreign policy matters... None of the [directors of the USIA], to the best of my knowledge ever suggested to the President of the United States, whoever he was, that certain foreign policy actions might or might not be taken.[16]

But by April 1961, in the wake of the failed CIA-orchestrated gambit at the Bay of Pigs, a manoeuvre that had taken place without Murrow's knowledge, public diplomacy's isolation from policymaking culminated in his now famous retort: "If they want me in on the crash landings, I'd better damn well be in on the takeoffs."[17] By the end of his involvement with the USIA in late 1963, Murrow had arrived at the conclusion that he had "never made it into the inner circles of the administration, for all the committees and task forces or his own seat on the NSC; it wasn't the NSC where Kennedy's policies were formulated...Above all the crash landings were outnumbering the takeoffs."[18] Although the Kennedy Administration originated the idea of using public diplomacy powers to advocate as well as advise on policy matters, implementation of that aspect would continue to plague the USIA beyond 1963.[19]

Six years later, President Richard Nixon and his powerful National Security Advisor, Henry Kissinger consolidated all foreign

---

[14] Dizard, *Inventing Public Diplomacy,* p. 67.

[15] A.M. Sperber, *Murrow: His Life and Times* (Freundlich Books, 1986), p. 677.

[16] Author's interview with Walter Roberts, 14 December 2006.

[17] Interview with Henry Loomis, 4 April 1985 in Sperber, *Murrow*, p. 624.

[18] Sperber, *Murrow*, p. 677.

[19] Gifford D. Malone, *Political Advocacy and Cultural Communication: Organizing the Nation's Public Diplomacy* (University Press of America, 1988), p. 20.

policymaking power in the NSC and limited participants to a highly selective group. The U.S. Advisory Commission on Information, then the chief oversight body for the USIA, produced annual reports during that time revealing a sense of exclusion, posing such desperate questions such as, "Should [the USIA] be more than an arm of foreign policy?" and "Should it play a role in the influence of policy as well as in its execution?"[20] In February 1969, the Commission sent a letter to President Nixon requesting that the USIA Director Frank Shakespeare attend all NSC meetings. The request was denied, with the exception of meetings in which matters of particular concern to USIA [were] under discussion."[21] Eventually Shakespeare, after threats of resignation, was allowed to attend all Cabinet and NSC meetings, but the deal reflected the resistance on the part of the Nixon White House to normalize the USIA-NSC relationship. The NSC invitation would never again be extended to USIA directors.

Outside the NSC, the Department of State offered a viable route to policy relevance for public diplomats, who might take their policy-related concerns through the Office of the Secretary to reach the cabinet level. With policy and communications interests overlapping, USIA and the Department were intrinsically linked. The creation of the USIA depended on a significant diversion of the Department's budget and human resources, including the redeployment of more than 40 per cent of its personnel temporarily housed under the U.S. International Information Administration, the Department's lead office on overseas policy information strategies from January 1952 to the USIA's inception in August 1953.[22] By its creation, the USIA's architects placed their hopes in a body that could command policy relevance without sacrificing communication savvy, but lawmakers regularly called this balance into question. Concern over the placement of policy information programs, for example, persisted within a litany Congressional studies conducted over much of the USIA's first twenty years.[23]

---

[20] United States Advisory Commission on Information. *Twenty-third Report* (Government Printing Office, 1968).

[21] *Foreign Relations of the United States, 1969–1976, Volume Two: Organization and Management of U.S. Foreign Policy, 1969–1972* (Government Printing Office, 2006), p. 36.

[22] Lois W. Roth, "Public Diplomacy and the Past: The Search for an American Style Propaganda (1952–1977)," *The Fletcher Forum* (Summer 1984): 365.

[23] U.S. Congress, Senate Foreign Relations Committee (Fulbright/Hickenlooper Committee), *Report of the Subcommittee on Overseas Information Programs* (Government Printing Office, 1953); U.S. President's Advisory Committee on Government

By the mid-1970's however, the existence of an independent agency for information programs seemed at last on the brink of either elimination or a dramatic reorganization. The 1975 Stanton Report represented a mediated solution between the two and somewhat blurry poles of political information and cultural information programmes. It proposed restoring the former to the Department while allowing the latter to reside in the still-independent USIA. The report asserted the need to "link policy formulation to articulation…ensuring that foreign public opinion was taken into account as policy was developed,"[24] but the more things changed, the more they stayed the same. The new Carter administration issued a reorganization plan (#2 of 1978) creating an entirely new agency, USICA [US Information and Cultural Agency?], comprised of both political and information programmes, administration of educational and cultural exchanges, and directorship of international broadcasting. For advice on policy, the USICA director would continue to send guidance through the Secretary of State.

The arrival of the Reagan administration opened yet another chapter in the application of public diplomacy for policy objectives. A far more aggressive stance on the communist threat, sparked by unfolding events in Eastern Europe and Central America, fuelled an equally more aggressive use of relevant agencies. By 1982 the USICA was once again reformed into the USIA, only this time much more concentrated on the task of enhancing the profile of the president and promoting American foreign policy overseas. All but forgotten were the stipulations laid out in the Carter administration's reorganization plan calling for the new USICA "to help insure that our government adequately understands foreign public opinion and culture for policy-making purposes".[25] In their place, the Reagan Administration viewed public diplomacy strictly as "those actions of the U.S. Government designed to generate support for our national security objectives".[26] While the

---

Organization (Rockefeller Committee), *Foreign Affairs Organization, Memorandum 14*, (Government Printing Office, 1953); U.S. President's Committee on International Information Activities, (Jackson Committee), *International Information Activities* (Government Printing Office, 1953).

[24] Malone, *Political Advocacy and Cultural Communication*, p. 37.

[25] Jimmy Carter, *Memorandum for the Director of the International Communication Agency*, 13 March 1978, quoted in Anna Tiedeman, "U.S. Public Diplomacy Lessons Learned from the Charlotte Beers Experience", 4 May 2004, http://uscpublicdiplomacy.com/pdfs/Anna_Tiedeman_Beers.pdf (accessed 21 October 2009).

[26] Ronald Reagan, *National Security Decision Directive 77: Management of Public Diplomacy Relative to National Security*, 14 January 1983, http://www.fas.org/irp/offdocs/nsdd/nsdd-077.htm (accessed 21 October 2009).

promises of USICA never lived up to their billing, the USIA of the 1980s aroused no expectations beyond serving as advocate to carry out the expressed will of the administration. USIA director Charles Z. Wick, a friend of President Reagan, with inexhaustible zeal built a modernized broadcasting component of global proportions so the agency could "tell America's story to the world".[27] Wick's commitment to policy advocacy and personal connection helped double the USIA's budget over the course of his eight-year directorship.[28] However, with resources poured into broadcasting, other functions suffered; educational and cultural exchanges waned until into Reagan's second term.

Meanwhile, policy advisory functions were still limited and largely beyond Reagan's public diplomacy purview. One former ambassador remarked in 1984 that the public aspects of policy were an "afterthought" in the Reagan White House.[29] The 1986 annual report of the U.S. Advisory Commission on Public Diplomacy found the agency was "still not asked to advise routinely on the public diplomacy impact of proposed policy options and new policies as they are being developed".[30] From July 1985 to July 1986, USIA director Wick attended only two NSC meetings, showing neither the interest nor the expertise to weigh in on policy matters.[31]

Deprived of the political will to use public diplomats as policy advisors, American practitioners endured the 1970s and 1980s, alternating between glimmers of an advisory role on policy and an abrupt return to the information approach stressing policy advocacy. The end of the Cold War ushered in a re-evaluation of the role of foreign policy institutions, coupled with a sharp drop in funding emblematic of the increased indifference of American lawmakers towards international affairs in the post-Soviet era. Courtesy of a motion first put before Congress in January 1995 by the Clinton administration's first Secretary of State, Warren Christopher, the option of merging the USIA with the Department of State was revived after more than three decades, a proposal gaining further momentum under the watchful eye of the chairman of the Senate Foreign Relations Committee, Jesse Helms.

---

[27] Malone, *Political Advocacy and Cultural Communication*, p. 64.

[28] Dizard, *Inventing Public Diplomacy*, p. 200.

[29] William H. Sullivan, "The Transformation of Diplomacy," *The Fletcher Forum* (Summer 1984), p. 293.

[30] U.S. Advisory Commission on Public Diplomacy, *1986 Report* (Government Printing Office, 1986).

[31] Edwin J. Feulner, Jr., Statement before the Subcommittee on International Operations, Committee on Foreign Affairs, House of Representatives, 16 July 1986.

Legislation introduced in following months and years supported the idea that the leadership of the Secretary of State should be strengthened through the consolidation of foreign affairs agencies, streamlining the Department's complex hierarchy by assigning the title of Under Secretar to former directors of those agencies. Changes that culminated in the 1999 merger of the USIA and the State Department demonstrated that public diplomacy had become no more effective; the U.S. Advisory Commission on Public Diplomacy's 2000 report found that the transferred responsibilities were "not seen as integral to the Department [of State], rather, peripheral".[32] Rather than the substantive work of advising to or advocating on behalf of policymakers, the first Under Secretary for Public Diplomacy and Public Affairs attended primarily to the administrative matter of facilitating the transfer into the Department's structure.

Public Diplomacy and Policy in the Post-9/11 United States

The administration of George W. Bush would be the latest to view duelling public diplomacy roles in these zero-sum terms, and it proceeded to shape new and existing organizations around an information approach reminiscent of the Wick USIA, setting out an aggressive information strategy to defend the administration's foreign policies. Ambitious broadcasting schemes, such as the new Arabic-language satellite television channel al-Hurra, were launched in pursuit of this goal, but these faced not only the challenge of the promotion of American foreign policy but also waning global sympathy for the United States after 9/11 and the outright hostility felt in many parts of the world over the 2003 invasion of Iraq.

Perhaps no single experience captures the estrangement between public diplomacy's advisory and advocacy roles better than the brief but eventful tenure of Charlotte Beers, the Bush administration's first of five Under Secretaries for Public Diplomacy and Public Affairs. The hiring of Beers, an advertising executive, cemented public diplomacy's isolation from substantive policy discussions, a separation that Beers, a

[32] U.S. Advisory Commission on Public Diplomacy, *Consolidation of the USIA Into the State Department: An Assessment After One Year*, Washington, DC: Department of State Publication 10781 (October 2000), p. 8.

policy neophyte, staunchly defended.[33] Her first significant act was to unleash a flashy, information-driven campaign, known as "Shared Values", to dampen rising anger in the geopolitically vital Arab-Muslim Middle East.

It missed the mark. The true concerns of the campaign's would-be audiences had less to do with Muslim life inside the United States than the impact of American foreign policy on Muslim life outside. According to Youssef Ibrahim of the Council on Foreign Relations, the campaign "failed because they weren't credible in the first place" and Beers was ill-suited to "put a gloss on policy" that curried no favor in the Arab-Muslim world.[34] In the end, the campaign's abject failure fuelled criticisms that Beers' unusual qualifications underestimated the importance of competency in the policy arena.

The Beers approach also drew fire from those expecting a precise form of policy advocacy to be included in the overarching public diplomacy strategy.[35] Beers steadfastly maintained that the Shared Values campaign was not intended as a policy communication but as an attempt to seek a dialogue beyond the parameters of policy.[36] In eschewing the policy debate in favour of value-laden themes like faith and family, Beers made the mistake of advocating a long-term strategy at a time when widespread disdain for American foreign policy dominated the moment. Skepticism mounted as reporters and pundits derided the selling of the United States in the same manner as a commercial item. "Can you sell Uncle Sam the way you sell Uncle Ben?" one writer asked, referring to the American instant rice product with which Beers first made her name in advertising.[37] The gulf between public diplomacy and policy goals was an insurmountable

---

[33] Remarks of Charlotte L. Beers, *CNN's NewsNight with Aaron Brown*, 16 January 2003, http://italy.usembassy.gov/viewer/article.asp?article=/file2003_01/alia/A3011719.htm (access 21 October 2009); Charlotte Beers, "*Public Diplomacy After September 11*," transcript of remarks to the *National Press Club*, December 18, 2002 http://www.state.gov/r/us/16269.htm

[34] National Public Radio, *Marketplace*, 16 January 2003.

[35] Robert Satloff, "Special Policy Forum Report: Battling for the Hearts and Minds in the Middle East: A Critique of U.S. Public Diplomacy, Post-September 11", *PolicyWatch #657*, The Washington Institute for Near East Policy, 17 September 2002.

[36] Beers, *Interview on CNN's NewsNight with Aaron Brown*; Charlotte Beers, "*Public Diplomacy After September 11*," transcript of remarks to the *National Press Club*, December 18, 2002 http://www.state.gov/r/us/16269.htm

[37] Nancy Snow, *Propaganda, Inc.: Selling America's Culture to the World* (New York: Seven Stories Press, 2002).

challenging for her glittering product, and as the Iraq War loomed in early 2003, Beers found herself mired in the contradictions of two campaigns, the public relations one that she championed and the impending military one. She expressed this frustration to the Senate Foreign Relations Committee on 27 February, "The gap between who we are and how we wish to be seen and how we are in fact seen, is frighteningly wide."[38] Four days later, Beers tendered her resignation.

One would be hard-pressed to note any positive impressions of Beers' accomplishments in the epitaph for her seventeen-month tenure in public service. Her Madison Avenue approach turned out to be a liability from start to finish as well as a miscalculation on the part of Powell. The message put forth by the communication-dominated public diplomacy strategy immediately after 9/11 assumed that "if only the United States clearly articulated its message…the rest of the world would jump on the American bandwagon".[39] But the idea that American values and way of life required some form of clarification missed the mark.

In truth, the larger portion of criticism over Beers dealt not with what she aspired to do but with what she did not do, which was to make policy discourses the focus of her public diplomacy strategy. "The problem is not our brand," wrote conservative scholar Joshua Muravchik, "it is their buying habits," as he suggested that fundamental changes must accompany the expression of American soft power if it was to win over those sceptical of the international endeavours of the United States.[40] By playing down the role of policy in the steadily rising anti-American tide abroad, Beers had unknowingly exacerbated two increasingly troublesome trends impeding U.S. public diplomacy.

Firstly, it had become evident that the ability of American Foreign Service Officers (FSOs) to advocate policy had been compromised. A 2003 survey of Public Affairs Officers (PAOs) posted in American embassies abroad found that, in the wake of the 9/11 attacks, opposition to U.S. foreign policy had become a moderate, major, or very major

---

[38] Charlotte Beers, Testimony to the Senate Foreign Relations Committee, 27 February 2003, http://foreign.senate.gov/testimony/2003/BeersTestimony030227.pdf (accessed 31 October 2009). Charlotte Beers, "*Public Diplomacy After September 11*," transcript of remarks to the *National Press Club*, December 18, 2002 http://www.state.gov/r/us/16269.htm

[39] David M. Edelstein and Ronald R. Krebs, "Washington's Troubling Obsession with Public Diplomacy," *Survival* (Spring 2005), 47:1, p. 90.

[40] Joshua Muravchik, *Hearts, Minds and the War against Terror* (American Enterprise Institute, 2002).

impediment for nearly 62 per cent of respondents aiming to achieve public diplomacy objectives in their host countries.[41] More tellingly, the survey found that approximately 71 per cent of PAOs had received some/little or no consultation from the Office of the Under Secretary or any other State Department or Administration leadership on the nature or implementation of policy initiatives.* A public relations-style plan led by Washington had the unintended effect of cutting out the FSO from the public diplomacy process.

Marginalising policy discourses from public diplomacy, Beers had overlooked the paramount causes for this grim reality, thereby obstructing the very "dialogue" she was attempting to promote. The primary cause of Arab resentment toward the United States, cited repeatedly by area scholars, pollsters, and analysts, is American foreign policy. Linked with a general character assessment of the United States, this invocation of policy supports arguments that Americans seek to dominate the Arab world and wage war against Islam. Thus it becomes clear as to why, for example, an Islamist such as Osama bin Laden and a secularist such as Saddam Hussein would each champion the Palestinian cause as well as their own at the same time.[42] Both recognized that citizens from around the Arab world, in spite of their many differences, share in their disaffection with American intentions and activities.

Of these primary policy disputes, the Israel-Palestine issue consistently ranks as the leading grievance over U.S. policy. When confronted with the question of what the United States should do to improve its relations with the Arab world, most respondents in each of eight countries surveyed responded that the U.S. should first and foremost change its position on Israel.[43] Issues surrounding the wars in Afghanistan and Iraq further damaged the credibility of the United States. For those who disapproved of the wars, the American decision to proceed in the face of resistance further widened the gulf with the United States and a host of other nations. Contrary to Beers presumption, the Pew report, *Views of A Changing World*, concluded that a majority of the more than

---

[41] United States Government Accountability Office, "U.S. Public Diplomacy: State Department Expands Efforts But Faces Significant Challenges," September 2003. The study was based on responses from 118 Public Affairs Officers.

[42] Fred Halliday, *Two Hours That Shook The World: September 11, 2001: Causes and Consequences* (Saqi, 2002), p. 40.

[43] James Zogby, "What Arabs Think: Values, Beliefs and Concerns," (Zogby International/The Arab Thought Foundation, September 2002), pp. 83–91.

66,000 participants in 49 countries accepted many of the espoused American ideals, such as democracy and the free market economic system.[44] In fourteen countries where the populations with a predominant or significant Muslim population, a majority of respondents expressed support for political and religious freedoms and affirmed the importance of a free press.[45] The true wedge issues with the United States lay, not so much in ideals and values, but rather in the preponderance of American power vis-à-vis its foreign policy.

Other evidence gathered by a consortium of public policy institutions suggests that American foreign policy was to a great extent heightening tensions with Europe as well. A project led by The German Marshall Fund of the United States and the Italian Compagnia di San Paolo, *Transatlantic Trends*, with responses from 8,000 Americans and Europeans showed a deepening apprehension of American power and an European view of U.S. unilateralism as a "possible threat" to international security by 2013.[46] European publics were largely united in their opposition to the Iraq War, influencing the outcomes of elections in France and Germany and later in Spain. Likewise, the survey captured trends in Europeans' diminishing favourable views of the United States, general disapproval of the foreign policy of the Bush administration, and antipathy towards an American exertion of global leadership.[47]

Conclusion

In its second term, the Bush administration could claim to have restored stability in the leadership of public diplomacy. In just over two years, Karen Hughes streamlined the "rapid response" communications of the U.S. government so that its message would appear more unified. Her successor James Glassman brought, from his former job as the chairman of the Broadcasting Board of Governors, a keen understanding of government-sponsored international broadcasting and a vision of how it can be modernized to compete in a saturated global

---

[44] Pew Research Center for the People and the Press, *Views of a Changing World, 2003* (Pew Research Center, 2003), pp. 7–11.

[45] Pew Research Center, *Views of a Changing World*, pp. 33–41.

[46] German Marshall Fund of the United States and the Compagnia di Sao Paolo, *Transatlantic Trends 2003*, p. 10.

[47] German Marshall Fund, *Transatlantic Trends*, pp. 4–6.

information climate. The budget for public diplomacy inched up slightly and global opinion polls late in the Bush presidency showed hostility toward the United States slowly abating in some crucial areas.[48]

However, this trend should not have overshadow the lack of progress on the critical question of what the proper role of public diplomacy should be in the current international environment, a problem that persists under the current administration of the internationally popular Barack Obama. Difficult questions remain: is it enough for powerful countries like the United States to advance agendas seemingly impervious to foreign public opinion? Should public diplomats get a fairer hearing in policy debates? In light of the problem of duelling roles, the following appear to be pertinent lessons:

Overemphasizing advocacy in public diplomacy creates a situation where policymakers are inoculated from important realities on the ground. Messages may be irrelevant, or worse, inappropriate. They may give the impression that the sentiments of target audiences are not being heard. (This lies at the core of the "listening" argument currently gathering momentum in the scholarship, the idea that acknowledging or showing understanding of the other's position will act as an emollient in policy implementation or, even better, produce a more effective and widely acceptable policy.) Extreme advocacy also challenges the credibility of practitioners, as can be seen in recurring conflicts within the U.S. government broadcasting establishment over how complicit it should be with administration policy positions.

Overemphasizing the advisory role, after a long period of continuous advocacy, creates confusion amongst public diplomats working abroad. Advocacy need not be "crude or blatant" and demands attention and effort. The USICA experience offers a glimpse into what may happen when public diplomacy architects go to the other extreme, a product of the 1970's aversion to all manner of propaganda and the "selling" of America. Change should come gradually, under steady guidance, and with the explicit backing of the executive.

Being neither here nor there is untenable. The case of Charlotte Beers shows us that one can nobly attempt to rise above the "takeoffs" and "crash landings" but find herself irritating all sides. Recusing herself from the advisory role, Beers signed off on a flawed and deeply

[48] Andrew Kohut and Richard Wike, "All the World's a Stage," *National Interest*, 6 June 2008, http://www.nationalinterest.org/Article.aspx?id=17502 (accessed on 12 October 2008).

unpopular policy that further alienated the very audience she was attempting to sway. On the other hand, paying no attention to advocacy left her diplomatic corps without guidance and unsure of what points they should be impressing upon local constituencies, which further marginalized and delegitimated public diplomacy at a time of great need.

Practitioners, when qualified and properly trained, do possess the ability to pursue both advocacy and advice to great effect. Forward thinking and innovative scholarship by enlightened observers, exploring the question of how best to reconcile the tension between public diplomacy roles, should offer an answer illuminating which of the roles is best suited to meet present needs.

LET'S MAKE THIS HAPPEN! THE TENSION OF THE UNIPOLAR IN US PUBLIC DIPLOMACY

Scott Lucas

In October 2008 Karen De Young and Walter Pincus, the *Washington Post*'s specialist journalists on military and intelligence matters, highlighted a little-known development. They reported, "The Defense Department will pay private U.S. contractors in Iraq up to $300 million over the next three years to produce news stories, entertainment programs and public service advertisements for the Iraqi media in an effort to "engage and inspire" the local population to support U.S. objectives and the Iraqi government." De Young and Pincus explained:

> The military's role in the war of ideas has been fundamentally transformed in recent years, the result of both the Pentagon's outsized resources and a counterinsurgency doctrine in which information control is considered key to success. Uniformed communications specialists and contractors are now an integral part of U.S. military operations from Eastern Europe to Afghanistan and beyond.[1]

The only problem with the exclusive is that it was far from new. Two years earlier, Pincus had revealed, "U.S. to Gauge Iraqi Support for Operations; Military Plans to Hire a Contractor to Conduct Polls and Set Up Focus Groups". The Lincoln Group, one of the four companies receiving the 2008 contracts to engage and inspire Iraqis, was "to assess the effectiveness of operations as they relate to gaining and maintaining popular support". The Department of the Army added, "Since the end of major combat operations in Operation Iraqi Freedom, Coalition Forces have sought to build robust and positive relations with the people of Iraq and to assist the Iraqi people in forming a new government."[2]

---

[1] Karen DeYoung and Walter Pincus, "U.S. to Fund Pro-American Publicity in Iraqi Media," *Washington Post*, 3 October 2008, http://www.washingtonpost.com/wp-dyn/content/article/2008/10/02/AR2008100204223.html (accessed 27 November 2008).

[2] Walter Pincus, "U.S. to Gauge Iraqi Support for Operations," *Washington Post*, 28 September 2006, http://www.washingtonpost.com/wp-dyn/content/article/2006/09/27/AR2006092701912.html (accessed 27 November 2008). The Lincoln Group won the contract despite revelations, in December 2005, "that it [had] paid Iraqi newspapers to carry positive news about U.S. efforts in Iraq". [Josh White and Bradley Graham, "Military Says It Paid Iraq Papers for News," *Washington Post*, 3 December 2005,

The tale of public relations companies making millions to sample the opinions on Iraqis after more than five years of American military occupation may not have been indicative of the general course of US public diplomacy, but it raises an important question. What would have happened in 2008 if the local population were not engaged and inspired but instead expressed general dissatisfaction with US policy, not only in the military sphere but also in the American political, economic, and cultural approach to the country and the region? Indeed, what happened in the 2006 consultation? Was there any change in Washington's strategy or programmes in response or was the emphasis simply on a better "presentation" of the US and its relationship with Iraq?

The practice of American public diplomacy has received extensive, exhaustive, arguably unprecedented attention since the tragedies of 11 September 2001 and their aftermath prompted the question, "Why do they hate us?" Yet in the myriad of studies from then to now, almost all focused on the mechanics of public diplomacy. There was the 2003 Council on Foreign Relations report, *Finding America's Voice*: "Many of the most controversial U.S. actions might have generated less antagonism with better presentation."[3] Months later, there was the State Department's *Changing Minds, Winning Peace: A New Strategic Direction for U.S. Public 0Diplomacy in the Arab and Muslim World*: "a new operating process and architecture are required for the transformation of public diplomacy".[4] Studies from 2001 to December 2007 by the Defense Science Board culminated in the proposals of "an independent, non-profit, and non-partisan Center for Global Engagement", "a permanent strategic communication structure within the WhiteHouse", enhanced "policy, budget and personnel authorities for the Under Secretary of State for Public Diplomacy and Public Affairs", and "a permanent Deputy Under Secretary of Defense for Strategic Communication".[5]

---

http://www.washingtonpost.com/wp-dyn/content/article/2005/12/02/AR2005120201454.html]

[3] Council on Foreign Relations, *Finding America's Voice: A Strategy for Reinvigorating U.S. Public Diplomacy* (2003) http://www.cfr.org/content/publications/attachments/public_diplomacy.pdf (accessed 27 November 2008)

[4] US State Department, *Changing Minds, Winning Peace: A New Strategic Direction for U.S. PublicDiplomacy in the Arab and Muslim World* (1 October 2003), http://www.state.gov/documents/organization/24882.pdf (accessed 27 November 2008).

[5] Defense Science Board, *Task Force on Strategic Communication* (January 2008), http://www.acq.osd.mil/dsb/reports/2008-01-Strategic_Communication.pdf(accessed 27 November 2008).

This work should not be devalued; indeed, one of the aims of this book is to feature analysis that can address these challenges and problems. However, in the attention to the role of the public diplomat, bureaucratic tensions, identification of audiences, and framing of issues, there is a risk that the central problem for public diplomacy is still not addressed. Authors may re-arrange the desk chairs—creatively, logically, efficiently—but in the case of the projection of "America", the *Titanic* continues to sink. To be blunt: how does the best public diplomacy cope with a flawed, even counter-productive, policy? Indeed, how can public diplomacy ever remedy the dilemma that this policy may rest on a conception that constrains and diminishes the foreign audience that public diplomacy is supposed to be engaging?

Approaches such as the "soft power/smart power" models promoted by Joseph Nye[6] will supposedly remedy defects in recent US foreign policy, in part through the incorporation and use of public diplomacy. Those approaches, however, did not challenge the source of those defects: the quest of the Bush Administration for a perpetual "preponderance of power".[7] Indeed, they continued to rest upon a quest for American primacy or, in Nye's definition, "the ability to get what you want by attracting and persuading others to adopt your goals".[8]

There has been no shortage of attention to the George W. Bush Administration's distinction in the pursuit of the unipolar. Supporters of the Administration such as Charles Krauthammer set out the conception as early as 1990, and it was elucidated as an official policy in the Administration of the elder George Bush:

> Our first objective [would be] to prevent the re-emergence of a new rival. This is a dominant consideration underlying the new regional defense strategy and requires that we endeavor to prevent any hostile power from dominating a region whose resources would, under consolidated control,

---

[6] Nye has developed the approach in books from *Bound to Lead* (Basic, 1990) to *The Powers to Lead* (Oxford University Press, 2008). See also Center for Strategic and International Studies, Commisson on Smart Power, *A Smarter, More Secure America* (6 November 2007), http://www.csis.org/media/csis/pubs/071106_csissmartpowerreport.pdf (accessed 27 November 2008).

[7] Scott Lucas and Maria Ryan, "Against Everyone and No-one: The Failure of the 'Unipolar' in Iraq and Beyond", in David Ryan and Patrick Kiely (eds.) *America and Iraq: Policy-Making, Intervention and Regional Politics Since 1958* (Routledge, 2009).

[8] Joseph Nye, "Propaganda Isn't the Way," *International Herald Tribune*, 10 January 2003, reprinted at http://ics.leeds.ac.uk/papers/vp01.cfm?outfit=pmt&folder=49&paper=221 (accessed 27 November 2008).

> be sufficient to generate global power. These regions include Western Europe, East Asia, the territory of the former Soviet Union, and Southwest Asia.[9]

Since 2001 the notion has been embedded in vibrant, if somewhat futile, debates over the nature, development, and value of an American imperium.[10]

Some authors have given substance to the quest for the unipolar through the identification of the demonstration case of US intervention in Iraq, through attention to the successful battle of a relatively small group of officials in pushing both unipolarity and Iraq to the top of the foreign policy agenda, and through study of the effect of the battle on Government functions such as intelligence-gathering, analysis, and overt and covert operations. Few, however, have interrogated the key shift in "power" in the attempted univocal era. "Power" was no longer just the means to obtain specific geopolitical, economic, and military ends but, expressed as the quest for American "full spectrum dominance", an overriding end in and of itself.

And so no one has noted the insoluble problem that the unipolar poses for public diplomacy. Jan Melissen has written:

> Modern public diplomacy is a "two-way street", even though the diplomat practising it will of course always have his own country's interests and foreign policy goals in mind (which most likely inspired his or her association with the public in the first place). It is persuasion by means of dialogue that is based on a liberal notion of communication with foreign publics.[11]

If the pursuit of the unipolar does not block this street, it turns it into a one-way avenue. Campaigns may claim to recognise and appreciate

---

[9] Charles Krauthammer, "The Unipolar Moment," *Foreign Affairs: America and the World 1990/91*, http://www.foreignaffairs.org/19910201faessay6067/charles-krauthammer/the-unipolar-moment.html (accessed 26 November 2008); "Excerpts From the Pentagon's Plan: 'Prevent the Re-emergence of a New Rival,'" *New York Times*, 8 March 1992, p. A14.

[10] See, for example, Michael Cox, "Empire, Imperialism and the Bush Doctrine," *Review of International Studies* (2004), 30: 585–608; John Gaddis and Paul Kennedy, "Kill the Empire!

(Or Not)," *New York Times*, 25 July 2004, http://query.nytimes.com/gst/fullpage.html?res=9905E5D7173AF936A754C0A9629C8B63 (accessed 27 November 2008); Robert Kagan, "The End of Dreams," *Policy Review* (August/September 2007), http://www.hoover.org/publications/policyreview/8552512.html; John Ikenberry et al. (ed.), *The End of the West? Crisis in the Atlantic Order* (Cornell University Press, 2008).

[11] Jan Melissen, "The New Public Diplomacy: Between Theory and Practise" in Jan Melissen (ed.), *The New Public Diplomacy* (Palgrave Macmillan, 2005), pp. 3–27.

the aspirations, activities, and values of others, but they are serving a policy which succeeds only if the American exceptional is rendered universal. American values must be enshrined as global values; American interests must be primary in a "balance of power that favors freedom". The process is not only positive in the demonstration and extension of a purportedly worthy unipolar but negative in the emptying or obliteration of existing political, economic, and cultural space.

But, of course, that space is not empty or blank. It is occupied by individuals, groups, and communities who favour their own interests, aspirations, and values. These are not necessarily "anti-American" but the approaches can be—indeed are likely to be—distinct from those pursued by US actors, be they policymakers or the public diplomats representing them. In such a context, how can Nye's baseline—the achievement of "our", i.e., American, goals—be defended?

One possible response was set out in 2006 in the model of the Princeton Project for National Security.[12] The product of more than 400 individuals, many with service in or connected to the US Government, over two years, the project was a clear attempt to deal with the perceived shortcomings of the Bush Administration's global strategy and its specific operations. While maintaining the military option emphasized by that Adminstration, the Project advocated "fusing hard power—the power to coerce—with soft power—the power to attract".[13] It pointedly rejected the Bushian unipolar:

> Power cannot be wielded unilaterally, and in the pursuit of a narrowly drawn definition of the national interest, because such actions breed growing resentment, fear, and resistance. We need to reassure other nations about our global role and win their support to tackle common problems.[14]

The Project did not premise its approach, as the Bush Administration had, upon a demonstration case. Indeed, it was a direct response to the case of Iraq, since that episode had damaged the American power to attract. It called for a restoration of proper channels and procedures for policymaking and decisions.

---

[12] G. John Ikenberry and Anne-Marie Slaughter (eds.), *Forging a World of Liberty Under Law: U.S. National Security in the 21st Century—Final Report of the Princeton Project on National Security* (27 September 2006), http://www.princeton.edu/~ppns/report/FinalReport.pdf (accessed 27 November 2008).

[13] Ikenberry and Slaughter, *Forging a World of Liberty*, p. 6.

[14] Ibid., p. 7.

Yet if Princeton clearly sought a reshaping of methods and approaches, including that of public diplomacy, in the conduct of US foreign policy, the question remains: approaches to what end? If the Project was notable in trying to establish a consensus within American political circles and society and in relations with political, economic, and academic elites in allied nations—a consensus akin to the American Cold War liberal consensus that held until the traumas of the Vietnam War—the ends for that consensus remained abstract. The Princeton report recognised this in its opening statement: "Americans need to recognize that ours is a world lacking a single organizing principle for foreign policy like anti-fascism or anti-communism."[15] Instead of delineating a considered response to the issues of specific regions or communities, and indeed to global problems linking these communities, the Project relied on the generalities of "Secure Homeland", "Healthy Global Economy", and "Benign International Environment", generalities that differed little from the 2002 National Security Strategy's invocation of the holy trinity of freedom, free trade, and free markets.

Rather than interrogate this sweeping proclamation, Princeton fell back upon the endpoint of "our" organisations and structures premised on shared, universalistic values:

> The United States should work with its friends and allies to develop a global "Concert of Democracies"—a new institution designed to strengthen security cooperation among the world's liberal democracies…If the United Nations cannot be reformed, the Concert would provide an alternative forum for liberal democracies to authorize collective action, including the use of force, by a supermajority vote.[16]

Bushian "preponderance of power" has simply been replaced by a "preponderance of democratic power" as an end in itself:

> Instead of insisting on a doctrine of primacy, the United States should aim to sustain the military predominance of liberal democracies and encourage the development of military capabilities by like-minded democracies in a way that is consistent with their security interests. The predominance of liberal democracies is necessary to prevent a return to destabilizing and dangerous great power security competition; it would also augment our capacity to meet the various threats and challenges that confront us.[17]

---

[15] Ibid., p. 13
[16] Ibid., p. 25.
[17] Ibid., p. 8.

With such an approach, the question becomes not that of the public diplomat (and, on occasion, the anguished policymaker[18]), "Do They Really Like Us?", but "Are "They" Really Like Us?"

Thus, from a starting point of a purported strategic as well as tactical response to the Bush Administration, the Princeton model moves to a possible convergence with the conceptions of that Administration and its supporters. Its call for military predominance is in step with the view of Robert Kagan:

> American predominance in the main categories of power persists as a key feature of the international system. The enormous and productive American economy remains at the center of the international economic system. American democratic principles are shared by over a hundred nations. The American military is not only the largest but the only one capable of projecting force into distant theaters.[19]

With its emphasis on predominance, Princeton's reference to the multilateral is complicated and its rejection of the unipolar is called into question. For it is rarely the case that the unipolar is pursued on a unilateral basis; instead, the goal is to ensure that other countries accept and follow your lead. So, by spring 2008, everyone—irrespective of how ardently he/she had supported the Iraq War—was a multilateralist from George W. Bush to the man who aspired to succeed him, John McCain.[20]

Indeed, Princeton's invocation of "values" merely enshrined American primacy. Its appeal complemented the rationalisation of power by historian John Gaddis, a favourite of the Bush Administration:

> Empire is as American as apple pie...It seems to me on balance American imperial power in the 20th century has been a remarkable force for good, for democracy, for prosperity. What is striking is that great opposition has not arisen to the American empire.[21]

---

[18] See, for example, President George W. Bush in a press conference on 11 October 2001: "I am amazed that there is such misunderstanding of what our country is about, that people would hate us. Because I know how good we are." [Quoted in David L. Greene and Paul West, "Bush Assails 'The Evil One'," *Baltimore Sun* (12 October 2001), http://cltv.trb.com/news/politics/bal-te.bush12oct12,0,3113511.story].

[19] Kagan, "End of Dreams".

[20] Larry Rohter, "McCain, in Foreign Policy Talk, Turns His Back on Unilateralism," *New York Times* (27 March 2008), http://www.nytimes.com/2008/03/27/us/politics/27campaign.html (accessed 27 November 2008); "Bush the Multilateralist," *Wall Street Journal* (28 March 2008), http://online.wsj.com/article/SB120666168987070241.html?mod=opinion_main_review_and_outlooks (accessed 27 November 2008).

[21] Gaddis and Kennedy, "Kill the Empire!".

Still, if the Princeton participants converged with Bushians on their promotion of a continuing American power, the question remained: how could and should the US Government make that power manifest? On the surface, the final report offered some indications of engagement, "The United States should make every effort to work with Islamic governments and Islamic/Islamist movements, including fundamentalists, as long as they disavow terrorism and other forms of civic violence." Specifically, "we must…be prepared to offer Iran assurances that assuage its legitimate fears".[22] Yet, beyond the condition placed on violence, the report did not answer the question, "What if a country proved unsatisfactory from an American perspective with respect to its policies, institutions, or values?" Would American engagement be replaced by the prospect of a US-led liberal intervention?[23]

At one level, the problem was that Princeton, despite any reference to the multilateral, swept aside international structures—"*if the United Nations cannot be reformed*"[24]—for its rather vague alternative of the Concert of Democracies. At a deeper one, the report merely compounded the risk of emptying or negating the political space of others. "Democracy" as an over-arching, US-defined concept sets the terms of the encounter. Other approaches—"Islamic democracy", "Arab democracy", "Iranian democracy", "Chinese democracy", "Latin American democracy"—have no standing. (Just before I wrote this, Condoleezza Rice amplified in an interview with the *New York Times*: "[International relations is] really recognizing that this is about a single answer to what is the right form of government, and that's democracy."[25])

At one point, the Princeton report recognised this pitfall, "Labeling countries as countries as democracies or non-democracies…needlessly complicates our relations with many nations and often undermines the very goals we seek to achieve,"[26] but it never confronted the problem set up by its own universal construction. Instead, specialists like Joseph Nye made artificial, often misleading divisions within

[22] Ikenberry and Slaughter (eds.), *Forging a World of Liberty*, p. 8.

[23] Conversely, the report never addressed the issue of American acceptance of "undemocratic" regimes because those countries a strategic function as political, economic, and/or military allies.

[24] Ikenberry and Slaughter (eds.), *Forging a World of Liberty*, p. 7.

[25] Quoted in Helene Cooper and Scott Malcomson, "Welcome to My World, Barack," *New York Times*, 13 November 2008, http://www.nytimes.com/2008/11/16/magazine/16rice-t.html (accessed 27 November 2008).

[26] Ikenberry and Slaughter (eds.), *Forging a World of Liberty*, p. 19.

nation-states, such as the juxtaposition of "mullahs" and the "younger generation" in Iran, and ponder why the optimal political system has not emerged, "Is it because people simply hate power?"[27] Thus the alternative of soft power, rather than dealing with emerging cases, avoided them: what of Hamas in Palestine? Hezbollah in Lebanon? Political parties in Iran and Iraq? Chavistas in Venezuela?

If Princeton were only just one report amongst many, one could be more sanguine about the objections to its purported alternative for US foreign policy. The study, however, served as a bellwether, promoting the ideas of a wide cross-section of policymakers, diplomats, officials, and academics. A year later, its findings were extended by another significant study, the "Smart Power" project of the Center for Strategic and International Studies.[28]

Led by Nye and Richard Armitage, the Undersecretary of State in the George W. Bush Administration from 2001 to 2005, the Smart Power project reiterated the assumption of co-operation through US primacy: "The United States must become a smarter power by once again investing in the global good—providing things people and governments in all quarters of the world want but cannot attain in the absence of American leadership." And, as with Princeton, that leadership would come through the fusion of "U.S. military and economic might with greater investments in soft power".[29]

There was a glimmer in the CSIS report that Smart Power might recognise the political, economic, and cultural positions of others: "Helping other nations and individuals achieve their aspirations is the best way to strengthen America's reputation abroad."[30] At the level of state interaction, the report added, America should renew its commitment to the current order and help find a way for today's norms and institutions to accommodate rising powers that may hold a different set of principles and values."[31] However, at no point in the 76-page report did the authors elucidate on these aspirations, principles and values. Nor did they confront the issue of communities and movements who may have had policies that did not sit easily with US interests: a

[27] See Nye's foreword to Yusushi Watanabe and David L. McConnell, *Soft Power Superpowers: Cultural and National Assets of Japan and the United States* (ME Sharpe, 2008).

[28] CSIS, *A Smarter, More Secure America.*

[29] Ibid., p. 5.

[30] Ibid., p. 5.

[31] Ibid., p. 10.

reference to "all parties involved in the Israeli-Palestinian conflict' did not extend to a specific recognition of Hamas.[32] Instead, the report fell back on a precedent which implied a restriction of the autonomy of others: "America can learn a lesson from certain elements of Great Britain's strategy in the nineteenth century, when it was the world's foremost power. Great Britain took the lead in maintaining the balance of power in Europe, promoting an international economic system and maintaining freedom of the seas."[33]

In "soft power", as defined by American practitioners, the issue is not "what they want' but "what we want". There is no debate over whether the US should spread its influence, merely discussion of the methods with which it should do so. The vision is of power moving one way, even as advocates assume that those on the "other side" are willing and ready to receive the message in the intended way. The attention to mechanics ignores the dictum, present in studies of the antecedents and elements of soft power such as "propaganda", "cultural diplomacy", and "political/psychological warfare", that no programme of public diplomacy can correct the deficiencies of flawed policies.

As George Kennan and his State Department Policy Planning Staff recognised in their seminal consideration of political warfare in 1947/48, if the projection of American power is not linked to a coherent strategy, it will probably fail.[34] If soft power is linked to a coherent strategy, but if that strategy is not supported by thoughtful and nuanced economic, social, and cultural planning—witness the case of Iraq 2003—it will probably fail. Even when soft power is linked to a coherent strategy and even when that strategy is supported by adequate planning, if it is perceived as imposition—including the imposition associated with "liberal intervention"—which does not recognise the autonomy of others, it will probably fail.

What implications does this have for public diplomacy, at least as conducted by practitioners of and connected with the US Government? If one accepts the definition offered by Representative Henry Hyde in 2002, as he introduced the Freedom Promotion Act, of public diplomacy as "systematic efforts to communicate not with foreign

[32] Ibid., p. 12.

[33] Ibid., pp. 12–13.

[34] Scott Lucas and Kaeten Mistry, "Illusions of Coherence: George F. Kennan, US Strategy and Political Warfare in the Early Cold War, 1946–1950," forthcoming in *Diplomatic History* (January 2009).

governments but with the people themselves", the tension raised during the George W. Bush era is apparent. For the strategy of that Administration was premised upon the need for an American predominance, extending the injunction of the 1992 Defense Planning Guidance to "prevent the re-emergence of a new rival", over those foreign governments. And that in turn, irrespective of attempts in the US Government's public diplomacy to separate governments from their populaces, meant an exertion of US power over "the people".

Of course, US officials would attempt to mask this, for example, through the invocation of powers to both rationalise and obscure the unipolar: the 2002 National Security Strategy referred repeatedly to "a balance of power that favors freedom".[35] They could present "America" as an economic commodity to be purchased by recipents. In the words of Secretary of State Colin Powell to his department staff, "What are we doing? We're selling a product. The product we are selling is democracy. It's the free enterprise system, the American value system. It's a product very much in demand. It's a product that is very much needed."[36]

Yet the fundamental problem remained. Because the unipolar would be jeopardised by an acceptance of the power of others, public diplomacy was in the position of both presenting the American exceptional and converting it into a universal to be adopted by others. The "Shared Values" initiative of websites and $15 million for television advertisement, for example, presented American Muslims both as part of an international Islamic community and as members who have advanced because of their location in the United States. The website "Muslim Life in America" featured the exceptional-to-universal conversion, "As Shahed Amanullah, an engineer who lives in San Francisco, California, puts it, 'American values are, by and large, very consistent with Islamic values, with a focus on family, faith, hard work, and an obligation to better self and society.' "[37]

---

[35] White House, *The National Security Strategy 2002* (17 September 2002), http://www.whitehouse.gov/nsc/nss/2002/index.html (accessed 27 November 2008).

[36] Colin Powell speech to State Department staff, 6 September 2001, in Maureen Sirhal, "State Department Looks to Technology to Boost Mission," *Government Executive Magazine* (7 September 2001), http://www.govexec.com/dailyfed/0901/090701td1.htm (accessed 27 November 2008).

[37] US State Department, International Information Programs, *Muslim Life in America*, http://usinfo.state.gov/products/pubs/muslimlife/ (accessed 27 November 2008).

While intervention in Iraq exacerbated the difficulties in this public diplomacy challenge, it did not create them. The Council on Foreign Relations noted by July 2002 the flaws of "a lack of political will, the absence of an overall strategy, a deficit of trained professionals, cultural constraints, structural shortcomings, and a scarcity of resources".[38] More importantly, the Pew Research Group identified the problem beyond that of mechanics and organisation, namely the international response to the American projection of power: "Images of the U.S. have been tarnished in all types of nations: among longtime NATO allies, in developing countries, in Eastern Europe and, most dramatically, in Muslim societies."[39] Even as the US Government re-doubled its efforts through new media and outlets, particularly in the Middle East, the comment of Osama Siblani, the publisher of the largest Arab-American newspaper in the United States, was on the verge of becoming an epitaph: "They could have the prophet Muhammad doing public relations and it wouldn't help."[40]

Well-intentioned observers have offered counsel to address this fundamental problem. For example, Mark Lynch wrote in 2003:

> America needs to approach regional public diplomacy in a fundamentally new way, opening a direct dialogue with the Arab and Islamic world through its already existing and increasingly influential transnational media. Such a dialogue could go a long way toward easing deep-seated anger over perceived American arrogance and hypocrisy and could address the corrosive skepticism about Washington's intentions, which colors attitudes toward virtually everything the United States does…
>
> Frequent and appropriately frank appearances in the new Arab media by American representatives could have a salutary effect on Arab attitudes simply by changing the pool of participants and the style of argument, creating new ways for individuals to stand out and enhance their reputation. They could open up a space for influential Arab intellectuals to triangulate between the extremes, staking out a new, reasonable middle ground.

[38] Council on Foreign Relations, "Public Diplomacy: A Strategy for Reform," 30 July 2002, http://www.cfr.org/pubs/Task-force_final2–19.pdf (accessed 27 November 2008).

[39] Pew Research Center, "What the World Thinks in 2002," 4 December 2002,http://people-press.org/reports/display.php3?ReportID=165 (accessed 27 November 2008).

[40] Quoted in William Douglas, "U.S. Turns to Madison Avenue for PR War," *Newsday,* 23 October 2001, reprinted at http://www.commondreams.org/headlines01/1024-06.htm (accessed 27 November 2008).

Such advice, however, inadvertently highlighted rather than redressed the problems. At no point did Lynch consider the issues and policies that may be sources of discontent with the United States. Indeed, his own advocacy reinforced public diplomacy as a vehicle for abstract American aims, detached from political, economic, and cultural realities, even as it claimed to establish a two-way interchange: "[The dialogue] might also help nurture the very kinds of Arab liberalization that the Bush administration claims to seek."[41]

The more detailed approach of R.S. Zaharna, working with the "soft power differential", has used comparative cases from the public diplomacy of NGOs and that of the US Government to set out the difference between "relational, network-centric" efforts and Washington's "outdated information, media-driven approach". Doing so, Zaharna aspires to offer the possibilities of "creating" rather than "wielding" soft power.[42] Unfortunately, this does not deal with the fundamental issue: because the "relational" is already set out in the conception of the unipolar, network-centric public diplomacy is precluded. Cowan and Arsenault may write of "moving from monologue to dialogue to collaboration"[43]; in the Bush years, American public diplomats have essentially spoken of collaboration while conducting a monologue.

Perhaps the most symbolic episode in the continuing, insoluble conflict between the theoretical dialogue of public diplomacy and the one-way strategic conception of the Bush Administration came in 2005 with the appointment of Karen Hughes as Under Secretary of State for Public Diplomacy and Public Affairs. Hughes, as a close advisor to Bush during his Presidential campaign and his early years as President, had been involved in the linkage of policy formation and the White House's promotion of that policy. Her initial tour of Saudi Arabia, Turkey, and Egypt in 2005 has become a staple of shock-and-horror public diplomatic legend, as she regaled women's groups about the wonders of being able to drive, seemingly oblivious to her audience's

---

[41] Marc Lynch, "Taking Arabs Seriously," *Foreign Affairs* (September/October 2003),http://www.foreignaffairs.org/20030901faessay82506/marc-lynch/taking-arabs-seriously.html (accessed 27 November 2008).

[42] R.S. Zaharana, "The Soft Power Differential: Network Communication and Mass Communication in Public Diplomacy," *The Hague Journal of Diplomacy* (October 2007), 2, pp. 213–228.

[43] Geoffrey Cowan and Amelia Arsenault, "Moving from Monologue to Dialogue to Collaboration: The Three Layers of Public Diplomacy," *The Annals of the American Academy of Political and Social Science* (2008), 616:1, pp. 10–30.

primary concern with developments in Iraq.[44] Less well-recited is the incident on her 2006 tour of the Arab world:

> "Tell me what we can do better," she said to a group of Moroccan business leaders, in a discussion about bridging the cultural gap. Soon, though, Hughes offered her own answer. "I keep thinking we need to do a reality-TV show of a Moroccan family living in America! Let's make this happen!"[45]

After trying—unsuccessfully—to elicit from Hughes "what she had heard and what she had learned" from the trip, Ilana Ozorgoy of *The Atlantic* concluded, "[Hughes] seems to ignore the obvious benefits that emanate from any conversation, one to one or millions to millions, in which each side feels the other is listening, not just talking."[46] It might be suggested that Hughes could not risk hearing and learning. When she was appointed, some of her new colleagues in the State Department were quick to point out, albeit on a confidential basis, "that the problem is American policy, not inadequate public relations, and that no amount of marketing will change minds in the Muslim world about the war in Iraq or American support of Israel".[47]

Three years after Hughes" excursion into public diplomacy, her successor James Glassman provided another example of the gap between a prescriptive American model and the engagement and networks sought by others. Launching the Democracy Video Challenge, which "invites citizens from around the world to create short videos that complete the phrase: 'Democracy is…'", Glassman proclaimed, "If the Challenge can generate thought and debate about democracy, on the medium of choice for young people, we'll have achieved success." Yet, as Ali Fisher has noted, the Challenge exemplified "the creation of a centralised emphasis of a judged competition, maintaining the we-know-best perspective, rather than a co-creational/collective effort of genuine open-source approach".[48]

---

[44] A collection of articles on Hughes' tour is at *Eccentric Star: A Public Diplomacy Weblog*, http://eccentricstar.typepad.com/public_diplomacy_weblog_n/2005/09/index.html (accessed 27 November 2008).

[45] Ilana Ozorgov, "Ears Wide Shut," *The Atlantic* (November 2006), http://www.theatlantic.com/doc/200611/karen-hughes (accessed 27 November 2008).

[46] Ozorgov, "Ears Wide Shut".

[47] Quoted in Elisabeth Bumiller, "Bush Picks Adviser to Repair Tarnished U.S. Image Abroad", *New York Times*, 12 March 2005, reprinted at http://www.commondreams.org/headlines05/0312-06.htm (accessed 21 October 2009).

[48] US State Department, "Video Contest Launched at UN to Promote Dialogue on Democracy," *http://www.videochallenge.america.gov/release3.html* (accessed 27

As the Princeton and CSIS reports demonstrate, this tension between the approach to US foreign policy and public diplomacy will not be resolved simply by a change in Administration. Even if the unipolar is explicitly rejected, the issues over American power remain. As long as such reports, and the policies of a new Administration from January 2009, are based on the assumption of American leadership and the goal of American primacy, then public diplomats can merely offer the illusion of a two-way relationship as they serve a one-way strategy. Glassman's first public speech as Undersecretary of State could not be clearer, "We want to influence foreign publics in the achievement of *our* foreign policy goals." The views, beliefs, and aspirations of other communities are marginal, even absent, in Glassman's representation: "We support constructive alternatives to violent extremism. In the war of ideas, our core task is not to promote our brand, but to destroy theirs."[49]

There may be talk of "change" in Washington under an Obama Administration; however, the formula of Robert Gates, Secretary of Defense in both the Bush and Obama Administrations, of "strengthening our capacity to use "soft" power and...better integrating it with "hard" power" is almost word-for-word the formula put forth by those supposedly advocating an alternative to the Bushian approach. Even more important is Gates" representation of power, drawing from Donald Kagan, in the post-Bush world: "What seems to work best in world affairs "is the possession by those states who wish to preserve the peace of the preponderant power and of the will to accept the burdens and responsibilities required to achieve that purpose"."[50]

In 2005, I wrote with Liam Kennedy:

> In the promotion of "freedom" to foreign audiences, public diplomacy is inextricably connected with the development and implementation of U.S. foreign policy, charged with the awkward task of reconciling interests

---

November 2008); Ali Fisher, comments to author. See also Ali Fisher, "Glassman in the UK," *Wandren PD*, 11 September 2008, http://wandrenpd.com/2008/09/11/glassman-in-the-uk (accessed 27 November 2008).

[49] James Glassman speech, "Public Diplomacy in the Twenty-First Century: Engaging in the Most Important Ideological Contest of Our Time," 30 June 2008, *Council on Foreign Relations*, http://www.cfr.org/publication/16719/public_diplomacy_in_the_twentyfirst_century.html?breadcrumb=/issue/50/public_diplomacy

[50] Robert Gates speech, 26 November 2007, *U.S. Deepartment of Defense*, http://www.defenselink.mil/speeches/speech.aspx?speechid=1199 (accessed 27 November 2008).

> and ideals. This reconciliation is always deferred, forever incomplete, yet it cannot be disavowed since it is the horizon of the imperial imaginary projected by the extension of the national security state.[51]

Amidst the continuing cases of US power and intervention, as well as US public diplomacy, in Iraq, Afghanistan, Pakistan, the Middle East, and beyond, I stand by that assessment.

---

[51] Liam Kennedy and Scott Lucas, "Enduring Freedom: Public Diplomacy and US Foreign Policy," *American Quarterly* (2005), 57:2, pp. 309–333.

THE DOTS ABOVE THE DETAIL: THE MYOPIA OF META-NARRATIVE IN GEORGE W. BUSH'S DECLARATIVE "WAR OF IDEAS"

David Ryan
University College Cork, Ireland

> Our age is involved in irony because so many dreams of our nation have been so cruelly refuted by history.[1]

Soon after 9/11 President Bush informed the nation that the attacks on the World Trade Center and the Pentagon were also attacks against American freedom, western civilisation and against tolerance and democracy. There is little doubt that these buildings were also symbols with other quite different points of reference in other narratives. These two architectural edifices were also concrete, steel and glass expressions of power, mastery, control and lordship.[2] The Twin Towers, constructed in 1973, coincided with the emergence of postmodernism, with the attendant decline of US power, the sense of meaning, the adherence of the meta-narrative of US history and diplomacy, the complication of identity politics centred on the post-Vietnam understanding of the US positioning in the world, the rise of gender politics and the Civil Rights movement that so thoroughly questioned traditional and collective assumptions on the United States character. The buildings are, in a sense, exemplary constructions that symbolise different things to different audiences. As Mark Kingwell has suggested,

> The World Trade Center never captured the imagination of New Yorkers, and the world, the way the Empire State has. It is not too harsh to say they are mourned more in memory than they were ever liked in fact; and the mourning is surely for loss of life, and innocence, rather than for any architectural or symbolic reason. Except in the pathological imagination of a terrorist, the World Trade Center never really symbolized anything,

[1] Rienhold Niebuhr, *The Irony of American History*, New York: Charles Scribner's Sons, 1952, 2.

[2] Wolfgang Schivelbusch, *The Culture of Defeat: On National Trauma, Mourning, and Recovery*, New York: Henry Holt, 2003, 292.

> except the bland face of late-twentieth-century capitalism, with whole floors occupied by traders and brokers, the phone-line and computer-screen workings of spectral wealth. And perhaps that, as much as any idea of America, is what Osama bin Laden was attacking.[3]

The Pentagon stood as two symbols in different narratives: the strategic node for the defence of the United States and the "free world" and simultaneously a concrete expression of US military power and hegemony. These two buildings also echoed two dominant theses on US foreign policy that pervaded the decade of the 1990s and were revived and contested after 9/11: that of the "end of History" and the so-called "Clash of Civilizations". These narratives subsequently, at least in initial stages, permeated the subsequent wars in both Afghanistan and Iraq with agendas of democratic transformation and the new "clash" in the war on terrorism.

As the ensuing war in Afghanistan and Iraq initially provided the United States with a greater sense of national unity and purpose, Bush's rhetoric and the emergent narratives – in which there was little consideration of the roots of such hatred and violence – juxtaposed terrorism against the benign framework of US history and diplomacy. The explicit and insidious strategy in the Government's narratives conjured up the vocabulary of civilizational conflict, providing both closure and explanation. Bush's rhetoric told stories about freedom, democracy and self-determination. He promised to bring justice to the world. Not only did the definition of the enemy enhance the Manichaean outlook, but the stories told by the President, newscasters, articles, op-ed pieces in the papers and magazines, further buttressed the basic dichotomy. The language used was performative and pervasive augmenting the idea that the new conflict filled the "space vacated by the unremitting bipolar war of ideas and values embodied in the unregretted Cold War." The conflict was not economic or social, as Edward Said posited, but ideological; the conflict was and is centred on one ideology, that of the west. Nevertheless, the conceptual framework focused on binary oppositions – that you are either with the terrorists or not – that was still a "framework separating us from them [which] is belligerent, constructed, and situational."[4] This is not to suggest that other views were

---

[3] Mark Kingwell, *Nearest Thing to Heaven: The Empire State Building and American Dreams*, New Haven: Yale University Press, 2006, 11–12.

[4] Edward Said, "The Clash of Definitions," in his *Reflections on Exile and Other Literary and Cultural Essays*, London: Granta, 2000, 570, 577.

not present, but they were marginal to the thrust of social preference and performance.

Contexts and settings were important: when Bush delivered his speeches in the National Cathedral or in the House of Congress, the location sent messages. It did so on the occasion when Bush climbed above the crowd at Ground Zero in New York, standing besides a firefighter, bullhorn raised. The audience chanted "USA! USA!" when Bush let them know, "The people who knocked these buildings down will hear all of us soon." (In the video sequence on the White House website one can hear the injunction, "Go get 'em'").[5] The situation is largely regarded as the moment when Bush found his voice in among the people; but that notion of "the people" is just as significant because it was itself a construction centred on the mood of defiance. (A mood that was not shared universally in the United States or even within various neighbourhoods that remained relatively "flag-free" in the days after 9/11).[6] The official narratives served as "gatekeepers ruling in or out options for groups, decision makers, and politicians." They reflected how the protagonists understood the impending wars and their own motivations. The stories provided "in-group support and solidarity that promote negative images of the enemy, escalatory actions, and offer little room for accommodation."[7] This is not to suggest that accommodation with the terrorists was desirable. What it does question is the effect of the rhetoric and public diplomacy in paving the way for the belligerent stance towards the regimes in Kabul and Baghdad. On the first, not all avenues of (private) diplomacy had been exhausted.[8] And on the second, the war on Iraq was simply unrelated and unnecessary, yet the power of the public diplomacy which was not only aimed at foreign audiences (a delineation that has become increasingly difficult over recent decades) but also at the US domestic audience.

---

[5] Remarks by the President to Police, Firemen and Rescue Workers, Murray and West Streets New York, The White House, http://www.whitehouse.gov/news/releases/2001/09/20010914-9.html, 14 September 2001.

[6] Susan Willis, "Old Glory," *The South Atlantic Quarterly* 101, no. 2 (Spring 2002), 376.

[7] Marc Howard Ross, "The Political Psychology of Competing Narratives: September 11 and Beyond," in Craig Calhoun, Paul Price and Ashley Timmer (eds.), *Understanding September 11*, New York: New Press, 2002, 304.

[8] Peter Singer, *The President of Good and Evil: The Ethics of George W. Bush*, New York: Dutton, 2004; David Ryan, *Frustrated Empire: US Foreign Policy, 9/11 to Iraq*, London: Pluto, 2007.

Still it was this use of public diplomacy as an instrument of power that eventually found such dissonance between US and foreign audiences.

A diversity of conditions and relevance to the crimes of 9/11 were conflated through various acts of rhetorical pronunciation. So for instance, within the constructed binary framework, the differences in terms of characteristics, involvement and agendas, between al Qaeda, the Taliban and Saddam Hussein were lost. The expectation that foreign audiences, especially within the region, would accept such rhetoric and public diplomacy was myopic in the extreme. A year after 9/11 the National Security Strategy informed us that "We will also wage a war of ideas to win the battle against international terrorism." The strategy was made up of various facets including the need to use "the full influence of the United States, and working closely with allies and friends, to make clear that all acts of terrorism are illegitimate so that terrorism will be viewed in the same light as slavery, piracy, or genocide: behavior that no respectable government can condone or support and all must oppose." The NSS indicated that Washington would support "moderate and modern" governments in the Muslim world, to inhibit the ideologies that promoted terrorism. Moreover, it would diminish "the underlying conditions that spawn terrorism by enlisting the international community to focus its efforts and resources on areas most at risk" and finally, it would use "effective public diplomacy to promote the free flow of information and ideas to kindle the hopes and aspirations of freedom of those in societies ruled by the sponsors of global terrorism."[9]

The NSS clearly sought to build upon the narrative established in the immediate aftermath of 9/11, yet for numerous observers, the promotion of the American vision failed. In 2006 Ambassador Pamela Hyde Smith reminded readers what the Pew Research Center's Global Attitudes Project had confirmed for the past four years: "World public opinion has turned ferociously against the United States." Quoting the columnist Roger Cohen, she added, "The world has 'stopped buying the American narrative.'"[10] Despite the attempts by the then British Prime Minister, Tony Blair, to remind audiences that the world was engaged in a "Battle for Global Values," he was quick to diffuse the

[9] White House, *The National Security Strategy of the United States of America*, Washington, D.C.: The White House (September 2002).

[10] Ambassador Pamela Hyde Smith, "The Hard Road Back to Soft Power," *Georgetown Journal of International Affairs* (Winter/Spring 2007), www.publicdiplomacy.org/76.htm.

notion that he was a foot soldier in the conventional framework by asserting that "this is not a clash between civilizations; it is a clash about civilization. It is the age-old battle between progress and reaction, between those who embrace the modern world and those who reject its existence – between optimism and hope, on the one hand, and pessimism and fear, on the other." He identified a crucial challenge as the battle for perception. As he argued in 2007, they could have chosen "security as the battleground", instead, "We chose values. We said that we did not want another Taliban or a different Saddam Hussein. We knew that you cannot defeat a fanatical ideology just by imposing or killing its leaders; you have to defeat its ideas." In a selective reading of history Blair argued that despite the early tolerance found in Islamic culture, by the twentieth century, "after the Renaissance, the Reformation, and the Enlightenment had swept over the Western world, the Muslim and Arab world was uncertain, insecure, and on the defensive." Radicalism, both political and religious, spread. It was then made respectable because those in power in the region accommodated the radicalism by incorporating certain leaders and their ideologies.[11] Despite these and similar attempts to reshape the perception and dominant narrative, Jürgen Habermas ultimately concluded, "the normative authority of the United States of America lies in ruins"[12] precisely because its actions ran counter to its preferred normative framework.

So what went wrong? Hyde Smith suggests that the most pressing problem for Karen Hughes, the Under Secretary, Public Diplomacy and Public Affairs from 2005, was to persuade President Bush to begin efforts to rebuild US credibility, moving away from the mega-phone diplomacy and unilateralism of earlier years. Various tactics to improve the American image were advanced. First, Washington had to work on the image of the US as honest broker; it had to treat other nations with renewed respect; they needed to listen better to the opinions around the world; policies had to be more closely aligned to traditional American ideals; and finally US public diplomacy, recently in decline, had to be bolstered.[13]

---

[11] Tony Blair, "A Battle for Global Values," *Foreign Affairs* online, January/February 2007; see also, Tony Blair, "A Clash about Civilization," International Relations and Security Network, 21 March 2006; idem., *A Global Alliance for Global Values*, The Foreign Policy Centre, London, 2006; idem., Address to Congress, 18 July 2003.

[12] Jurgen Habermas, *The Divided West* (Cambridge: Polity, 2006).

[13] Ambassador Pamela Hyde Smith, "The Hard Road Back to Soft Power," *Georgetown Journal of International Affairs* (Winter/Spring 2007), www.publicdiplomacy.org/76.htm.

Other observers suggested further sophisticated devices and methods for targeting information more effectively and scripting it to resonate with particular audiences. "Disaggregation" as a "strategic direction for public diplomacy" might yield better results and a more favourable disposition towards the United States and its foreign policies. They proposed a shift from simple "message management" and deployment of abstractions to US engagement with localised "communication infrastructures ... where populations make sense of ambiguous or threatening events through public discourse", further research on local "markets", and more attention to the " 'granular' nature of communication practice in local cultures". These suggestions could be incorporated into a more systematic approach to public diplomacy through the consideration and management of three dimensions relating to daily communications necessary to explain to particular audiences the essential context of various events. Secondly, strategic communication developed around a set of simple themes needed to be enhanced. Finally, Washington needed to develop lasting and credible relationships centred on various programmes involving: scholarship, exchange, seminars, conferences, and other initiatives.[14]

There might have been some merit to those pieces of advice, tailoring a more effective message that is sustained through a consistent engagement and exchange of ideas, but the far more widespread problem, the concept of "the tension between national and universal values", transcended the particular discussion on tactics. Far too much public diplomacy linked the United States and its foreign policies to the benign meta-narratives of US history (or more accurately, its constructed collective memory).[15] A range of large and simple themes were deployed far too frequently on democracy, liberty, self-determination, individualism and opportunity which are often juxtaposed with simple alternatives. These alternatives, constructed through a series of conflations, came to represent certain essences such as the "old world" of the eighteenth and nineteenth centuries or the "global communism" of the Cold War years – even after the myth of monolithic communism had been exposed and derided, there was no sense of irony in the tone or content of the Reagan administration's message

[14] Craig Hayden, "Disaggregate: A Strategic Direction for Public Diplomacy," USC Center on Public Diplomacy, blog, 15 March 2007.

[15] See for instance David Ryan, *US Foreign Policy in World History*, London: Routledge, 2000.

on communism in Nicaragua or Central America or the Bush administration's depictions of the threat faced by the United States in Iraq prior to invasion. These essences do not bear a significant relationship to the actuality of experience within the various situations, nor do the depictions find a comfortable home in the perceptions of many audiences. The facile and utilitarian conflations represented by Bush's infamous phrases as the "terrorists and the tyrants" at West Point in June 2002, paving the road to Baghdad would ultimately undermine US credibility.

These meta-narratives not only led to the strategic tensions between US public diplomacy and its policies but also, they often appeared incongruous and incoherent when set against counter-narratives and the blizzard of images of the US at war. Falluja, Abu Ghraib, Guantanamo, and Haditha were cases in point, but there were no end of examples from the Cold War era and earlier. There is incoherence at the heart of US foreign policy that is difficult to reconcile, especially at times of crisis or war, in which various actions associated with US national security undermine the traditional reading and articulation of American values. This incoherence was identified in 1955 by Louis Hartz in his discourse on the two American nationalisms. One wellspring of nationalism was associated with the collective memories of those "universal" values and the other associated with the pursuit of the US national interest, national security, the state and its foreign policies.[16] Serge Ricard, in his work on American exceptionalism, clearly identified the irreducible contradiction that would forever vitiate US foreign policy: the tensions between the universal and the particular.[17]

These narrative tensions can be seen within the United States at most points of its expansion in the internal debates and division that attended the foreign policies of 1823, 1848, 1898, 1946, the 1960s, the 1980s and since 2003. Over time the tensions and divisions abate through the desire for reconciliation, community and a restored sense of identity and shared sense of collective memory within the nation, and of course public diplomacy is also about explaining and contextualising for various domestic audiences. The Obama Administration might well provide such an opportunity; words of unity might transcend the

---

[16] Louis Hartz, *The Liberal Tradition in America*, New York: Harcourt, Brace, 1955, 289.

[17] Serge Ricard, *The Manifest Destiny of the United States in the 19th Century*, Paris: Didier Erudition-CNED, 1999.

discourse of division and Obama might, like Lincoln, construct another metaphorical Gettysburg Address, with "everyone in that vast throng of thousands…having their intellectual pocket picked" and the crowd "depart[ing] with a new thing in its ideological luggage".[18]

But if such periodic reconciliation is attractive and desired within the United States, facilitated by ideologies that bridge the gap between the ways things actually are and the way they ought to be, no such mechanisms work effectively to many other audiences around the world. Such meta-narratives, cast amongst the plurality of interpretive networks outside the United States and juxtaposed with counter-narratives, bitter experiences, or alternative interpretations of US foreign policies, produce strategic tensions that are too acute to reconcile. It is too difficult to negotiate the differences between things as they seemingly are elsewhere and as they are presented to be in US public diplomacy. In the case of the Iraq war, it seems that no matter how subtle, soft and sophisticated public diplomacy might aspire to be, the message, especially set against the megaphone diplomacy and rhetorical inclinations of President Bush, did not and could not effectively speak to US allies, let alone adversaries or even well-disposed yet sceptical audiences.

In 2003, the Pew Global Attitudes surveys revealed that many respondents, even in states not generally considered favourably disposed to the United States and in countries in the Middle East, those surveyed did not have issues or problems with democracy, liberty, and progress; indeed there was considerable desire for them. What the respondents had a problem with was the application of US power, not only hard power but the soft power that linked these concepts to phrases such as "American values".[19] The mingling of the universal with the particular seemed incoherent, especially when set against the history of US support for authoritarian regimes, its continued support for such regimes in the Middle East, the failure of the "transformative" project in the region, and the attendant support for regimes throughout Central Asia in the Long War.

Secondly, if experience might be one mitigating factor that inhibits the impact of public diplomacy, another might be the too pervasive declarative tone in much of its rhetoric. US public diplomacy, the

[18] Garry Wills, *Lincoln at Gettysburg: The Words That Remade America*. New York: Touchstone, 1992, 146–147.

[19] Pew Global Attitudes Project, *Views of a Changing World*, Washington, D.C.: Pew Center for the People and the Press (June 2003), 6.

associated rhetoric, and its delivery is often not subtle or sophisticated enough for many audiences. Far too frequently there is the reliance on assertion in the absence of argument or explanation that undermines the tone and plausibility of the message. The frequent and oft-repeated words associated with US foreign policy, such as liberty and democracy, are thrown out like confetti in public discourse, paying little attention to the recipient audiences. So for instance these messages are received by audiences living under authoritarian regimes supported by the United States without any sense of irony or insincerity. The ontological powers of US public diplomacy are ultimately counterproductive. If they determine the meaning and applicability of words like democracy or liberty and if they can decide with shifting criteria which elections to recognise or regimes to characterise as democratic and which to support and which to oppose—frequently through unilateral action, interpretation, or definition—such inclinations obviously and necessarily generate narratives on double standards and antipathy towards US power and its foreign policy.

In the 1950s Hans Morgenthau characterised public diplomacy as a process in which politicians and others appealed to the world rather than privately to each other. When George Bush and Tony Blair decided to position the various crises following 9/11 within the context of a battle over values, as opposed to security of necessity, they had to appeal to the world through the "word" rather than address particular issues with particular regimes through quiet diplomacy. Frequently, the processes of public diplomacy necessitated the vilification of a significant Other, in Morgenthau's era the US opponents in the Cold War, and more recently the conversion of Saddam Hussein and others into the "axis of evil" (itself a referent conflation of signifiers relating to World War II and Reagan's characterisation of the Soviet Union). This conversion occurred despite the extensive contact with Saddam Hussein through the 1970s and 1980s and the muted response to his worst atrocities across that decade for strategic reasons, which of course local populations and audiences well remember.

Such characterisations subsequently make it difficult to conduct private diplomacy, to negotiate, and to compromise, for example on an Iraqi withdrawal from Kuwait in very early January 1991, with the Sandinistas during the 1980s, or over Kosovo in 1999. As Ambassador Charles Freeman said:

> If there is no private diplomacy, there can be no public diplomacy. And as we all know, Americans no longer do diplomacy ourselves. We are very concerned that, by talking to foreigners with whom we disagree, we

> might inadvertently suggest that we respect them and are prepared to work with them rather than preparing to bomb them into peaceful coexistence. Both at home and abroad we respond to critics by stigmatizing them and ostracising them. To avoid sending a signal of reasonableness or willingness to engage in dialogue, we do threats, not diplomacy. That's something we outsource to whomever we can find to take on the morally reprehensible task of conducting it.[20]

Such attitudes might go some way to explaining the reaction to Presidential candidate Barack Obama's indication that he would be willing to talk to regimes such as Iran. Without the serious attempt to diplomatically engage opponents before the use of force is employed, US credibility is undermined and its image as an aggressive power is enhanced; there is little that public diplomacy can effect to bring about changes in attitude.

Finally, the more parochial elements of the US National Security Strategy of both 2002 and 2006, when linked to the sentiments of the Defense Planning Guidance document of 1992 and the similar messages that emanated from the Reagan National Security Council in 1982 on the inclinations towards unilateralism, undermine the narratives of universal or shared values through these rhetorical projections of the US national interest and its power.[21] The demonstrations of unilateralism and isolation on a range of issues from the Kyoto process to the International Criminal Court undermine US diplomatic credibility and the US potential for leadership on a range of other, perhaps more pressing issues. If the United States expects to maintain its leadership and develop or maintain the substantial reservoir of "soft power" that it harbours, it will need to listen more effectively, negotiate more sincerely through quiet diplomacy, and, at least for Joseph Nye, "define [its] national interest in a broad and farsighted way that incorporates global interests".[22]

In May 2010 a new National Security Strategy was unveiled by the Obama Administration. The document declared:

---

[20] Chas W. Freeman, "Why not Let Them Hate Us, as Long as They Fear Us," remarks to the United States Information Agency Alumni Association, 4 October 2006, Washington, D.C., www.publicdiplomacy.org/71.htm.

[21] National Security Strategy 2002.

[22] Joseph Nye, *The Paradox of American Power: Why the World's Only Superpower Can't Go It Alone*, Oxford: Oxford University Press, 2002, 157–159; Jessica T. Matthews, "Estranged Partners," *Foreign Policy* (November / December 2001), 48–49; Michael Cox, "American Power Before and After 11 September: Dizzy with Success?" *International Affairs* 78, no. 2 (2002), 264.

> Our national security strategy is, therefore, focused on renewing American leadership so that we can more effectively advance our interests in the 21st century. We will do so by building upon the sources of our strength at home, while shaping an international order that can meet the challenges of our time. This strategy recognizes the fundamental connection between our national security, our national competitiveness, resilience, and moral example. And it reaffirms America's commitment to pursue our interests through an international system in which all nations have certain rights and responsibilities.[23]

For some, this implicit rejection of the unipolar emphasis of the early years of the Bush Administration, accompanied by the dropping of the phrase "War on Terror", was a new course for US foreign policy. Obama's notion of engagement was proclaimed to be "on behalf of a world in which individuals enjoy more freedom and opportunity, and nations have incentives to act responsibly, while facing consequences when they do not". However, in practice, if not rhetoric, the Administration faced a fundamental question, 18 months into its handling of issues from Afghanistan to Iran to the Middle East to Latin America. Did its commitment to "a stronger foundation for American leadership" offer a significant difference for the rest of the world?

In his address to the USIA Alumni Association, Charles Freeman rejected Caligula's maxim, "Why not let them hate us, as long as they fear us", because of its long-term impact on US foreign policy, leadership, and the prospects for democracy promotion. This had to be replaced…

> …with our traditional respect for the opinion of mankind. I do not think it is beyond us to do so. We are a far better and more courageous people than we currently appear. But when we do restore ourselves to mental balance, we will, I fear, find that decades are required … to rebuild the appeal and influence our post-9/11 psychoses took a mere five years to destroy.[24]

---

[23] US National Security Strategy, May 2010, http://www.whitehouse.gov/sites/default/files/rss_viewer/national_security_strategy.pdf (accessed 08 June 2010)

[24] Chas W. Freeman, "Why not Let Them Hate Us, as Long as They Fear Us," remarks to the United States Information Agency Alumni Association, 4 October 2006, Washington, D.C., www.publicdiplomacy.org/71.htm

SOFT POWER, US PUBLIC DIPLOMACY AND GLOBAL RISK

Giles Scott-Smith

It is clear that the events of 2008 will go down as a turning-point in world politics, if not in the sense of the US view on the world, certainly in the sense of the rest of the world's view of the US. The sudden, precipitous unravelling of the Wall Street-led financial system in August and September, coupled with a calamitous week of turmoil on Capitol Hill as Congress strived to reach consensus on a heavily criticised Federal bail-out plan, have released shock-waves not just of doubt but of disbelief that the US still possesses the capability for world leadership. Commentary on the significance of these events is fast increasing and declarations of the end of empire, not so long since it was announced in the first place, will be dominating much International Relations and Politics discourse for some time to come.[1] President Obama has taken these seismic changes into account, but since taking office he has struggled to overcome the image of being both winner and loser. The damage to American political, economic, and financial credibility that occurred during the eight years of the Bush presidency is something that is inescapable, and credibility is a crucial factor in the projection of soft power. This chapter focuses on some central issues that need to be faced in the future in terms of re-aligning US national interest and rebuilding its soft power potential. Above all, there needs to be a conscious effort to understand what it means to be one nation among many, even if transferring this into a political platform is not going to be easy.

Soft Power and Public Diplomacy since the End of the Cold War

It is somewhat ironic that in a decade when hard power has largely set the tone for the US foreign policy approach, soft power has become

[1] For some early contributions to this field see Aziz Huq, "How to Manage Imperial Decline," *Asia Times*, 18 October 2008; "The End of Arrogance: America Loses its Dominant Economic Role," *Der Spiegel*, 30 September 2008, http://www.spiegel.de/international/world/0,1518,581502,00.html (accessed 24 October 2008).

the passion of analysts and academics alike. Underlying this "movement" is a renewed liberal wish for a peaceful paradigm in international relations that eschews the use of force, but there is also an understanding that competition between state entities is now as much about imagery and values as it is about power in the traditional sense "of getting others to do what you want". At the forefront of this exercise has been Joseph Nye, who since the late 1980s has led the way in explicating and promoting cross-border, cross-cultural interaction.[2] The genealogy of the term stretches back several decades, but it is Nye who has given us a relatively clear interpretation: "the ability to shape the preferences of others...[which] tends to be associated with intangible assets such as an attractive personality, culture, political values and institutions, and policies that are seen as legitimate or having moral authority". This is a form of "co-optive" rather than command power.[3]

From the broad starting-point of soft power, public diplomacy can achieve more specific goals. If soft power emanates from a nation's culture, political values, and foreign policies, then "public diplomacy is an instrument that governments use to mobilize [soft power] resources to communicate with and attract the publics of other countries, rather than merely their governments".[4] Creating a favourable international environment with this instrument, a nation can more easily claim legitimacy as it seeks to "shape international rules that are consistent with its interests and values" and so achieve its foreign policy objectives.[5] At the same time, not all foreign relations are reduced to the indirect machinations of public diplomacy, since hard power is still required to enforce the national interest if necessary. Credibility is as important with the threat or actual use of force as it is with persuading others to accept your viewpoint as being in their general interest. Hence the recent articulation, by Nye and influential colleagues, of "smart power" as a combination of the hard and soft varieties.[6]

---

[2] See Nye, *Bound to Lead: The Changing Nature of American Power* (Basic Books, 1990).

[3] Nye, *Soft Power* (Public Affairs, 2004), pp. 5–7. Nye refers to his source as Peter Bachrach and Morton Baratz, "Decisions and Non-Decisions: An Analytical Framework," *American Political Science Review*, 57 (1963), pp. 632–642.

[4] Nye, "Public Diplomacy and Soft Power," *Annals of the American Academy of Political and Social Science*, 616 (March 2008), p. 95.

[5] Nye, *Soft Power*, p. 10.

[6] See the Commission on Smart Power, "A Smarter, More Secure America" (Washington DC: Center for Strategic International Studies, 2007), http://www.csis.org/component/option,com_csis_pubs/task,view/id,4156/type,1 (accessed 11 September 2008).

The logic of this combination is both appealing and compelling. Any emphasis on the ability to achieve goals without resort to the use of force or coercion and in the general interest is a welcome shift in the post-9/11, post-Iraq world. The challenges to implementing this model are formidable, however. Authors including Nye have commented on how the changing nature of the global political environment since the end of the Cold War has affected the ability of states to achieve particular goals.

These changes can be broadly collected under three headings: political democratisation, media diversification, and the US-led normative world order.[7] There is no doubt that the wave of democratisation that occurred in the early 1990s raised hopes of realising the Kantian "democratic peace". It also elevated the factor of public opinion in calculations on foreign policies. The significance of democratisation is questionable, however, if it merely leads to states battling each other in brand-wars over who is most "liked". Then there are the limits to the process. The focus on either the inauguration of elections or the extension of the franchise to women within the "liberalisation" of the world falls short of its goal when the rationality of voters is not in alignment with the assumptions of Fukuyaman "progress", democracy in Palestine and the electoral success of Hamas being only one recent example. This political complexity is the structural problem of the limits to democratic control at the national level, brought on by fundamental shifts in global political economy. Since the 1970s national socio-economic, fiscal, monetary, and trade policies have become increasingly circumscribed by the "new constitutionalism" of binding agreements arranged at the regional (EU) or global (IMF, World Bank, WTO) levels.[8] National economic sovereignty has been diminished in favour of transnational neoliberal efficiency, particularly in the field of finance, where bilateral and multilateral rules have ensured that footloose capital remains outside of the reach of possible democratic "expropriation".[9] The US-led system of "globalisation

---

[7] See Joseph Nye, "The Information Revolution and American Soft Power," *Asia-Pacific Review*, 9 (2002), pp. 60–76;
Robin Brown, "Information Technology and the Transformation of Democracy," *Knowledge, Technology and Policy*, 18 (Summer 2004), pp. 14–29;
Ben D. Mor, "Public Diplomacy in Grand Strategy," *Foreign Policy Analysis*, 2 (2006), pp. 157–176.

[8] Stephen Gill, "Globalisation, Market Civilisation and Disciplinary Neoliberalism," *Millennium*, 24 (1995), pp. 399–422.

[9] David Schneiderman, "Investment Rules and the New Constitutionalism," *Law and Social Inquiry* 24 (Summer 2000), pp. 757–787.

from above" has generated an angry dispossessed "globalisation from below".[10]

Closely connected to the issue of public opinion is the transformation in communication and media. The dramatic diversification of channels and the resulting spread of information has led to a wider diffusion of power with states no longer able to act as the principal provider. Diplomacy, often unwillingly, is made more transparent, and non-state actors can assume pivotal roles in undermining, strengthening, or even setting the dominant discourse on world events. The outcome of this has been a realisation that the state has to realign itself as one player among many competing for airtime. The credibility of the "official" voice is no longer taken for granted, and importance is placed on "branding" to reinforce credibility. This challenges one of the fundamental precepts of realist thinking in international relations, namely that the state, even in the context of complex interdependence, remains the prime actor for decision-making and agenda-setting.

The responses to this situation have been mixed, but the path of the United States has revealed an inability to accept this new global contested environment. In particular, the determination of the U.S. military to apply psychological warfare practices and strategic thinking to the information field has overshadowed all attempts to upgrade public diplomacy in the post-9/11 period. The focus over the past eight years on short-term, rapid-reaction information management instead of long-term alliance-building.[11] Above all, the trend from 2000–2008 was dominated by a nationalist perspective, highlighting the merits of the United States, at the expense of a transnational perspective finding common ground with others across a range of policies. This perspective has been driven by national security concerns as an addendum to the War on Terror, resulting only in the fall-out of declining legitimacy and credibility of the U.S. position. In the midst of the credit crisis in September 2008, President Bush addressed the UN General Assembly

---

[10] See Richard Falk, "Resisting 'Globalization from Above' through 'Globalization from Below'," in Barry Gills (ed.), *Globalization and the Politics of Resistance* (Basingstoke: Macmillan, 2000), pp. 46–56.

[11] Roula Khalaf, "With friends like these, who needs enemies," *Financial Times,* 15 September2008,http://www.ft.com/cms/s/0/9bfea064-833a-11dd-907e-000077b07658.html?nclick_check=1 (accessed 17 September 2008).

for the eighth time and to the general disbelief of those present he focused yet again on the issues of terrorism and terrorist regimes.

The third element of the post-Cold War environment, the US-inspired normative order that was largely created during and after World War II, is now also increasingly being questioned. The post-war framework centred upon NATO has come under increasing criticism from Russia. In July 2008 a set of propositions were floated by the Russian ambassador to NATO, Dmitri Rogozin, as part of a developing Russian concept to re-structure the Eurasian security architecture, reduce the importance of NATO and the Organization for Security and Cooperation in Europe, and involve other powers such as China and India.[12] Yet although the United States with its post-9/11 unilateralism has set the standard in rejecting Cold War security structures, ending the Anti-Ballistic Missile Treaty and agreeing to a nuclear deal with India in defiance of the Non-Proliferation Treaty, there is little willingness to allow other powers to do the same.

The call to restructure in the field of economics and finance goes beyond Washington. The Bretton Woods institutions were created for a post-World War II world framed around US leadership. During the 1990s criticism of the dismal failure of the "Washington Consensus" in reducing global poverty escalated, fuelled by the International Monetary Fund's disastrous reactions to the Asian crisis, the World Bank's dismal environmental record, and the World Trade Organization's inability to resolve deadlock between the global North and South. As a result, in the 21st century all three institutions have suffered from a serious decline in legitimacy and credibility.[13] On 18 April 2008 British Prime Minister Gordon Brown spoke of "reframing the international architecture" to accommodate the rise of new economic powers, and the credit crisis has given a further boost to critics of

[12] "Russian proposal for European security would sideline NATO," *International Herald Tribune*, 27 July 2008, http://www.iht.com/articles/2008/07/27/europe/nato.php (accessed 17 September 2008); "Russia's security proposal doesn't threaten NATO, official said," *International Herald Tribune*, 28 July 2008, http://www.iht.com/articles/2008/07/28/europe/nato.php (accessed 17 September 2008).

[13] On the World Bank see the unprecedented criticism by its former chief economist Joseph Stiglitz in *Globalization and its Discontents* (Penguin: Harmondsworth, 2003).

deregulated neoliberalism such as Angela Merkel.[14] The IMF's hope to gain more supervisory power out of this crisis situation (as it has tried to do during previous crisis situations) is almost certainly going to meet with indifference from many nations around the world.

This situation has been exacerbated by the steep rise in energy prices, redistributing wealth and economic power. The emerging "axis of oil", made up of "a loose and shifting coalition of energy-exporting and – importing states, anchored by Russia and China," is potentially a serious counterweight to US global influence, a process given extra impetus by the decline of the US dollar and the inexorable rise of US trade and budget deficits.[15] Up till now this has been no more than an act of "soft balancing", but there are clear signs of greater assertiveness, best exemplified by the Shanghai Development Corporation's efforts for economic, political, and security cooperation in central Asia and Hugo Chavez's oil-fuelled counter-hegemonic strategy in Latin America and beyond.[16]

There has been little evidence, outside of a consistently militant rhetoric, of the United States accommodating itself to this changing global environment. The ideology of the George W. Bush years was driven by the militarised vision of "full spectrum dominance" and the insistence that there should be no challenger to the undisputed global reach of US power. The assumption of US leadership in the world and that without it there is far less chance of achieving progress in the general interest is not the exclusive preserve of the Bush Administration, however. In the words of Madeleine Albright, Secretary of State under President Clinton, the United States is the "indispensable nation".[17] Joseph Nye's continued insistence that the US is pivotal for shaping the path that global governance will take is also indicative of this

---

[14] "Brown urges new US-Europe links," *BBC News*, 18 April 2008, http://news.bbc.co.uk/1/hi/uk_politics/7353824.stm (accessed 17 September 2008).

[15] See Flynt Leverett, "Black is the new Green," *The National Interest* (January–February 2008).

[16] See Marcel de Haas & Frans-Paul van der Putten, *The Shanghai Cooperation Organisation: Towards a Full-Grown Security Alliance?*, Netherlands Institute of International Relations, November 2007;

Kishore Mahbubani, *The New Asian Hemisphere: The Irresistible Shift of Global Power to the East* (PublicAffairs, 2008).

[17] "A Political Diplomat: Madeleine Korbel Albright," *New York Times*, 6 December 1996, http://query.nytimes.com/gst/fullpage.html?res=9903E0DE143FF935A35751C1A960958260&sec=&spon=&pagewanted=all (accessed 18 September 2008).

thinking,[18] as is Arquilla and Ronfeldt's analysis of the global "noosphere" (realm of ideas) that includes "much that America stands for: openness, freedom, democracy, the rule of law, humane behaviour, respect for human rights, a preference for peaceful conflict resolution". The "complex organizational and technological bases" required in this evolving realm are held by the United States, which remains the only country "who can pull this off".[19] This is despite the fact that the War on Terror has been used as justification for a series of transgressions of international law (for instance rendition, Guantanamo, use of torture), a trend that has further undermined the very normative order that the US itself claims to uphold.

It remains to be seen whether the new era of soft power will still be the era of US leadership. Dense, intricate, multilayered interlinkages beyond inter-state contacts are working in tandem with or often bypassing the state in order to achieve socio-economic, cultural, and political goals. Other nations and non-state actors are realising this quicker than the US. As Paul Cammack argues, Nye's arguments are underpinned by the assumptions "that America (and America alone) can and should lead; and that American leaders can win domestic and international support for their leadership", and yet both are highly problematic in an era when the US has done everything to undermine the bases of multilateralism. Cammack concludes that "American leadership is a massive *obstacle* to the development of a constructive international agenda".[20]

Successful public diplomacy is being able to merge the interests of others with those of your own. Nye is correct that the delivery of "global public goods" is going to be a crucial feature in the politics of the 21st century;[21] however, much of this is dependent not on US leadership *per se* but the style of leadership. The challenge is how to shift US public diplomacy, and diplomacy in general, away from realpolitik and

---

[18] See Joseph Nye, *The Powers to Lead: Soft, Hard, and Smart* (New York: Oxford University Press, 2008).

[19] David Ronfeldt and John Arquilla, "The Promise of Noöpolitik," *First Monday* (July 2007), www.firstmonday.org/issues/issue12_8/ronfeldt/index.html (accessed 18 September 2008).

[20] Paul Cammack, "Smart Power and US Leadership," *49th Parallel* (Autumn 2008). http://www.49thparallel.bham.ac.uk/back/issue22/1_Cammack.pdf (accessed 18 September 2008).

[21] See Joseph Nye, "Recovering American Leadership," *Survival* (2008), 50, p. 64.

towards the realities of 21st-century interdependence, even if US involvement remains a *sine qua non* for successful outcomes.

Challenge Number 1: Curbing the Pentagon's Strategic Influence

On 20 September 2001 President Bush declared to a joint session of Congress that the war on terror against Al Qaeda and all terrorist organizations had begun. With military operations soon to begin in Afghanistan, it was clear that the Pentagon would occupy the driving role, including in the field of communications. Yet as one influential report stated in 2003, the result is that…

> … the role the Defense Department plays in public diplomacy is neither broadly recognized nor well coordinated…While the State Department is considered the lead agency…we are concerned that the Defense Department, with resources that dwarf those of all other agencies of government, is not fully integrated into the public diplomacy architecture.[22]

The Pentagon's wish to control information and media affairs is based on its aim to secure "strategic influence" and "influence opinions, attitudes, and behaviour of foreign groups in ways that will promote US national objectives".[23] However, the methods to achieve this have crossed into explicit propaganda and psychological warfare operations. The determination to dominate the infosphere since the onset of the Afghan and Iraq campaigns has its roots in Gulf War I (or Vietnam, for those with a longer historical perspective), its perfect gestation in Kosovo, and its ultimate expression in the targeting (both verbally and militarily) of Al Jazeera; the outcome is a severe case of "mission creep" as the Pentagon's information operations, given legitimacy by the War on Terror, demonstrated no limits, either geographically or ethically.

In October 2001 the Defense Department set up the Office of Strategic Influence (OSI), which had the task of conducting covert disinformation and deception operations, including planting false news items with disguised origins in the media abroad. In February 2002 the *New York Times* revealed the OSI's intention to have these fabricated

---

[22] "Changing Minds, Winning Peace," *Advisory Group on Public Diplomacy for the Arab and Muslim World*, October 2003, Washington DC, p. 68, www.state.gov/documents/organization/24882.pdf (accessed 18 September 2008).

[23] Susan L. Gough, "The Evolution of Strategic Influence," *USAWC Strategy Research Project*, 2003, http:www.fas.org/irp/eprint/gough.pdf (accessed 18 September 2008).

news reports picked up by American news media and distributed in the United States to bolster domestic support for US actions overseas. Following the leak Rumsfeld was forced to shut down the organization, but the office's operations were effectively passed to another unit called the Information Operations Task Force (IOTF), and the goals did not change.[24] In October 2003 the Defense Department issued the Information Operations Roadmap, which called for the formation of a strategic psychological operations unit and increased budgetary support for these activities. This was supported by the National Defense Strategy of March 2005, which included within the US military's dossier the intention to help "change Muslim misperceptions of the United States and the West" and to project the message that the war on terror "is not a war against Islam".[25]

The Pentagon has worked closely with the private sector in this pursuit of strategic influence. In October 2001 a contract worth $16 million was awarded to John Rendon, leader of the public relations firm the Rendon Group and a well-known practitioner of "perception management". Rendon had received several large-scale contracts since the Gulf War in 1991 and had been closely involved with first the CIA and then the Pentagon in undermining Saddam Hussein's regime and promoting the dissident Iraqi National Congress of Ahmed Chalabi. In 2001 Rendon was given the task of reversing the negative image of the United States abroad by tracking the global news cycle on a 24-hour basis and responding instantly to significant breaking news items. The Group effectively ran an Information War Room in the Pentagon's IOTF; its principal target was the Qatar-based satellite channel Al-Jazeera, which the Pentagon considered its chief adversary in the War on Terror's information campaign. Rendon's task extended to cooperation with US allies (Saudi Arabia, Turkey, Egypt, Indonesia, Pakistan, and Uzbekistan) "in developing and delivering specific messages to the local population, combatants, front-line states, the media and the international community" in support of US objectives.[26]

---

[24] See James Bamford, *A Pretext for War: 9/11, Iraq, and the Abuse of America's Intelligence Agencies* (New York: Doubleday, 2005).

[25] National Defense Strategy of the United States (2005), http://www.globalsecurity.org/military/library/policy/dod/nds-usa_mar2005.htm (accessed 18 September 2008).

[26] James Bamford, "The Rendon Group," *Rolling Stone*, 988 (2005). Online, available at http://www.rollingstone.com/politics/story/8798997/the_man_who_sold_the_war (18 September 2008).

In November 2007 Robert Gates, the successor to Donald Rumsfeld as Secretary of Defense, spoke of the need "to make the case for strengthening our capacity to use 'soft' power and for better integrating it with 'hard' power". Declaring that the civilian tools of government must be upgraded, Gates continued, "Public relations was invented in the United States, yet we are miserable at communicating to the rest of the world what we are about as a society and a culture, about freedom and democracy, about our policies and out goals."[27] To illustrate his point, he noted that the State Department's foreign affairs budget of $36 billion was less than what the Pentagon spent on health care.

Yet, despite Gates' concerns, the Pentagon's public diplomacy role has been further established. In late 2004 the Defense Science Board Task Force on Strategic Communication stated that "public diplomacy, public affairs, psychological operations (PSYOP) and open military information operations must be coordinated and energized", and it recommended a more streamlined infrastructure linking the White House, the National Security Council, and the Defense and State Departments.[28] The document emphasised strategic communication, which required…

> …a sophisticated method that maps perceptions and influence networks, identifies policy priorities, formulates objectives, focuses on "doable tasks," develops themes and messages, employs relevant channels, leverages new strategic and tactical dynamics, and monitors success. This approach will build on indepth knowledge of other cultures and factors that motivate human behavior. It will adapt techniques of skillful political campaigning, even as it avoids slogans, quick fixes, and mind sets of winners and losers. It will search out credible messengers and create message authority. It will seek to persuade within news cycles, weeks, and months. It will engage in a respectful dialogue of ideas that begins with listening and assumes decades of sustained effort.[29]

The reference to "a respectful dialogue of ideas" may be well-meant, but it remains an anomaly. The driving force behind the report's recommendations is control of the infosphere in support of realpolitik.

With the "militarisation" of US public diplomacy and the continuing "spill-over" of Pentagon programmes into State Department terri-

---

[27] Speech online, available at http://www.defenselink.mil/speeches/speech.aspx?speechid+1199 (2 June 2008).

[28] Report is available online at http://www.publicdiplomacy.org/37.htm (18 September 2008).

[29] Ibid.

tory, the question is how "limited firewalls" can contribute to rebuilding credibility.[30] In December 2006 Gates created a new position, the Deputy Assistant Secretary of Defense for Support to Public Diplomacy. The occupant of the post, Michael Doran, spoke in late 2007 of acting as "a transmission belt between the Department of State and Defense." Crucially, he noted the "current governmental structure [that] was not meant to resolve the problems of the global Information Age – the mismatch between authorities for public diplomacy in State and the resources in DOD – being one obvious proof of this".[31] To rectify this mismatch in authority and resources, proposals were launched for the revision of the Information and Educational Exchange Act of 1948 (the Smith-Mundt Act), the original legislation authorising the State Department to conduct information and cultural activities abroad. According to Pentagon officials, Smith-Mundt, which precluded the dissemination of information within the United States, was based on "an outdated model of global communication".[32] Significantly, in September 2008 the White House nominated Doran for the position of Assistant Secretary of State for International Information Programs in the State Department. As an independent report stated in October 2008:

> The "militarization of diplomacy" is noticeably expanding as DOD personnel assume public diplomacy and assistance responsibilities that the civilian agencies do not have the trained staff to fill. In the area of security assistance…a number of new DOD authorities have been created, reducing the role of the Secretary of State even more in this vital area of US foreign policy.[33]

How the credit crisis will impact on the gigantic military budget remains to be seen, and current opinion remains divided on

---

[30] See Bruce Gregory, "Public Diplomacy and Strategic Communication: Cultures, Firewalls, and Imported Norms," *APSA Conference on International Communication and Conflict*, George Washington University, Washington DC, 31 August 2005, www8.georgetown.edu/cct/apsa/papers/gregory.pdf (accessed 18 September 2008). Gregory was a member of the Defense Science Board Task Force.

[31] Michael Doran, statement to the House Armed Services Committee, 15 November 2007, www.armedservices.house.gov/pdfs/TUTC111507/Doran_Testimony111507.pdf (accessed 18 September 2008).

[32] "Bill would amend Smith-Mundt Act," *Inside the Pentagon*, 17 July 2008, www.insidedefense.com.

[33] "A Foreign Affairs Budget for the Future," *American Academy of Diplomacy*, October 2008, p. 4 www.academyofdiplomacy.org/publications/FAB_report_2008.pdf (accessed 24 October 2008).

this point.[34] The war in Afghanistan has put pressure on Obama and the Pentagon to deliver success after the Iraqi failure, yet the tensions evident between White House and general staff, as shown by the debacle of General McChrystal being fired in summer 2010, does not bode well for constructive solutions. But a necessary cut-back in the military budget, accompanied by a regeneration of the State Department and a large-scale improvement in diplomatic resources, could be the best possible outcome from the credit crisis and resulting financial turmoil.

Challenge Number 2: Building a New Consensus around a Global Community of Fate?

At present, the public diplomacy outlook of the United States is marked by a recognition of the changing global environment but a desire to do nothing but control it. The challenge for the coming decade is to accommodate the rising powers of the 21st century within a credible institutional framework of rules and norms before the existing post-WW II structures are undermined further, for example through "axis of oil" alternatives creating a "world without the West".[35] There are precedents, such as the gradual incorporation of Japan into the structures of global governance via the OECD, the Trilateral Commission, and the original G6, and analysts such as John Ikenberry have argued that "Chinese economic interests are quite congruent with the current global economic system – a system that is open and loosely institutionalized and that China has enthusiastically embraced and thrived in".[36] The appointment of Justin Lin Yifu as the World Bank's chief economist was a clear step in this direction, and large-scale Chinese investments to shore up Citibank, Morgan Stanley, and Merrill Lynch in 2007 and 2008 demonstrated the interest of Beijing in maintaining a stable financial environment.[37] By the end of January 2008 there were

---

[34] See for instance Matthew Yglesias, "The Coming Military Spending Surge," *American Prospect*, 16 October 2008, http://www.prospect.org/cs/articles?article=the_coming_military_spending_surge (accessed 24 October 2008);

Nancy Youssef, "Both McCain and McCain would Rebuild US Forces," *McClatchy Newspapers*, 22 October 2008, http://news.yahoo.com/s/mcclatchy/20081022/pl_mcclatchy/3079604 (accessed 24 October 2008).

[35] Steven Weber, "A World without the West," *The National Interest* (Jan 2007).

[36] G. John Ikenberry, "The Rise of China and the Future of the West," *Foreign Affairs* (Jan-Feb 2008).

[37] "The citadels of the global economy are yielding to China's battering ram," *The Guardian*, 23 April 2008;

at least $60 billion of East Asian investments in American, British, and Swiss banks, and this trend has continued through the year as the credit crisis battered major banks across the US and Europe. In the energy sectors, some have floated the idea of a "consumer cartel" of oil-using nations, led by the US and China, to bear down on the increasing resource-led power of the axis of oil.[38]

The conditions do exist for the building of transnational networks to manage an international system based on multipolarity and power-sharing, not on implicit or explicit US hegemony. Indeed, the situation can be compared to that of the early 1970s, when US faced damaged prestige, a weakening economic position, and the need to engage with others to solve common problems such as environmental decline. Building a public diplomacy approach for these challenges, the State Dept's Bureau of Educational and Cultural Exchange in 1973 advocated the direction of exchange programmes "to stimulate institutional development in directions which favourably affect mutual comprehension". The study of interdependence[39] led to a growing focus on "transnational as well as transgovernmental coalition-building" and the role of knowledge-based or issue-based communities in achieving consensus and establishing norms for the management of common problems.[40] These ideas have recently been updated by, among others, Anne-Marie Slaughter.[41] It is worth considering in this context the work of Ulrich Beck, the developer of the "risk society" thesis.[42] In *Power in the Global Age* Beck talks of the need to forge a transnational cooperative public sphere that coordinates itself with the realities of globalisation. The resultant "strategic power" stems not from its cover for the extension of national power and the right of imperial-style intervention (the national writ universal, as appears to be the case in

"Foreign investments in US banks draw attention," *National Public Radio*, 6 February 2008, http://www.npr.org/templates/story/story.php?storyId=18754222 (accessed 18 September 2008).

[38] Joshua Kurlantzick, "Can Public Diplomacy counter Resource Nationalism," *USC Public Diplomacy Blog*, 28 September 2008, http://uscpublicdiplomacy.com/index.php/newsroom/pdblog_detail/060928_can_public_diplomacy_counter_resource_nationalism (accessed 24 October 2008).

[39] See Robert Keohane and Joseph Nye, "Transgovernmental Relations and International Organizations," *World Politics* 27 (1974), pp. 39–62.

[40] Thomas Risse-Kappen, *Bringing Transnational Relations Back In* (Cambridge University Press, 1995), p. 30;

Risse-Kappen, *Cooperation Among Democracies: The European Influence on US Foreign Policy* (Princeton University Press, 1995), p. 38.

[41] Anne-Marie Slaughter, *A New World Order* (Princeton University Press, 2004).

[42] See Ulrich Beck, *Risk Society: Towards a New Modernity* (Sage, 1992).

Nye and Slaughter) but from its creation of new forms of governance that transform the defensive hierarchical nation-state into the progressive "network state".[43] Beck's call for a reconfiguration of global politics may conveniently bypass the realities of the shifting distribution of global power, but it is still necessary.

The assumption of Nye, Arquilla/Ronfeldt, and others is that the Soft Powers of the 21st century will be those who abide by a normative set of ideas that are close to prevailing global norms such as liberalism, pluralism, and autonomy and that have access to multiple channels of communication, enabling a greater influence over how issues are framed.[44] However, the critical factor enabling a state to take on a leading role that others will follow—the factor of credibility—is at present a limitation. As Habermas appositely put it, "The normative authority of the United States lies in tatters."[45]

Nevertheless, there are possibilities. American ideals continue to resonate around the globe, and no other system offers such powerful symbols and motivating narratives. In the Middle East, for instance, many still hope to "replace the Arab nightmare with the American dream".[46] However, the United States needs to increasingly become one nation among many, recognising its ideals appeal widely but equally accepting that their appropriateness for universal application is not taken for granted.[47] The issue is towards which goals these ideals should be directed. Beck argues for a necessary shift away from realpolitik and mercantilist national interest towards an appreciation of the "global community of fate" in the context of global risk, which currently presents itself in the dimensions of environmental decline, financial instability, and terrorism. So far only the cause of anti-terrorism has led to an American demand for increased transnational cooperation,

---

[43] Ulrich Beck, *Power in the Global Age: A New Global Political Economy* (Polity, 2005), pp. 18, 219, 231.

[44] Nye, "The Information Revolution," p. 70;
Ronfeldt and Arquilla, "The Promise of Noöpolitik".

[45] See Jurgen Habermas, *The Divided West* (Cambridge: Polity, 2006).

[46] An Al Jazeera television producer, quoted in the documentary *Control Room* (Jehaine Noujaim, 2004).

[47] See Anne-Marie Slaughter, "Reviving American Ideals," *International Herald Tribune* (18 May 2007), and the subsequent response from those who objected to its continuing unipolarity and one-sidedness, such as David Rieff's criticism, "Slaughter's entire argument, for all its talk of the need for humility, is a reiteration of this 'exceptionalist' conception," http://www.iht.com/articles/2007/05/23/opinion/edlet.php (accessed 24 September 2008).

and even then this has been in the context of constructing a US-centred global "surveillance state" that transverses – both openly and surreptitiously – all other jurisdictions.[48] So far we have witnessed only a "false cosmopolitanism" that continues to pursue the confluence of American (national) and global (universal) interests. The insistence on maintaining sovereignty and autonomy in an era of increasingly fluid boundaries can only lead to a downward spiral of negative regulation.

Where does this place public diplomacy? There is a desperate need, above all, to move away from an insistence on developing strategic communication in support of a narrowly-defined national interest. The emphasis on managing the news cycle, the central drive in US public diplomacy in recent years, can be dated back to the Clinton administration and the inability to explain the US position or deal with misinformation during the Kosovo and Haiti crises.[49] Under George W. Bush this emphasis escalated across the whole spectrum of government, from the Pentagon to the White House (Office of Global Communications 2002–2005) and the State Department (Under-Secretary of State for Public Diplomacy and Public Affairs). Former Secretary of State Condoleeza Rice's implementation of transformational diplomacy, "to work with our many partners around the world to build and sustain democratic, well-governed states that will respond to the needs of their people – and conduct themselves responsibly in the international system,"[50] may have been continued by her successor Hilary Clinton, but it is being hard pressed to succeed in a more challenging global environment. While it proclaims the aim to be building democratic societies around the world, the necessary corresponding components for this, such as the securing in basic needs, have been disregarded and funding for the US Agency for International Development has been cut.[51]

---

[48] Ulrich Beck, "The Terrorist Threat: World Risk Society Revisited," *Theory Culture and Society*, 19 (2002), pp. 39–55;
Beck, *Power*, p. 12.

[49] See the information on the FAS website concerning "International Public Information," Presidential Decision Directive (PDD) 68, 30 April 1999, http://www.fas.org/irp/offdocs/pdd/pdd-68.htm (accessed 24 September 2008).

[50] Fact Sheet, Department of State, http://www.state.gov/r/pa/prs/ps/2006/59339.htm (accessed 24 September 2008).

[51] See Giles Scott-Smith and Martijn Mos, "Democracy Promotion and the New Public Diplomacy," in Inderjeet Parmar, Linda Miller, and Mark Ledwidge (eds.), *New Directions in U.S. Foreign Policy* (Routledge, forthcoming 2009).

The American approach can be contrasted with the so-called New Public Diplomacy, an outlook that recognises the need for governments, in an era of increasing information awareness, to connect with their publics to carry out foreign policy. The merits of this are twofold. Firstly, it will foster and maintain a greater democratic legitimacy for policies. Secondly, it will open up opportunities to make use of the extra reach, both in terms of issues and access, of private citizens, businesses, and non-governmental organisations abroad.[52]

This is a fundamental shift away from much of the debate surrounding US public diplomacy, which tends to focus on the "narrow, mechanistic terms of delivery rather than content" and the assessment of information as no more than "an area of increasing strategic competition."[53] The issue of global warming could be one important catalyst that both causes a gradual shift in perception on national interest and lays the basis for a New Public Diplomacy strategy. In the face of resistance to climate change legislation by the federal government, by June 2006 nine US states had passed greenhouse gas emission reduction targets, and more than half of all states now use public funds for energy efficiency and renewable energy programmes.[54] This widespread constituency could be tapped in combination with a reconfiguration of US national interest and an increasing interaction with other nation-state, business, and NGO partners.

However, these transitions are going to be difficult to negotiate, particularly in a world where competition and resource nationalism are becoming ever more pronounced, and US credibility is stretched on all fronts. What is becoming more acute in this scenario is the spiral of violence that can be released when nationalism, undermined by the integrative forces of globalisation, resorts in response to the best means

---

[52] Jan Melissen, "The New Public Diplomacy: Between Theory and Practice," in Jan Melissen (ed), *The New Public Diplomacy: Soft Power in International Relations* (London: Macmillan, 2005).

[53] Scott Lucas, "The Past, Present, and Futures of Public Diplomacy and Political Warfare," *Libertas*, http://www.libertas.bham.ac.uk/publications/articles/index.htm (accessed 24 September 2008);

Rhiannon Vickers, "A New Public Diplomacy for the Information Age," paper presented at the International Studies Association annual conference, New Orleans, March 2002.

[54] H. Selin and S. Van Deever, "Political Science and Prediction: What's Next for US Climate Change Policy?", *Review of Policy Research*, 24 (2007), pp. 1–27.

to sustain itself, namely war. Even though "the 'control' of a state is finally the work of social, legal, political, and economic forces that operate within a nominal geopolitical 'territory'," the determination to exercise military solutions in the name of security will continue (to fail).[55] The "Westfailure system" led by the United States is therefore going to experience a permanent crisis as (modern) political discourse and state-level practice remain caught within their evident limitations and contradictions.[56] Writing during an ongoing financial crisis on a scale beyond that of 1929, it is worth reflecting on how the American twentieth century was closely associated with a grand narrative of abundance. If the twenty-first century is going to have a grand narrative of anything, it is going to be based on dealing with scarcity. The shifts in interest-recognition and self-perception that will be required to deal with this are way beyond anything that has so far emerged from the petty debates over the US image and how to repair it. The Obama presidency is aware of the stakes involved, but it will take far more than one well-meaning President to overcome this situation.

[55] See John Carlos Rowe, "European Lessons in Imperialism: A Letter to America," *Journal of Transatlantic Studies* 6 (August 2008), p. 185.

[56] Susan Strange, "The Westfailure System," *Review of International Studies* 25 (1999), pp. 345–354.

KAREN HUGHES AND THE BREZHNEV SYNDROME: THE TRIAL OF PUBLIC DIPLOMACY AS DOMESTIC PERFORMANCE

Nicholas J. Cull

In 1992 British intelligence received an offer it could not refuse (though the CIA had just done exactly that). An elderly Russian named Vasili Mitrokhin, who happened to be the former archivist of the KGB, proposed to defect and bring with him 25,000 pages of records of Soviet secret activities around the world throughout the Cold War period. In due course he published these materials in collaboration with the distinguished historian of British intelligence, Christopher Andrew. The documents included expected tales of spies, lies and intrigue, but one aspect came as a surprise: the immense scale of KGB resources devoted to engaging international opinion, and more specifically, faking evidence of international admiration for the Soviet way of life in the developing world. As the idealism of the Khrushchev-era gave way to the more cynical grip of Leonid Brezhnev, and as the international buzz around the Soviet conquest of space was eclipsed by the American landing on the moon and discomfort with the intervention in Czechoslovakia, the KGB moved to take up the slack. In addition to the millions of rubbles spent on sustaining cultural exchanges and Soviet artistic exports, soon rupees, pesos, Egyptian pounds and other currencies flowed freely to ensure the requisite number of "spontaneous" demonstrations outside Soviet embassies and in the wake of visiting Soviet dignitaries.

These initiatives suggested that one important goal of Soviet engagement with foreign publics was the production of positive images for domestic consumption; the Kremlin knew the value of telling their own population that the Soviet society remained the admiration of the world. Apparently genuine attempts to engage with foreign audiences in the Khrushchev-era had given way to a new kind of activity, not public diplomacy as a form of foreign policy but foreign engagement of the crudest kind as a blunt instrument of domestic propaganda. Yet, if the tactic helped Brezhnev preserve his regime and appease his home audience, it also set a trap. The Soviet leadership was caught in their own narrative, forgetting that they had hired their admirers. Like a car driver who sticks a piece of tape over a dashboard warning light, they masked the warning signs of their declining world role until it was too late.[1]

While the Brezhnev-era case is an extreme example, it shows that engagement with foreign publics is not always conducted with international objectives in mind; sometimes public diplomacy has a short-term domestic motive. Hitler's Olympics make more sense as a domestic display than a genuine international gambit, and the same might be said for Victorian England's Great Exhibition or the frenetic bi-lateral cultural diplomacy of early Bolshevik Russia. The combination of massive expenditure and monumental cynicism sets Brezhnev at the top of the pile and deserving giving his name to the entire phenomenon. Scholars should be mindful of the Brezhnev Syndrome, a public diplomacy pursued according to domestic priorities, and practitioners cognizant of its consequences. The state which operates in this manner way not only risks undermining its own public diplomacy but also faces the long-term consequences of deceiving its own population.

This essay will consider the Brezhnev Syndrome as a mechanism for understanding the public diplomacy of two major contemporary players – China and the United States. Having considered public diplomacy as it is, the essay will then turn to what it ought to be.

China and the Brezhnev Syndrome

The rise of Chinese public diplomacy has been one of the most spectacular features of the post-Cold War field. It began in the wake of the Tiananmen Square incident of 1989, when the Chinese government hired the services of the international public relations firm of Hill and Knowlton to begin the process of rebuilding their reputation. In 1991 the regime reconfigured all domestic and international information and propaganda work under a single State Council Information Office (SCIO).[2] The work of SCIO kicked into high gear under the dynamic

---

[1] For a full description of the campaign and the element of self deception, see Christopher Andrew and Vasili Mitrokhin, *The World Was Going Our Way: The KGB and the Battle for The Third World*. (Basic Books, 2005).

[2] Ingrid d'Hooghe, "Public Diplomacy in the People's Republic of China", in Jan Melissen (ed.), *The New Public Diplomacy: Soft Power in International Relations* (Palgrave, 2005), pp. 92 and 98–99.

leadership of a former vice mayor of Shanghai, Minister Zhao Qizheng, who led the office from 1998 to 2005. Zhao's radical approach began with a willingness to concede Chinese errors for the sake of credibility. He chose his words carefully, avoiding the traditional Chinese term for his work, "*xuan chuan*" or propaganda, as he understood that the translation fell awkwardly on western ears. He preferred to speak of "explaining" China ["*shuo ming*"].[3]

Zhao's initiatives included a sustained upgrading of all the usual elements of public diplomacy. In the field of listening, he launched a series of polls to track China's standing in the world.[4] In the field of advocacy, he enhanced China's ability to address the foreign media, astonishing a gathering of journalists in December 2004 with the names and phone numbers of the seventy-five spokespersons of every ministry and commission under the State Council.[5] In cultural diplomacy, he delivered a relentless succession of major exhibitions, "China Weeks," and tours for artists around the world, and he embarked on the launch and rapid expansion of the Confucius Institutes, culture and language teaching institutes located within world universities generally operated in partnership with Chinese institutions.[6] Zhao concluded new bilateral agreements with partners around the world for exchanges and expanded the recruitment of international students, bringing twenty percent more each year.[7] In the field of international broadcasting, China Central Television launched CCTV 9 a round-the-clock English-language TV news channel in September 2000. Rupert Murdoch

---

[3] For an early concession of error see Erik Eckholm, "China admits ecological sins played role in flood disaster," *New York Times*, 26 August 1998, p. A1.

Todd Crowell and David Hsieh, "Beijing's spin doctor," *Asia Week*, 22 September 2000. In 2005 an anthology of Zhao Qizheng's speeches appeared with the title *Xiang Shijie Shuoming Zhongguo* (Explain China to the World).

See also "Hong Kong daily analyses official's role in improving China's public image," *BBC Monitoring International Reports*, 7 June 2005.

[4] "Chinese, Japanese NGOs release poll on bilateral relations," *Xinhua*, 24 August 2005.

[5] "China makes public names of government spokespersons for the first time," *Xinhua*, 28 December 2004, and "Hong Kong daily analyses official's role in improving China's public image," *BBC Monitoring International Reports*, 7 June 2005.

[6] "Confucius Institute: promoting language, culture and friendliness," *Xinhua*, 2 October 2006.

[7] "Number of foreign students in China rises 20 percent annually," *Xinhua*, 19 January 2006 as cited in

Joshua Kurlantzick, *Charm Offensive* (Yale University Press, 2007), p. 118.

obligingly carried the signal on his Sky satellite service, and further language services followed.[8]

The debt of these initiatives to the domestic audience arises from the recognition that whatever the Chinese government has to gain from wooing the citizens of Chicago, it has much more to risk from losing the citizens of Shanghai. In Chinese doctrine, the phrase "public diplomacy" was initially used exclusively to refer to the task of explaining foreign policy at home.[9] Coverage of public diplomacy programmes was typified by the breathy style of *Xinghua* headlines: "Overseas craze for Chinese spreads from universities to schools" and "110 British headmasters visit China for language teaching co-op". Whereas rice or steel production was once the performance indicator for the effectiveness of the state, now it was international interest in learning Chinese. In 2006 Beijing promised its people a network of more than one hundred Confucius Institutes within five years,[10] and in June 2007 the Office of the Chinese Language Council proudly declared that 30 million people around the world were now learning Chinese and predicted that this figure would hit 100 million by 2010.[11] The "real" benefit of these initiatives is still debatable. Anecdotal evidence suggests that the Confucius programs are more for show than content. Relations with Chinese partner institutions have been strained and the quality and morale of the Chinese teachers imported to deliver the curriculum have been patchy. Some, as Don Starr has noted, have been over qualified. Imagine the chagrin of a specialist on classical philosophy,

---

[8] "China to launch all-English channel tomorrow," *Xinhua*, 24 September 2000.

On the Murdoch deals see Danny Gittings and Julian Borger, "Homer and Bart realize Murdoch's dream of China coup," *The Guardian*, 6 September 2001, p. 3.

On China in Africa see Adam Clayton Powell III, "Chinese TV extends its reach into Africa," 19 December 2005, *USC Center on Public Diplomacy*, http://uscpublicdiplomacy.com/index.php/newsroom/journal_detail/051219_chinese_tv_extends_its_reach_into_africa/

[9] Wang Yiwei, "Public Diplomacy and the Rise of Chinese Soft Power," in Geoffrey Cowan and Nicholas J. Cull eds, "Public Diplomacy in a changing world," published in *ANNALS of the American Academy of Political and Social Science*, vol. 616, March 2008: 257–273.

[10] "Confucius Institute: promoting language, culture and friendliness," *Xinhua*, 2 October 2006.

[11] "Overseas craze for Chinese spreads from universities to schools," *Xinhua*, 26 June 2007.

See also "Foreign headmasters follow Chinese language teaching trail," *Xinhua*, 20 June 2007

and "110 British headmasters visit China for language teaching co-op." *Xinhua*, 27 May 2007.

arriving in Europe to discover that he or she is required to teach Mandarin conversation. Standards of teaching are reportedly low and, in the United States at least, the Institutes seem to function more as a rallying point for Chinese students studying abroad than as bridgeheads to the outward march of Chinese culture.[12]

In addition to wielding the tools of Soft Power, China is also ready to deploy the most obvious of hard power levers – bribery – to elicit to headlines and fraternal conference that play so well at home. Beijing wooed nations in Latin America, the Middle East and above all Africa with lavish no-strings-attached gifts. Southern African nations were offered either a new headquarters for their ruling party or a sports stadium.[13]

The ultimate Brezhnev Syndrome project was one that Brezhnev himself had used: the Olympic Games. China's bid and successful hosting of the Beijing Olympics was the heart of a web of domestic propaganda about the arrival of China on the world stage. The Beijing Olympics were planned on a vast scale, costing over $42 billion.[14] Every aspect from the buildings to the performance of the Chinese athletes to the experience of foreign spectators was carefully engineered to show China at its best. At the same time, planners worked to head off potential negatives. They tried to improve the appalling air quality in the Beijing region by relocating some of the worst offending factories. They trained the people of Beijing in acceptable cheers and refined public manners with the avoidance of spitting, smoking and littering. The eleventh day of each month in the run up to the Games became "queuing day", as citizens of Beijing were surrounded with slogans: "I participate, I contribute, I enjoy."[15] As Zhao Qizheng noted approvingly in his new capacity as a member of the National Committee of the Chinese People's Political Consultative Conference (a rough analogue to the British House of Lords), "It often is the small things that really hurt China's national image."[16]

---

[12] The author has benefited from an excellent unpublished essay on the institutes by Don Starr of Durham University, "Creating a World Language: Chinese Government Policy and the Confucius Institute Programme viewed from a British Perspective."

[13] For a survey of this work see Kurlantzick, *Charm Offensive*.

[14] "Economist: Olympics raise global profile of China," *Xinhua*, 12 August, 2008.

[15] Wang Wei, presentation at University of Southern California, 15 May 2007.

See also Li Baojie, Cheng Yifeng and Wang Mian, "Soft Power a new focus at China's Two Sessions." *Xinhua*, 14 March 2007.

[16] Li Baojie, Cheng Yifeng and Wang Mian, "Soft Power a new focus at China's Two Sessions." *Xinhua*, 14 March 2007.

The final spectacle at the Games was almost too much to be effective. The opening ceremony with its two thousand and eight drummers seemed threatening in its scale, and revelations of splicing of special effects shots into the telecast or the replacement of the girl singing the opening anthem with a "more attractive" body-double raised eyebrows overseas. But the moment belonged to China, as a fine haul of medals followed the grand opening. The Beijing government had no plans to rest on its laurels. The dust had hardly settled on the "Bird's Nest" stadium before the Chinese media began the build up for its next mega-event: the Shanghai Expo of 2010. One unbudgeted cost of the "perfect Olympics" was paid in public health. In the course of September 2008 it emerged that the government had delayed the release of news that much of China's milk was tainted with melanin to preserve the nation's image before the world.[17]

Considering the surge in Chinese public diplomacy as a manifestation of the Brezhnev Syndrome reveals a vulnerability of the Chinese state. The intense public diplomacy activities give the Chinese government an international exposure raising the traditional inter-personal Chinese concepts of "face" (*Lian* meaning personal honor and moral worth, and *Mianzi,* social prestige).[18] While the new wave of Chinese public diplomacy may be aimed at pleasing the audience at home, it also allows foreign states and citizens groups to engage the Chinese government. Recognising the Chinese wish to be part of the world, foreign governments could indulge their desire for concessions or increase the price for playing Beijing's game. This engagement in the run-up to the Olympics included pro-Tibet protests, disruption of the Olympic Torch relay, and the application of leverage against Chinese support for the regime in Sudan.

Appreciation of the Chinese effort also refines anticipation of future behaviour. The international community now expects a steady stream of cultural investment and projects to raise prestige and unify the "nation" in the foreseeable future. While limiting any gains that China might expect from the element of "surprise", this may be a positive outcome of the Brezhnev Syndrome. Mounting the Shanghai Expo in 2010

---

[17] Richard Spencer, "China accused over contaminated baby milk," 15 September 2008, http://www.telegraph.co.uk/news/worldnews/asia/china/2963808/China-accused-over-contaminated-baby-milk.html

[18] For a classic exploration of the concepts see David Yau-Fai Ho, "On the Concept of Face," *American Journal of Sociology*, Vol. 81 (4), 1976, pp. 867–884.

is fairly inoffensive compared to other projects which Beijing might have embraced to impress the home audience, such as a drive for reunification with Taiwan.

The United States and the Brezhnev Syndrome

The Brezhnev Syndrome afflicts American public diplomacy in a rather different way from the effect on China. It has played out in three scenarios. The first is the periodic entry of the issue of public diplomacy into mainstream national politics. The second is the expression of local ethnic politics in public diplomacy policy. The third, and most problematic, is the on-going conduct of public diplomacy with the domestic audience in mind.

It is a feature of American democracy that neither the people nor the Congress have historically been comfortable with a government role in communication, whether at home of abroad. The massive apparatus for public diplomacy created during the Great War was demolished at the war's end and the apparatus built during World War Two survived only because of a belated realization of the scale of the ideological threat posed by the USSR. As David Krugler has documented, criticism of American public diplomacy became a favourite avenue of attack for Republicans seeking to make inroads against the Truman administration. Favourite themes included allegations that Voice of America was a nest of liberals.[19] In this tradition, sniping at Voice of America and other outlets of American public diplomacy remains today a favourite sport of conservative columnists, and being targeted in the domestic media is an occupational hazard of life in American public diplomacy. One recent victim was Larry Register, embattled News Director of the Arabic TV channel al-Hurra, funded by the US Government. Register resigned in the summer of 2007 after a drubbing in the pages of the *Wall Street Journal* for the sin of allowing too much coverage of the Iranian and Jihadist points of view.[20] On a more positive note, several successful election campaigns have featured pledges to reform U.S. public diplomacy and address issues of

---

[19] David Krugler, *The Voice of America and the Domestic Propaganda Battles, 1945–1953* (University of Missouri Press, 2000).

[20] For comment see Marc Lynch, "The failure of public diplomacy," *The Guardian*, 16 June 2007, http://www.guardian.co.uk/commentisfree/2007/jun/16/alhurramarti

international prestige overseas. Eisenhower, Kennedy, Carter, and Reagan all raised the issue in their campaigns, and all delivered on their election promises.[21]

Lobbies have also loomed large in the history of American public diplomacy. In the 1950s the southern states, with their objections to "beating up on the South", occasionally skewed U.S. public diplomacy away from a balanced representation of Civil Rights issues.[22] The Eastern European exile communities provided a powerful hinterland for operation of the surrogate radio stations Radio Free Europe and Radio Liberty, which were so powerfully connected to the conservative community in the US that they radically distorted the process of consolidating American international broadcasting in the early 1990s. One lobby proved unmatched in its ability to influence American public diplomacy: that of Cuba. This emerged in the later 1970s, when activists began a campaign to strike back against Castro through a dedicated surrogate radio station. Since the concentration of Cuban Americans in Miami gave them an electoral significance that a more dispersed community could not muster, the Reagan Administration and its successors had a vested interest in keeping them happy. Radio Martí, created in the Reagan years was partially jammed by Castro, but the signal at least got through. The follow-on project was not so fortunate. TV Martí, which began trials in 1990 with broadcasts from a transmitter suspended from a balloon on the Florida Keys, was much more easily jammed. Soon the U.S. government was spending millions of dollars on a television station that virtually no one could watch. The expenditure seemed absurd, but as one international broadcasting executive explained to the present author in 1995, "Some people believe that an entire presidential election could be won or lost on votes cast in Florida."[23]

Finally, the domestic sphere impinges on the day-to-day operation of U.S. public diplomacy. One of the features of the 21st-century public

---

[21] See Nicholas J. Cull, *The Cold War and the USIA: American propaganda and public diplomacy, 1945–1989* (Cambridge University Press, 2008), pp. 78–79, 181–183, 358, and 399–400.

[22] The classic case of this is the attack on the U.S. pavilion at the Brussels World's Fair. See Michael L. Krenn, "'Unfinished Business': Segregation and U.S. Diplomacy at the 1958 World's Fair." *Diplomatic History*, 20, no. 4, (Fall 1996): 591–612.

[23] On the origins of Radio Martí see Cull, *The Cold War and the United States Information Agency*, pp. 395, 407, 449–450, 499.

See also Alvin Snyder, *Warriors of Disinformation: American Propaganda, Soviet Lies and the Winning of the Cold War* (Arcade Publishing, 1995).

diplomacy environment is the collapse of the gap between the domestic and the international news spheres. In the world of the internet, ever-vigilant bloggers, and real-time satellite television, a word spoken by the president in Kansas is heard in Kandahar. George W. Bush found this out to his cost in the immediate wake of 9/11 when, with a domestic audience in mind, he referred to the coming struggle as a "crusade."[24] His slip caused outrage in the Islamic world. Only slightly better received was Bush's use of the Wild West rhetoric of "wanted dead or alive", which alarmed Western Europe.[25] The logic of this new transparency should have been the assurance that the international audience was considered in the framing of domestic statements. Instead, the reverse happened: words were being spoken in Kandahar, Cairo and Karachi with an eye on their impact on Kansas.

The situation was not helped by the decision in the last months of the Clinton administration to return the United States Information Agency, the organization which had served as the home for US public diplomacy since 1953, to the State Department. Beyond the saving of money, the concept was that public diplomacy was now so central to the conduct of foreign policy that the entire U.S foreign policy machine should be imbued with its spirit. By mixing personnel from USIA into the main body of the Department of State, the public diplomats would act like a leaven, raising the dough of stodgy, hide-bound, conventional diplomacy.

This did not occur. The elements from USIA were too dispensed and cut off from leadership to function properly, and they became prisoners of the priorities of their respective regional bureaus. The senior administrator for Public Diplomacy was double-hatted as Under Secretary of State for Public Diplomacy and Public Affairs (an awkward hybrid of international and domestic concerns), and though the administrative structure preserved a firewall between the two functions, public affairs priorities bled into the working of public diplomacy in the field. The story circulated that under USIA, if you went to a foreign post and asked the senior Public Affairs Officer about media in his locality he or she would talk at length about the nuances of the press in that country; after the amalgamation his harried successor

---

[24] Peter Ford, "Europe cringes at Bush 'Crusade' against terrorists." *Christian Science Monitor,* 19 September 1991.

[25] Michael White and Lucy Ward, "Blair distances UK from 'dead or alive' claim," *Guardian,* 19 September 2001, p. 1.

would answer the same question by listing recent visits from American journalists.

Although the decline in the international reputation of the United States was not a major issue in the election of 2004, it was clear that something needed to be done to address the situation. The president's nominee for Secretary of State, Condoleezza Rice, told her Senate confirmation hearing on 18 January 2005, "If I am confirmed, public diplomacy will be a top priority for me and for the professionals I lead."[26] Meanwhile, in the Senate, Richard Lugar introduced S. 192: "A bill to provide for the improvement of foreign stabilization and reconstruction capabilities of the United States Government". This included measures for an enhanced use of public diplomacy in nation-building operations.[27]

On 12 March 2005, the newspapers announced the President's choice for Under Secretary of State for Public Diplomacy and Public Affairs: Karen Hughes. The nomination caused an immediate stir. Hughes was known as a close friend of George W. Bush, a trusted advisor who had been crucial in both his gubernatorial and first presidential campaigns, and a director communications both in Texas and in the early White House years. If someone with her clout could not fix American public diplomacy, it was hard to see how anyone could.[28] Hughes did not accept her new post immediately. She requested that her appointment not begin until her son left for college in the summer of 2005. After Bush agreed, Hughes began work in Washington on 15 August and was sworn in on 9 September.[29]

---

[26] For text of Rice's testimony, see http://foreign.senate.gov/testimony/2005/RiceTestimony050118.pdf.

[27] Section 4 of S.192 called for a Presidential directive to: "(1) to better understand global public opinion about the United States, and to communicate with global audiences; (2) to coordinate all components of strategic communication, including public diplomacy, public affairs, and international broadcasting; and (3) to provide a foundation for new legislation on the planning, coordination, conduct, and funding of strategic communication." http://thomas.loc.gov/cgi-bin/query/z?c109:S.192.

[28] Peter Baker, "Karen Hughes to work on the world's view of U.S." *Washington Post*, 12 March 2005, p. A3;

Elizabeth Bumiller, "Bush picks adviser to repair tarnished U.S. image abroad," *New York Times*, 12 March 2005, p. A2.

[29] For commentary on her book see Tina Brown, "Cranking out the volumes on George Bush," *Washington Post*, 8 April 2004, p. C1.

and Elisabeth Bumiller and Richard W. Stevenson, "A trusted Bush aide returns to center stage," *New York Times*, 28 March 2004, p. A28.

For commentary on her return, see Steven R. Wiseman, "Bush confidante begins task of repairing America's image abroad," *New York Times*, 21 August 2005, p. A6.

The period between Hughes' nomination and her arrival in Washington saw a dramatic worsening of America's position in the world. In June the ultra-conservative major of Tehran, Mahmoud Ahmadinejad, won the presidency of Iran. In July the Venezuelan president Hugo Chávez, a long-time antagonist of the Bush administration, launched TeleSur, a Latin America-wide cable and satellite news channel. Capitol Hill bristled with talk of a new propaganda war with Venezuela.[30] Then, in the final days of August 2005, Hurricane Katrina tore into New Orleans and the surrounding coast, revealing shameful images of African-American poverty in the South and the inability of the United States government to respond effectively to a disaster on its own soil.[31]

At her confirmation hearing in July, Hughes expressed her priorities as Under Secretary in terms of the "four Es": engagement, exchanges, education and empowerment. Implicit in the engagement was Hughes' declared intent to improve the listening dimension of public diplomacy. "I am mindful," she told the world, "that before we seek to be understood, we must first work to understand."[32] To this end she announced that her first move would be to begin a program of "listening tours" of the Middle East and Europe.[33]

In late September 2005 Hughes set out on her first listening tour, which took her to Turkey, Saudi Arabia and Egypt. Her key approach was to present herself not as a politician but as an ordinary American "working mom". Her emphasis on her home life seemed considered, like a hostage negotiator's trick of using first names to heighten rapport before beginning to bargain for concessions. But Hughes made

---

[30] For the anti-Chavez broadcasts proposed by Connie Mack (R-Fl) see HR 2601, Sec. 106 (5), 22 July 2005 and S 600 I (b), Sec. 111;

Humberto Marquez, "United States plans to invade Venezuelan airwaves in propaganda strike," *Inter Press Service*, 22 July 2005;

William Fisher, "U.S. anti-Chavez broadcasts may be hot air," *Inter Press Service*, 28 July 2005;

Andres Oppenheimer, "U.S. shouldn't try to counter Chavez TV network," *Miami Herald*, 4 August 2005, p. 8.

[31] "How Could It Happen? World Reaction to Hurricane Katrina" 10 September 2005, posted at http://www.publicdiplomacy.org/53.htm

[32] State Department, IIP press release, "Public Diplomacy chief-designate seeks dialogue and advocacy," 22 July 2005.

[33] Anne Applebaum, "Think Again, Karen Hughes," *Washington Post*, 27 July 2005, p. A21;

State Department IIP press release, "Public Diplomacy chief-designate seeks dialogue and advocacy," 22 July 2005.

one critical error at the outset, and reflective of the early on-set of the Brezhnev Syndrome. She travelled with a sizeable American press corps. With Bush's foreign policy on trial, she then allowed herself to be drawn into counter-productive bouts of defending the administration rather than focusing on her declared objective of listening. Possibly Hughes had become a victim of her double-hated office which, compelled attention to both international and domestic audiences. Possibly her reaction was just the reflex of a seasoned campaigner who could not help but come out swinging. Whatever the reason, the tour generated an almost wholly negative press at home and overseas. Arab writers scoffed at her inability to address their actual concerns with US foreign policy. USIA's veteran Arabists winced when Hughes suggested to Saudi women that in the U.S. they would be allowed to drive cars, only to be told that they had no wish to do this. The American press made merry when she mistakenly cited the phrase "one nation, under God", from the Eisenhower-era Pledge of Allegiance, as a line from the Constitution. Doves, growing ever bolder in their opposition to the war in Iraq, and hawks, who disliked the very idea of listening or engaging other than in a military fashion, prepared to see off Hughes as they had seen off George Bush's first Under Secretary, Charlotte Beers.

To her credit Hughes learned from the experience. She did not take the press on her subsequent listening tours of Latin America and Africa.[34] She also brought home a message that American policies were the root of regional anger. "One of the things that I heard as I traveled throughout the Middle East," she told National Public Radio in spring 2006, "is concern about the Israeli-Palestinian policy." On her return she told the President and Secretary of State that the US needed to be "seen as visibly working to improve life for the Palestinian people".[35] They concurred, and for a season US foreign policy moved subtly to address the region's main issue, apart from the American presence in Iraq. This approach was abruptly halted, however, following the election victory of Hamas in the Gaza Strip in spring 2006.

[34] For a summary, see Tom Regan, "US State Department 'charm offensive' hits bumps" *Christian Science Monitor,* 24 October 2005, http://www.csmonitor.com/2005/1024/dailyUpdate.html.

[35] Steve Inskeep, "Hughes: no short term fix for U.S. image abroad," *NPR Morning Edition,* 28 March 2006, http://www.npr.org/templates/story/story.php?storyId=5304491.

Hughes was able to strengthen the operation of American public diplomacy, building a structure for the rapid rebuttal of false stories and strengthening the hand of the Department of State in the inter-agency process, but she could do little to address the problem of selling what was essentially bad policy. She resigned in October 2007, leaving a better-funded and slightly more efficient operation to the next presidential administration.

Conclusion: Burying Brezhnev, Public Diplomacy as it Ought to Be

One core problem for "public diplomacy" is that, despite having a convenient name as an umbrella, there are many ways in which an international actor conducts foreign policy by engaging with a foreign public. These approaches – listening, advocacy, culture, exchange, and international broadcasting – each have their own sources of credibility, each require their own structures, and perhaps most importantly, each work over a different time-scale. Advocacy, needing to be close to the source of foreign policy to be useful and credible, works in the short term. Cultural diplomacy works in the medium and long term and requires a structure rooted in artistic integrity rather than the

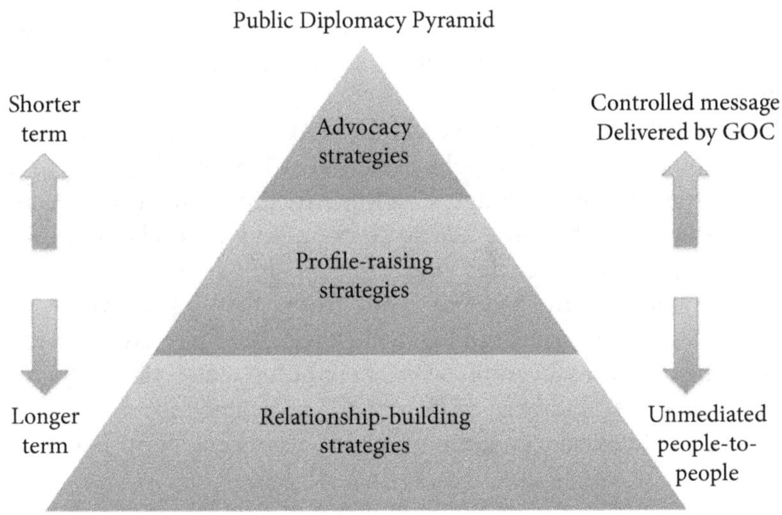

Figure 1: The Public Diplomacy Pyramid, Foreign Affairs Canada, 2005, (GOC = Government of Canada).

immediate needs of foreign policy. International broadcasting works similarly but draws its credibility from the mores of international journalism. Exchange work has the longest-term perspective. Investments are made in exposing individuals to the lived experience of another country, and it can be decades before the state receives its dividend. All of these activities are necessary and have their place in the range of tools deployed by an international actor. The Canadian government has recently imagined them as a pyramid with advocacy at the point and relationship building strategies like exchange at the base.

The problem is that a state which is running its public diplomacy to please a home audience will tend to select activities which show the most easily demonstrable results. In a democracy, public diplomacy can become hostage to electoral cycles and may be unduly biased to advocacy operations and the crudest measures of success from millions of pamphlets printed to purported audience share for radio broadcasts. In Washington DC during the early years of the War on Terror, this politically-driven short-termism was expressed in the ubiquitous question, "Does it help to move the needle?" The chairman of the Board of Governors, Kenneth Tomlinson, compared the attitude of Capitol Hill towards public diplomacy to that of toddlers on a car journey, tormenting their father by asking. "Are we there yet?"[36] The truth is that important parts of public diplomacy are often more an act of faith than an act of science, and the long-term practice seems to bear out the text which Einstein hung on his office wall at Princeton: "Not everything that can be counted counts, and not everything that counts can be counted."

In Britain, Germany, and several other European countries the influence of domestic politics in public diplomacy has been kept to a minimum by the structure through which public diplomacy is conducted. Broadcasters like the BBC World Service and *Deutsche Welle* and cultural diplomacy agencies like the British Council and Goethe Institute operate with minimal input from their respective foreign ministries. At times they appear to behave more like NGOs with a passing historical association with their home states rather than as extensions of it. Editorial and artistic independence is jealously guarded, as statesmen including Helmut Kohl and Tony Blair have

---

[36] Tomlinson speech to Media Institute, 22 September 2005, http://www.mediainstitute.org/Speeches/Tomlinson_09222005.pdf.

discovered when they made noises about impinging on the independence of these agencies.

Neither German nor British public diplomacy has suffered as a result. The Foreign Office and *Auswärtiges Amt* have their own mechanisms for short- and medium-term policy advocacy, such as the network of German Information Centres. The Goethe Institute, British Council, *Deutsche Welle* and BBC have enhanced credibility because of their autonomy, and the issue of cross-agency coordination has the handled with obvious care. British public diplomacy is coordinated by an inter-agency board, chaired from the Foreign Office, around a small set of strategic policy objectives. These have emphasized broad issues such as climate security and anti-terrorism, rather than blind boosterism for the UK.[37]

The question for a country like the United States, where domestic politics has tended to distort public diplomacy, is how to reduce that distortion. One obvious channel would be to move closer to an Anglo-German model and abstract key elements of public diplomacy from a politicized environment. It is difficult to see what American cultural diplomacy gains from being located within the Department of State. Every other major democratic player in the world has preferred to establish an arms-length agency to handle this sort of work.

The State Department's grip on cultural diplomacy owes more to a desire to maximize budgets than to any sense of being especially fit for purpose. The artistic integrity and credibility of the program suffer as a result. A similar argument could be made about the structure of American international broadcasting. The Broadcasting Board of Governors was created in the mid-1990s as a parent agency for America's international stations (Voice of America, Radio Free Europe/Radio Liberty, Radio Free Asia, Radio and TV Martí and the stations of the Middle East Broadcasting Network), but it is made up of political appointees. Expected to function as a mechanism for keeping partisan influence out of public diplomacy, it has instead walled that influence in and magnified it through the obsessions of particular board members. A more effective board would be representative of the full range of U.S. society or could even have board members appointed

[37] This paragraph has benefited from conversations with serving British and German public diplomats, including Dr. Georg Schulze Zumkley of the German Embassy in Washington DC.

on an *ex officio* basis, drawing on figures like the director of the Smithsonian Institution or the editor of the *Washington Post* whose roles give them special insight into the proper conduct of international broadcasting and representation of the American way.

The political ascendancy secured by Barak Obama and the Democratic Party in November 2008 provided political capital for a radical restructuring of U.S. public diplomacy to begin. Unfortunately the administration had other priorities. Its public diplomacy focused on presidential speeches and much rhetoric about "engagement" and "smart power" rather than any actual reform of or investment in the public diplomacy apparatus. Routine housekeeping tasks like nominating members for the broadcasting board of governors were slow to happen. Ironically, the international appeal of the charismatic president provided exactly the sort of "good news" headlines and poll numbers that the Bush administration craved, without the Obama administration changing much of substance. With domestic public opinion pressing elsewhere, substantial reform of U.S. public diplomacy now seems unlikely. This is not a solution, but merely a postponement of the break with the follies of the post-USIA era. In the final analysis, the only antidote to the Brezhnev syndrome is leadership at the State Department and White House: leadership with the character and sense to defy the columnists, take a stand against domestic short-termism, and ensure that public diplomacy really is driven by the need to engage international opinion in its own terms and not to conduct domestic politics by proxy.

PUBLIC DIPLOMACY IN THE MIDDLE EAST: DYNAMICS OF SUCCESS AND FAILURE

Lina Khatib

The events of September 11 brought an increased attention to public diplomacy in the Middle East. In particular, American public diplomacy measures were re-invigorated after a period of decreased attention to the region following the end of the Cold War. The war on Iraq in 2003 was an occasion for further American public diplomacy efforts, this time mainly channeled through the broadcast media. It is understandable, therefore, that critiques have focused on the United States as the primary public diplomacy actor in the region.

Attention needs to be paid, however, to other state and non-state actors engaging in public diplomacy. Adopting a wider perspective offers a critical assessment of the dynamics of success and failure of public diplomacy efforts in the region. This chapter aims to achieve this through the analysis of public diplomacy by the United States, by the state of Qatar, and by Hizbullah, three actors who provide diverse yet complementary case studies.

Drivers of Public Diplomacy

The term "public diplomacy" has numerous, sometimes competing, definitions. While some equate public diplomacy with propaganda[1], others have tried to separate the two. In 1987, the US Department of State's Dictionary of International Relations Terms defined public diplomacy as "government-sponsored programs intended to inform or influence public opinion in other countries; its chief instruments are publications, motion pictures, cultural exchanges, radio and television".[2] Ten years later, the Planning Group for Integration of USIA into the Department of State asserted, "Public Diplomacy seeks to promote

---

[1] Monroe E. Price, *Media and Sovereignty: The Global Information Revolution and its Challenges to State Power* (MIT Press, 2002).

[2] US Department of State, *Dictionary of International Relations Terms* (Government Printing Office, 1987), p. 85.

the national interest of the United States through understanding, informing and influencing foreign audiences"[3], adding "understanding" to the objectives of "informing" and "influencing". The link between these three words is clearest in the definition of public diplomacy adopted by the British Government's Foreign and Commonwealth Office, "work aiming to inform and engage individuals and organisations overseas, in order to improve understanding of and influence for the United Kingdom in a manner consistent with governmental medium and long term goals".[4]

In each of the three objectives, despite the different levels of cushioning used in terminology, it is evident that public diplomacy is a form of exercise of power. Joseph Nye has coined the term "soft power" for …

> … the ability to get what you want through attraction rather than coercion or payments. It arises from the attractiveness of a country's culture, political ideals, and policies. When our policies are seen as legitimate in the eyes of others, our soft power is enhanced.[5]

Nye has followed up this definition with the claim that "attraction often leads to acquiescence".[6]

Public Diplomacy through Broadcasting

The sharp increase of American public diplomacy efforts in the Middle East after September 11 was fostered by US military action, first in Afghanistan, and then in Iraq. The United States needed to frame its use of force as legitimate; as Jamie Metzl argues, "[w]ithout winning the struggle to define the interpretation of state actions, the physical acts themselves become less effective".[7] Indeed, Metzl's advocacy of the use of communication technologies like the internet and satellite

---

[3] Quoted in Public Diplomacy Alumni Association, *What is Public Diplomacy* (2008), http://www.publicdiplomacy.org/1.htm (accessed 13 November 2008).

[4] Lord Carter of Coles *Review of Public Diplomacy* (2005), http://www.fco.gov.uk/publicdiplomacyreview (accessed 13 November 2008).

[5] Joseph S. Nye, *Soft Power: The Means to Success in World Politics* (Public Affairs, 2004) p. x.

[6] Nye, *Soft Power*, p. 6.

[7] Jamie Frederic Metzl, "Popular Diplomacy", *Daedalus* (Spring 1999), 128: 2, p. 178.

television for "defining the legitimacy of the use of force"[8] was supported by the United States Government's use of radio and television to reach audiences in the Middle East in general and the Arab world in particular.

Using broadcasting during the 2003 war on Iraq was not a new development. American public diplomacy in the country dates back to the 1950s when the United States subsidized newspapers and produced programs for Radio Baghdad to disseminate anti-communist propaganda.[9] American reliance on Arabic-language media to target Iraq was also employed during the 1991 Gulf War when the United States used a government transmitter based in Kuwait to broadcast Iraqi opposition propaganda on the Iraqi Broadcasting Corporation and Radio Hurriah (Radio Freedom).[10] Before the war on Iraq in 2003, the United States started a global public relations campaign through the Office of Global Communications to generate support for American foreign policy in the Middle East.[11]

The Arab satellite television landscape encouraged the use of this medium by the US government to appeal to Arab audiences. This was mainly due to the rise of Al-Jazeera after September 11 as the Arab world's primary source of news, an image cultivated after its broadcasting of several messages by Osama bin Laden after September 11. The exaggeration of the impact of satellite television in the Middle East[12] and the perception that Al-Jazeera was presenting anti-American views prompted the US Government to launch the Middle Eastern Television Network, otherwise known as Al-Hurra.[13] Al-Hurra's birth was not entirely due to the war on Iraq, however. The United States Government's development of Radio Sawa predated September 11, and plans were rushed after that date in an attempt at "rebranding" the United States. Radio Sawa (meaning Radio Together) was formed to

---

[8] Ibid.

[9] Sue Curry Jansen. "Foreign Policy, Public Diplomacy and Public Relations: Selling American to the World" in Lee Arts and Yayha R. Kamalipour (eds.), *Bring 'Em On: Media and Politics in the Iraq War*, (Rowman and Littlefield, 2005), pp. 51–66.

[10] Laura Miller, John Stauber and Sheldon Rampton, "War is Sell" in David Miller (ed.), *Tell Me Lies: Propaganda and Media Distortion in the Attack on Iraq* (Pluto, 2004), pp. 41–51.

[11] Ibid.

[12] David Hoffman, "Beyond Public Diplomacy", *Foreign Affairs* (March/April 2002), 81:2, pp. 83–95.

[13] Edward Kaufman, "A Broadcasting Strategy to Win Media Wars", *The Washington Quarterly* (Spring 2002), 25:2, p. 123.

reach "the new young mainstream of educated Arabs under 30 and the emerging Arab leadership".[14]

The United States is not the only actor utilizing broadcasting as a public diplomacy tool in the Middle East. Iran also launched an Arabic-language satellite television channel, Al-Alam (The World) during the war on Iraq. The channel labeled the conflict "Harb al-Soltah" (War of Domination) and referred to the American army in Iraq as the "occupiers", in line with Al-Jazeera's coverage of the war.[15] Russia and the United Kingdom jumped on the bandwagon, with the former launching Russia Al-Yawm (Russia Today), a government-owned Arabic-language satellite channel, and the latter supporting the launch of BBC Arabic television.

Gadi Wolfsfeld's "political contest model" tries to understand power relationships in setting the news agenda, contending, "[t]he best way to understand the role of the news media in politics is to view the competition over the news media as part of a larger and more significant contest among political antagonists for political control".[16] Wolfsfeld divides political antagonists into the more powerful "authorities" and the less powerful "challengers".[17] Both sides, according to his model, engage in two simultaneous battles: the "structural dimension" over access to the news media and "the cultural dimension" over the construction of meaning in the media.[18] Wolfsfeld argues that the relationship between antagonists and the media is one of mutual dependency, whereby the antagonists rely on the media to send their messages and the media rely on the antagonists for information. Launching public diplomacy broadcasting stations challenges this dependency, giving governments guaranteed access to the media and complete control over the construction of messages disseminated through their outlets, and thus a potential advantage over competitors in the battle for political control.

---

[14] Quoted in Price, *Media and Sovereignty*, p. 222.

[15] Nadim Badii, "Iranians and Media Coverage of the War in Iraq: Rhetoric, Propaganda and Contradiction", in Yahya Kamalipour and Nancy Snow (eds.), *War, Media, and Propaganda: A Global Perspective* (Rowman and Littlefield, 2004), pp. 171–178.

[16] Gadi Wolfsfeld, "The Political Contest Model", in Simon Cattle (ed.), *News, Public Relations and Power* (London: Sage, 2003), p. 81.

[17] Ibid.

[18] Wolfsfeld, "Political Contest Model", p. 83.

This theoretical advantage is not manifest in practice, however. Although Radio Sawa airs a mixture of pop songs and news, it has been regarded by Nancy Snow as an example of psychological operations, "planned psychological activities in peace and war directed at enemy, friendly and neutral audiences in order to influence attitudes and behavior affecting the achievement of political and military objectives".[19] Audience research suggests that Sawa is not entirely successful in achieving these objectives, as listeners seem to tune out when news is broadcast. Similarly, research on Al-Hurra suggests that it is failing to have the desired impact due to deep mistrust of its content by Arab audiences who perceive it as a propaganda tool by the American government.[20] This perception is not surprising. As Mornoe Price argues:

> "International broadcasting" is the elegant term for a complex combination of state-sponsored news, information, and entertainment directed at a population outside the sponsoring state's boundaries. It is the use of electronic media by one society to shape the opinion of the people and leaders of another. It involves what was once with pride called propaganda.[21]

Despite this objection, the United States has tried to step up its investment in Al-Hurra, with the planned establishment of new channel bureaus in the Arab world.

Diplomacy and Public Diplomacy

In addition to broadcasting, the United States has expanded its other public diplomacy initiatives in the Middle East. Following the 2006 Israeli attack on Lebanon, the United States invested in reconstruction projects across the country to help rebuild the infrastructure. The US Agency for International Development is also highly active in educational and cultural programs in the region. One project completed in Lebanon in the summer of 2008 aims at trust-building among Lebanon's different religious communities, creating four interconnected community theatre groups in four villages (one Christian, two

---

[19] Nancy Snow, "Brainscrubbing: The Failures of US Public Diplomacy After 9/11", in Miller (ed.), *Tell Me Lies*, p. 54.

[20] Marway M. Kraidy, *Arab Media and US Policy: A Public Diplomacy Reset* (The Stanley Foundation, 2008), http://www.stanleyfoundation.org/publications/pab/PAB08Kraidy.pdf (accessed 13 November 2008).

[21] Price, *Media and Sovereignty*, p. 200.

Shiite, and one Druze) in Lebanon. The project emphasizes the United States' role in Lebanon as one promoting national cohesion—an attempt at departing from the negative image of the USA generated in response to the United States' supportive stance towards Israel in the 2006 war.

This characterization of reconstruction and cultural programs as elements of public diplomacy is not universal. A 2005 roundtable on the issue at the Aspen Institute for example failed to reach a consensus on whether foreign assistance constitutes public diplomacy.[22] I would argue, however, that today's interconnected world demands a holistic outlook on public diplomacy that takes it beyond the rigid confines of communication messages. This conception also mediates the difference between diplomacy and public diplomacy. Christopher Ross distinguishes between the two, saying that the first aims at engaging foreign governments, while the second aims at engaging foreign publics.[23] However, as Hoffman has argued, the "communications revolution has made diplomacy more public, exposing the once-secret work of diplomats to the global fishbowl of life in the twenty-first century".[24]

In this context, it is useful to examine a case where diplomacy and foreign assistance have blended with communication-based messages to constitute an emerging form of public diplomacy. Qatar is a small Gulf state, but it is gaining a higher profile in regional politics in the Middle East through its role as a mediator. For example, in 2006, it tried to engage Hamas and the Palestinian Authority in negotiations to establish a Palestinian unity government. On 14 April 2008, it orchestrated the first public meeting between the Israeli and Omani foreign ministers.[25] And in May 2008, it hosted the Doha Conference, a five-day meeting between Lebanese factions that ended an 18-month period of political deadlock in the country.

---

[22] Shanthi Kalathil, *Soft Power, Hard Issues: Reports of the 2005 Aspen Institute Forum on Communications and Society and the Roundtable on Public Diplomacy and the Middle East* (Aspen: The Aspen Institute, 2006).

[23] Christopher Ross, "Public Diplomacy Comes of Age", *The Washington Quarterly* (Spring 2002), 25:2, pp. 75–83.

[24] Hoffman, "Beyond Public Diplomacy", p. 84.

[25] "Israeli Foreign Minister Meets Omani Counterpart in First Meeting of its Kind", *Al-Arabiya*, 14 April 2008, http://www.alarabiya.net/articles/2008/04/14/48274.html (accessed 13 November 2008).

Qatar's involvement in Lebanese issues predates this conference. The country is funding the building of the Lebanese National Library. Following the 2006 Israeli attack, Qatar made a commitment to the rebuilding of destroyed places of worship in the whole of South Lebanon and to the reconstruction of schools, public buildings, and infrastructure in the southern villages of Khiam, Bint Jbeil, Ayta Al-Shaab and Aynata.[26] These reconstruction efforts have been coupled with visual statements. Within a month of the end of the 2006 war, Qatari flags could be seen hanging in some of the villages it was helping rebuild. In April 2007, Hizbullah-owned Al-Manar television aired a song titled "Thank you, Qatar", complete with a specially-commissioned music video. The video opens with footage from the attacks on the South, followed by shots of Qatari rescue teams working in South Lebanon, before-and-after images of buildings reconstructed with Qatari support, and footage of churches and mosques being rebuilt. These images are intercut with others of the Qatari flag and of Qatari politicians at the Security Council. The song's lyrics are written from a Qatari perspective, saying, "We have come to rebuild Lebanon, defying death...We've rebuilt churches and mosques, a thorn in the eye of the greedy enemy." In the period surrounding the second anniversary of the 2006 war, the website of the town of Bint Jbeil displayed a banner declaring, in English, "Recognition of Honesty to the Loyal Country of Qatar". The banner referenced one of Hizbullah's slogans following the 2006 war ("God's promise was true") by declaring "[Qatar] was true to its promise".[27]

Qatar built on this image in the Doha Conference of 2008. After the failure to elect a Lebanese president upon the end of former president Emile Lahoud's term in November 2007 and after a protest camp set up by Hizbullah and its allies paralyzed life in downtown Beirut from December 2006 to May 2008, the country saw the worst sectarian conflict since the days of the Civil War. On 7 May 2008, a week of street fighting broke out between Shiite and Sunni factions in areas of West Beirut, with Hizbullah and its allies sending militiamen to take over those areas by force. Amidst fears that Lebanon was on the verge of another civil war, and after several failed attempts by the Arab League

[26] See *Khiyam: Qatar Governmental Aid* (2008), http://khiyam.com/qatar/index.php (accessed 13 November 2008).

[27] See *Bint Jbeil* (2008), http://www.bintjbeil.com (accessed 13 November 2008).

to mediate between the warring sides, Qatar stepped in, inviting key Lebanese leaders to meet in Doha for negotiations.

The negotiations were heavily reported in the Lebanese and pan-Arab media. After five intense days, including a well-covered story of the Emir of Qatar stepping in to rescue failed talks at midnight, the Doha Conference ended with a compromise agreement between the Lebanese government and its opposition. A Lebanese president was elected three days later, and a new "national unity" government was formed. Throughout the Conference, the Lebanese media praised Qatar for its "neutrality" in the negotiations, and afterwards, posters bearing the image of the Emir of Qatar were distributed on the streets of Beirut.

The media coverage, visibility of the Emir of Qatar's role, and on-the-ground activities to boost Qatar's image like the distribution of posters are all examples challenging the binary model of diplomacy/public diplomacy. Qatar succeeded in building a positive image of itself in Lebanon. The heavy coverage of the achievements of the Doha Conference in the pan-Arab media (including the Qatar-based Al-Jazeera) ensured that this image was a region-wide one, rather than being restricted to the Lebanese arena.

Qatari Successes versus American Failures

Qatar's success was due to a number of factors, all of which highlight the difference between the Qatari and American approaches to public diplomacy in the Middle East. Primary among these is Qatar's non-reliance on state-owned media to construct its new image. Robert Satloff argues that US public diplomacy initiatives should have three components:

1. Explaining U.S. policy, candidly and without apology.
2. Providing alternative sources of credible, factual, relevant information, especially about the wider world but also about the local countries in which listeners and viewers live.
3. Projecting those core U.S. values that characterize U.S. society.[28]

[28] Robert Satloff, *The Battle of Ideas in the War on Terror: Essays on U.S. Public Diplomacy in the Middle East* (Washington Institute for Near East Policy, 2004), pp. 3–4.

American public diplomacy initiatives in the Middle East have embraced these three components, with Al-Hurra television explaining and justifying the American angle towards US activities in the Middle East while emphasizing the compatibility of those activities with "values" such as freedom and democracy. At the same time as it promotes the goals of the US state, the channel claims to be a credible source of news in the region.

Although Al-Jazeera is a Qatar-based channel, it has not packaged itself as one disseminating the official Qatari point of view. With a long-established suspicion amongst Arab audiences of information disseminated through state-owned channels, Al-Jazeera has managed to cultivate credibility through its perceived independence, a reputation that al-Hurra simply cannot achieve. When Al-Jazeera covered the Doha Conference extensively, Qatar refrained from foregrounding its own media as a source of credible information during that period, instead using other means of communication like posters and banners on the street as well as relying on the reporting of the pan-Arab and Lebanese media.

The second reason for success is the construction of an image of Qatar as a neutral agent. Ross mirrors the other two points in Satloff's model by framing public diplomacy as being about the communication of policy on one hand and about the development of understanding and appreciation of the communicating agent on the other.[29] Once again, the Doha Conference was a vital example of this neutrality. The gathering marked a change in the role of Gulf states in Lebanon. Previously, Saudi Arabia was the primary Gulf player in Lebanese affairs, but Saudi Arabia's closeness to the Hariri family negatively affected its position in Lebanon, so that instead of being seen as an outside mediator – the classic role it had played since the 1980s – it was now viewed as an ally of the March 14 coalition. Qatar, on the other hand, prided itself on its impartiality. At the same time, although Qatar's activities in May 2008 brought greater appreciation in Lebanon and the Arab world, the state's objectives were not foregrounded, in contrast to the perception of the United States as a beggar for appreciation in the region.

In 2000, the Foreign Policy Centre in London published a short book, *Going Public: Diplomacy for the Information Society*, with

---

[29] See Ross, "Public Diplomacy Comes of Age".

guidelines for the British Government in the battle for "winning hearts and minds". One section in the book states, "It is as important to prove our relevance as it is to win other countries' trust".[30] Another section, titled "The New Diplomacy: Fusing Traditional and Public Diplomacy", states that international politics "must be a set of deep relationships that are based on mutual benefit. This means that government will often act as a facilitator—supporting the activities of others".[31] Qatar's case is an illustration of those guidelines in action. Its higher profile points to a shift in the balance of power in the region in its favour. It has managed both to capitalize on its outside status to play the role of facilitator and to use this role to prove its relevance as a serious political agent.

The final reason for success is Qatar's non-reliance on the communication of values. This can be contrasted with Nye's proposal that soft power "appeal to a sense of attraction, love, or duty in… [a] relationship and appeal to… shared values about the justness of contributing to those shared values and purposes".[32] The United States had attempted to implement this approach after September 11 when it launched a campaign, "Shared Values", targeted at Muslim audiences outside the USA. The campaign emphasized the contributions of Muslims to American life through a series of videos for broadcast outside the USA. The broadcasts, however, received little attention from the intended audience, who were more concerned with US foreign policy than domestic policy.[33] Practical issues of policy overshadowed values.

There are three other problems with the reliance on values as an element of public diplomacy. The first two emanate from a gap between idealistic values and facts on the ground. Nancy Snow argues that the challenges facing the United States in this context are that American interests (economic access supported by military action) do not match "American values".[34] Secondly, value-based public diplomacy campaigns after September 11 lack credibility in light of "Guantanamo detentions, FBI interrogations of Arab Americans, US deportations and new visa restrictions".[35] As Mark Bowden wrote in 2004, "[t]he photos

---

[30] Mark Leonard and Vidhya Alakeson, *Going Public: Diplomacy for the Information Society* (Foreign Policy Centre, 2000), p. 40.

[31] Leonard and Alakeson, *Going Public*, pp. 59–60.

[32] Nye, *Soft Power*, p. 7.

[33] See Nye, *Soft Power*.

[34] See Snow, "Brainscrubbing".

[35] Curry Jansen, "Foreign Policy, Public Diplomacy and Public Relations", p. 59.

from Abu Ghraib prison portray Americans as exactly the sexually obsessed, crude, arrogant, godless occupiers that our enemies say we are".[36] The final obstacle for the reliance on values is their vagueness. Nancy Snow contends that American public diplomacy favours " 'glittering generalities' like nebulous American values of freedom and democracy that are rarely defined".[37]

In leading the negotiations between the conflicting Lebanese factions, Qatar did not present its actions as aiming at sustaining democracy or freedom in Lebanon. Instead, it stuck to specific, operationally-defined, verifiable aims: the election of a Lebanese president, the formation of a national unity government, and the cessation of hostilities on the ground. Doing so, it has avoided the exposure of potential gaps between words and deeds.

Non-State Public Diplomacy: The Case of Hizbullah

It is not only states who are engaging in public diplomacy in the Middle East. Non-state actors are also involved, although their activities are rarely framed as such. For example, although Jan Melissen acknowledges that "non-state actors, and supranational and subnational players develop public diplomacy policies of their own", he limits examples of such public diplomacy efforts to the work of NGOs.[38]

Paramilitary groups also pursue public diplomacy, with the Lebanese Hizbullah the leading practitioner in the Middle East. Distinctively, Hizbullah targets the Lebanese and Middle Eastern audiences but also sometimes seeks global audiences. It is an example of Melissen's contention that the " 'interconnected' realities of global relationships" mean that it is becoming increasingly difficult to separate "public affairs (aimed at domestic audiences) from public diplomacy (dealing with overseas target groups)".[39]

Hizbullah's public diplomacy efforts utilize a mixture of media messages, aid initiatives and military actions. Hizbullah has had a

---

[36] Mark Bowden, "Lessons of Abu Ghraib", *The Atlantic* (July/August 2004), http://www.theatlantic.com/doc/200407/bowden (accessed 13 November 2008).

[37] Snow, "Brainscrubbing", p. 60.

[38] Jan Melissen, "The New Public Diplomacy: Between Theory and Practice" in Jan Melissen (ed.), *The New Public Diplomacy: Soft Power in International Relations* (Palgrave Macmillan, 2005), p. 12.

[39] Melissen, "The New Public Diplomacy", p. 13.

dedicated media bureau almost since its inception. Throughout its existence, it has used the latest technologies in its communication strategies, from cassette tapes in the 1980s to all forms of mediated visual and oral communication today. It owns radio and television stations and several websites. It sells branded merchandize, from calendars to lighters to T-shirts. Hizbullah's approach to diverse audiences was illustrated, following its war with Israel in 2006, when it employed a public relations company to design its "Divine Victory" campaign. This used billboards on the streets of Beirut displaying photographic images from the 2006 war with the slogan written in Arabic, English and French.

It is curious that several of Hizbullah's activities mirror United States' public diplomacy initiatives. Both have made efforts to engage with Arab populations through educational, social and reconstruction programmes. Hizbullah has dedicated social and educational services bureaus, while the United States relies on a number of agencies like USAID. Following the 2006 war, Hizbullah funded the rebuilding of bridges in South Beirut while the USA funded reconstruction of the Mdairej Bridge in Mount Lebanon. Both use the media as a mouthpiece in addressing Arab audiences: the United States has al-Hurra television and Radio Sawa; Hizbullah has al-Manar television and al-Nour radio.

Hizbullah's communication strategies have largely been successful, helping the group to sustain its presence as a key political player in the region. Part of this success is due to its choice of messages—whether visual (posters), rhetorical (speeches) or practical (social programmes)—that resonate with its audiences. Its messages are constantly evolving, changing in line with the political context, and consequently allowing the group to adapt its public image. As an Islamist militia created in 1982 for the establishment of an Islamic state, Hizbullah presented itself as an anti-Israeli resistance movement, first in the Lebanese and then the Arab arenas. Later it transformed into a key participant in Lebanese politics, initially as an Islamic group, then a resistance group, and later a national group. And, since the 2006 war, Hizbullah has widened its network of audiences and developed itself as a heroic brand across the Arab world.

The importance of this brand is that it has merged and streamlined Hizbullah's political transformations to lend the group credibility. At every stage, Hizbullah has been able to back up its transforming image with an evolving yet responsive political agenda coupled with visible "results", be they military, political, social, or educational. For example, since Hizbullah sold its resistance activities to Israeli occupation in South Lebanon in the 1980s and 1990s as attempts at evicting Israeli troops from Lebanese soil, the Israeli withdrawal from South Lebanon in 2000 was "proof" of Hizbullah's credibility. Similarly, Hizbullah leader Hassan Nasrallah declared that the 2006 war was aimed at returning Lebanese detainees in Israeli prisons, and the release was anticipated through the branding of the conflict as the "True Promise" war, with dissemination through an integrated multiplatform media campaign. Thus the release of those detainees in June 2008 was marketed by Hizbullah as further proof of credibility.

Joseph Nye argues that future public diplomacy battles between different political agents will be "a contest of credibility".[40] R.S. Zaharna adds, "[t]he persuasive value of public diplomacy is tied to its credibility: the more credible a government's public diplomacy is, the more persuasive it is".[41] By consistently backing its media messages with verifiable results, and then using the media to publicize those results, Hizbullah has been successful in creating a snowball effect that has increased its credibility and visibility. Hizbullah has therefore been successful in ensuring that its public diplomacy messages are harmonious with its military and political actions, a condition of success for public diplomacy aims.[42]

Conclusion: Lessons of Public Diplomacy in the Middle East

In 2002 Antony J. Blinken wrote, "[t]he war of ideologies is over. The war of ideas is just beginning".[43] For Blinken, American concern had shifted into bridging the gap between the way it perceived itself and the way others perceive it, rather than remaining focused on the validity of its ideologies vis-à-vis those of others. The lesser the distance between perceptions, the higher the degree of success of public diplomacy efforts. By that standard, however, the US is failing in its efforts, as opinion polls in the Arab world show a great degree of disparity

[40] Joseph S. Nye, *The Paradox of Power* (Oxford University Press, 2003), p. 68.

[41] R.S. Zaharna, "From Propaganda to Public Diplomacy in the Information Age", in Kamalipour and Snow (eds.), *War, Media, and Propaganda*, p. 223.

[42] See Melissen, "The New Public Diplomacy".

[43] Antony J. Blinken, "Winning the War of Ideas", *The Washington Quarterly* (Spring 2002), 25:2, p. 102.

between the two.[44] In the case of Qatar, its perceived neutral background has transformed it into a *tabula rasa* that aids in the construction of an image of itself in line with its political ambitions. However, perhaps the most successful example of the blending of perceptions is that of Hizbullah.

The presentation of these cases offers other lessons. First, while public diplomacy in the Middle East is primarily seen as revolving around the use of the media, it encompasses other forms of action like foreign and domestic aid which cannot be detached from the communication context. Second, the line between public diplomacy and diplomacy, as demonstrated in the case of Qatar's involvement in Lebanon, is becoming increasingly blurred. Third, while some have argued that policy advocacy must be at the core of public diplomacy[45], the challenge remains: no matter how sophisticated public diplomacy efforts are, if the policies they are advocating are not acceptable to the targeted audience, those efforts are doomed to failure. Fourth, the reliance on vague terms like "values" and "democracy" in public diplomacy campaigns will not lead to measurable results. The US Government, in line with recommendations such as those of David Hoffman and Joseph Nye, may be using the "greatest weapon" of its values to "brand" itself as a democratic nation that appeals to the rest of the world.[46] Both those statements are constructed on the assumption that values have a universal appeal. The case of Qatar demonstrates, however, that it is much more effective to focus on small, measurable aims than to advocate abstract terms like "freedom" or "democracy". The more concrete the result of a public diplomacy effort, the more credible the message will appear.

This leads to the fifth point, which is that no public diplomacy act will succeed if it lacks credibility. Both the United States and Hizbullah rely on notions of justice and liberty to prove their legitimacy to their audiences. The United States presents itself as a model of democracy and an example of liberty to be emulated by other nations; Hizbullah claims to represent the voices of the people and to seek "justice" for victims of Israeli aggression, while branding itself as a "liberator" of

[44] Fares Braizat, *Revisiting the Arab Street*. (University of Jordan, 2005), http://www.jcss.org/SubDefault.aspx?PageId=55&PubType=1 (accessed 13 November 2008).

[45] See Satloff, *The Battle for Ideas in the War on Terror*.

[46] See Hoffman, "Beyond Public Diplomacy"; Joseph S. Nye, "The Decline of America's Soft Power: Why Washington Should Worry", *Foreign Affairs* (May/June 2004), 83:3, pp. 16–20.

land and people. However, while Hizbullah has managed to back up its image and rhetoric with parallel acts on the ground, the United States has not managed to cultivate a wide sense of credibility because of the gap between its public discourse and its actions in and policies towards the Middle East.

Two other factors can be deduced from the case studies discussed in this chapter. The first is the importance of constructing public diplomacy around the notion of agency. American public diplomacy in the Middle East has been accused of being marred by basing its discourse "on the erroneous assumption that extremists in the region misunderstand and deliberately distort U.S. goals and actions", which necessitates repackaging "the U.S. image and policies in a manner more appealing to a presumably alien and less intelligent culture".[47] This position is echoed by Penny M. Von Eschen, who says that public diplomacy initiatives in the Middle East "have typically been aimed at a populace…whom policy makers and purveyors of U.S. propaganda rarely imagined as legitimate political agents".[48] Hizbullah in particular has reversed this notion through its presentation of itself as a heroic representative of an empowered people, be they Lebanese or Arab.

The second factor is the need for a dynamic relationship between public diplomacy and changing political contexts. In the case of the United States, despite its efforts to rebrand itself as a world helper, those efforts have been marred by the reinforcement of its perception in the Middle East as an imperialist power with the wars on Afghanistan and Iraq. Qatar on the other hand was able to take advantage of Saudi Arabia's eclipsing role in Lebanon to claim a higher profile for itself in Arab politics. However the most illustrative case is that of Hizbullah. Examining Hizbullah's communication strategies through the prism of public diplomacy reveals sophisticated processes in creating an image of the group that matches evolving political contexts and in using a variety of methods to communicate this image to a variety of audiences. Perhaps most importantly, it reveals a fine balance between political adaptability and reliability, which in turn generates trust. This formula is perhaps the hardest to crack by anyone involved in public diplomacy.

[47] Lamis Andoni, "Deeds Speak Louder than Words", *The Washington Quarterly* (Spring 2002), 25:2, p. 86.

[48] Penny Von Eschen, "Enduring Public Diplomacy", *American Quarterly* (April 2005), 57:2, p. 336.

THE LONGER TERM IMPACT OF U.S. PUBLIC DIPLOMACY IN THE AMERICAS DURING WWII

Elizabeth Fox

In the period leading up to the Second World War, many of the general goals of the public diplomacy of the United States towards Latin America were similar to those of today, promoting the commercial interests of US companies in the region and ensuring favorable public opinion towards the United States, its government, policies, and people. During the war, these goals also included combating the propaganda efforts of the Axis powers and strengthening an emerging Latin American commercial broadcasting system modeled on the one evolving in the United States. More than sixty years later, the longer term impact of US public diplomacy in Latin American during the war can be seen in the structures and functions of the Latin American broadcasting systems, and, in some ways, also in the strength of the US private commercial as opposed to public or government-owned broadcasting systems as the main vehicle of public diplomacy. The impact of US public diplomacy during the formative years of Latin American radio and television, and in some cases press was the product of the partnerships and tensions between the supporters of US commercial media and the supporters of US Government-owned broadcasting over who executed public diplomacy. The results of these tensions are still felt across the region.

Governments, private sectors, and civil society have long been part of an interlocking and, often, competing webs of public diplomacy. Today, much has changed in technologies and the structure of the Latin American and global broadcasting industries, with internet, satellites, and cell phones replacing shortwave radio in all locations except, perhaps, the case of Cuba. The debate over how and through which sector the public diplomacy message is best delivered and received, however, is still current. That debate has intersected with a long-term and not unintended consequence, the growth of a commercial broadcasting system fashioned after the model of commercial broadcasting in the United States, the content of which would generally support US economic and political interests in the region.

The Latin American media developed roughly at the same time as they did in the United States, film and radio in the 1920s and television in the 1950s. During the early years, a key public diplomacy goal of the US Government was to counter the control of radio and television stations by a foreign power or local political actor hostile to US interests, notably Nazi Germany and what were perceived then as communist or socialist tendencies of some Latin American political movements. Meanwhile, the US Government and US commercial broadcasters worked in tandem in Latin America to promote private ownership and the flow of US programs and recordings into the region. The ultimate goal was to reach Latin American publics with images and messages that reflected and supported US values and policy objectives and expanded markets for US goods and services.

As commercial radio was beginning in Latin America, some European countries were setting up government-owned shortwave radio stations with the power to broadcast directly into homes in another country. Shortwave broadcasting such as Radio Moscow in 1929, the British Broadcasting Corporation in 1932, and the Foreign Radio Section in Germany under Adolf Hitler after 1933 changed the conduct of public diplomacy. This "capability of states to penetrate territorial frontiers at will via radio and thereby directly influence foreign public opinion significantly altered the international environment of the new administration of President Roosevelt",[1] forcing the US Government to adopt a position on the use of broadcasting as an instrument of foreign policy.

In the spring of 1934, the development of foreign, government-owned shortwave stations broadcasting directly into Latin America prompted a State Department proposal to establish a government-owned and operated shortwave radio station in the United States. The struggle over who would carry out public diplomacy, the government or the private sector, however, was already an issue. Before the bill authorizing funding of a government-owned station was sent to Congress, a representative of the American Telephone and Telegraph Company (AT&T) effectively blocked the proposal by informing the State Department that his company "would be glad to cooperate in any way possible in the development of the very best means of

[1] Bruce Gregory, *The Broadcasting Service: An Administrative History* (USIA, 1970). p. I–9.

communication with the Latin American countries.[2] The bill authorizing the station was never tabled.

In 1937, support for a government effort in international broadcasting was again taken up by the US Congress, in particular with the Celler Bill calling for the establishment of a government-owned radio station broadcasting to Latin America. Forced by the public profile of the debate to make a decision, President Roosevelt stopped short of supporting the Celler Bill as a result of the vigorous public opposition of the U.S private broadcasting industry. Instead he authorised a series of interim measures that, "while they did not close the door to a publicly-owned broadcasting service, had the effect of expanding the use of privately-owned facilities as a means of achieving the foreign policy objectives envisaged by the proponents of a government-owned and operated radio station".[3]

The National Broadcasting Corporation (NBC) had become the first private commercial broadcaster to provide shortwave services to Latin America, transmitting programs directly to listeners and making them available for re-broadcast by Latin American radio stations in 1934. In 1937, the Columbia Broadcasting System (CBS) set up a small, separate shortwave program bureau and began regular international broadcasting to Europe and Latin America. Three other commercial companies, General Electric, Westinghouse, and the Crosley Corporation,[4] also had regular shortwave broadcasts to Latin America. These commercial broadcasters felt the entrance of the government in the field of international broadcasting would "unnecessarily duplicate existing private stations and would constitute an entering wedge for public control and operation of all domestic broadcasting in the United States."[5]

Commercial broadcasters, invited to present their views in hearings, strongly opposed bills introduced in 1938 to set up a government shortwave station to combat Fascist propaganda in South America and

---

[2] Gregory, *The Broadcasting Service*, p. I–28.

[3] Gregory, *The Broadcasting Service*, p. II–2.

[4] The *Federal Communications Commission* (FCC) ruled that the Crosley station, WLW, had to reduce its power to 50,000 watts in 1939 because it interfered with other stations. During *World War II*, the higher power of WLW was utilized again, and the station could be heard throughout most of the world. The 500-kilowatt transmitter was eventually crated up for shipment for use in Asia, but the war ended before it was shipped. WLW's engineers also built high-power shortwave transmitters that became the Voice of America.

[5] Gregory, *The Broadcasting Service*, p. II–22.

to establish in the State Department an Institute of Friendly American Relations which included a Government station for broadcast to the US and other American Republics.[6] Mark Ethridge, President of the National Association of Broadcasters, forcefully stated his argument against this role for US Government broadcasting:

> It is desirable for the United States to impress its culture on Latin America by indirection and to further the Good Neighbor policy by projecting a living pattern of our democracy, presenting the best of our music, institutions, traditions of liberty and freedom, programs of entertainment, and the news of the day, uncolored and uncensored. While this can be done by government, under the existing system of broadcasting in the United States, it can be better and more effectively accomplished by private entrepreneurs.[7]

The New York Times reported, "Uncle Sam himself has withdrawn, at least temporarily, from competing in any 'battle of the wave-lengths' to 'peddle isms' by radio to South America."[8]

Only with the exigencies of war did the U.S. Government decide to undertake international broadcasting for public diplomacy on a massive scale. In Latin America, the challenge was heightened by the increasing propaganda efforts of Germany in the 1930s. The National Socialist government escalated its state-directed and subsidized broadcasting and cultural activities in and to Latin America, sponsoring schools, cultural centers, athletic clubs, and other societies, subsidising press agencies and radio stations, and distributing German motion pictures.

The strategic relationship between Latin American and the United States at the start of the war was important because many strategic materials could no longer be obtained from areas that had fallen under control of the Axis powers. US purchases from Latin America would contribute to the Latin American economies, helping maintain employment, preventing discontent and disorder, and eliminating a fertile field for Nazi propaganda.[9] To implement this strategy, in 1940 Nelson

---

[6] "Shelve Radio Plan For Latin America; House Committeemen Defer Action on Proposal for Government System. Companies Oppose Bill. G. E, Westinghouse and Columbia Cite Facilities Now Ready for Broadcasting," *Time* (23 May 1938).

[7] Quoted in Gregory, *The Broadcasting Service*, p. II–59.

[8] "Legislation for construction and operation of a 'good-will' broadcasting service to South and Central America. The station to be owned and operated by the government apparently died today when the House Committee on Naval Affairs postponed indefinitely further hearings on the Celler bill," *New York Times* (18 May 1938), p. 14.

[9] *History of Office of the Coordinator of Inter-American Affairs* (Government Printing Office, 1947).

Rockefeller was named coordinator of the Office for Coordination of Commercial and Cultural Relations between the American Republics, renamed in 1941 Office of the Coordinator of Inter-American Affairs (CIAA). Rockefeller was responsible for a programme for the use of government and private facilities in Latin America in the arts and sciences, education, travel, radio, press, and cinema.

The CIAA information programme informed public opinion in the Americas about the "significance of the events that are taking place at home and abroad [in an] attempt to meet and counteract the propaganda program of the Axis powers on radio, in news columns, and the subsidized press, and through other means of communication."[10] The Press Division of CIAA furnished news and features to more than a thousand Latin American newspapers, magazines, and radio stations. News was transmitted by shortwave radio as well as distributed directly in the form of feature articles, news photographs, pamphlets, and cartoons, and in a magazine *En Guardia*. The radio division of the CIAA produced its own programs, which it distributed through private broadcasters such as the local affiliate chains of NBC and CBS in Latin America. The Motion Picture Division produced and distributed its own films and worked with film companies like Walt Disney Productions to produce and distribute newsreels and films in the region. Other CIAA programmes helped US companies place advertising in pro-Allied Latin American media outlets and supplied newsprint to publishers friendly with the Allied cause.

A handbook prepared by the director of the CIAA Communication Division described situations where US firms were found to be placing advertising on German news programs on Latin American radio stations:

> In many of the Republics American advertising budgets are, due to the low purchasing potential of the population, necessarily small. Some firms could afford to buy time on a station for a newscast broadcast, but could not afford to buy United Press or Associated Press news. Neither could the stations afford to buy the high priced American news services. Committed to broadcasting news for an American product – without money enough to buy "good news" – some of the stations probably found it profitable to use the news they could obtain at no cost from European propaganda sources. Some American advertisers have admitted that they

[10] US Congress, House of Representative Hearings, Second Deficiency Appropriations Bill, 1941, p. 688, cited in *History of the Office of the Coordinator of Inter-American Affairs*, p. 41.

> did not know the sources of the news they were sponsoring, though they did know it could not be that from American news.[11]

In 1940, twelve US commercial shortwave stations were broadcasting to Latin America (CBS 2, Crosley Corporation 1, General Electric 3, NBC 2, Western Electric 2, and World Wide Broadcasting Foundation 2), but they were operating with much less power than the foreign government-owed stations in London, Berlin and Rome. The CIAA concluded that the only practical way to reach a large audience was to place programmes on the domestic commercial radio stations already operating in Latin American countries. In April 1941, broadcasts compiled by CBS were sent by AT&T radio telephone to the Latin American countries. There they were picked up by the International Telephone and Telegraph Company and distributed for broadcasting over a network of domestic long- and shortwave radio stations. CIAA worked with NBC and CBS studios to produce Spanish and Portuguese programmes under the companies" logos, and they established contracts with the US shortwave stations for the use of their transmitting facilities and the production of programmes, including the writing of scripts and the hiring of announcers. These contracts also covered station time in Latin American countries for re-broadcasting programmes from the United States. By the fall of 1943, CIAA radio activities had grown to 200 hours per week of shortwave broadcasts from the United States and local rebroadcasts on about 190 local stations.[12]

The Motion Picture Division of CIAA was concerned with increasing the production of US films for exhibition in Latin America and with eliminating newsreels from Axis countries in Latin American theatres. The Motion Picture Division also hoped to supply production capital, technical assistance, and equipment for the support of the Latin American film industry. The aim was to produce feature films presenting the case for hemisphere solidarity in the war against the Axis powers, using the rationale that Latin American films reached a different audience than US films and would be not be suspected of being a part of a US Government propaganda campaign. The US was able to establish support to the Latin American film industry in Mexico. Support consisted of the sale of US-made motion picture equipment to the two

---

[11] Francisco, RG 229, Box 43, USIA Historical Collection, US Department of State.

[12] *History of the Office of the Coordinator of Inter-American Affairs, A Historical Report on War Administration*, pp. 58–59.

leading film studios in Mexico City, technical training to Mexican technicians, special products, and cooperation with the Mexican film in film distribution. Undeterred by the partial success of such ventures, Rockefeller testified before the House Appropriations Committee:

> We are faced, as we see it, with a very serious aspect of the defense program. The front line is the aide-to-England program. The second line of defense is the hemisphere programs. At the present time, it is not a military basis but we are faced with an economic defense problem and with a psychological defense problem as against propaganda from abroad controlled by Axis groups...Axis propaganda has swept over the entire hemisphere. The intellectual imperialism of ideas is at the moment just as serious a threat to the security and defense of the hemisphere as the possibility of a military invasion.[13]

Transition to Peace and the Cold War

In addition to their direct support for the expansion of the U.S. broadcasting industry in Latin America, the activities of the CIAA had a profound effect on the development of the Latin American media. Under government supervision and support during the war years, the U.S. private broadcasters had seen their initial shortwave and direct radio station investments in Latin America expand into a much wider range of media activities. For the first time, U.S. news services were widely used in the region. U.S. motion pictures were easily available and without competition, and U.S. radio programming and news, produced by government services and by private broadcasters was aggressively disseminated and used by domestic radio stations throughout the region. Even the U.S. advertising industry was coordinated in the effort to work with U.S. exports to Latin America.

After the war, with the exception of the U.S. Government shortwave radio broadcasts, most of the communication and media activities of the CIAA were transferred or returned to the private sector. With the return of peace, for a short time, the commercial broadcasters continued to produce programs for the Voice of America on a contract basis. Soon, however, the U.S. Government completely took over VOA activities.

---

[13] *History of the Office of the Coordinator of Inter-American Affairs, A Historical Report on War Administration*, p. 168.

While the economic recovery of Europe, the first priority of the US Government, shaped its approach to communication and culture,[14] Washington's concern over the attitudes toward communism of Latin American populations paralleled its attention to Europe. A study carried out for USIA in urban Chile in 1953 specifically addressed the relationship between public attitudes towards communism and exposure to US media. The study found that with the exception of Santiago, the capital, Chileans exposed to US media were more likely than others to believe that communism brought no special benefit to the workers of the country.[15] Such findings provided further justification for the international expansion of U.S. broadcasters.

There was cause for the U.S. Government to be concerned about the political stability of Latin America after the Second World War. The chronic foreign exchange shortages of many Latin American countries had made it impossible to satisfy the rising demands of their populations. Populist leaders such as Juan Peron in Argentina, Getulio Vargas in Brazil, and Gustavo Rojas Pinilla in Colombia were losing their dynamism and political support. In there desperation, they often resorted to harsh censorship and control of the media. Although newspapers suffered the most, radio journalists, magazines, popular entertainers, and musicians also felt the heavy hand of the increasingly authoritarian regimes. When the populist regimes fell, Vargas in 1954, Peron in 1955, Rojas Pinilla in 1957, their attempts to censor and, at the same time, their nationalistic protection of the development of domestic media industries through tariffs, subsidies, and state ownership collapsed.

---

[14] This need was argued by Charles D. Jackson, an officer under General Robert A. McClure in the Anglo-American Psychological Warfare Division of Eisenhower's Headquarters Staff (SHAEF), "In the cold war of words all our deeds abroad, all our writings, all our publications, all our expressions of thought, must be weighed according to their propaganda impact. This is why all private activities affecting public opinion abroad have, in effect, a propaganda aspect, using the word without an invidious sense and in its true meaning. That is why in the Economic Recovery Plan, specific provision was made for helping to promote the circulation of American publications and American ideas in Europe."

Charles Jackson, "Private Media and Public Policy," in Daniel Lerner (ed.), *Propaganda in War and Crisis: Materials for American Policy* (George W. Steward, 1951) p. 328.

[15] International Public Opinion Research, *A Report on Attitudes toward the United States and on Exposure to the Mass media and to the United States Information Program in Chile*, a report submitted to the Office of Research and Evaluation, United States Information Agency, January 1954.

Following the War, rather than combating the Axis propaganda in Latin America, the concerns of the commercial broadcasters in the United States, especially after the Cuban Revolution in 1959, were directed against movements toward state-ownership or control of media. The US broadcasters were firm supporters of the development of private, commercially-operated media industries. Thus the 1950s and 1960s brought a period of sustained expansion of privately owned commercial print and electronic media in Latin America, often with substantial investments from the fast growing US commercial broadcasters, including NBC, CBS, ABC, and Time Life. ABC, the largest investor, had investments in TV stations in Argentina, Chile, Colombia, cost Rica, Dominican Republic, Ecuador, El Salvador, Guatemala, Honduras, Panama, Uruguay and Venezuela. NBC, CBS and Time-Life all had investments in TV stations in Argentina, Peru, and Venezuela.

By then, the commercial nature of Latin American broadcasting had been firmly established. It would have been almost impossible for state owned or public radio and television to survive on a large scale in Latin America in the face of the pressures and inducements of the US capital, industries, and, and least at the beginning, government. Once the commercial nature of Latin American broadcasting was established – that the media would be operated for profit, not for public service, and financed by advertising, not by state subsidies – the nature of the industry that evolved in each country was the result of the different domestic forces at play. In those countries under one-party, non-democratic regimes, the media industries developed in a highly monopolistic fashion, ignoring any public service or watchdog function. In countries under more democratic rule, private commercial broadcasting was subject to regulation, often reflecting broader public interests, and the media developed in a more diverse, competitive environment. The growth of powerful domestic media monopolies in Latin America was not inevitable. Each country's policies, types of party structures, and the strengths and weakness of its civil and political society determined the nature of the broadcasting media industries that evolved in that country.

US direct investment in Latin American broadcasting began to decrease in the late 1970s. Indirect influence or investment from the US, however, continued through sales of TV programming from the major US networks, in some countries as high as three-quarters of the content of local stations. But, as domestic broadcasters grew and home-grown productions replaced imports, American programming lost its allure among Latin American audiences. Although TV series and films remained popular among more educated audiences, Latin American productions attracted larger and larger portions of the middle and lower income audiences, and locally or regionally produced music, soap operas and even documentaries took the place of US series. U.S. film and TV exports were limited to the more technically sophisticated and costly action and adventure series. Even these eventually would be overtaken replaced by the boom in Mexican, Brazilian, and Venezuelan productions.

What the public diplomacy efforts of the US during the Second World War accomplished was more subtle and harder to quantify than changes in public opinion regarding the US and its policies, although these were the immediate effects of the programs of the CIAA. By edging out almost all Government-backed European media and cultural exchange, libraries, film series, schools and clubs and replacing them with a US commercial broadcasting model, US public diplomacy efforts during the war contributed to setting the course of how the Latin American broadcasters would develop based on a commercial broadcasting structure similar to that in the United States.

Some US Government public diplomacy efforts to Latin American did continued after the Second World War – direct shortwave radio, and later television broadcasts under the Voice of America, and, later Radio and TV Marti broadcasts to Cuba. US Government shortwave broadcasts also continued in other areas of the world. The shortwave broadcasts of Radio Free Europe were crucial during the Cold War to the Soviet Union and other countries of Eastern Europe. A similar model of shortwave broadcasts was applied again, many years later in 1994 with Radio Free Asia, a private, non-profit corporation funded by an annual federal grant from Congress via the Broadcasting Board of Governors, broadcasting in nine languages to countries in Asia. The most recent US Government radio station, launched in 2002, was Radio Sawa, an Arabic language radio station combining western and Arab popular music with news broadcasts and specialized programming. Al-Hurra TV, a satellite channel followed in 2004, with a typical American commercial network look with more time devoted to news programming. None of these broadcasting efforts, however, were ever considered a real threat to US commercial radio or television in the regions where they broadcast, if these existed at all. By the time these stations were established, the tensions between the public diplomacy goals of the US Government and the commercial expansion goals of U.S. commercial broadcasting had been largely resolved.

The goals of U.S. commercial broadcasters – to expand their markets – and the goals of public diplomacy – to expand the support for the Allied powers and to eliminate propaganda from the Axis powers during the Second World War, coalesced in Latin America during the war to help form a commercial broadcast system modeled on the U.S. The initial tension over the challenge to the private sector posed by the US Government broadcasting to the region disappeared when the country declared war on Germany and private and public sectors began to work in tandem. These tensions did not reappear after the war, as the U.S. public diplomacy goals were well-served by the private sector, even if over the years, the reliance on the private sector to deliver messages that explain and support broader US interests has not always been certain.

The case of Latin America was unique. The tensions and convergence between public diplomacy and commercial broadcasters did not occur in other regions. In the case of most Asian and Arab countries, by the time they became the recipients of international broadcasts, they had developed their own government or public broadcasting systems.

COMPETING NARRATIVES: US PUBLIC DIPLOMACY AND THE PROBLEMATIC CASE OF LATIN AMERICA

Bevan Sewell

Ideally Public Diplomacy (PD) should function as a two-way, trans-national exchange of ideas; it should avoid the notion of power or of a dominant partner and, instead, develop as an exercise in communication, "listening" as well as exporting one's own message.[1] The establishment and creation of collaborative communications networks has to work both ways and has to transcend state-to-state interactions, if it is to be truly effective in terms of shaping perceptions. This is a concept that will take time to come to fruition; successful PD cannot be achieved overnight.[2]

In practice, the reality is somewhat different. While trans-national groups, organisations and networks do strive to implement PD in the ways outlined above, there is a point of tension between this model and the way that governments—particularly the US government—utilise it. For officials in Washington, the ultimate objective is not so much increased communication and understanding as it is increased success at improving receptiveness toward US objectives in order that American goals—and American power—can be attained. Even then it seems logical that, in the pursuit of power, increased influence can only be achieved via the notion of "soft power", "getting others to appreciate you to the extent that they change your behaviour to your liking", if persuasion is accompanied by reception.[3] However, broader domestic and international contexts are not conducive to implementing PD in this pure form. The frameworks of the War on Terror and recurrent electoral cycles have worked, as Philip Taylor has argued, to

[1] See Ali Fisher and Scott Lucas, Introduction to this volume, pp. 6–9.

[2] Philip Taylor, "Public Diplomacy and Strategic Communications", Nancy Snow and Philip Taylor (eds), *The Routledge Handbook of Public Diplomacy* (New York: Routledge, 2009) p. 14–15.

[3] Nancy Snow, "Rethinking Public Diplomacy", Nancy Snow and Philip Taylor (eds), *The Routledge Handbook of Public Diplomacy* (2009) pp. 3–5; Joseph Nye, *Soft Power: The Means to Success in World Politics* (New York: Public Affairs, 2004).

bastardise PD when employed directly by governments. "The objective of modern democratic politicians," he writes, "is to win at the next election rather than serve the nation's long-term interests. This absence of vision has characterized the western response to 9/11."[4]

After the September 2001 terrorist attacks, the George W. Bush administration adopted a PD model that adhered to part of Nye's conception in the desire to persuade but which avoided any acceptance of two-way communication or of the possibility that this could be a long-term approach. Swift results were deemed to be of paramount importance in repairing America's image and gaining the initiative in the Global War on Terror. Indeed, PD as practised by the US government since 9/11 has often become conflated, or synonymous, with Public Relations (PR). "In the last few years," as Liam Kennedy and Scott Lucas have argued, "US public diplomacy has undergone intensive reorganization and retooling as it takes on a more prominent propaganda role in the efforts to win the hearts and minds of foreign publics."[5] Though this is perhaps inevitable when governments and states become directly involved in implementation, it has a significant impact on the way that foreign policy is determined and on the necessity for the state to be able to "shape" the prevailing message.

This chapter will examine a region where the quest to shape the message and established the dominant narrative has proven to be difficult for the US: Latin America. The Bush administration's attempts during its second term in office to improve the climate of inter-American relations via PR and PD proved to be highly unsuccessful. Put simply, US officials were never in a position whereby they could control the predominant dialogue of inter-American relations; and they were unsuccessful in this due to the shared history between the US and the Latin American states, one characterised predominantly, especially during the Cold War, by instances of US intervention.[6]

PD, PR, and propaganda of course were all commonplace during the Cold War: each would be pursued repeatedly in an effort not just to

[4] Philip Taylor, "Public Diplomacy and Strategic Communications" (2009) p. 14; David Ryan, *Frustrated Empire: US Foreign Policy, 9/11 to Iraq* (Ann Arbor, Michigan: Pluto Press, 2007).

[5] Liam Kennedy and Scott Lucas, "Enduring Freedom: Public Diplomacy and US Foreign Policy," *American Quarterly* Volume 57, No. 2 (June 2005) p. 310.

[6] See: Juan Cole, "Anti-Americanism: It's the Policies", *American Historical Review*, Volume 111, No. 4 (October 2006).

undermine the cohesion of the Soviet Union, but also to maintain the solidarity of the western cause at home and abroad.[7] In Latin America, though, US officials between 1954 and 1973 would often consider and often resort to intervention to resolve emergent difficulties, even though they recognised the deleterious impact that this would have on the climate of intra-hemispheric relations. These actions have, unsurprisingly, cast a shadow over the inter-American relationship – one that the Bush administration not only failed to fully comprehend, but which it continued to believe it could effectively override with continued statements about its commitment toward economic fulfilment and social betterment in the region. In the spring of 2007, President Bush toured the region in an effort to use the power of the presidency and of public relationsto undermine Venezuelan leader, Hugo Chavez's, efforts to spread discord about the US and to generate a renewed sense of goodwill in inter-American relations.[8] According to the White House, the trip was an effort to "demonstrate" Washington's commitment to those nations south of the Rio Grande; to show, in the president's words, that "we care about your plight".[9] The unspoken, but nevertheless implicit, connotation was that, in doing so, the climate of US-Latin American relations would be improved.

Central within this assumption was the archetypal belief in American exceptionalism and moral sanctity that permeates much of the ideological underpinnings of US policy. This, as Piero Gleijeses has noted, "is a common refrain in American interpretations of US

---

[7] On Cold War efforts to utilise PR and propaganda, and to shape the message at home and abroad:

Kenneth Osgood, *Total Cold War: Eisenhower's Secret Propaganda Battle at Home and Abroad* (Lawrence, Kansas: University Press of Kansas, 2006);

Nick Cull, *The Cold War and the United States Information Agency: American Propaganda and Public Diplomacy, 1945–1989* (Cambridge, UK: Cambridge University Press, 2008);

Marc Selverstone, *Creating the Monolith: The United States, Great Britain, and International Communism, 1945–1950* (Cambridge, Massachusetts: Harvard University Press, 2009);

Scott Lucas, *Freedom's War: The US Crusade against the Soviet Union, 1945–1956* (Manchester: Manchester University Press, 1999).

[8] Bevan Sewell, "The Problems of Public Relations: Eisenhower, Latin America and the Potential Problems for the Bush Administration", *Comparative American Studies* Volume 6, No. 3 (September 2008) pp. 295–312.

[9] Address by President Bush on the Western Hemisphere, Ronald Reagan Building and International Trade Centre, March 5 2007. Taken From: http://www.whitehouse.gov/news/releases/2007/03/20070305-6.html Accessed on March 6 2007.

foreign policy: even when the United States has erred, its intentions were pure. The United States always means well. It is the city on the hill."[10] In accepting this theory so readily, Bush and his advisors were overlooking a crucial problem. While that might be the narrative that Washington was promoting, it was certainly not the narrative that the Latin Americans were reading. The problems and engrained memories of the long history of the relationship between the US and Latin America could, in the eyes of the Bush administration, be absolved by this "new" phase in intra-hemispheric relations. But for the Latin Americans, who were the supposed to beneficiaries of this approach, the traumatic legacies of their history with the US could not be forgotten so readily.

The Latin American case study, therefore, demonstrates the inherent difficulty in a US-centric model of public diplomacy. Any attempt by the US to pursue an effective public diplomacy strategy in Latin America first needs to navigate a way past the long-standing antipathy that many elements in Latin America feel (and have traditionally felt) toward the US.[11] The use of private and non-governmental organisations, of course, can begin to break these barriers down; but this cannot happen until the White House relinquishes the mantle of PD in Latin America, or at least until there is a significant shift in the tone and delivery of the message. Public diplomacy, as practiced by the US government, cannot ignore the shared legacy between the US and the Latin American nations. "Successive administrations," writes Nick Cull, "have fallen into the trap of overemphasizing the distance between public diplomacy and regular diplomacy and ignoring the degree to which public diplomacy is inextricably tied to the whole".[12] The message that the US would like to convey in Latin America – one of partnership, kinship and cooperation – will struggle to succeed until there is a tacit shift in emphasis that jettisons long-held beliefs about US superiority and power and accepts the notions of equivalence and receptivity.

---

[10] Piero Gleijeses, "Afterword" in Nick Cullather, *Secret History: The CIA's Classified Account of its Operations in Guatemala, 1952–1954* (Stanford, California: Stanford University Press, 1999) p. xxviii.

[11] Alan McPherson, *Yankee No!: Anti-Americanism in US-Latin American Relations* (Cambridge, Massachusetts: Harvard University Press, 2003) p. 11.

[12] Nick Cull, *The Cold War and the United States Information Agency:* (2008) p. 496.

Ideological Themes and Anti-Americanism

Latin American hostility toward the United States, which greatly undermines any attempts to improve the cultural climate of relations through propaganda, cultural relations, business exchanges and presidential rhetoric, can be traced back to two recurrent themes in inter-American relations: the obvious power imbalance between Washington and the Latin American nations and the projection of American influence - both physical and cultural - across the region. US policy has been motivated by a complex mixture of stark national interest and ideology - the belief that, in terms of development and racial hierarchies, the Latin Americans are inferior to United States "Americans" is coupled with the abundant capacity of the US to pursue its own interests in the region. While the Latin Americans have, beyond question, been able to interpose their own interests and objectives onto this relationship, it has not by any measure been an equal one.[13] Mark Gilderhus, concluding his book *The Second Century*, notes, "'The Western Hemisphere idea', to the extent that it applies at all, has conveyed a pro-US orientation, constricting the range of choice for Latin Americans."[14]

At first, such wilfulness on the part of the US appears self-defeating. Ignoring the desires and objectives of the Latin Americans, after all, seems a sure-fire way of exacerbating anti-American tensions in the region. That wilfulness, however, has been conditioned by an ideological mindset that legitimates the belief that innate American superiority over the Latin Americans renders such imbalances irrelevant. Dominating the outlook of US officials, Lars Schoultz argues, "are the underlying beliefs that US officials hold about Latin Americans and, specifically, their belief that Latin Americans are an inferior people".[15] The mind-set can be identified in Thomas Jefferson's sentiments,

[13] For a contemporary examination of the capacity of the Latin Americans, especially during the Cold War, to pursue their own interests in their dealings with the Latin Americans, see:

Max Paul Friedman, "Retiring the Puppets, Bringing Latin America Back In: Recent Scholarship on United States-Latin American Relations", *Diplomatic History* Volume 27, No. 5 (November 2003) pp. 621–636.

[14] Mark Gilderhus, *The Second Century: US-Latin American Relations since 1889* (Wilmington, Delaware: Scholarly Resources Inc, 2000) p. 246–247.

[15] Lars Schoultz, *Beneath the United States: A History of US Policy Toward Latin America* (Cambridge, Massachusetts: Harvard University Press, 1998) p. 374.

outlined in a letter of 1813, when he wrote that he did not believe that Latin Americans were "capable of maintaining a free government. Their people are immersed in the darkest ignorance, and brutalised by bigotry and superstition."[16] More than one hundred and seventy years later, it can be identified in Ronald Reagan's desire to make the rebellious Sandanistas "say uncle" and George H.W. Bush's derogatory labelling of Panamanian leader, Manuel Noriega, as a "small man".[17]

The continued prevalence of these ideologies has exacerbated the sense of ill-feeling in the region toward the United States.[18] It does not hold, however, that this has led to an endemic culture of anti-Americanism in the region. As an ideology and as a manifestation of antipathy toward the US, anti-Americanism is built on firmer foundations; it is not a reflexive and irrational hatred of all things American, rather it is a reaction to US policies.[19] Many Latin Americans continue to buy into "America" as a cultural, commercial and metaphysical entity. (In fact, in the economic sphere there are signs of some Latin American nations moving toward the US, rather than away).[20] Alan McPherson has argued that hostility to the US has "almost always been, and often primarily was, not an *a priori* ideology but a response to US policy. The more US policy offended, the more widespread, deep, and visceral anti-US sentiment became."[21] Similarly, Max Paul Friedman has suggested: "Rather than anti-Americanism causing negative response to US actions, we see US actions sometimes generating increased negative views of the United States... Using anti-Americanism to explain the cause of opposition to US policies does not just put the cart

---

[16] Jefferson quoted in: Odd Arne Westad, *The Global Cold War: Third World Interventions and the Making of our Times* (Cambridge: Cambridge University Press, 2005) p. 10.

[17] Reagan Quoted in: David Ryan, *US Foreign Policy in World History* (London: Routledge, 2000) p. 178; For Bush, see Lars Schoultz, *Beneath the United States* (1998) p. xi.

[18] For an outlining of these themes and the way they developed, see: Michael Hunt, *Ideology and US Foreign Policy* (New Haven: Yale University Press, 1987).

[19] Juan Cole, "Anti-Americanism: It's the Policies" (2006).

[20] Jean Grugel, Pia Riggirozzi and Ben Thirkel-White, "Beyond the Washington Consensus? Asia and Latin America in Search of more Autonomous Development", *International Affairs* Volume 84, No. 3 (2008) pp. 499–517;

Ian Jackson, "The Geopolitics of President George W. Bush's Foreign Economic Policy" in *International Politics* (2007) 44 pp. 572–295.

[21] Alan McPherson, "Common Findings and New Directions" in Alan McPherson (eds), *Anti-Americanism in Latin America and the Caribbean* (New York: Beghahn Books, 2006) p. 271.

before the horse, it says the cart is the horse – it reverses causality."[22] It is in the shared history of the United States and the nations of Latin America that we can discern the reasons for the inevitable failure of any US public diplomacy strategy in the region. And though PD can, to an extent, transcend this bitterness it is always going to be susceptible to wider diplomatic relations.

A useful example of this is Brazil in the 1950s. There, the efforts of private citizens in Brazil ameliorated some of the ill feeling that had developed as a result of official US diplomacy. Far more cognisant of Latin America's history, its traditions and the desires of its people than government strategists in Washington, Nelson Rockefeller and Henry Kaiser were able to encourage a moderate air of goodwill in US-Brazilian relations through their commercial and philanthropic endeavours.[23] This could, though, only extend so far: "Within the larger Latin American context…the Kaiser-Rockefeller activities could do little, limited as they were, to ameliorate the oppressiveness of the power imbalance between North and South."[24] Relations between Washington and Brazil could be slightly improved by the actions of private individuals, but the official diplomatic relationship continued to exert far more influence. The Dwight D. Eisenhower administration's refusal to sanction increased levels of developmental loans or prolong the life of the Joint Brazil United States Economic Development Commission brought a significant level of resentment into the bilateral relationship that could not be countered by the efforts of Kaiser and Rockefeller. US officials, furthermore, were well aware that their approach was winning them few friends in Brazil (and, more broadly, the region). In September 1953, Walter Walmsley, an official working in the US Embassy in Rio de Janeiro, informed Assistant Secretary of State John Moors Cabot: "I agree that we should avoid being "propositioned with bigger and better Brazilian plans", and I think we can do so, but we can not expect to keep friends by blows."[25]

---

[22] Max Paul Friedman, "Anti-Americanism and US Foreign Relations", *Diplomatic History* Volume 32, No. 4 (September 2008) p. 504.

[23] "The private activities of Rockefeller and Kaiser," writes Elizabeth Cobbs, "were counterweights to the worsening trend of official US-Brazil relations." Elizabeth Cobbs, *The Rich Neighbor Policy: Rockefeller and Kaiser in Brazil* (New Haven: Yale University Press, 1992) p. 251.

[24] Ibid.

[25] Letter from the Chargé in Rio, Walter N. Walmsley, to the Assistant Secretary of State for Inter-American Affairs, John Moors Cabot, September 24 1953, Folder – Brazil, Box No. 1, Record Group 59, Entry 1131, Records for the Assistant Secretary

Thus, the unequal relationship – at least in terms of impact – between policy (or diplomacy) and PD, is one that has continued to blight US efforts in Latin America in the contemporary era. During their successful run for office in 2000, the George W. Bush campaign team sought to present a different aspect of US-Latin American relations; Bush promised that, if elected, he would seek to transform inter-American relations into a flourishing partnership. In a speech at Florida International University in Miami, candidate Bush stated: "Our future cannot be separated from the future of Latin America. Should I became the president, I will look south not as an afterthought, but as a fundamental commitment."[26] However, such sentiments fell by the wayside in the post-9/11 transformation of the Bush administration's foreign policy: the creation and implementation of the Bush Doctrine, the onset of the "War on Terror", and the evolving global situation conspired to move the administration's focus away from the region.[27] Within nine months of coming to office, the gaze of Bush and his advisors had shifted irrevocably away from the Western Hemisphere.

By 2007, though, the administration was coming under increasing pressure to pay more attention to Latin America. As the US had been fighting wars in Afghanistan and Iraq, Washington's standing in the region had been falling; moreover, Hugo Chavez – and like-minded Latin American leaders – had been working to usher in leftist governments across the region. In an effort to combat this, the Bush administration sought to publicise the level of harmony in inter-American relations and, in a clear nod to PD, to seize control of the inter-American narrative.

This was clear from the administration's statements about the trip. But while President Bush's National Security Advisor, Steven Hadley,

of State for Inter-American Affairs, John M Cabot, Country File, Lot 56 D 13, National Archives, College Park, Maryland.

[26] The 2000 Campaign: The Texas Governor; Bush Vows to put Greater US Focus on Latin America", *New York Times*, August 26 2000.

[27] On Bush's foreign policy, especially since 9/11, see: David Dunn, "A Doctrine Worthy of the Name?: George W. Bush and the Limits of Pre-Emption, Pre-Eminence, and Unilateralism", *Diplomacy and Statecraft* Volume 17, No. 1 (2006) p. 1–29;

Rob Singh and Mary Buckley (eds), *The Bush Doctrine and the War on Terrorism: Global Responses, Global Consequences* (London: Routledge, 2004);

Melvyn Leffler, "9/11 and American Foreign Policy", *Diplomatic History* Volume 29, No. 3 (June 2005) pp. 395–413.

could outline to a press conference – albeit rather inelegantly – the supposed benevolence behind the 2007 trip, it was a sentiment unlikely to convince the listening Latin Americans unless it was matched by tangible developments. As Hadley told a press conference:

> That's one of the reasons we're doing this trip, to both make it clear to the people of Latin America, really, three things: one, that we are committed through democracy and economic opportunity to help bring the people of Latin America out of poverty; secondly, that we...have made an enormous contribution to that; and, third, that we remain committed and have some additional ways of providing initiative to trying to achieve those objectives.[28]

In their efforts to control the diplomatic narrative, therefore, US officials were neglecting to address the broader range of ideological and anti-American constructs that permeate the inter-American relationship. Effective PD networks, operating at a level beneath that of states and governments, can avoid some of these pitfalls. But the slow-burning nature of this approach clearly did not suit the Bush administration. Consequently, the room within which PD networks could function was, in 2007, taken up by the US government as immediate strategic gain outweighed other factors.

An additional complication and barrier to successful US PD in Latin America is the need for US politicians – particularly those on the right, but also on the left, too – to appear "strong" on national defence. In the Latin American context this has often – although not exclusively – focused on maintaining a strong stance on Cuba. In 2004, for example, President Bush told an audience Miami, "When I say something, I mean it. We will not rest until the Cuban people enjoy the same freedoms in Havana that they receive here in America."[29] Similarly, Rudy Giuliani made a strong statement of intent with respect to Cuba in an article on *Foreign Affairs*. America, he wrote, "must stand ready to help the Cuban people reclaim their liberty and resist any step that allows a decrepit, corrupt regime from consolidating its power under Raúl Castro. Only a commitment to free people and free markets will

---

[28] Press Briefing on the President's trip to Latin America by National Security Advisor Steven Hadley, March 5 2007. Taken From: http://www.whitehouse.gov/news/releases/2007/03/20070305-3.html Accessed on March 7 2007.

[29] Remarks by President Bush in Miami, August 27 2004, taken from: http://www.presidency.ucsb.edu/ws/index.php?pid=62574&st=cuba&st1 Accessed on March 5 2008.

bring a prosperous future to Cuba and all of Latin America."[30] Politically, such statements made practical sense for Bush and Giuliani; but this commitment to stand firm with respect to Cuba has an adverse effect in Latin America where, irrespective of their views on Cuba or the Castro regime, the Latin Americans are understandably nervy of any sense of prospective US intervention in the region.[31] While on one level US officials are cognisant of this fact, they remain wedded to long-standing ideological constructs that suggest that the mutuality of inter-American interests, coupled with broadly expounded sentiments of hemispheric comity, will be enough to alleviate the situation.

This has been repeatedly demonstrated by the recurrent nature of US interventions in the region, where short-term gain has been prioritised over long-term impact. The fact that US officials recognised this effect, moreover, provides a huge challenge for PD practitioners – including the US government – in Latin America.

Intervention, anti-Americanism and Short-Term Gain for Washington

The insertion of American troops into Latin America – whether to restore order, protect US interests, overthrow a government or aid a revolution – has cast an indelible shadow over the inter-American relationship. During the nineteenth century, instances of concern in Latin America were often, though crucially not always, met with a show of force. It is instructive, as Jay Sexton has argued, that an occasion such as US action toward Cuba following a rebellion in 1875 saw the pursuit of a multi-, rather than uni-, lateral initiative; a stance that, it bears noting, provoked a far less febrile response than that prompted by more traditional instances of overt US intervention.[32] Such responses, however, were far from typical. From the Civil War until the advent of dollar diplomacy, Washington's stock reaction to problems in

---

[30] Rudy Giuliani, "Toward a Realistic Peace: Defending Civilization and Defeating Terrorists by Making the International System Work", *Foreign Affairs* (September/October 2007).

[31] For a recent study of US interventions in the Cold War – albeit one that avoids an examination of the impact this has had on inter-American relations – see:

Michael Grow, *US Presidents and Latin American Interventions: Pursuing Regime Change in the Cold War* (Lawrence, Kansas: University Press of Kansas, 2008).

[32] Jay Sexton, "The United States, the Cuban Rebellion, and the Multilateral Initiative of 1875", *Diplomatic History* Volume 30, No. 3 (June 2006) pp. 335–365.

the region was to react with force – either by dispatching the marines, or the US Navy or by implementing crippling economic sanctions.[33]

Typically, instances of US intervention had been motivated by short-term strategic or economic benefits. In the post-1945 era, though, the traditional parameters of US-Latin American relations became complicated by the emergence of a dominant Cold War framework. Political and social change, economic development, local issues regarding security and population control, all came under the umbrella of the stand-off between Washington and Moscow. The result, as Gilbert Joseph has perceptively argued, was a traumatic period for the region.

> The dynamics of the Latin American Cold War are embedded in a particularly ferocious dialectic linking reformist and revolutionary projects for social change and national development and the excessive counter-revolutionary responses they triggered in the years following World War II.[34]

Episodes of US intervention (covert or overt) during this Cold War period provoked tragic outcomes. Throughout the region, the legacy of US involvement was repression, underdevelopment, absence of democratic mechanisms, social inequalities and, in the very worst cases, mass murder. The collective memory of these events lingers in Latin American minds; recollections remain vivid, Washington remains culpable, and contemporary policymakers continue to struggle with the failure of their predecessors to heed warnings as to the broader impact of their policies. In short, it is a huge legacy for PD to try and surmount. And in three cases of intervention in particular – Guatemala, the Dominican Republic and Chile – US officials went ahead despite clearly recognising that to do so would have a major impact on Latin American appraisals of the US.

The tale of US intervention in Guatemala to overthrow the president, Jacobo Arbenz, is an oft-told one.[35] Less well-told, however, is the

---

[33] Mark Gilderhus, *The Second Century* (2000) pp. 1–71; Joseph Smith, *The United States and Latin America: A History of American Diplomacy, 1776–2000* (London: Routledge, 2005) pp. 21–91.

[34] Gilbert Joseph, "What We Now Know and Should Know: Bringing Latin America More Meaningfully into Cold War Studies" in Gilbert Joseph and Daniella Spenser (eds), *In from the Cold: Latin America's New Encounter with the Cold War* (Durham, North Carolina: Duke University Press, 2008) pp. 3–7.

[35] There are many sources that deal with this topic. A good selection is: James Siekmeier, *Aid, Nationalism and Inter-American Relations: Bolivia, Guatemala and the United States, 1945–1961* (New York: Edward Mellen Press, 1999);

tale of the impact that this had on the standing of the US in Latin America (one notable exception here is the effect that the events had on Ernesto "Che" Guevara, who was in Guatemala City at the time of Arbenz's overthrow).[36] Despite exhaustive attempts by the Eisenhower administration to seek hemispheric approval for Arbenz's removal from office at the Caracas Conference in March 1954, efforts by the CIA to keep US involvement hidden, and the administration's subsequent attempt to portray the coup as an internal Guatemalan uprising to reject Communist rule, Washington's hand in the events was all too apparent to Latin American observers. Both before and after the coup, there was a significant and well-orchestrated effort by the United States Information Agency (USIA) to spread anti-Guatemalan propaganda throughout the region; any links between Arbenz and Communist groups, however tenuous, were broadcast around the hemisphere. "Developments in Guatemala," notes Kenneth Osgood, "reverberated throughout the region in US propaganda programs."[37] But while these projects, at least to some extent, achieved their immediate aims, they ensured that Washington's complicity in both the propaganda programme and the actual overthrow of Arbenz was clearly apparent.

The rush to intervention, hailed by the administration in its immediate aftermath, cast a long shadow over the region. "An unprecedented wave of angry demonstrations in cities and legislatures across the region" quickly broke out following Arbenz's removal. These protests, as outlined by Max Friedman, were "attributed by Eisenhower officials to anti-Americanism, which they explained as the result of Latin Americans" immaturity and irresponsibility".[38] US officials, taking the

---

Piero Gleijeses, *Shattered Hope: The United States and the Guatemalan Revolution, 1944–1954* (Princeton, New Jersey: Princeton University Press, 1991);

Stephen Rabe, *Eisenhower: The Foreign Policy of Anticommunism and Latin America* (Chapel Hill: University of North Carolina Press, 1988) Chap 3;

Richard Immerman, *The CIA in Guatemala: The Foreign Policy of Intervention* (Austin, TX: University of Texas Press, 1982).

[36] On Guevara's involvement and subsequent impact: Jon Lee Anderson, *Che Guevara: A Revolutionary Life* (London: Bantam Books, 1997) pp. 148–159.

[37] Kenneth Osgood, *Total Cold War: Eisenhower's Secret Propaganda Battle at Home and Abroad* (Lawrence, Kansas: University of Kansas Press, 2006) pp. 145–148;

Nick Cullather, *Secret History: The CIA's Classified Account of Its Operations in Guatemala, 1952–1954* (Stanford, California: Stanford University Press, 1999).

[38] Max Paul Friedman, "Anti-Americanism and US Foreign Relations" (2008) p. 506–507.

approach that offered the most immediate resolution, explained the protests as reflexive anti-American tendencies in Latin America; the broader point, which they avoided, was that it was US actions over Guatemala that had provoked the protests. Moreover, the enmity that was apparent was unlikely to subside quickly. As Mark Hove has recently outlined, "Scholars generally agree that the overthrow of the democratically elected [Arbenz] stunned and angered Latin Americans, and haunted US relations with the region, as well as with the developing world, long after Arbenz resigned and fled the Guatemalan capital." In Chile, Hove has argued, the legacy of US intervention in Guatemala began a set of circumstances that led to the emergence of the Salvador Allende government in the 1970s. "With the overthrow of Arbenz," argues Hove, "US policymakers self-inflicted a wound that hobbled US policy and relations toward Chile." The broader point was made most vociferously by Chilean Socialist leader Oscar Weiss who, in the aftermath of the 1954 coup, stated, "It is certain that [the United States] has lost more than it has gained…it has lost forever the friendship of the peoples of Latin America…Latin Americans will not forget Guatemala so easily."[39] For Eisenhower, John Foster Dulles and the majority of their advisors, the strategic necessity of ousting Arbenz had triumphed over any potential concern as to the impact it might have on the region. For the concept of PD, however, the Guatemalan intervention – and the murderous fall-out that followed[40] – set the tone for an environment rarely conducive to shared messages of cooperation.

After Guatemala, each instance of US Cold War intervention in Latin America, irrespective of its causes and relative justifications, brought back memories of this earlier case and, later, the debacle surrounding the 1961 Bay of Pigs invasion.[41] Lyndon Johnson's decision to send US troops into the Dominican Republic in 1965 again raised Latin American ire, especially as it came so soon after a stand-off with

---

[39] All quotes here, from: Mark Hove, "The Arbenz Factor: Salvador Allende, US-Chilean Relations, and the 1954 US Intervention in Guatemala", *Diplomatic History* Volume 31, No 5 (November 2007) pp. 623–663.

[40] Nick Cullather, *Secret History* (1999); Greg Grandin, *The Lost Colonial Massacre: Latin America in the Cold War* (Chicago: University of Chicago Press, 2004)

[41] See: Lawrence Freedman, *Kennedy's Wars: Berlin, Cuba, Laos and Vietnam* (New York: Oxford University Press, 2000);

Piero Gleijeses, "Ships in the Night: The CIA, the White House and the Bay of Pigs," *Journal of Latin American Studies* Volume 27, No. 1 (February 1995) pp. 1–42.

Panama over riots in the Canal Zone (an event that the Panamanians publicly reframed as an anti-colonial struggle to meet their own objectives).[42] In a meeting in Johnson's cabinet room, soon after US troops had begun operations on the ground in the Dominican Republic, Averell Harriman – who was serving as LBJ's Ambassador at Large – noted that while many Latin American leaders "were personally behind President Johnson's action in the Dominican Republic", each of them had identified "reasons why local domestic problems prevented these government officials from making public statement to this effect".[43] By intervening, moreover, Johnson inadvertently caused the tone of the protests in the Dominican Republic to become anti-American in nature, rather than the internal civil problem it had begun as.[44]

Even though the Johnson Administration managed to extricate itself from the Dominican Republic relatively successfully, the episode highlighted the extent to which memories of previous interventions lingered. Johnson was well aware of this. Weighing up the consequences of US intervention, the President "sighed that he was in a hell of a shape either way. If I take over, I can't live in the world. If I let them take over, I can't live here."[45] For Johnson, it had come down to the fact that strategic necessity trumped protecting inter-American comity. Such episodes were central in creating a Latin American narrative of resentment and anger, one that ran contrary to the hopes and desires of the US (and PD strategists and practitioners) and one which would be made even more trenchant by US intervention in Chile.

The Nixon administration's decision to collude in the removal of Chilean leader Salvador Allende from office has become a testament to the devastating impact that a rigidly-applied Cold War paradigm can have on US policy in Latin America.[46] Prior to Allende's election in

---

[42] On Panama: Alan McPherson, "Courts of World Opinion: Trying the Panama Flag Riots of 1964", *Diplomatic History* Volume 28, No. 1 (January 2004) pp. 83–112.

[43] Memorandum for the Record, Meeting in the White House, May 8 1965, *Foreign Relations of the United States 1964–1968 Volume XXXII* (Washington: United States Government Printing Office) p. 141.

[44] Alan McPherson, *Yankee No!* (2003) Ch. 4.

[45] LBJ quoted in: Odd Arne Westad, *The Global Cold War* (2005) p. 151;
Randall Woods, "Conflicted Hegemon: LBJ and the Dominican Republic," *Diplomatic History* Volume 32, No. 5 (November 2008).

[46] For an outline of the events in Chile and the reasons for US intervention – which touched on economic, strategic, domestic and ideological factors – see: Michael Grow, *US Presidents and Latin American Interventions* (2008) pp. 93–113.

1970, neither Nixon nor his National Security Advisor, Henry Kissinger, had believed Latin America to be very important.[47] As with earlier instances of intervention, US officials sensed that a visible Washington hand in events could have a negative impact on the view of the US in the region. However, as with Guatemala, the immediate strategic issues related to Allende's avowed Marxism and his links with Moscow and Havana came to outweigh these broader concerns.

Throughout the process of destabilisation, incitement of the public, and undermining of the Chilean state that had been pursued since Allende won the 1970 election, efforts concentrated on presenting the emergence of the Allende government as a major setback for the world; achieving this impression would give US actions a veneer of legitimacy and aid ongoing attempts to secure the support of the Chilean (and Latin American) publics. When a report generated by the CIA station in Santiago conceded that, "as short as ten days ago there seemed to be almost no feeling outside of Chile and very little mass feeling within Chile that the election of Allende was necessarily an evil", a psychological warfare strategy was constructed to alter this perception. "The key is psych[ological] war[fare] in Chile," the report noted. "We cannot endeavour to ignite the world if Chile itself is a placid lake."[48] Considerations as to what long-term impact this creation of a climate conducive to revolution would have on inter-American relations were barely visible; the only concerns on this front, in fact, focused on making sure this did not look like a US intervention. Acting without due legitimacy, acting unilaterally, or failing to create the impression that an Allende government was a stark national security threat could severely undermine the Nixon administration's position in Latin America. Kissinger outlined this for the President:

> We are strongly on record in support of self-determination and respect for free election; you are firmly on record for non-intervention in the internal affairs of this hemisphere and of accepting nations "as they are". It would therefore be very costly for us to act in ways that appear to

[47] Mark Atwood Lawrence, "History from Below: The United States and Latin America in the Nixon Years" in Frederik Logevall and Andrew Preston (eds), *Nixon in the World: American Foreign Relations, 1969–1977* (New York: Oxford University Press, 2008).

[48] Cable from CIA Headquarters in Santiago, Chile, "Blueprint for Fomenting a Coup Climate," September 27 1970, in: Peter Kornbluh, *The Pinochet File: A National Security Archive Book* (New York: The New Press, 2003) pp. 50–56.

> violate those principles, and Latin Americans and others in the world will view our policy as a test of the credibility of our rhetoric.[49]

A subsequent National Security Decision Memorandum from the President's desk made it clear that the US *had* to work with the other Latin American nations in opposing Allende and, moreover, ensure that the urgent need to bring about his removal was made demonstrably clear.[50] US disappointment that efforts to destabilise Chile enough to prevent Allende assuming office in 1970 were tempered three years later when a longer-term project of destabilisation led to a military coup that saw Allende replaced with General Pinochet.[51] Prior considerations as to how this made the US look, though, remained pertinent; Washington's hand – or, at least, strong assistance – was strongly suspected to be behind the coup and the net outcome in the region was an escalation in anti-American sentiments.[52] Nixon, like Eisenhower, Kennedy and Johnson before him, had believed the immediate strategic priorities he perceived in the region to be more important than the long-term climate in the area. It was a sentiment thrown into sharp relief in a perceptive report by *New York Times* reporter, James Reston, in 1975. "In the long run, the security of the United States and even its relations with the rest of the world, may very well depend on the stability of the Americas as a whole," he wrote. "Ideology is a matter of transitory opinion, but geography is an enduring fact, and this is an immediate problem in our relations with the rest of the hemisphere."[53] The subsequent reversion to intervention, under Ronald Reagan and George H.W. Bush, suggested that little heed had been paid to the lessons of earlier incursions. Short-term strategic gain continued to trump the long-term comity outlined by James Reston in 1975.

What, though, does this recurrent tale of ideology, anti-Americanism and interventions tell us about the prospects for public diplomacy

[49] Memorandum from National Security Advisor Henry Kissinger to President Nixon, November 5 1970, in: Peter Kornbluh, *The Pinochet File* (2003) pp. 121–128.

[50] National Security Decision Memorandum 93, "Policy Towards Chile," November 9 1970, in: Peter Kornbluh, *The Pinochet File* (2003) pp. 129–131.

[51] On these events and the US role: Robert Dallek, *Nixon and Kissinger: Partners in Power* (London: Penguin Books, 2008) pp. 509–515.

[52] "The Bloody End of a Marxist Dream," *Time*, September 24 1973.

[53] James Reston, "The Forgotten Americans," *New York Times*, August 17 1975, p. 167;

Hal Brands, "Third World Politics in an Age of Global Turmoil: The Latin American Challenge to US and Western Hegemony, 1965–1975," *Diplomatic History* Volume 32, No. 1 (January 2008) pp. 105–138.

in Latin America? PD in its most effective format could well leave behind the role of the state and instead function as a series of transnational and interrelated networks that operates not only in the realm of governments but, more importantly, at a much lower level. To function effectively, however, PD practitioners and governments will have to find some way of negotiating the complexities of their relationship. State management of PD, after all, is always going to prioritise immediate gain and interests.[54] Even the onset of the Obama era, it bears noting, has not brought about any separation between PD and American power (or interests).[55] But if the US government continues to utilise its own conception of PD in Latin America then it is going to keep running up against the roadblock that is the long, shared history between North and South America.

There is something for PD advocates and practitioners to work with in Latin America. As contemporary examinations of anti-Americanism in the region have determined, there is nothing irrational or all-encompassing about Latin American antipathy toward the US.[56] Indeed, a report by the Pew Global Attitudes Project in 2007 described: "while opinion of the U.S. has slipped in Latin America over the past five years, majorities in such countries as Mexico, Peru and even Venezuela still say they have a positive opinion of their large neighbor to the north."[57] "Public diplomacy," as Robert Kelley has suggested, "is fundamentally a two-part process shared by the substance of foreign policymaking and the message exchange capacity of international communications."[58] Yet it is within this shared space that divisive

---

[54] Liam Kennedy and Scott Lucas, "Enduring Freedom" (2005) pp. 324–329; also see, for instance, the words of James Glassman – one of the leading US public diplomats – in describing how PD works in US foreign policy.

James Glassman speaking at Council on Foreign Relations, June 30, 2008, http://www.america.gov/st/texttransenglish/2008/July/20080702123054xjsnommis0.3188745.html#ixzz0I1ryWoiy&D.

[55] Ali Fisher and Scott Lucas, Introduction to this volume (2009) p. 9.

[56] For good examples, Alan McPherson, *Yankee No!* (2003); Max Paul Friedman, "Anti-Americanism and US Foreign Relations" (2008);

Greg Grandin, "Your Americanism and Mine: Americanism and Anti-Americanism in the Americas", *American Historical Review* Volume 111, No. 4 (October 2006).

[57] "Global Unease with Major World Powers: Rising Environmental Concern in 47-nation Survey," *Pew Global Attitudes Project*, June 27 2007. Taken From: http://pewglobal.org/reports/display.php?ReportID=256 Accessed on May 19 2009.

[58] John Robert Kelley, "Between 'Take Offs' and 'Crash Landings': Situational Aspects of Public Diplomacy", Nancy Snow and Philip Taylor (eds), *The Routledge Public Diplomacy Handbook* (2008) p. 72–73.

tensions emerge; tensions that, if un-addressed, can totally undermine the potential for PD to work successfully.

The case study of Latin America – resplendent with recurrent instances of US interventions; interventions that, almost without exception, US officials undertook while knowing they would severely destabilise the level of accord in inter-American relations – provides a stark illustration of the problems confronting PD in the twenty-first century. Washington can talk a good game and make the right noises about cooperation – as President Bush and his advisors did in 2007 – but they are highly unlikely to relinquish their broader goals and objectives in the region in an effort to buttress PD operations. During her run for the Democratic nomination for the presidency, Hillary Clinton – then Senator, now Obama's Secretary of State – wrote of the need to improve inter-American relations. "At our peril," she wrote, "the Bush administration has neglected our neighbors to the south…We must return to a policy of vigorous engagement; this is too critical a region for the United States to stand idly by…we must work with our allies to provide sustainable-development programs that promote economic opportunity and reduce inequality for the citizens of Latin America."[59] Such sentiments, however, need to be matched by equivalent actions if progress is to be made.

Recently, President Obama has begun to try and break down some of the old barriers and address the problems that have blighted US-Latin American relations. Possible signs of reconciliation with Cuba and, to a lesser extent, Venezuela have suggested a new US approach toward the region – "one defined in terms of a willingness to engage with countries whose interests and ideas might diverge from Washington's."[60] But few would suggest – or expect – that he is doing so for any other reason than to promote US interests. Robert Sandels has suggested that while Obama is getting credit in the region for "not being George W. Bush", his approach toward Cuba will still be developed around notions of US interests and credibility.[61] Signs that US

[59] Hillary Rodham Clinton, "Security and Opportunity for the Twenty-First Century", *Foreign Affairs* (November/December 2007).

[60] Greg Grandin, "Obama and Latin America," *The Nation*, April 22 2009. Taken From: http://www.thenation.com/doc/20090511/grandin Accessed on June 15 2009.

[61] Robert Sandels, "Obama and Latin America: No Light, All Tunnel," *Counterpunch*, May 13 2009. Taken From: http://www.counterpunch.org/sandels05132009.html Accessed on June 15 2009.

actions are to the detriment of the Latin Americans or are unduly weighted toward American interests, will soon provoke opposition among the Latin Americans.

By operating outside of this state-centred nexus, PD can provide an opportunity to build bridges in areas where governments would encounter major problems. Spreading the American message to the Latin American people is notoriously difficult for a bureaucratic structure more used to government-to-government interaction and who are labouring to throw off the legacy of intervention and anti-Americanism outlined above. Thus far, however, there is little evidence that the US government is prepared to relinquish its control of PD efforts, or even to reconsider the way its PD policies are implemented. One possible solution is to use emergent technologies and media outlets – like Facebook, Twitter and Myspace – to spread the US message. At the time of writing, however, there is little evidence that Washington has developed an effective strategy on this front that would enable them to appeal to the general population. Facebook's vice president of Global Communications, Eliot Schrage, outlined this in an interview with the Council on Foreign Relations where he argued: "The challenge is, how do we move the dialogue away from a government-to-government dialogue, and more toward engaging citizens on the ground. I don't think the United States has a particularly strong track record of doing that successfully."[62]

Consequently, US officials continue to encounter a situation whereby there is a need, as outlined at the start of this chapter, to try and control the narrative. Obama's attempts to alter the dynamics of the relationship, for example, are evidence of this.[63] Achieving this, though, is difficult; and it is a problem that the Bush administration, during their 2007 visit, found insurmountable. Throughout the trip, journalists – and those from US news outlets in particular – sought to portray the visit as a clash between Bush and Chavez. For the US, this undermined their attempts to portray the trip as being one motivated by US efforts

---

[62] "New Media Tools and Public Diplomacy," Interview between Elliot Schrage, Vice President of Global Communications for Facebook, and Lee Hudson Telik of www.cfp.org, May 11 2009 Taken From: http://www.cfr.org/publication/19300/new_media_tools_and_public_diplomacy.html?breadcrumb=%2Fissue%2Fpublication_list%3Fgroupby%3D0%26id%3D50%26filter%3D210 Accessed on June 16 2009.

[63] See: Seth McLaughlin, "Summit of the Americas: A New Regional Narrative," *World Politics Review*, April 15 2009. Taken From: http://www.worldpoliticsreview.com/article.aspx?id=3613 Accessed on June 16 2009.

to work with the Latin Americans. Bush's press secretary, Tony Snow, grew so incensed at this that, during a press briefing, he exclaimed:

> It's the narrative you guys are bringing. There is an active agenda on these meetings and it's worth covering, because the United States is making an active difference…You've got a President who at every stop makes the point that the success of these countries is good for the United States. So that's the narrative we're bringing. We didn't pack anybody else in our luggage.[64]

While there is, then, clearly room for successful US PD operations in Latin America, it is far less clear that the US will be able to negotiate the endemic culture of anti-American sentiment that persists as a legacy of US intervention; it will require a reframing of US methodology which takes an intersubjective approach to understanding communities in the region.[65]

[64] Press Gaggle by Dan Fisk, Thomas Shannon and Tony Snow, Air Force One en route to Guatemala City, March 11 2007. Taken From: http://www.whitehouse.gov/news/releases/2007/03/20070311-3.html Accessed on March 12 2007.

[65] Ichheiser's Structure and Dynamics of interpersonal relations and E. Goffman The presentation of self in everyday life provide an insight into the development of intersubjective thinking.

THE PUBLIC DIPLOMACY OF TOMORROW

THE SEVEN PARADOXES OF PUBLIC DIPLOMACY

Daryl Copeland

The World is Ready for PD ...

In recent years there has been a striking resurgence of international interest in public diplomacy (PD). Foreign ministries, universities, think tanks, and consultants have engaged with the practice with marked enthusiasm. A profusion of new programmes, courses, books, journals, articles, and conference panels have bolstered a burgeoning literature and provided form and direction to this renaissance. Drawing on insights gleaned from the fields of international relations, public administration, communications, political science, and anthropology, amongst others, public diplomacy may even be emerging as a new academic discipline.

I am a strong proponent of PD, especially as an alternative to traditional, state-to-state diplomacy or—and all the more so—to sending in the marines. After 11 September 2001, many governments have returned to the use of armed force, especially in prosecuting the U.S.-led Global War on Terror. The means of violence are readily available, and the ongoing militarization of international policy has corresponded with the agenda of certain powerful special interest groups.

In my view, the military has proven a rather blunt, costly, and in important respects inappropriate instrument in dealing with the essential threats and challenges associated with the globalization age. The results of relying on defence rather than diplomacy or development have been mixed, if not counter-productive—rather like using a hammer when a scalpel, or an outstretched hand, was required. Whether in Iraq for the US, Afghanistan for NATO, Darfur for the African Union, or Gaza for Israel, the balance of experience to date indicates that, notwithstanding recent efforts to update and re-tune counterinsurgency doctrine, armies are not the most effective option to resolve complex differences or to achieve ambitious political goals.

Treating terrorists as criminals, rather than dignifying them as warriors, would place a much greater reliance on police and intelligence work. Over the longer term, I see a need to address the essential drivers of insecurity and underdevelopment – poverty, inequality, distributive injustice and poor governance. This is where diplomacy in general, and an emphasis on PD in particular, comes to the fore.

PD, with its emphasis on talking rather than fighting, on cross-cultural literacy, on shared interests, and on meaningful exchange, holds out the prospect of improved performance at much lower cost. It is a more suitable international policy instrument for dealing with the range of pressing issues which are rooted in science and propelled by technology: climate change and resource shortages; pandemic disease and environmental collapse; genomics and species extinction. These multi-dimensional, transnational issues, as well as the uneven and polarizing impacts that are characteristic of globalization, are much better suited to treatment through public diplomatic means than through recourse to violence, either state or non-state sponsored.

The continuing incidence of conflict, the range of unaddressed threats, and the prevalence of misery and suffering indicate that much work remains to be done. In my view, PD can and should be germane to any agenda addressing these concerns. On this small, democratizing, globalizing planet, the views of the public are of increasing importance in shaping and determining outcomes. PD's time is now.

... But is PD Ready for the World?

Centre stage is a demanding place to be: are diplomats, foreign ministries and governments prepared to mainstream PD? This question remains open. It certainly seems prudent to re-examine PD, which came of age during the Cold War, in the context of a highly ideological struggle for hearts and minds, and a territorially expressed contest for proxies and client states.

In the rush to re-think and re-tool PD, inadequate attention has been paid to the elaboration of its constraints and limitations. In other words, PD is not only under-theorized, it is under-criticized. There is a danger that a surfeit of naïve boosterism could lead to unrealistic expectations and, later, to the damage associated with negative overreaction. That would be most unfortunate, because in my view it is both important, and urgent that governments commit to PD as the international policy instrument of choice.

Although one of the mature pleasures of adulthood is learning to live with paradox, the severity of the challenges facing PD is not to be underestimated. I offer an admittedly personal take on the seven central paradoxes of public diplomacy, some related to the activity itself and others to its broader frame of reference.

1. *Definitional Disorder*

The standard definition of PD is so broad that it can include elements inimical to the ethic of PD and subversive of its purpose and promise. When seeking to identify the distinctive characteristics of an academic or professional discipline, especially a potentially new one, definitional clarity is paramount. At the highest level of analysis, diplomacy is a non-violent approach to the management of international relations and global issues through negotiation and compromise. Within that ambit, PD is usually thought of as the sum of efforts on the part of governments to achieve identified outcomes by connecting with populations, establishing networks, building relationships and influencing public opinion abroad. It is essentially a triangulated tool, designed to sway the decisions of foreign governments by working, in the first instance, through their publics.[1] What, then, is missing?

In my conception, what sets PD apart from, say, marketing or branding—not to mention information warfare—are the elements of dialogue, two-way information flows, and *meaningful* exchange, with the feedback of the results of the dialogue in both directions, resulting in changes in policy and behaviour at each end of the conversation. But is this actually what most governments want, or are prepared to engage in? It is at this point where the distinction between PD and branding comes into play.

Engineering a positive predisposition—that is, when association with a specific nationality evokes in the first instance a smile rather than a scowl—might be thought of as the ultimate end of branding, and for obvious reasons it is clearly favoured by governments. Yet by virtue of its origins in advertising and marketing places and products, branding is reliant more upon projection and is less dependent upon interactive communication.

A brand is what sets you apart, what makes you distinct, what differentiates you from others. Good brands are suffused with attitude.

[1] There are certain monologic, uni-directional forms of PD intended to communicate politically through the media or to influence governments directly, such as communiqués or major speeches by foreign ministers or heads of state. This is especially the case where bilateral diplomatic relations have broken down or are non-existent. Relatively rare, this type of PD requires a category of its own.

They are positive. They have soul and seek to establish or maintain an emotional attachment. Nation-branding involves telling a unique story and expressing that story as an integrated narrative with clear shape and direction. The resulting brand will represent the distillation and conveyance of that story in a manner supportive of national values, policies and interests. Country brands help citizens to clarify and crystallize their national identity, as well as those of others, in a confusing and sometimes threatening world. This type of branding, even if not especially interactive, nonetheless has useful effects both inwards and outwards as a political communications tool.

If public diplomacy is thought of as a nation's book, then a nation's brand is something like its cover, designed to appeal viscerally to the consumers of international policy by encouraging potential buyers to open the book (or visit the country, buy the product, or support the international policy objective). Because the market evolves quickly, however, the cover's design may need attention—re-branding—even before the book requires revision and a new edition can be released.

If branding means consistency, conformity, and staying *on message,* and the communications content is paramount, then public diplomacy means *explaining* the message, asking for comments, and reporting the response. PD is about style as much substance, the *how* as much as the *what.* PD enlarges understanding by creating a common frame of reference, and weds communication to action with the demonstration effect. If branding is about selling dreams, public diplomacy is about sharing them.

Brands take years to build but are easily damaged and will erode if not cultivated constantly. When the image, or brand, is positive, it will be immeasurably easier to draw others into the conversation. When countries fail to live up to the brand promise being promoted, they risk losing credibility and running down their soft power.

Branding and PD, though not interchangeable, certainly resemble each other more closely than some other practices which also fit under a broad definition of PD. Branding, for example, does rely on market testing, on knowing the audience, and on customer or client feedback, so there is at least an element of two-way flow. Yet there are other activities which fall within a wide interpretation of PD and directly undermine its premise and prospects. These include propaganda, disinformation campaigns, psychological operations, and information warfare, all of which seek to condition, if not to dominate, the communications landscape. They differ from earned media, from partnerships with civil society, from joint ventures with the like-minded, and from the building of enduring relationships based on confidence, trust and respect. These aspects are elemental to my understanding of PD.

Enlightened governments are determined to actively manage their country's image and reputation, its global brand.[2] Because of that determination, however, their PD strategies have come to rely upon the one way flow of information, upon getting the message right, upon *diktat* more than dialogue. If the definition of PD were refined to exclude most monologic practices, we might get out of the thicket – but only to enter the woods.

2. *Vitiated Messaging*

Diplomats, however well-intentioned, are hardly disinterested parties – they work for governments,[3] and this can make them suspect from the start. The messenger can vitiate the message.[4]

Governments exist to defend and pursue national interests, to advocate policies, and to promote values. In these respects they rely on the apparatus of the state, of which diplomats are an integral part. When members of civil society encounter diplomats, therefore, the encounter is not likely to be entirely unconditional, and this can give rise to suspicion and mistrust. Chances are that the diplomat, especially if he or she have initiated the exchange, will almost certainly be after something—an expression of support, a shift in position, a useful insight, a gem of intelligence. There is nothing wrong with this, but it is not a neutral point of departure. Just as the best communications cannot compensate for flawed policy, no amount of active listening can overcome the handicap of seeking scripted outcomes or pre-ordained conclusions. While this does not necessarily undermine or devalue the activity *per se*, it does leave open the possibility of eroding the integrity of the exchange, and in so doing could prejudice the chances of arriving at a mutually beneficial outcome.

---

[2] In this respect diplomats on assignment abroad can be seen to serve as local brand managers, foreign ministers as international branding coordinators, and the foreign ministry as world headquarters.

[3] Some diplomats also work for multilateral organizations such the United Nations and NATO. They are not included in the discussion here.

[4] For this precise formulation I am indebted to my colleague Martin Rose, Director of the British Council in Canada.

Governments are fond of saying that "PD is for everyone" The implication? The best public diplomats might not be members of foreign services at all, but business people, artists, entertainers, travellers, or NGO representatives whose particular networks, contacts, fans, or client base can make them indispensable as partners. One caveat is necessary, though—no matter who is carrying out the activity, if it is disconnected from the management of international relations and the objectives of government policy, then while it may be international public relations or culture or commerce, it is not PD.

3. *Dysfunctional Diplomats*

Many, if not most serving diplomats are without the temperament, skills, and experience required for excellence in public diplomacy. Elsewhere I have written that:

> The public diplomat's core values and ideals include continuous and lifelong learning, historical knowledge and cultural understanding. Public service will serve as a primary motivator, although the desire to pursue national interests will not be far behind. Dialogue and communication will be favoured over compulsion or force, just as cooperation and teamwork will be preferred over "one-upmanship" and showboating. A dedication to reason, fairness and the rule of law will be a prominent professional characteristic. Professional integrity, the absence of a "say-do gap" between words and deeds, and moral courage, by which I mean the wherewithal to stand up both for one's country abroad and, when necessary, to one's country at home, will be central. Humanism, a real interest in people, and an abiding commitment to humanitarian thought and action, provide the firm foundation upon which these values rest.
>
> The public diplomat must be capable not just of exchanging views with interlocutors at the foreign ministry or chatting with other diplomats, but of swimming without effort in the sea of the people beyond the embassy gates. Personable and enthusiastic, the public diplomat will display a set of clearly defined attributes which flow from vitality and a positive disposition, as well as the possession of natural curiosity, an open, enquiring mind and a critical consciousness. Cultural sensitivity and personal awareness will lead naturally to the display of empathy and compassion, just as the capacity for quick study will find expression in improvisation, creativity and innovation. This kind of work will require ample and equal reserves of determination and commitment, energy and resilience, flexibility and adaptability. An affinity for risk management, collaboration and team-building will be crucial in establishing partnerships and mobilizing coalitions of the similarly inclined. A high

> tolerance of, if not a taste for uncertainty and ambiguity will be essential.[5]

Well beyond any formal qualifications, specified experience, and personal suitability, public diplomats, if I may borrow from Jennifer Welsh, should be "at home in the world."[6] This will involve traits which are as likely to have been acquired over years spent exploring the world at ground level as over semesters studying in Ivy League colleges. The public diplomat will need all the capacities and qualities of the traditional diplomat—tact, judgement, intellect, objectivity, political sense, discretion—any a good many more, including competencies as varied as technological savvy and a demonstrated interest in engaging with diaspora communities domestically.[7]

The issue here? Far too many diplomats resemble dinosaurs more than they do dynamos. The archetypal portrait of the public diplomat does not correspond to the disposition or profile of most diplomats I know. Most tend to prefer chatting with others of their ilk about what might be going on "out there" rather than experiencing it first-hand. The right thing won't work if it is being done by the wrong people.

4. *Institutional Crisis*

If not entirely obsolete, the institutional home of PD, the foreign ministry, is rarely found on the cutting edge of public administration.

Public diplomats do not just materialize, and public diplomacy does not just happen. It is practiced by people who work for foreign ministries and embassies in home and host countries. PD, moreover, is not just one programme among many, but a diplomatic business model. As such, it should be at the core of a foreign ministry's planning and operations. It is not.

Foreign ministries generically are facing a rough patch. Their one-time near monopoly on the management of international policy and

[5] See Daryl Copeland, "No dangling conversation: portrait of the public diplomat," in *Engagement: Public Diplomacy in a Globalized World* (Foreign and Commonwealth Office, 2008), pp. 134–144.

[6] Jennifer Welsh, *At Home in the World: Canada's Global Vision for the 21st Century* (Toronto: HarperCollins, 2004).

[7] Much of this could be accomplished through more targeted, strategic use of the interactive capabilities of the internet. Although some foreign ministries encourage blogging and many make much better use of their web sites through web 2.0 and even more sophisticated applications, more remains to be done.

relations has been broken, and while the diminishing importance of states *per se* in the age of globalization explains this in part, there is more to the story. There has been a general, debilitating trend towards the migration of decision-making authority and other high-end functions, such as policy advice and development, away from foreign ministries and towards central agencies, such as the Prime Minister's Office, Cabinet Office, and the White House. Beyond the centralization within national governments, power and influence have shifted upwards to supranational institutions, outwards to business, other government departments, civil society, and even individuals, and downwards to other levels of government (provincial, state, and municipal). This has been accompanied by the erosion of the position of foreign minister in favour of defence ministers and heads of state or government.

Internally, effective public diplomacy requires of its practitioners not only a high degree agility and acuity, but also a substantial measure of autonomy. Senior managers and decision-makers must have the confidence of their ministerial masters and the trust of those in the trenches, at home and abroad. Creativity, responsiveness, and comfort with risk and a willingness to devolve authority are crucial. This description does not correspond to the culture of most foreign ministries that I have studied.

Why are foreign ministries like this, and why have both they, and diplomatic practice proven so notoriously resistant to reform? One reason might simply be age. Not only are foreign ministries unlike other government departments, they are unlike other organisations generally. While many other government departments come and go, foreign ministries, along with central banks and departments of finance and defence, persist since the management of a country's international relations represent one of the core responsibilities of national governments. Venerable institutions such as these are typically wedded to tradition: conservative, predictable, and change-averse. Hierarchic structures and top-down social relations are defining characteristics. Dissent is generally discouraged, unquestioning loyalty and faithful service rewarded.[8] Blessing the received wisdom and running with the

---

[8] The FCO in the UK has in recent years produced three noteworthy dissenters, all of whom left the service:

Sean Riordan, who is now consulting and writing on foreign ministries out of Madrid; Rory Stewart, who writes travel books and has founded the NGO *Turquoise*

herd, often under the guise of team playing, can be the keys to advancement. More than a few successful careers have been made by specializing in making the boss look good.

It has been my experience that there is something uniquely corrosive about bureaucracies in general, and quite possibly about foreign ministries in particular. By this I mean that I no longer recognize the personalities of many of those with whom I joined the Canadian foreign service more than 25 years ago. Former friends and colleagues have become strangers.

It is my sense that all of those years of steeping in the particular foreign ministerial broth has had a unique and powerful effect on perceptions and behaviour. Ideas are judged more on their provenance than their strength. As is the case with most large organizations, about half of the decisions that really count can be attributed to factors perhaps best described as personal and situational—who knows whom and what is going on where. Another thirty per cent or so of what happens tends to turn on matters of chance and timing. That leaves typically only twenty per cent of decisions which are taken primarily on the basis of objective circumstances or the strength of an analysis or business case. Meritocracy and objectivity are not unknown, but nor are they as commonplace as might be thought or desired.

And the representational platform abroad? It, too, is infirm. Some diplomatic missions are being reduced to whole-of-government points of service overseas, with career diplomats often outnumbered by the employees of other government departments. That might be fine—except that too often those despatched are being exiled for other reasons or lack the personal suitability for representational work. Larger chancelleries tend to be structured as miniature replicas of headquarters operations, while most everywhere else the representational profile, or diplomatic footprint, is not as supple, flexible, or adaptable as it might be. Standard mission moulds, featuring fixed terms and conditions are still in wide use.

A cookie cutter is clearly the wrong instrument in the face of the unlimited variability required to suit ever-changing circumstances. In some places the footprint needs to be large and visible, for example in a global network node such as London. In other places, small and light

Mountain in Kabul, and is now a Conservative MP for Penrith and The Border, and; Carne Ross, founder of the NGO *Independent Diplomat* and author of a book by that title (Hurst &Co., 2007).

is just about right. Why not experiment, where appropriate, with in-country residence but without support staff, Chancellery, or an Official Residence? Gateway missions, hub and spoke arrangements, shared services and co-location with the like-minded, additional honorary consuls are all possibilities. In certain settings, such as conflict zones, complete portability, using a secure satellite uplink for communications but leaving no physical trace, may be most appropriate. The point is flexibility—sometimes internet conferencing or a brass plaque on a hotel room door for a few days will be enough.

Do the foreign ministries that we have resemble the foreign ministries we need? Not by my reckoning. If they had a vision of their place in the machinery of government, foreign ministries might see themselves as central agencies for the management of globalisation, with a cross-cutting writ vis-a-vis other government departments and with authority supported at the highest political levels. They could, and I think should be, at the centre of international policy development. They are not, however, lacking the domestic influence, the budgetary strength, the analytical depth, the specialized skills and the subtle, supple capacity required. A foreign ministry whose mandate is under siege and whose workforce is populated by the wrong kind of employee will not be able to develop or implement innovative international policy in difficult environments, especially if under-resourced and disconnected from the levers of domestic power. In my experience, if they are not completely dysfunctional, most foreign ministries, and their outposts abroad, are in very serious need of repair.

5. *Transactional Triumph*

Not only are foreign ministries being downgraded and sidelined within government, reduced sometimes to the role of landlords and common service providers to other government departments,[9] but they are being hollowed out from within. Bureaucratic process and administrative busy-work is overtaking international policy leadership, analysis and formulation; the administrative tail is wagging the policy dog.

---

[9] At Canada's Department of Foreign Affairs and International Trade, this model has been christened the "international platform". One colleague commented recently that it looked more like a formula for becoming a global doormat.

What is left in foreign ministries is not exactly the stuff of statecraft.

- preparation of briefing materials, media lines and routine communications, parliamentary questions and answers;
- incoming and outgoing visits planning and implementation;
- minimal maintenance of multilateral and international legal obligations;
- consular assistance (a boom industry in the of wake more nationals travelling and living abroad);
- crisis management (e.g., SARS, BSE, evacuations, natural disasters);
- maintenance of the physical and information technology (IT) infrastructure, with special attention to communications security;
- common service provision to their own employees and those of other government departments (the latter who now comprise a majority at many missions abroad);
- protocol;
- endless administrative processes (reorganizations; regulations; audits; performance and publications reviews; access to administration and privacy requests; and other tasks).

Whatever the merits of these sorts of activities, they are a far cry from what most people would associate with diplomacy or international policy. It is not so much that the mainstay of foreign ministries, bilateral relationship management, has disappeared entirely, but rather that its currency, and that of geographic relations generally, has been devalued.

6. *Constituency Envy*

Unlike the case with many other government departments, such as social services, transport, environment, and immigration, there is no large domestic audience or base of support for international policy or the work of the foreign ministry. The days of the foreign ministry cruising on its vestigial prestige and mystique, with its face to the world but its back to the capital, have long passed. Yet nothing has been substituted to help keep its place near the commanding heights of national government. With the domestic environment in flux, constituency building is especially difficult for those who are without any natural or permanent allies within their borders.

While the expansion, seen by some as encroachment, of other government departments into areas previously believed to be the exclusive preserve of the foreign ministry has been going on for years, there has been little compensatory effort to insert the foreign ministry into domestic debates or to underline its relevance to the national security and domestic prosperity. There has been no concentrated, sustained, or strategic effort to develop a durable base at home. This has hurt because the proximate environment for international policy formulation frames and conditions the entire exercise: if messages are to be carried abroad, they must resonate at home. At a time of maximum need, domestic support for public diplomacy is more limited than ever.

Diplomats, foreign ministries and international policy once carried more weight on the home front, but whatever public or political consensus may once have existed has now has fissured. What's different now? It is ironic that even as populations become daily more cosmopolitan and charge ahead ever more completely into the culture and ethos of globalization, the domestic coverage of international affairs in the mainstream media – television, radio, newspapers – continues to diminish. Be it the side-swiping of a national economy, the migration of jobs or a run on the currency as a result of financial decisions taken elsewhere; shifting patterns of land use and settlement due to climate change, or; the impact of tourism and investment decisions on current accounts, there is no doubt that all countries are exquisitely, and increasingly vulnerable and exposed to events initiated beyond their frontiers.

This reality, however, is rarely reflected in the daily news cycle and even less so in the content behind the headlines. Why? Reasons include media multiplication and segmentation, budget and personnel cuts, a loss of institutional memory, the closing or consolidation of foreign bureaux, infrequent and shorter stories, an absence of analysis, and a fixation on the visually and emotionally sensational such as earthquakes, plane and train wrecks, and tidal waves. Fewer journalists, with increasingly stretched resources, are covering the international relations "beat", and there appears to be a widespread conviction among media managers that their readers are not interested in world affairs. Those who are have little choice but to rely upon specialised sources and the Internet for anything but the most basic information.

These changes in the structure of media coverage have both prefigured and reflected major shifts in the public environment, which has also been subject to the powerful historical currents of globalization. This is producing a new division of labour at all levels, fracturing some communities while creating others, splintering populations, generating wealth and re-distributing it at the same time.

To be sure, the public environment for international policy is at the best of times uncertain. Still, it was not that long ago there existed a broad, comfortable, middle-class consensus around the most central aspects of international policy, such as containment, deterrence, or trade liberalization. But that entente has been riven and its demise hastened by the growing popularity of highly particularistic, single-interest lobbies on rainforest or reefs, Timor or Tibet, gender or human rights, small arms or child soldiers. It is difficult to reach, let alone attempt to draw together, such a fragmented constituency.

The unravelling of a supportive domestic environment for public diplomacy goes well beyond the blurring of the lines between the national and the global, the rising prominence government of departments outside the purview of the foreign ministry, or the activism of other levels of government such as cities. Trends in the domestic polity are now deeply influenced by the activities of non-state actors ranging from Al Qa'eda to philanthropic NGOs and from transnational businesses to the preoccupations of prominent individuals such as Bono, Bill Gates, and George Soros. The rise of issue-driven advocacy, job insecurity, generational change and growing disquiet over matters closer to home have increased levels of discomfort but have also induced fatigue, apathy, and cynicism.

Perhaps feeling adrift in this turbulent and confusing world, it appears that many citizens have redrawn the lines of their individual moral engagement in closer proximity to the front door. Beset by lingering doubts about governance at home and facing a range of vexing, if not intractable, challenges abroad, many seem to be looking inwards just when they should be looking out. In developed countries most people now see their government's priorities as overwhelmingly domestic. Health care, education, the environment, and management of the economy dominate, with all aspects of international affairs (defence, aid, and foreign policy) barely registering in comparison.

Spoon-fed by embedded journalists and anaesthetized by spin doctors, people everywhere seem to be paying less attention to either the world or to their place in it. There are occasional spikes in interest—the aftermath of 9/11, the decision to abstain from the invasion of Iraq, echoes from events in Iran or North Korea—but these are at best minor peaks in a valley of indifference. Global issues, including the hardy perennials of peace, development and human rights, often register but are rarely rated among the top three popular pre-occupations.

International policy has become somewhat of an exotic, far removed from their more pressing concerns. It exists in a kind of floating world, a disconnected bubble somehow severed from the everyday and animated more by a sense of visceral values than an appreciation of concrete interests.

7. *Policy Militarization*

The substitution of defence for diplomacy at the center of international policy has exacerbated all six of the paradoxes sketched above and is making the world a less secure place. Diplomacy is mostly about talking rather than fighting, about finding reasonable accommodation, about conflict resolution, and about crafting win/win solutions to difficult problems. Recourse to armed force, on the other hand, is about compelling others to do your bidding. Public diplomacy becomes at best window-dressing, and at worst non-existent, when the latter trumps the former.

During the Cold War, the West organized its international policy around the objective of "containment" by blocking, and wherever possible, rolling back what was seen as a monolithic Communist threat. Nuclear deterrence and the spectre of mutually assured destruction served to keep local conflicts from expanding or escalating out of control. Diplomacy figured centrally in episodes such as the Cuban Missile Crisis, but on balance departments of defence were favoured over foreign ministries and, for that matter, development assistance agencies. President Eisenhower warned of the consequences or this trend when he spoke of the dangers associated with the ascent of the military-industrial complex, yet the same patterns have continued into age of globalization and asymmetrical warfare.

For the first years after the Cold War walls came down in Europe, threat conjurers had a difficult time identifying credible enemies, and it looked, fleetingly, like a peace dividend just might be paid. The tragedy of 9/11 changed all that, and a similarly open-ended group of impulses and functions were resurrected and now find expression in the Global War on Terror, which has been substituted for the Cold War just as terrorists have been substituted for Communists. The principal expressions of these Cold War carry-overs include:

- the adoption of a binary world view, which reduces complexity to a matter of us versus them – "you are with us, or with the terrorists";

- the use of fear to galvanize domestic support by characterizing the threat as urgent, universal, and undifferentiated – "they not only out there, everywhere, but they are among us and could strike anywhere, anytime"[10];
- a preference for the use of armed force in responding to perceived threats, favouring defence over diplomacy or development in what might be reasonably described as the militarization of international policy.[11]

This ideological transfer has meant that for almost two decades the scope for applying alternative approaches, such as diplomacy, to the resolution of international differences has been very limited. Most foreign ministries have paid a high price.

It is no small irony that public diplomacy played a significant role during the Cold War in efforts to win the "hearts and minds" of potential clients among the new and decolonising states of what would come to be known as the developing world.[12] Money was poured into cultural, scientific, educational, and artistic programs designed to display the wonders of one or the other system. Cold War public diplomacy did show that by connecting directly with populations and, in so doing, reaching out to the distressed, the disempowered, and disenfranchised, it could address not only the immediate drivers of insecurity—anxiety, anger and recrimination—but also the longer-term, underlying causes rooted in structural and political relationships.

As globalisation accelerates, its polarising effect is exacerbating inequalities and generating insecurity for those on its underside or periphery, while at the same time contributing to prosperity and progress elsewhere.[13] Yet even more than during the Cold War, the tendency to react to terrorism and religious extremism by militarising international policy is showing its limits. Current efforts, especially those pursued

---

[10] A superb treatment of this theme is offered by Adam Curtis in his three-part documentary for BBC 2, *The Power of Nightmares,* http://video.google.com/videosearch?q=power+of+nightmares (accessed 29 November 2008).

[11] For a summary with reference to the experience of the USA, see Mel Goodman, "The militarization of U.S. foreign policy," *FPIF Policy Brief* (February 2004). 9:1, http://www.fpif.org/pdf/vol9/01military.pdf (accessed 29 November 2008).

[12] See, for example, James Critchlow, "Public diplomacy during the Cold War," *Journal of Cold War Studies* (Winter 2004), 6:1, pp. 75–89.

[13] There is a vast, and still growing literature on the issue of inequality, and little agreement on whether or not it is increasing or diminishing as a result of globalisation. For an overview, see World Bank, *World Development Report 2006: Equity and Development* (World Bank, 2007).

within the framework of the Global War on Terror, are not going well.[14]

While present tribulations have resulted in an enormous misallocation of international policy resources, the pre-occupation with the military and defence has obscured appreciation of the emergence of a new range of threats and challenges, most rooted in science and driven by technology. This new constellation is in different in kind from previous territorial and ideologically-based disputes.[15] Global issues such as climate change, environmental collapse, energy supply, pandemic disease, genomics, resource depletion, and weapons of mass destruction all carry the potential to cause serious disruption, if not disaster. None is susceptible to being detained, garrisoned, extraordinarily rendered, or taken out in an air strike.

By linking development and security through the medium of international policy, diplomacy and especially public diplomacy should again find itself front and centre in governmental action. Neither members of the military nor aid workers, NGO representatives nor journalists have the span of engagement, the particular skill set, or the knowledge of the broader policy and political context which might permit them to substitute in this critical role.

The Way Ahead

Addressing the paradoxes set out above, there are no quick fixes, but there are a few obvious steps which can and should be taken. While not much can be done about the fact that most public diplomats will continue to work for governments, adhering in practice to a more rigorous definition of their role will help to ensure that outcomes are both mutually beneficial, and seen to be so.

The problem of diplomatic dysfunction can be remedied, to some extent, by providing additional resources and adjusting antiquated

---

[14] It is a very short road from heresy to received wisdom. For a sampling of what is quickly becoming the new mainstream, see Paul Rogers, *Why We're Losing the War on Terror* (Polity, 2007); Philip Gordon, *Winning the Right War* (Brookings, 2007); Mel Gurtov, *Superpower on Crusade: the Bush Doctrine in US Foreign Policy* (Lynne Rienner, 2007).

[15] An increasing number of analysts are reaching similar conclusions regarding real threats. The Oxford Research Group, for example, cite climate change, competition over resources the marginalization of the majority; and militarization as the main drivers of insecurity. See Chris Abbott et. al., *Beyond Terror: The Truth About the Real Threats to Our World*. (Rider and Co., 2007).

policies related to recruitment, training, and professional development. More enlightened policies, however, will in large part depend on reforming and engineering a cultural shift within foreign ministries, and that will almost certainly prove be a much harder nut to crack. Even if the bureaucratic culture could somehow be transformed, crucial issues related to the restoration of international policy leadership, substantial work content, and operational centrality remain. All of this is to considerable extent dependent upon building an effective domestic constituency and cultivating a more conducive public environment, neither of which appear to be priorities for foreign ministries at present.

This brings us to the seventh paradox, which is perhaps the most vexing of all. If international policy is to be de-militarized, then diplomats are going to have to show that they are capable of providing effective alternatives.[16] In the globalization age it is economic and political underdevelopment which drives insecurity. To flip this formulation over, if development has emerged as a precondition for lasting security, then diplomacy will have to become much more concerned with addressing issues of underdevelopment. Diffusing the anger and resentment that find expression in violence and religious extremism means committing to a more equitable and sustainable division of the world's wealth and resources. Bombs and guns can't deliver that dispensation. Public diplomacy, on the other hand, by virtue of its cross-cultural, dialogical and win/win orientation, is ideally suited to taking on the challenge.

One way to encourage this reformation, and to contribute to demonstrable diplomatic relevance and effectiveness, might be to place science and technology at the centre of the international policy agenda. This point deserves special emphasis. Science creates new knowledge, which assists us in understanding the world around us. Through research and development, we can test and apply that new knowledge in reference to specific problems or challenges such as alternative energy sources, pollution control, or disease-resistant grains. From the

[16] When governments favour military over diplomatic options, most diplomats swallow hard and get on with it. There are exceptions, however. Veteran US foreign service officers J. Brady Kiesling, John Brown, and Ann Wright resigned in March 2003 over the decision to invade Iraq. The text of Kiesling's memorable letter of resignation available at: http://www.truthout.org/cgi-bin/artman/exec/view.cgi?archive=1&num=61 (accessed 29 November 2008). See also his 19 March 3003 interview with *Salon*, http://dir.salon.com/story/news/feature/2003/03/19/_kiesling/index.html (accessed 29 November 2008).

research and development process comes the technological innovations intended to redress those problems. And those technologies can be disseminated and implemented, not just through market forces and specialized international organizations, but through science diplomacy, which will in turn contribute to addressing the problems of underdevelopment and insecurity.

Neither Endgame, nor Grand Illusions

In this brief overview of the seven paradoxes of public diplomacy, I have tried to assess the nature and origins of the current diplomatic performance gap and capacity deficit. At present, and this may be the over-arching issue, public diplomacy tends to work best in metropolitan centres and when applied to relations between advanced states. Little attention has been paid to adapting public diplomacy practices for use elsewhere, either in the developing world or, at the sharp end, in counter-insurgency.

The over-riding purpose of public diplomacy in a world of insecurity should be to address the root causes of underdevelopment. The place in the globalization age for diplomacy and the foreign ministry, as the agents best able to cohere the national interest and to manage it strategically, is at the nexus between security and development. If development is the new security and if security is best achieved through talking rather than fighting, then public diplomacy must be adapted to function not only in what used to be referred to as the Third and Fourth worlds, but also in conflict zones.[17]

Governments, for their part, must find better ways to deliver on the promise of public diplomacy, not least because the alternatives—continued confrontation, worsening conflict, and the costly, debilitating militarization of international policy—are unpalatable. While public diplomacy is the plumbing, at the end of the day it is what is in the pipe that will make or break the prospects for a better world. It is that content which will provide the vital diplomatic elements of credibility and legitimacy. Absent those key attributes, including walking the talk and bridging the say/do gap, the foundations of peace and progress—confidence, trust and respect—will be impossible to construct. Soldiers can't do this. Public diplomats can.

---

[17] For an elaboration on this point, see Daryl Copeland, *Guerrilla Diplomacy: Rethinking International Relations* (Lynne Rienner, 2009).

THE PUBLIC DIPLOMACY CHALLENGES OF STRATEGIC STAKEHOLDER ENGAGEMENT

R.S. Zaharna

"Strategic stakeholder engagement," as a term, concept, or practice has yet to gain wide currency among public diplomacy scholars and practitioners. That gap, however, may soon close as the international arena transitions from the information age, dominated by the mass media and message-driven strategies, to the global communication era dominated by the social media and relational and network strategies.[1] The shift represents more than a rush to incorporate the latest technology into a public diplomacy initiative. In fact, it is less about the technological tools that connect people and more about the communication strategies that provide the motivation and platform for people to want to connect with others and stay connected long after a public diplomat returns home.

For public diplomats, strategic stakeholder engagement represents a two-fold challenge. The first challenge is identifying the "who." Who is a strategic stakeholder in public diplomacy? Within the literature, the term stakeholder is being used in ways that suggest either domestic agents or audiences. As agents, stakeholders share a political entity's goals and may serve to augment the reach and effectiveness of a public diplomacy initiative.[2] The British Foreign and Commonwealth Office (FCO), for example, lists its key stakeholder groups as think tanks, regional outreach champions, businesses, trades unions, and faith groups.[3] This

---

[1] John Arquilla and David Ronfeldt, *Networks and Netwars: The Future of Terror, Crime, and Militancy* (Santa Monica, CA: RAND, 2001); Ronald J. Deibert, *Parchment, Printing and Hypermedia: Communication World Order Transformation*. (New York: Columbia University Press, 1997); D. J. Rothkopf, "Cyberpolitik: The Changing Nature of Power in the Information Age," *Journal of International Affairs*, 51, 2 (1998), pp. 325–359; and R.S. Zaharna, *Battles to Bridges: U.S. Strategic Communication and Public Diplomacy after 9/11* (Basingstoke: Palgrave-Macmillan, 2010).

[2] My thanks to Bruce Gregory for the label of agency and agents of public diplomacy and its link to representation in traditional diplomacy.

[3] FCO, "Working with Stakeholder Groups," accessed July 6, 2009, http://www.fco.gov.uk/en/about-the-fco/what-we-do/building-strong-relationships-ol/stakeholder-groups/. See, also, Foreign and Commonwealth Office Stakeholder Survey 2008, Overview Report," prepared by Jigsaw Research, London, June 19, 2008: The 2008

internal domestic constituency is similar to the principal stakeholders identified in U.S. public diplomacy reports.[4] The term stakeholder is also increasingly being used in lieu of external audience and publics. Such stakeholders may or may not share a political sponsor's goals. Public diplomats would need to identify potential stakeholders and find where their shared interests and goals intersect within a public diplomacy initiative.

A second challenge is the "what." What constitutes strategic engagement? The term engagement has appeared with greater frequency but perhaps with even less clarity than stakeholder. In traditional government to government diplomacy, there are fairly clear demarcation lines of engagement that range from diplomatic isolation up the ladder to contact between senior officials to the heads of state or government. In public diplomacy, however, the term engagement has been used more broadly. It is often used to suggest audience involvement or participation in a public diplomacy initiative, including relationship-building.[5] Prior to September 2001, an oft-cited shorthand for public diplomacy was "understanding, informing, and influencing foreign audiences."[6] In 2003, a prominent U.S. public diplomacy report added the word "engage" to the list.[7] Interestingly, engagement is increasingly being used as a substitute for public diplomacy. In 2008, the British FCO entitled its major report on public diplomacy, "Engagement."[8] In the introduction of the report, Jim Murphy advocated that engagement

---

British FCO's survey of "stakeholders" involved individuals at a "very senior level" and who appeared to share the goal of "representing the UK position and interests well."

[4] Shortly after the start of Obama administration, a group of 70 "principal stakeholders" prepared the 2009 White Oak public diplomacy called for a "Holistic Stakeholder Approach: Public diplomacy is relevant to a broad array of strategic interests and has multiple stakeholders: military and non-military, Executive and Congressional, public and private sector. We need to identify the needs and strengths of each stakeholder and determine together how to best play to (support, staff and fund) the strengths of each." See, White Oak Public Diplomacy Recommendations, January 30-February 1, 2009 (available online).

[5] John Robert Kelley, "Between "Take-offs" and "Crash Landings," Situational Aspects of Public Diplomacy," in N. Snow and P. Taylor (eds.), *Routledge Handbook of Public Diplomacy,* (New York: Routledge, 2008), pp. 72–85; also, Kathy R. Fitzpatrick, *The Future of U.S. Public Diplomacy*: *Uncertain Fate*. (Boston: Brill, 2010), p. 105.

[6] U.S. Public Diplomacy Council (www.publicdiplomacycouncil.org).

[7] U.S. Advisory Group on Public Diplomacy for the Arab and Muslim World, "Changing Minds, Winning Peace: A New Strategic Direction for US Public Diplomacy in the Arab & Muslim World," U.S. State Department, Washington, DC, October 2003.

[8] *Engagement*, London, Foreign and Commonwealth Office, June 2008.

"must be the hallmark of contemporary public diplomacy."[9] In U.S. public diplomacy, soon after President Barack Obama took office in early 2009, public diplomacy and soft power were gradually being replaced by engagement and smart power.[10] The shift intensified with the interest in network diplomacy and the desire to connect and interact with publics.[11] By mid-2010, Kristin Lord and Marc Lynch called engagement "a pillar and guiding principle of President Barack Obama's foreign policy."[12] Despite the shift in terms, the activities of "engagement" appear to mirror those of public diplomacy.

Even as stakeholder and engagement gain currency, both terms still remain loosely defined in public diplomacy. This chapter looks at strategic stakeholder engagement through these dual lenses – the who and the what. The first section looks at information initiatives, including information broadcasts, information campaigns, nation branding and media relations. The second section surveys engagement strategies in relational initiatives, specifically relationship-building campaigns and cultural programs. The third section explores complex engagement strategies in non-policy and policy networking initiatives. The final section recaps the insights about strategic stakeholder engagement across the various types of initiatives. The intent of this chapter is to hopefully expand the boundaries of analytical thinking and creative imagination of strategic stakeholder engagement for public diplomats.

Stakeholder Engagement—The Who & What

The use of the term "stakeholder" in public diplomacy belies the evolution in thinking across a variety of communication-related fields. In the dawn of communication theory, it was all very simple: sender→message→receiver. The sender and receiver were distinct, separate entities. There was no blurring of attributes, responsibilities, or

---

[9] Jim Murphy, "Engagement," in *Engagement*, London, Foreign and Commonwealth Office, June 2008.

[10] John Brown, "Smart Power In, Public Diplomacy Out?" John Brown's Notes and Essays, posted March 2, 2009. http://johnbrownnotesandessays.blogspot.com/

[11] Anne-Marie Slaughter, "America's Edge," *Foreign Affairs*, January/February 2009, pp. 114; Kristin Lord, "Engaging the Private Sector for the Public Good: The Power of Network Diplomacy," Policy Brief, Center for a New American Security, January 2010.

[12] Kristin M. Lord and Marc Lynch, *America's Extended Hand: Assessing the Obama Administration*, Center for New American Security, June 2010.

territory. The goal of communication was how to transmit the message from the sender to the receiver. Coincidentally, the communication terms closely parallel those used in traditional diplomacy, *sending* nation and *receiving* nation of diplomatic envoys.

Since the flood of new interest in public diplomacy after September 2001, various terms from different fields and professions have been used to connate receivers. From marketing and public relations comes the terms audience, consumers, and even "publics" with an "s." In political science, which focuses on persuasion, attitude change and public opinion, the term public, is also used along with opinion leaders, and influential elites. These conceptions of the public or audience, however, are based on mass media models. As communication scholar Jon Anderson points out, the basic assumptions about mass media models, such as a few senders and many receivers, or who produces and who consumes messages, are contradicted by the social media.[13] The interactive capabilities of digital technologies and connective ability of the internet that underlie the social media has usurped the power of production once held by the mass media and blurred the difference between sender and receiver. Some even suggest that the social media has shifted the power from senders to receivers.[14] Indeed, as Anderson asks, "What sort of public is this, if it cannot be thought of as an audience or mass opinion?"[15] For public diplomacy, what does this say about opinion leaders and influential elites?

The use of the term "stakeholder" has gained traction in public relations as the field moves from compliance-gaining to relationship-building strategies.[16] In his 1984 path breaking work, *Strategic Management: A Stakeholder Approach*, Edward Freeman first advocated practitioners shift their focus from the broad general public to more specific primary and secondary stakeholders.[17] Writing more

---

[13] Jon Anderson, "New media, New publics: Reconfiguring the Public Sphere of Islam," *Social Research*, 70, 3 (Fall 2003), pp. 887–903.

[14] Rian van der Merwe, Leyland F. Pitt, and Russell Abratt, "Stakeholder Strength: PR Survival Strategies for the Internet Age," *Public Relations Quarterly*, 50, 1 (Spring 2005), pp. 39–48.

[15] Jon Anderson, "New media, New publics", p. 891.

[16] Kathy R. Fitzpatrick, "Advancing the New Public Diplomacy: A Public Relations Perspective," *Hague Journal of Diplomacy*. 2 (2007), p. 205.

[17] R. Edward Freeman, *Strategic Management: A Stakeholder Approach* (Boston: Pitman/Ballinger, 1984).

recently, Brad Rawlins' probing work also significantly advanced techniques for identifying stakeholders.[18] Richard Edelman explains the shift from passive publics to more active stakeholders in his piece "The Relationship Imperative."[19] Edelman (head of Edelman Public Relations, one of the largest international public relations firms), argued that the old mass media pyramid, with the organization at the top passing information to the few elites down to the masses at the base of the pyramid has become obsolete. Instead of a pyramid with the organization at the top, he suggests a circle or "sphere of cross influence" with the organization in the middle. Edelman's sphere of cross influence includes NGOs, media, employees, consumers and other major groups that try to influence the organization. For public diplomacy, one might adapt the sphere by including the domestic public, political allies on an issue/conflict, political adversaries on an issue/conflict, and international organizations as additional stakeholders. Noteworthy, most public diplomacy discussions still view the organization as the "influencer" – not the center of a "sphere of influence."

These various groups that comprise what Edelman calls a sphere of influence is what other public communication professionals are increasingly referring to as "stakeholders." Stakeholders in general have a vested interest or stake in an organization or program, hence the term stakeholder. Edelman draws attention to a group that organizations should be particularly alert to – the "catalysts." His description is different from the traditional mass media opinion leaders or influential elites: "Catalysts are self-appointed leaders in their area of expertise…They are rapid and passionate communicators…They are media-attentive and have a narrow focus. While catalysts differ by activities and interests, they share a personality trait, a missionary zeal… Catalysts are experienced at building and nurturing virtual communities around their core interests."[20] Catalysts do not yet appear to be on public diplomacy's radar screen. However given their specialized knowledge, motivation and social media skills, catalysts may well represent the most formidable allies or foes for a public diplomat.

---

[18] Brad L. Rawlins, "Prioritizing Stakeholders for Public Relations," Gold Standard Paper of the Commission of Public Relations Measurement and Evaluation, Institute of Public Relations (www.instituteforpr.org), March 2006.

[19] Richard Edelman, "The Relationship Imperative," *Journal of Integrated Communications*, 2003–2004, pp. 1–12.

[20] Richard Edelman, "The Relationship Imperative," p. 10.

Another area that refers to publics as stakeholders and even specifically focuses on "stakeholder engagement" is corporate social responsibility (CSR). CRS is not new. In Western settings, CSR includes a company's philanthropic activities such as establishing scholarships, donating to charities, or sponsoring community functions. Recently, in fact, more recent than the explosion of interest in public diplomacy, CSR has been receiving attention as an important component for gaining access and acceptance to consumers in profitable emerging markets.[21] CSR has a direct effect on a company's image and reputation in these markets. Although research is still new, and best practices are still sketchy, effective "stakeholder engagement" appears to be a pivotal component of successful CSR programs. It is important to note that most stakeholder engagements are not one-time projects, but on-going programs. Of note for public diplomacy, skilled CSR organizations appear to be proactive in identifying stakeholders impacted by an organization's policies or activities and in developing programs related to the stakeholders' interests/concerns. Additionally, it appears that tangible projects tended to receive more recognition by stakeholders than intangible ones.[22] Finally, some of the most innovative initiatives were those that used the organization's "core competency" or core strength as an anchor for a CSR program. For public diplomacy, this might be the equivalent of tying public diplomacy initiatives to a nation's strength. The idea of core competency may reinforce Cooper's discussion of niche diplomacy.[23]

Stakeholder has long been the preferred term used in participatory communication. Participatory communication and social marketing

---

[21] For resources, see, International Finance Corporation (IFC) website, George Lodge and Craig Wilson, *Corporate Solution to Global Poverty: How Multinationals Can Help the Poor and Invigorate Their Own Legitimacy* (New Haven: Princeton University Press, 2006); Gerald Davis, M. von Neumann Whitman, and Mayer Zald, "The Responsibility Paradox: Multinational Firms and Global Corporate Social Responsibility," University of Michigan, n.d., Feng Zhang, "Corporate Social Responsibility in Emerging Markets: The Role of Multinational Corporations," The Foreign Policy Center in association with Coca-Cola Great Britain, London, March 2008.

[22] This may explain why some public diplomacy and aid programs do not receive the attention that sponsors and donors expect. For more complete discussion, see interview with Richard Welford, head of CSR consultancy firm in Asia, by Miguel R. Camus, "CSR as an Investment," *BusinessMirror.com*, May 21, 2009.

[23] Andrew F. Cooper (ed.) *Niche Diplomacy: Middle Powers after the Cold War* (Basingstoke: Palgrave Macmillan, 1997).

are two dominant approaches used in development projects to communicate with publics about social issues such as health, education, or the environment.[24] The migration of language from development projects into public diplomacy is perhaps a reflection of the growing trend to highlight development assistance as part of a country's public diplomacy[25] as well as the growth of more explicitly politically-oriented development projects.[26] In participatory communication, stakeholder refers to any party that has a stake, potential benefit or consequence of the program. Several features of participatory communication indeed invite stakeholder participation. This includes horizontal communication; valuing the process instead of the final campaign; adopting a long-term process designed to build capacity versus short-term planning that responds to external "results framework"; using specific rather than massive scale; designing messages *with* versus *for* stakeholders, and finally, seeking to "raise consciousness" about social problems and solutions versus persuasion for short-term behavioral changes that are only sustainable with continuous campaigns."[27] As will be seen shortly, some of these elements of participatory communication are echoed in the more innovative public diplomacy initiatives.

Possible refinement of the term stakeholder comes from aid development programs, specifically the growing literature on multi-stakeholder partnerships (MSP).[28] Whereas the term "stakeholder" refers to all actors who have an interest in the initiative, "partners" refers to

---

[24] Jan Servaes, *Communication for Development: One World, Multiple Cultures*, (Cresskill, NJ: Hampton Press, 1999); and Silvio Waisbord, "Fifty Years of Development Communication: What Works," Presentation to the Inter-American Development Bank, Washington, DC, July 1, 2003. (Available online).

[25] As Fiske de Gouveia noted, "[humanitarian aid and assistance] has an important public diplomacy function: it is important not only that aid be given but that it is seen to be given." In Philip Fiske de Gouveia with Hester Plumridge, *European Infopolitik: Developing EU Public Diplomacy Strategy*, London, Foreign Policy Centre, November 2005, p. 17.

[26] For example of a participatory approach used in political project in Afghanistan, see, Wendy Quarry, "Decision Makers Do Want Communication – But They May not Want Participation," *Glocal Times*, Issue #10, February 2008. (Available online).

[27] Alfonso Dumicio Dagron, *Making Waves*, New York, The Rockefeller Foundation, 2001, p. 35.

[28] According to the U.N., "multi-stakeholder partnership" (MSP) is defined as a "voluntary and collaborative relationships between various parties, both State and non-state, in which all participants agree to work together to achieve a common purpose or undertake a specific task and to share risks and responsibilities, resources and benefits." (U. N. General Assembly Resolution, "Toward Global Partnerships," December 5, 2007).

the actors who jointly plan and implement activities, mobilize and share resources and agree on how the resources are managed.[29] The field also exposes the often overlooked stakeholder identified by Walker as the "silent stakeholder," or the people on the receiving end.[30] The distinction between stakeholders and partners as well as the importance of silent stakeholders are evident in some of the more complex relational initiatives such as the relationship-building campaigns in public diplomacy.

Finally, stakeholder has received increasing attention within traditional diplomacy, particularly in discussions related to global governance. Diplomatic scholar Brian Hocking has broken new ground in public diplomacy by his applications of multi-stakeholder dynamics in complex policy networks.[31] He distinguishes between stakeholders as "targets or consumers" typically found in competitive public diplomacy (bilateral diplomacy) and stakeholders as "partners and producers" found in collaborative public diplomacy (multilateral or multi-stakeholder diplomacy).[32] Much like traditional diplomats, he counsels public diplomats to determine the status, credentials, capabilities, and expectations of potential stakeholders and then the interests and needs of actual stakeholders.

The above insights from other fields are helpful for thinking about the first challenge of stakeholder engagement in public diplomacy, namely, how practitioners and scholars can identify stakeholders. A second challenge is to identify the types of engagement strategies for the different types of stakeholders. As a means for expanding the

---

[29] Will Crichley, Miranda Verburg and Laurens van Velhuizen, Facilitating Multi-stakeholder Partnerships: Lessons from PROLINNOVA," [The Netherlands] International Institute of Rural Reconstruction, December 2006, p. 2.

[30] Peter, L. Walker, "Aid Recipients, Engaging the Silent Stakeholder," Transformation Public Diplomacy, The Diplomatic Academy of London, Westminster University, April 23–24, 2008.

[31] See, Brian Hocking, "Catalytic Diplomacy: Beyond 'Newness' and 'Decline,'" in Jan Melissen (ed.) Innovation in Diplomatic Practice, (Basingstoke: Palgrave Macmillan, 1999), Brian Hocking, "Diplomacy: New Agendas and Changing Strategies," *iMP Magazine* (July 2001), Brian Hocking, "Reconfiguring Public Diplomacy: From Competition to Collaboration," in *Engagement*, London, Foreign and Commonwealth Office, June 2008.

[32] Brian Hocking, "Multistakeholder Diplomacy: Foundations, Forms, Functions and Frustrations," International Conference on Multistakeholder Diplomacy, Malta, February 11–13, 2005; and Brian Hocking, "Reconfiguring Public Diplomacy: From Competition to Collaboration," in *Engagement*, London, Foreign and Commonwealth Office, June 2008.

notion of stakeholder engagement, the next several sections look at the who and what of stakeholder engagement across various public diplomacy initiatives.

Information Initiatives

The most basic types of stakeholder engagement are found in information initiatives that stress designing and disseminating information. Salient features of information initiatives include messaging strategies, sponsor control, reliance on mass media channels, and goal orientation as well as restricted or limited interaction between the political sponsor and the public.[33] Information initiatives appear to vary in terms of their level of stakeholder engagement. For example, initiatives that seek to inform or raise awareness about an issue may have a very low level of stakeholder engagement.[34] Initiatives that seek to influence, either create or modify attitudes about an issue, would require a higher or more focused level of engagement. Initiatives that seek behavior change would demand intensive and even sustained engagement. It is possible to suggest that the lower level of stakeholder engagement, the lower the persuasive power of the initiatives. The level of stakeholder engagement also appears inversely proportional to the amount of control by the sponsor. The more control a political sponsor has over the research, design, and implementation of an initiative, the less space there is for stakeholders to meaningfully engage in the initiatives. The different stakeholder dynamics are discussed below.

Information Dissemination – Print, Radio, Television, and Internet

Information dissemination as been a foundation activity of public diplomacy and includes print publications, international broadcasting (radio, television, and satellite) and now internet webcasts, podcasts,

[33] Zaharna, *Battles to Bridges*, pp. 138–146.

[34] As may be surmised, I tend to view persuasive communication, and by extension public diplomacy, as a progress from changing knowledge, to changing attitude, to ultimately, changing behavior, should behavior change be the desired goal. While U.K. and U.S. public diplomacy tend to stress behavior change, a behavioral focus and outcome does not appear to be the defining concern for public diplomacy initiatives of all countries or political entities across the globe. See, for example, Wilkins, K. G. "Japanese Approaches to, Development Communication," *Keico Communication Review* 25 (2003), pp. 19–37.

and even Twitter. Traditionally, information dissemination via mass media channels represents limited, if any, stakeholder engagement. The sponsor is the initiator and is responsible for the communication. The political sponsor develops the content, typically news, commentary and information programming and disseminates it over controlled channels or partner stations.

It is important to point out that audience reach is not the same thing as stakeholder engagement. Simply because a public diplomacy initiative may be successful in distributing X number of pamphlets or securing X number of listeners does not mean that any of those recipients will accept or even acknowledge the message. This point does need stressing because it is still common for officials, in their drive to account for the bottom line, to cite output measurements as a sign that they have engaged an audience.

While the mass media presupposes a passive audience, the social media is predicated on the notion of an active audience. In an attempt to "engage" the public, some public diplomacy initiatives have grafted interactive media (email, chat rooms, telephone call-in programs, etc.) onto mass media platform. The audience uses the interactive features to express their views, provide feedback, and try to influence the programming (content). However while adding interactive technology to mass media initiative may create the illusion of interactivity with foreign audiences, the limits of that interactivity or stakeholder engagement are often strictly circumscribed. The audience may use the interactive features to enhance their own communication experience and even be effective in changing the content of the mass media programming. However, the extent of stakeholder engagement tends to stop at the level of directly influencing political policy. While the goal of the public diplomacy initiative may be to change the attitudes and even behavior of the audience; the reciprocal process of the audience being able to change or influence the policy of the political entity is not normally part of the rules of stakeholder engagement.

The use of social media in information dissemination represents a potential cross over from purely passive media viewers to more active stakeholder engagement. Several of the international broadcasting giants have started to incorporate social media components. The U.S. State Department International Information Programs has added "IIP-chat," a tool many news media outlets use to generate audience interest and interactivity on its featured stories. Similarly, the Obama administration has developed Facebook and YouTube sites for the various

U.S. agencies, not just the State Department.[35] This move to social media across the whole of government gives the Obama administration not just a domestic presence but larger global presence via the internet.

An interesting example of "core competency" is the British Broadcasting Corporation (BBC) language site. The BBC is one of the oldest and largest international broadcasters. Its broadcasts represent a treasure trove of news and feature stories in variety of languages. Some of these stories are used in a robust language learning site that features Chinese, French, German, Spanish, and other languages.[36]

Another example of information dissemination that has broken the mold is the Israeli public diplomacy use of Twitter during its military operation in Gaza. On December 30, 2008, the Israeli Consulate held the first ever "citizens press conference," which allowed the mission to achieve its goal of "sharing our POV (point of view)," while taking questions from the global audience. The Israeli government also posted video of aerial views of its bombing in Gaza on YouTube. In one sense, the use of YouTube, with its motto of "Broadcast Yourself," is information dissemination. The sense of stakeholder engagement emerges with the use of the platform. YouTube is a social networking site that enables users as opposed to merely passive viewers, to share and comment on videos. These two aspects are a qualitative step up in stakeholder engagement from a state-run media outlet with limited audience feedback.

Information Campaigns

Information campaigns can represent a step up from information dissemination. The communication goals move from disseminating information that informs publics and promotes public awareness, to a more systematic, structured presentation of information that can influence public attitudes and even behaviors. Most information campaigns closely parallel the four-stage Western public relations model. The preliminary research stage gathers information on the communication environment, public and possible messaging strategies. The planning stage entails formulating key objectives, identifying target audiences,

---

[35] Michael Scherer, "Obama and Twitter: White House Social-Networking," *Time Magazine*, May 6, 2009.

[36] http://www.bbc.co.uk/languages/

and defining strategies and tactics. The implementation stage involves developing and delivering the messages to the target audience. Finally, the evaluation stage assesses the specific outcomes and overall effectiveness of the campaign. While the campaign may be "audience-centered" in terms of campaign design and messaging strategies, the campaign sponsor retains sole control over the decision-making throughout the four-stage process. Audience engagement is limited to circumscribed participation as defined by the sponsor.

An example of an information campaign that incorporated aspects of stakeholder engagement is "Telling Our Stories" launched by U.S. Agency for International Development (USAID) in 2003. The double-entendre of the USAID campaign title, "our stories," reflects the sophistication of the initiative. The web-based campaign consists of solicited stories from beneficiaries of the USAID-sponsored projects. By soliciting and posting these stories, USAID translated its on-the-ground involvement with stakeholders in its development projects to online stakeholders for its public diplomacy initiative. The online engagement may technically be with the individual stakeholders who submit the stories, but the stories are framed as representative of the larger beneficiary community or nation, that is, many more stakeholders. This is one aspect of the campaign's sophistication. The other aspect is the nature of the stories and their pre-scripted formats. The "stories" are, in fact, personal testimonials, one of the most powerful tools used in persuasion. Testimonials also suggest a deeply personal level of stakeholder engagement and endorsement. USAID lays out strict guidelines in story format, length, language and accompanying photos or graphics for submission of personal testimonials. Applicants must select and follow one of five story formats, including visual requirements. Ultimately, USAID retains control over which stories are posted and how they are posted. An analysis of the stories and guidelines by Zehra Rizavi, revealed underlying frames that are more about shaping audience perception than simply telling their story, and even more important as a public diplomacy initiative, telling America's story.[37]

Nation Branding

On the surface, nation branding campaigns appear very similar to information campaigns in that both share basic components such as

[37] Zehra Rizavi, "Telling Our Stories," Unpublished Masters Capstone Project, American University, May 2007.

audience research, campaign design and implementation, and evaluation. Additionally, most nation branding, like persuasive information campaigns, tend to speak of "target audience" and specific goals such as enhancing a national image or increasing foreign investment or tourism. While stakeholder engagement is not normally discussed in nation branding, it does seem to be a hidden aspect of successful ones. However, the principal stakeholders are not foreign audiences, but the domestic public, which at the end of the day has the most to gain by a successful initiative.

Colombia es pasión, (*Colombia is passion*) is an example of strong domestic stakeholder engagement.[38] Colombia's export, tourism and investment promotion agency, Proexport, initiated the program as an internal or national domestic campaign in which different Colombian sectors, including the government, worked together to improve the image of the country on a national and international scale. Soon after its debut, the campaign logo and slogan was readily adopted by Colombian companies, trade unions, state and local entities, associations and federations, as well as an airline and even bicycling team.[39] The campaign became a source of national identity and pride for the country's citizens, who, in turn, made a personal effort to improve individual service and attention in their tourism and investment activities with foreign publics.[40] Fiona Gilmore called the "spirit of the people," the heart of the brand of countries.[41] When Colombia did move to external promotion activities aimed at foreign audience, the country realized increased tourism and investment benefits from the program much earlier and stronger than originally anticipated.

As the Colombian example suggests, domestic stakeholders can play a decisive role in effective public diplomacy initiatives. Conversely, weak or absent domestic stakeholder engagement may cause nation

[38] http://www.colombiaespasion.com/VBeContent/home.asp

[39] The campaign slogan, however, did not resonate as well with some non-Colombians, see, Simon Jenkins, "Passion Alone Won't Rescue Colombia from its Narco-Economy Stigma," *The Guardian*, February 2, 2007; and Matt Moffett, "Colombia Wants the World to Recognize Its Passion: Latin American Nation Trots Out a New Slogan, Seeking to Rehabilitate Its Brand After Years of Violence and Corruption," *Wall Street Journal*, October 27, 2008.

[40] Silvia Marquine, "Nation Branding Campaigns in Latin America," Unpublished Masters Capstone Project, American University, May 2009; and Margarita Arango, "Colombian Nation Branding Campaign: Colombia is Passion," Unpublished Masters Capstone Project, American University, May 2008.

[41] Fiona Gilmore, "A Country – can it be repositioned? Spain – the success story of country branding," *Journal of Brand Management*, 9 (April 2002), p. 286.

branding campaigns to falter. "Gifted by Nature," for example, launched by Uganda in 2005 failed to take root. The initiative was funded by the USAID and designed by U.K.-based public relations firm Hill & Knowlton, but it lacked a domestic buy-in.[42] The importance of domestic stakeholders as the principal stakeholders in an initiative may represent the strategic linchpin in "policy-based branding," proposed by Simon Anholt. Anholt, a leading consultant on nation branding, spoke of the idea of "policy-based branding," in which a nation focuses on changing and implementing policies that can help create a stronger, more positive national appeal than simply nation branding.[43]

Media Relations

Media relations are another form of information initiatives. Here one could view the relationship between the political entity and the media as a form of stakeholder engagement, as both have a stake in disseminating information. The political entity is seeking to get the information out, or have its story told. Members of the media, in turn, want access to information so that they can get their story out. Lower levels of engagement focus more on information dissemination, such as writing and issuing press releases or holding press briefings. Cultivating personal relations through lunches or social functions, providing leads, access to sources, and accurate and timely information are all ways to increase engagement. The stronger and more positive the engagement with the foreign media, the more likely the political entity is to have its perspective reflected in their news reports. A particularly innovative approach to media relations was developed by the press secretary and spokesperson of the Embassy of Finland in Washington. He used the sauna housed in the embassy basement to host much coveted informal gatherings of prominent journalists and politicians.[44]

It is important to note that media relations can differ dramatically across countries. According to Katerina Tsetsura who is conducting a

---

[42] "Tourism Promoters Reject Uganda's "Gifted By Nature" Brand." All Africa.com, March 17, 2009. (http://www.eturbonews.com); Western PR Company to Sell Uganda, BBC News, May 19, 2005.

[43] Simon Anholt, "The Importance of National Reputation," *Engagement: Public Diplomacy* (UK: Foreign Commonwealth Office, July 2008).

[44] Jason Horowitz, "At Finnish Embassy, the Heat Is On," *Washington Post*, March 18, 2010.

global study of media practices, in an overwhelming number of countries, monetary payment, "subsidies," or gifts are often expected in exchange for favorable media coverage.[45] In other countries, extensive late night dining and socializing may be the norm for cultivating strong media relations. Sriramesh's personal influence model was built on strong and highly personalized relations with members of the local media.[46] Other countries such as the United States have strict codes of journalism ethics that restrict certain practices. With such variance, public diplomats need to be alert to such differences as well as their potential implications for official diplomatic relations.

It is also important to note that creating a mass media venture such as a new radio or television station would perhaps be a lower level of stakeholder engagement with foreign publics than relying on the indigenous mass media outlets which that public habitually uses. The reason goes back to sponsor control-stakeholder engagement equation: the lower the level of sponsor control, the higher the level of engagement. Possible ranking of stakeholder media outlets: highest engagement would be securing coverage by an indigenous media outlet (least control over information by sponsor); helping to establish an indigenous media outlet (some control over information, stakeholder contribution); establishing a media outlet (greatest control over information).

Relational Initiatives

Relational initiatives focus on relationship strategies, coordination, interaction with publics, use of interactive and interpersonal communication channels, and sustainability.[47]

Relational initiatives stress participation over presentation. Stakeholder engagement is evident on several levels and parallels the sophistication of relationship-building strategies in the initiatives. For example, the level of participation, or number of stakeholders, can range from a limited involvement of pre-selected individuals for a

---

[45] Katerina Tsetsura and Dean Kruckeberg, *Transparency, Public Relations and Mass Media: Combating Media Bribery Worldwide* (Routledge, forthcoming).

[46] Krishnamurthy Sriramesh "Societal Culture and Public Relations: Ethnographic Evidence from India," *Public Relations Review* 18, 2 (1992), pp. 201–211.

[47] Zaharna, *Battles to Bridges*, pp. 146–152.

pre-defined time period to institutional involvement over an open-ended time horizon. Ideally, a relational approach adopted by the leadership of a political entity would span across all levels of engagement from the leaders, to officials, to specialized publics, to institutions, to the general public. At the leadership level, stakeholders may be described as "partners," while general publics may be viewed as participants or even constituencies instead of the more passive, anonymous mass "audience."

Another aspect of relational initiatives is the degree of coordination or involvement a sponsor has with the stakeholders. In information initiatives the sponsor is responsible for the research, planning, design, implementation and evaluation of a public diplomacy initiative. In relational initiatives, sponsors may engage stakeholders in decision-making throughout the process. Stakeholders who invest early or heavily in a program often tend to feel a sense of ownership in the program, including the initiative's success. A distinct benefit of having in-country stakeholders involved in the program design and implementation is that they can provide valuable cultural knowledge and local connections that foreign sponsors may lack. While there are several levels and types of relational initiatives, relationship-building campaigns provide a window into stakeholder engagement.

Relationship-Building Campaigns

Similar to information campaigns, relationship-building campaigns can have a predefined campaign goal, set time frame, specific public, and entail research, planning, implementation, and evaluation, or follow-up assessments. However, the primary goal is to build relationships with publics, rather than disseminate information to publics or enhance a country's image. A campaign that stresses other motives over relationship-building may lessen the initiative's relational value for stakeholders. Campaigns that stress relationship-building tend to involve a high degree of coordination or stakeholder involvement, even team work to successfully design and execute a campaign. The campaign would begin by developing partnerships with co-sponsors in the host country, then actively designing and developing campaign goals and strategies together. Such campaigns often feature participation or stakeholder engagement across several levels, ranging from high level officials to the general public. Finally, campaign effectiveness is more aptly gauged by relationship strength and expansion, rather than opinion surveys.[48] Successful relational initiatives appear to exhibit more extensive and intensive interaction among publics or stakeholders with greater perceived satisfaction among the parties.

An example of a relationship-building campaign is the British Foreign Commonwealth Office (FCO) initiative *Think UK*, conducted in China from April 2003 to January 2004.[49] The "relationship-building campaign," as the FCO described it, was initiated in response to poor perceptions of the U.K. in China and recognition of China's growing influence. The purpose of the campaign was to provide greater access to innovative and creative ideas from contemporary Britain. In this respect, the campaign rationale and goal appeared to be prompted more by unilateral promotion than shared interests. Nevertheless, other campaign elements heavily stressed stakeholder engagement across several levels. At the level of planning and implementation, the campaign activities were developed through the coordination of more than one hundred Chinese and U.K. partner organizations working together. The thirty plus in-country events featured British and Chinese scientists, sculptors and writers teaming up for public concerts, exhibitions, competitions and discussion forums that actively engaged the Chinese public. The campaign illustrated the difference between "passive engagement" such as viewing a cultural exhibit, and "active engagement" in which the public actually assisted in an art installation. For example, one of the most popular events featured a prominent British sculptor working with villagers in southern China to create a sculpture garden of more than 100,000 palm-size figures made from clay indigenous to the region. The then Prime Minister Tony Blair toured the sculpture garden during his visit to China for the opening of the campaign. This one event illustrates the multiple levels of stakeholder engagement, from the leadership to the public. Other events included a robot design competition and interactive interior design challenge. The highly participatory and imaginative public events received extensive coverage by the Chinese media and formed

[48] The "mixed" results of the Think UK campaign may be because officials sought to use public opinion polls as measurement tools.

[49] Think UK, Final Report, Foreign & Commonwealth Office and British Council, London, February 2004; ThinkUKFinal_ReportFebruary2004.pdf.

the basis of a Chinese television series "U.K.-China Challenge." Developing strong in-country media relations and relying on the local media is an important relational activity that offers other dividends long after a campaign is completed. A final critical note that speaks volumes about a sponsor's commitment to its stakeholders was Britain's decision to adhere to the campaign's time schedule and events even when, just as the campaign was due to launch, China was hit by SARS flu epidemic.

Although not specifically labeled a relationship-building campaign, a fairly recent cultural and language initiative by Turkey contains several creative features of stakeholder engagement. The innovative initiative is not a new institute, but rather an annual language Olympics. According to its website, the International Turkish Language Olympics (*Uluslararasi Türkçe Olimpiyatlari*) are "designed to bridge people from all over the world on the common denominator of spoken and written Turkish and contribute to the unity, love and peaceful understanding among world countries (www.turkceolimpiyatlari.org). The 10-day event brings students of the Turkish language to Ankara from around the world to participate in poetry, song, drama, dance and grammar competitions. The Olympics is organized by the Turkish Education Association in collaboration with the Government of Turkey, the Ministry or National Education, the Turkish Language Authority, Turkish History Authority and host of Turkish business sponsors, including the Turkish airlines which provide transportation for the contestants. Immediately evident is the domestic stakeholder engagement that spans, at a fairly high level, both public-private sectors.

Participation has grown from an initial representation of 62 students from 17 countries in 2003, to 750 students from 120 countries in 2010. In the 2008 Olympics, not only do some students wear their traditional dress of their home country during the competitions held before the public, there is also a special cultural exhibition in which participants from each country introduce their respective cultures to the Turkish people. Over 200,000 people attended the cultural exhibition. Some of the event activities were held in various provinces around Turkey, while the competition finals were broadcast live nationally. Turkish celebrities helped coach the students before their broadcast performance and the public helped vote on the winners. The Turkish Prime Minister and Parliament Speaker participated in the award ceremony, which was broadcast live. Among the Turkish Language Olympics medal winners were students from Mozambique, Indonesia, Papua New Guinea, Mongolia, Vietnam, Cameroon, and Ghana. Although the initiative was controlled by the sponsor, it featured domestic engagement across the public and private sectors, interaction between domestic and foreign stakeholders, mutual learning and exchanges, had several layers of stakeholder involvement, and rested upon a global network of language teachers and learners.

Networking Initiatives

Networking initiatives – both non-policy and policy networking schemas – entail the most sophisticated, and indeed most challenging level of stakeholder engagement for a political entity. The relative sophistication as well as the challenge stems from the basic premise that the clearest sign of a successful networking initiative is when the stakeholders take over responsibility for engagement from the sponsor. The sponsor provides the initial platform for stakeholders to engage, assists in the initial weaving of the network, and then, yields control so that the network can grow and flourish.[50]

Stakeholder engagement occurs across the three dimensions of the network communication approach: network structure, network synergy and network strategy.[51] In terms of network structure, the network structure of stakeholder engagement allows for an efficient flow of information among members. Network synergy stems from the internal and external relationship building activities as well as the incorporation of diversity. Finally, network strategy is the process of using information to co-create shared identity and master narratives. As can be seen in the cases, the stakeholders in these initiatives would tend to be similar to the catalysts (described earlier by Edelman) who are experienced at building and nurturing virtual communities around their core interests. The following examples highlight stakeholder engagement in non-policy and policy networking schemas.

Cultural-Education Network

Many countries have established cultural institutes. The overwhelming majority of these institutes are stand-alone facilities. China's Confucius

---

[50] For discussion and examples of public diplomats "weaving" networks, see, Ali Fisher, Mapping the Great Beyond: Identifying Meaningful Networks in Public Diplomacy, USC Center for Public Diplomacy, Paper 2 (April) 2010.

[51] Zaharna, *Battles to Bridges*, pp. 92–114.

Institutes are unique in that they not only partner with host institutions, but are interwoven together in a way that resembles a non-policy networking schema. As such, the entire initiative as well as the individual institutes have strong stakeholder engagement features. The Institute, headquartered in Beijing and sponsored by China's National Office for Teaching Chinese as a Foreign Language (NOCFL, or Hanban), has grown from 1 pilot institute in 2004 to more than 256 institutes in 81 countries by March 2009.[52] However, more important than the numbers of the individual institutes is the interlocking network working strategy that underlies the initiative's conception and design. Unlike other cultural institutes that are individually and independently planted in a foreign country, the Confucius Institutes are grafted into the local cultural setting through their partnerships with prominent indigenous educational institutions. The Confucius Institute in Britain, for example, is housed in the London School of Economics and paired with Qinghau University in Beijing.[53] In terms of stakeholder engagement, such partnerships represent a higher level of coordination and commitment than independent cultural institutes and provide important platforms direct interpersonal communication. The collaboration and cooperation efforts and activities also represent a bonding feature for sustained stakeholder engagement.[54]

The foreign-located Institutes are not only linked with a Chinese academic institute, all the institutes are linked to the Beijing headquarters. This headquarter, in effect, becomes a network hub, which in turn, serves as an indirect link for all other Confucius Institutes around the world to connect with each other.[55] In 2006, Beijing headquarters began hosting its annual Confucius Institute Conference for current and prospective Institutes. The conference not only gives delegates the opportunity to meet like-minded others, share experiences, and

---

[52] "Ministry of Education, Hanban talking about the development of the Confucius Institute." March 15, 2009. http://www.gov.cn/gzdt/2009-03/15/content_1260011.htm

[53] Purnendra Jain and Gerry Groot, "Beijing's 'soft power' Offensive," *Asia Times* Online, May, 17, 2006.

[54] Although not usually mentioned in discussions of Confucius Institute, China's scholarship programs and expansion of student visas for study in China can be viewed as an important corollary reinforcing mechanism that adds to the pragmatic appeal and sustainability of the Institute initiative.

[55] One of the features of the network communication approach is the potential for synergy drawn from all the various Institutes operating in different cultures around the world. Innovations and techniques learned in one location can be circulated throughout the network.

exchange ideas, it represents the addition of direct interpersonal communication to global stakeholder engagement process.

Probing deeper into the official Confucius network is the unofficial networks that have been created by the students in the institutes. The patterned distribution of Confucius Institutes does not appear to be random, and, the informal student networks and the students' use of social media take on particular significance. In 2006, Sheng Ding and Robert Saunders drew attention to an early pattern of distribution based on political ideology, specifically Western liberal democracies (US, UK, Canada, Australia, and New Zealand France, Italy, German, Sweden, Belgium).[56] The distribution of Institutes also appears strongly weighted in China's regional sphere (Korea, Japan, Thailand, Philippines, Bangladesh, and India). Both of these distribution patterns allow for stakeholders to find commonality among themselves, perhaps even more so than with their Beijing sponsor.[57] This commonality, combined with the relative tech-savvy nature of the students of these countries, is fertile ground for a student-generated global network of catalysts, which has indeed sprung up. Students have started Facebook pages for "their" Confucius Institute - and are easily found and linked with their fellow institutes. Other students, such as those at the Michigan State University's Confucius Institute, have created an educational island for learners of Chinese in the virtual world of Second Life. Chinese officials appear to have realized the importance of online presence and social networking potential of the Institute for today's digital generation. Beijing quickly established a Confucius Institute Online in English and Chinese, which provides lists of Confucius Institutes around the world, by region, country, and specific academic institution.[58] The site is highly interactive, containing Chinese podcast lessons, a resource pool as well as cultural features. Undoubtedly the students are likely to expand the site as a social forum. Graduates may well develop a Confucius Institute alumni network to

---

[56] Sheng Ding and Robert Saunders, "Talking Up China: An analysis of China's Rising Cultural Power and Global Promotion of the Chinese Language," *East Asia*, 23, (Summer 2006) p. 22

[57] The foreign students represent an interesting blurring of stakeholder internal-external boundaries. On one level the students are external stakeholders whom Chinese public diplomacy is trying to reach and engage. On another level, as members of their own self-generated social network of student enrolled in Confucius Institutes, the students become very close to being internal stakeholders of Chinese public diplomacy and augment the government's efforts to reach out to other students.

[58] Confucius Institute Online http://www.confuciusinstitute.net/

draw upon after they finish their studies and utilize it as a type of *guanxi* throughout their professional careers.

Non-political Networking Schema

Non-political networking schema are public diplomacy initiatives that seek to link citizens or institutions together in a network so that they can work together on non-political issues such as science, medicine, education, or environmental issues.[59] Although networks have gained increasing prominence for their efficient information-sharing organizational structures, networks are fundamentally relationship structures. Robust networks tend to have what Krebs and Holley call a "network weaver," who creates links with other members and thus expands the network: "The network weaver catalyzes interaction in complex human systems via introductions, collaborations, mentoring, creating new partnerships, clusters, innovations and economic activities."[60] In non-political networking schemes, public diplomacy officers are essentially network weavers who build relationships between like-minded individuals or institutions.[61]

An example of a non-political networking scheme is the UK Science and Innovation Network (SIN) launched by the British FCO in 2000.[62] SIN seeks to integrate science and diplomacy on the international stage. "Making science central to diplomacy is vital," for confronting challenges such as climate change, energy security, and global pandemics said the then British Foreign Secretary Jack Straw. The initiative consists of a network of SIN attachés in nearly thirty countries who are continuously monitoring scientific developments and opportunities in their assigned countries for scientific collaboration on major

---

[59] Naturally, political sponsors may have a strong, underlying political agenda for initiating a network around science, medicine, sports, or the arts. Advocates of cultural and arts diplomacy have long argued that part of the effectiveness of these vehicles for engagement is because they are perceived as not overtly political. I am using the term "non-political" here in contrast with policy formation networks in which political agendas are explicitly articulated and advanced.

[60] Valdis Krebs and June Holley, "Building Smart Communities through Network Weaving," *Orgnet.com* (2002), www.orgnet.com/BuildingNetworks.pdf.

[61] For discussion and examples of public diplomats weaving a network, see, Ali Fisher, Mapping the Great Beyond: Identifying Meaningful Networks in Public Diplomacy, USC Center for Public Diplomacy, Paper 2 (April) 2010.

[62] Foreign & Commonwealth Office, "Science and Innovation Network, Science & Innovation Annual Report," (July 2006), www.fco.gov.uk/science (accessed April 28, 2007).

projects and research and then facilitating those links. These SIN attachés represent a new breed of public diplomacy network weavers. A special feature of the country-specific research collaboration is that they are "bottom up," meaning that the researchers determine the direction and topics. Such collaboration, like the nature of scientific research, is long term. Relational and networking initiatives tend to focus on establishing interactive communication channels, and then seeking ways to enhance, facilitate or expand those channels. For example, a British Council initiative for young scientists found that periodic face-to-face contact between collaborators was important for sustaining the relationships, and thus sponsored visits and forums for the participants to meet their counterparts.

Policy Formation Network

A final example of stakeholder engagement is found in policy formation networks.[63] Brian Hocking spoke about the growing symbiosis between state and non-state activities as "catalytic diplomacy," in which political entities act in coalitions rather than relying on their individual resources.[64] Shaun Riordan called it "dialogue-based public diplomacy," which he said constitutes a new collaborative foreign policy paradigm.[65] In his catalytic model, Hockings describes the diplomat as "manager, co-coordinator, and integrator".[66] These tasks are very similar to the network weaver's tasks.

Canada and Norway stand out in this diplomatic area of relationship and network-building.[67] Alan Henrikson described Canadian and

---

[63] For more comprehensive discussion, see, Zaharna, "The Soft Power Differential: Network Communication and Mass Communication in Battles to Bridges, pp. 92–112.

[64] Brian Hocking, "Catalytic Diplomacy: Beyond 'Newness' and 'Decline,'" in Jan Melissen (ed.) *Innovation in Diplomatic Practice*, (Basingstoke: Palgrave Macmillan, 1999).

[65] Shaun Riordan, "Dialogue-based Public Diplomacy: A new Foreign Policy Paradigm?" Discussion Papers in Diplomacy, Netherlands Institute of International Relations Clingendael, November 2004.

[66] Brian Hocking, "Catalytic Diplomacy."

[67] See, Evan H. Potter, "Canada and the New Public Diplomacy," Clingendael Discussion Paper in Diplomacy 81, The Hague, Clingendael Institute, July 2002; and Alan Henrikson, "Niche Diplomacy in the World Public Arena: The Global 'Corners' of Canada and Norway", in Jan Melissen (ed.), *The New Public Diplomacy: Soft Power in International Relations* (Basingstoke: Palgrave) pp. 67–82.

Norwegian officials and diplomacy as "master networkers."[68] Among the most prominent case examples is that of the Canadian foreign minister Lloyd Axworthy. Axworthy teamed with Jodi Williams of the International Campaign to Ban Landmines (ICBL) to lead the "Ottawa Process" that help secure ratification of the landmine treaty in an astonishing 18 months by networking and coordinating with other state and nonstate actors. Relationship-building occurred internally to solidify dynamic teams within organizations and externally with coalition partners to form a multi-stakeholder network. The adoption and use of technology emphasized information sharing, connectivity and interactivity. The importance of credibility is seen in the way the network handled information. Williams described the Ottawa Process as a "new model of diplomacy … that makes smaller and mid-size countries working together with civil society a potential superpower."[69] In 1997, Jodi Williams and the ICBL were awarded the Nobel Peace prize. Other examples include the treaty establishing the International Criminal Court[70] and the Kimberly Process that help restrict the trade in conflict or blood diamonds.[71]

Conclusion: The Challenges of Strategic Stakeholder Engagement

Throughout this piece I have avoided using the term strategic to describe any type of stakeholder and engagement. For, like communication itself, there are too many variations and being strategic depends on the context, purpose, and goal. The brief survey of initiatives does highlight several challenges for public diplomats.

An initial challenge is identifying potential stakeholders. Who or which groups have a potential stake by a public diplomacy initiative? Public diplomats need to think carefully about the full spectrum of stakeholders, domestic as well as foreign.[72] As was seen earlier, and

---

[68] Henrikson, "Niche Diplomacy in the World Public Arena," p. 70.

[69] Jody Williams, 1997 Nobel Lecture, December 10, 1997. [www.wagingpeace.org/articles/nobel_lecture_97_williams.html]

[70] David Davenport, "The New Diplomacy," Policy Review, 116 (December 2002/January 2003), pp. 17–31.

[71] Brian Hocking, "Diplomacy: New Agendas and Changing Strategies," *iMP Magazine* (July 2001). http://www.usip.org/virtualdiplomacy/publications/reports/14b.html.

[72] U.S. public diplomacy, as stipulated in the Smith-Mundt Act of 1948 explicitly assumes a separation of domestic and foreign publics, and even exclusion of the U.S. domestic public from U.S. public diplomacy activities intended for foreign audiences.

particularly in the case of nation branding, strong domestic stakeholder engagement can be pivotal to successful initiatives. Conversely, weak or absent domestic stakeholder engagement can cause an initiative to falter. When it comes to identifying foreign stakeholders, public diplomats need to be as nuanced about individual stakeholders and groups abroad as they are at home. Foreign stakeholders cannot be ignored or lumped together. Public diplomats need to move beyond the generalized notion of communicating with "the public" or "target audiences," or "elites" and "masses." They also need familiarity with the political, social and economic terrain to identify important stakeholder groups and their variations within a particular country or region. Identifying faith-based or religious stakeholders may not be as straightforward or as easy as it at first glance.

After identifying potential stakeholders, public diplomats must assess the specific needs or interests which might prompt or sustain stakeholder engagement. Why would a stakeholder group benefit specifically, concretely, or even eventually from a particular public diplomacy initiative? Does the initiative have enough significance for sustained stakeholder engagement? The more an initiative resonates with shared and specific interests and goals of stakeholders, the more stakeholders will be drawn into an initiative. Listening and dialogue appear to be a prerequisite for being able to identify stakeholders and verify their specific interests in initiative.

Public diplomats must also assess the potential level and type of engagement for each stakeholder. For most stakeholders, the level of interest may parallel the level of engagement, but not always. Not all stakeholders have the potential to engage extensively in an initiative. In some settings, a public diplomat may find a high level of stakeholder interest, such as an empowerment program. However, the level of actual engagement may be unexpectedly low. The public diplomat may need to be creative in finding suitable channels for engagement, such as a local social institution rather than foreign office, or even bring in another stakeholder group to serve as a bridge for engagement. A public diplomat can also be creative in terms of selecting different vehicles for engagement, such as culture, sports, science or medicine.

Many other countries tend to assume that the domestic public is an intregal part of the country's overall efforts to enhance their national image both at home and abroad.

The public diplomat may also select a public diplomacy initiative that has a lower level of engagement to stimulate interest or provide a stepping stone for initiating stakeholder engagement. As was seen in the examples, not all public diplomacy initiatives require a high or sustained level of stakeholder engagement. Public diplomats must match level of stakeholder engagement with the goals of the public diplomacy initiative. The level of engagement tends to vary with the amount of control a sponsor has over the initiative; strong control tends to result in lower levels of stakeholder engagement. For example, contrast the degree of sponsor control in information broadcasts versus networking schemas. If retaining control over an initiative (or message) is an important goal, a public diplomat may seek to limit engagement. Open source initiatives, such as that proposed by Ali Fisher, require yielding significant control and thus may only be suitable for some types of stakeholders or initiatives.[73]

It may be particularly important to assess the potential for engagement among influential elites, opinion leaders and catalysts. These stakeholder groups have different interests and their engagement impact the initiative differently. Catalytic stakeholders eager for change may have a higher potential level of engagement than elite stakeholders. They may be early adopters or active participants in a sponsored initiative, but only have minimal influence on the wider public. However, elites may have a higher impact even with modest levels of engagement than catalysts. As Fisher pointed out in his piece on power, influential elites may be well positioned to impact the larger public.[74] However, their proximity to power tends to put their interests close to the leadership status quo and thus may require more sophisticated strategies and even continuous attention to retain a high level of engagement if the public diplomacy initiative is counter to the prevailing status quo.[75] Controversial initiatives may be more appealing to the catalysts, a sector of stakeholders that correspond to Fisher's power position on the peripheral. Designing a strategic stakeholder

---

[73] Ali Fisher, "Music for the Jilted Generation: Open Source Public Diplomacy," *The Hague Journal of Diploamcy*, 3 (2008), pp. 1–24.

[74] Ali Fisher, "Looking at the man in the mirror, understanding of power and influence in public diplomacy," *Trials of Engagement*, pp 271–295.

[75] For discussion of external and internal influence models see, Helmut Anheier, Hagai Katz and Marcus Lam, "Diffusion Models and Global Civil Society," in Martin Albrow, Helmut Anheier, Marlies Cglasius, Monroe E. Price, Mary Kaldor (Eds.) *Global Civil Society* 2007/8 (Los Angeles, CA: Sage, 2008) (Available online, Centre for the Study of Global Governance, LSE, USC).

engagement for catalysts would more likely involve finding a spark (motivating interest) and platform for high-level engagement.

Finally, initiatives built around a political entity's "core competence" are likely to be perceived by potential stakeholders as the most credible. Higher perceived credibility is likely to translate into stronger drawing power for a greater number of stakeholders as well as higher levels of stakeholder engagement. Core competence underlies the credibility of cultural institutes. Alliance Française or Goethe Institut may be viewed as prime authoritative sources respectively for learning about the French or German culture and language. Core competence also appears to be especially critical for sparking catalysts to join strategic stakeholder initiatives.

While this chapter offers a rough sketch of emerging best practices of strategic stakeholder engagement in public diplomacy, public diplomats can be aided by much needed research in several areas. This review has focused on the positive examples. Further research on the difficulties of stakeholder engagement is critical. Hocking touched on an area that is likely to receive increased attention as stakeholder engagement gains prominence, namely, the murky area of expectations and "rules of engagement."[76] Whereas traditional diplomacy has greatly been aided by established protocols and conventions, public diplomacy has yet to develop a shared language of interaction. The absence of rules or even norms makes the area of conflict mediation and management among stakeholders pressing research concern.

The potential for stakeholder conflict appears conspicuously absent in public diplomacy discussions. As mentioned in the chapter opening, both U.K. and U.S. public diplomacy assumed that the stakeholders are domestic and share the government's goals. A 2009 professional workshop for senior Italian diplomats spoke of foreign stakeholders, but assumed a shared goal.[77] The narrow inclusion of allied or advocacy stakeholders is dangerous and hints at some of the

[76] Brian Hocking, "Multistakeholder Diplomacy: Foundations, Forms, Functions and Frustrations," International Conference on Multistakeholder Diplomacy, Malta, February 11–13, 2005.

[77] Professional workshop organized by FERPI (Italian federation of public relations) and the Instituto Diplomatico of the Italian Ministry of Foreign Affairs for 25 senior Italian diplomats described public diplomacy as "a new approach for governing effective relationships with foreign stakeholder communities to reinforce the identity of Italy." http://www.prconversations.com/wp-content/uploads/2009/02/english_program.pdf

underlying failings of recent public diplomacy initiatives. Having a "stake" or vested interest in a public diplomacy initiative may be critical for identifying potential stakeholders, but the public diplomat must carefully identify the direction (positive or negative) as well as intensity (weak or strong) of that interest. Not all those with a potential stake in a public diplomacy initiative may be favorably disposed. Public diplomats need to be particularly alert to stakeholders who may be threatened by an initiative or have a vested interest in the failure of the initiative. Collin Irwin, in his study of peace negotiations, raised the importance to "adversarial stakeholders" in determining the success and failures in initiatives.[78] Much work is needed to develop effective engagement strategies for adversarial stakeholders. To dismiss or try to ignore such stakeholders may drain a sponsor's credibility in the eyes of publics who do not see such stakeholders as adversarial or threatening. Additionally, being able to engage adversarial stakeholders may give legitimacy to a controversial initiative and dissuade others who might sabotage the initiative. Public diplomats need to be alert in identifying *all* parties that might be impacted by an initiative – positively as well as negatively – and include both in their plan of stakeholder engagement.

The potential for stakeholder conflict represents an ever present challenge for public diplomats even with stakeholder who do share an entity's goals. The stakeholder dispute may be over the means to achieve the goal or specific aspects of the goal rather than the goal itself. Calls for more dialogue and exchange programs tend to suggest only positive outcomes and downplay problems of bringing stakeholders of diverse values, beliefs and backgrounds together. As long noted in psychologist Gordon Allport's 1954 "contact theory," positive interaction between divergent groups tends to occur under specific circumstances.[79] Perhaps counter-intuitively, dialogue can be particularly problematic.[80] Much research is needed to explore the various

[78] Colin Irwin "Research Ethic and Peacemaking," in Donna M. Mertens and Pauline E. Ginsberg (eds.) *Handbook of Social Research Ethics* (Sage, 2008), pp. 259–276.

[79] For discussion of contact theory in public diplomacy, see, Geoffrey Cowan and Amelia Arsenault, "Moving from Monologue to Dialogue to Collaboration: The Three Layers of Public Diplomacy," *The ANNALS of the American Academy of Political and Social Science*, 618 (2008), pp. 20–21.

[80] Scott Hammond, Rob Anderson, and Kenneth N. Cissna, "The Problematics of Dialogue and Power," in Pamela J. Kalbfleisch (ed.) *Communication Yearbook 27* (London: Lawrence Erlbaum, 2003), pp. 125–157.

conditions that distinguish positive and sustained engagement from that which is unexpectedly negative and short lived. A related difficulty for public diplomats is when different stakeholder groups present competing claims or expectations on a single sponsor. This complication can be seen in the shadow that the Israeli-Palestinian conflict casts over US public diplomacy initiatives in the Middle East. Identifying specific areas and strategies for conflict management among stakeholders represents a much needed avenue of research in public diplomacy.

Stakeholder engagement is becoming the new norm in public diplomacy. As the use of social media deepens and relational and networking strategies become more sophisticated, *strategic* stakeholder engagement will become a distinguishing feature of effective public diplomacy initiatives that seek to involve the public. Strategic stakeholder engagement rests on aligning the right type of stakeholders with the right level of engagement with the goal of the public diplomacy initiative. As is hopefully evident, much work is still need to identify the different types of stakeholders as well as the levels of engagement in order to determine who are really the "strategic stakeholders" and what is "strategic engagement." While scholars can offer points of cross-fertilization from other fields, it is likely that much more of the refinement will come from the trials – both cases and challenges – of public diplomats working to put into practice strategic stakeholder engagement.

SKILLS OF THE PUBLIC DIPLOMAT: LANGUAGE, NARRATIVE AND ALLEGIANCE

Biljana Scott

Introduction

What are the skills required of a public diplomat? Since public diplomacy is an umbrella term which involves countless practices and players, this question may appear impossibly broad. Surely the answer is "horses for courses": the wider the skill set and more diverse the gene pool, the better. This paper argues, however, that if there is a single overriding accomplishment that all public diplomats should hone, it is language awareness. More particularly, they should pursue (1) a mastery of language and rhetoric, (2) an aptitude for narrative, both with regard to its creation and interpretation, and (3) a heightened awareness of the elements that contribute to allegiance, as well as an awareness of the influence of language and narrative on the positioning and repositioning of allegiance. These skills contribute significantly to the most valuable asset in public diplomacy – credibility.

Profile and problem

The public diplomat, as characterised in existing literature, is a cross between a Boy's Own derring-do hero, a Renaissance man, a Nietzschian Übermensch, a futuristic transhumanist, and a minister plenipotentiary. Given this characterisation, we should all aspire to be public diplomats.

Shaun Riordan, in "Practitioners as PD Entrepreneurs",[1] envisages the future diplomat as a travelling entrepreneur, laptop and mobile in hand, roaming around looking for networking opportunities and keeping in touch with a greatly trimmed-down embassy. Foremost

[1] Shaun Riordan, "Dialogue-based Public Diplomacy: a New Foreign Policy Paradigm?" *Clingendael Discussion Papers in Diplomacy*, Number 95, November 2004, http://www.clingendael.nl/publications/2004/20041100_cli_paper_dip_issue95.pdf (accessed) 10 October 2010.

among the revolutionary changes he envisages is a willingness to take risks and go off-message:

> Diplomats will continue to have an important role in engaging political elites, in many cases including key journalists and commentators. To do so they will need to be more open and willing to go "off-message" and to engage in genuine dialogue and debate… To perform this role successfully, they will need to be encouraged to, and rewarded for, taking risks.[2]

Daryl Copeland provides a particularly colourful portrait of the skills and attributes required of the future public diplomat,[3] whom he characterises as a new age polymath, a versatile guerrilla fighter, and more:

> The perfectly formed public diplomat, then, should combine the skills of a professional negotiator with the attributes of a renaissance humanist and the temperament of a hardy handyman. For the public diplomat, developing a capacity for something referred to in French as "*aisance*", a combination of personal and social comfort and ease, is crucial. And whether nurtured in university or developed in the field, nothing in public diplomacy has greater utility than having learned how to think (reflection, analysis and praxis), communicate persuasively and act effectively.[4]

In the same volume, Alex Evans and David Steven suggest that "The new public diplomat should therefore not be seen as a particular *kind* of diplomat, but rather, simply, as *tomorrow's* diplomat", who is best characterised by an investment mindset:

> Instead of behaving like a bank manager – with a large portfolio, low-risk appetite and a desire for incremental returns – the new public diplomat acts like a venture capitalist, focusing on a smaller portfolio, tolerating risk and aspiring to achieve transformational change.[5]

However attractive this new breed of diplomat may appear, two problems arise. The first is the impractical vagueness of the skill sets, which are more rousingly hyperbolic than readily applicable or measurable. Moreover, many of these skills (thinking, acting effectively,

---

[2] Riordan, "Dialogue-based Public Diplomacy", pp. 14–15.

[3] Daryl Copeland, "No dangling conversation: portrait of the public diplomat" in J. Welsh and D. Fearn (eds.), *Engagement: Public Diplomacy in a Globalised World* (Foreign and Commonwealth Office, 2008), http://www.fco.gov.uk/en/about-the-fco/publications/publications/pd-publication/dangling-conversation.

[4] Copeland, "No dangling conversation", pp. 141–142.

[5] Alex Evans and David Steven, "Towards a theory of influence for twenty-first-century foreign policy: public diplomacy in a globalised world," in Welsh and Fearn (eds.), *Engagement*.

communicating persuasively) are the minimum requirements of any white-collar worker. By what criteria are persuasiveness and effectiveness to be measured and how is one to evaluate (and *who* is to evaluate) the cost and gain of the risks advocated above?

The second problem is the plethora of conflicting messages likely to emerge on a stage where players write their own scripts, improvising as they go along. Cohesion is put at risk, as is credibility and with it, integrity. Where there are many voices, each hawking its own story, which one should we listen to, and which one should we trust? In so far as the public diplomat is concerned with stories, how can he ensure not just an audience but a loyal audience? These questions raise the "paradox of plenty" and the theory of influence.[6]

Information has traditionally been linked with power on the grounds that where information is a scarce resource, those in possession of it are at an advantage. In the wake of the communication revolution, however, information is readily available. The scarce resource is now attention, and it is this dearth of attention arising from a glut of information which is referred to as the "paradox of plenty". Today the people who wield power are those who are able to capture our attention. According to Joseph Nye, politics in an information age can therefore be seen as a "contest of competitive credibility", one in which success is measured by "whose story wins".[7]

The paradox of plenty not only begs the question of how one ensures a winning story but exposes the underlying assumption that stories are necessarily in competition with each other.[8] This view is embodied in common expressions such as "the *battle*" or "*struggle* for minds and wills", and "*winning* hearts and minds". The approach and associated terminology fail to distinguish between competitive versus collaborative dimensions of public diplomacy; a "winning" story might well be a compelling one, rather than a victorious one. We could conceive of it as a narrative that draws its listeners into its sphere of influence through the gentler arts of rhetoric and persuasion. It accommodates other stories, even contradictory ones, within its embrace. It adapts as it unfolds,

---

[6] Joseph S. Nye, Jr., *Soft Power: The Means to Success in World Politics*. (Public Affairs, 2004), p.106.

[7] Ibid.

[8] Evans and Steven, in "Towards a theory of influence", ask "whether people are joining forces with us, or with other tribes."

rather than offering a fixed narrative which proclaims itself king of the castle after it has defeated all other contestants.

Collaborative public diplomacy would comply with Richard Rorty's belief in a plurality of standpoints whose acceptance and value is determined by their utility in the here and now,[9] whereas competitive public diplomacy presupposes a "final vocabulary" and a God's-eye viewpoint which is the "right" one and should rightfully win. The problem with the latter, apart from risk of violence, is the tendency towards entrenched beliefs. Voltaire subtly notes in *Candide* that when, after a battle "on the orders of the two kings, the *Te Deum* was being sung in both camps",[10] those with entrenched beliefs are more open to their own narrative than to the facts.

Language

What is the relationship between language and a "winning story"? In a word: rhetoric. The art of persuasion begins with a heightened awareness of the resources of language. To achieve desired objectives, those resources should fit the nature of the audience and the mood of the moment. I am tempted to say that the aim is to "win an audience over", but I shy away from the connotations of exclusive victory that the word "win" (if not the collocation "to win over") might trigger. The speaker's aim may be to convince the audience that we are not necessarily limited to a choice between competing stories; instead, we may opt for a superordinate, inclusive story, one which may indeed contain certain tensions and contradictions but makes a virtue of this negative capability.[11]

So "winning" in the sense of "winning against" is not at issue as much as "winning over".[12] This is precisely the kind of semantic

---

[9] Richard Rorty *Irony, Contingency and Solidarity*. (Cambridge UP, 1989).

[10] Voltaire, *Candide*, (London: Penguin, 2001), pp. 6–7, from the French "… les deux rois faisaient chanter des *Te Deum*, chacun dans son camp".

[11] John Keats coined and defined the term as follows: "Negative Capability, that is when man is capable of being in uncertainties, Mysteries, doubts without any irritable reaching after fact & reason", and believed that this quality "went to form a Man of Achievement, especially in literature". Letter to G and T Keats, 22 December 1817, in *The Complete Poetical Works of John Keats*, ed. Horace Elisha Scudder (Riverside Press, 1899), p. 277.

[12] One could of course argue that the superordinate story I advocate is an exclusive alternative and that, having won over the reader to adopting it, I have defeated the alternative view which sees stories in a competitive light.

distinction to which an orator – and a public diplomat – should be sensitive. He would also need to be sensitive to whether such a distinction is worth drawing out, depending on the sensibilities and expectations of the audience. Pedantic though many semantic distinctions may seem, they should not be underestimated since the actions ultimately adopted often depend not only on the choice of words but also on inferences drawn from the gaps between words.

Given the diversity of linguistic resources relevant to rhetoric, I shall limit discussion to four rhetorical devices: metaphor-cum-analogy, connotation, ambiguity, and irony. An example of metaphor and analogy has already been encountered in the descriptions of the public diplomat as a *venture capitalist* and a *guerrilla fighter*. These characterisations represent, as in the case of all metaphors, the "tip of a submerged model".[13] In these two examples, we find that although there are a number of common denominators, namely adaptability, resourcefulness, speed of response, and a certain risk-lust, the images that come to mind differ with regard to dress, tactics, terrain, and purpose.[14]

Although these metaphors and analogies advocate a new breed of public diplomat, description of a diplomat as a guerrilla fighter may create cognitive dissonance for many people. One of the aims of a diplomat, who is an official representative, is to promote peaceful relationships between countries, whereas the aims of a guerrilla fighter are to disrupt and antagonise the powers that be, primarily through violent action, to undermine their authority and wrest influence from them. Similarly, the image of a public diplomat as a venture capitalist may prove inappropriate for those who feel that the reputation and influence of a country should not be put at risk for uncertain returns. Responsibility and accountability, they would argue, must take precedence over the potentially reckless adventurism of the new-breed public diplomat.

The images conjured by metaphors may differ across cultures (professional and other) and across individuals. These differences determine whether a person buys into the worldview presented by a metaphor, which in turn further influences thought and action.

[13] Max Black, "More about Metaphor", in *Metaphor & Thought*, ed. Andrew Ortony (Cambridge University Press, 1993), p. 30.

[14] When I say "images", I refer to the power of metaphor (defined by Aristotle as "the application to one thing of the name belonging to another"), to convey an instant picture in the mind which we then spell out as and when needed.

Mastery of language therefore requires a firm grasp of the way in which a single word or phrase can carry an entire story. This is certainly true of metaphors, which can be thought of as stories in a capsule. Unpack a metaphor, and you find a rich web of connotations and entailments, all of which suggest a particular conceptual structure.[15]

Connotations can also influence perception and associated action. Their power is illustrated by the terms *global warming*, *climate change* and *climate security*. The term "global warming" has not proven credible to many people who, instead of experiencing a rise in local temperatures, have found that their summers are turning colder and wetter. If these people are to be persuade, the title must be changed to match the content of the story. This is one of the reasons for replacing "global warming" with "climate change", which does not set up any expectation regarding temperature. However, the term "change" does not suggest urgency—change has always taken place and always will. To insert the necessary note of urgency and relevance, the term "climate security" has recently been introduced. "Security", with the connotations of national security, portrays an immediate threat that affects us all and needs to be addressed in a concerted fashion.

Consider also the connotations of the terms "soft" and "hard" in relation to power. Much of the ambivalence surrounding the merits of soft power arise from conflicting connotations surrounding the term "soft". Soft is presented as morally strong. It is good, healthy, eco-friendly, and persuasive rather than coercive. It is evidence of "being in touch with one's feminine side". These connotations arise from collocations such as the following soft answer (good-tempered), soft-centred/hearted (kind), soft detergent (biodegradable), soft drink (non-alcoholic), soft landing (one without damage), soft sell (low-key but persuasive salesmanship), to soft pedal (use restraint), to soft-soap (persuade with flattery). Yet to some, "soft" connotes weakness and may even act as a provocation. This interpretation is corroborated by the following collocations: soft touch (gullible person, pushover), soft

---

[15] The literature on metaphor is extensive. A good introduction is George Lakoff, "Metaphor and War: The Metaphor System Used to Justify War in the Gulf," 1991, http://lists.village.virginia.edu/sixties/HTML_docs/Texts/Scholarly/Lakoff_Gulf_Metaphor_1.html (accessed 14 November 2008);

Susan Sontag, *Illness as Metaphor; AIDS and its Metaphors* (Penguin, 1991);

George Lakoff and Mark Johnson, *Metaphors We Live By* (University of Chicago Press, 1980).

option (the easier option, cop-out), soft subject (one lacking in intellectual rigor), to "go soft" or "be soft" (unmanly).

Similarly the adjective "hard", with its connotations of virility, physical strength, persistence and intransigence, is admirable to some but despicable to others. Critics deem the coercive "might is right" approach that "hard power" presupposes as uncivilized, unsophisticated, and unfit for the subtleties of present-day politics. This ambivalence over the terms soft and hard arises from the following ambiguity: whereas "soft" is physically weak but morally strong, "hard" is physically strong but, in our day and age, morally suspect if not outright immoral. Physical and moral strength are thus in conflict. In this context, it is unsurprising that "theory of influence" is increasingly replacing the term "soft power".

"Climate security" offers a further example of the way in which connotations and ambiguity frame issues. The term begs the question: security *for* whom and *against* what? Are we securing ourselves against climate change, a formulation which suggests that climate change is a given and that we need to adapt to the likely consequences? Or are we securing the climate against us, a formulation which prescribes a course of pre-emptive measures to mitigate the damage we are doing? How we fill in the relationship in this nominal compound between "climate" and "security" affects the policies that we promote. Securing ourselves against climate change entails an adaptation framework, whereas securing the climate against us entails a mitigation frame and associated course of action. A similar ambiguity is to be found in the nominal compound "public diplomacy": is it diplomacy "for" or "by" the public, or does some other relationship hold between the two words, and if so, how should it best be translated into languages whose structure does not give rise to such ambiguity? Even one-word terms, such as "power" are ambiguous between "power over" and "power to".

My final example of a rhetorical device relevant to the art of persuasion is irony. Irony is a notoriously risky resource for diplomats for three reasons: first, more than any other rhetorical device, irony depends on an implied innuendo rather than a stated message and therefore appeals to one's powers of inference; second, irony tends to carry a moral judgement; and third, irony tends to create a divide between an ingroup (those privy to the subtlety and moral position of the ironist) and an outgroup (those against whom the irony is directed).[17] With both moral judgement and divisive power, irony thus raises the issue of allegiance.

Voltaire's depiction of the *Te Deum* sung to God's glory on the orders of the two kings is illustrative. One must be sufficiently aware of cultural practices to recognise its significance, and this knowledge is not given but assumed. It is unlikely that after a battle both sides should be victorious (a draw or inconclusive outcome is nothing to write home – or sing to God – about), yet by having the *Te Deum* sung, each king is clearly laying claim to victory. The likelihood therefore is that at least one of the kings is deluding himself as to the results of the battle. Yet this probability is not made explicit; on the contrary, it is embedded in a subordinate clause which sounds like a throwaway remark. Subordinate it may be syntactically, but insignificant it certainly is not, since the ability of those in power to delude themselves and thereby mislead their people is no small concern. Voltaire ridicules the blind vanity of kings, as well as the blind *naiveté* of subjects such as Dr Pangloss and Candide, and invites his readers to join sides with him in doing so. At the same time, in the second-order subtlety of his ironical aside, he ridicules us, the reader, and anyone who thinks he can afford to dismiss the foibles of kings as inconsequential.

What lesson might be drawn here for the public diplomat? The Voltaire quote exemplifies the way in which a huge amount can be communicated through a minimum of words. In this case: cultural knowledge of the rituals of victory in a Christian context, the fallacious discrepancy between cause (victory) and effect (the *Te Deum*), the tendency towards self-delusion among those in power, the danger of not recognising this tendency and the consequences it wreaks (a Panglossian point of view), the danger of laughing off our own recognition of this danger as just part of a good read, and the possibility that a parody such as *Candide* might not just be a source of light entertainment but an important critique of the world. Voltaire, in cautioning us about the state of the world and our own liability, might be considered the ultimate public diplomat of the future. Rather than promote the interests of a nation-state, and rather than hector us about how we should think and act, he presents the interests of mankind

---

[17] For an overview of theories of irony, see Biljana Scott, "Picturing Irony: the subversive power of photography" in Theo Van Leuwen (ed.) *Visual Communication* (February 2004), 3:1, http://www.biscott.co.uk/publications/documents/irony.htm.

through a multi-level narrative that invites us to think both more comprehensively and more carefully in order to secure not just a better future, but a future at all.

Entailments, connotations, and implications are all instrumental in shaping perception and influencing action, but their presence is not always recognised, let alone their power. It is always more effective to involve interlocutors and have them come to desired conclusions through their own thoughts than to tell them directly what to think and do. To the extent that the public diplomat prefers dialogue over diktat yet nevertheless wishes to persuade others to join him, an essential skill to master is how to use metaphor and other rhetorical resources to influence an interlocutor's train of thought.

Narrative

Narrative has become a buzz-word in politics in the last few years and is well worth exploring as such.[18] It is also directly relevant to this paper, since the paradox of plenty puts the focus on narrative and credibility as the primary source of influence in an era characterised by an excess of information and a shortage of attention. The relevance of narrative to politics and diplomacy is readily demonstrated both by historical epics, such as Virgil's *Aeneid*, and by contemporary "political narratives". These are stories told about (and often self-promulgated by) a politician to capture the imagination, create coherence, provide momentum and direction and, if possible, a sense of destiny.

The Aeneid, commissioned by Augustus, was an obvious example of the retelling of history to better situate the Emperor as not just the legitimate heir but the destined Roman descendant of the original Trojan hero, Aeneas. This self-mythologising is not uncommon among leaders. Today in the USA, Barack Obama has presented himself as a "man of destiny" calling for a "politics of hope" and has suggested that the choices he has made "were never truly mine alone", inviting us to

---

[18] See for instance: Tristram Hunt, "Once upon a time, a man with a quiff… Why do all politicians now need a 'narrative'", *New Statesman*, 25 June 2001, http://www.newstatesman.com:80/200106250022; transcript of BBC Radio 4's Analysis, "Jackanory Politics," 21 February 2008 http://news.bbc.co.uk/1/hi/programmes/analysis/7251302.stm; transcript of ABC Counterpoint, "Political Narrative" (1 September 2008), http://www.abc.net.au/rn/counterpoint/stories/2008/2351855.htm.

believe that "the forces now carrying him to the White House are part of a larger historical process, beyond his control".[19] Paul Waldon argues, "Of all the things Barack Obama has done right in this campaign, none may be more important than the fact that he has told a story perfectly keyed to the current moment in history."[20] Similarly, Bill Clinton in his aptly-named 1992 Democratic Convention film "The Man from Hope", included an image of his handshake in 1963 with President John F. Kennedy to promote the story of being singled out by the country's most popular president whose own hopes would be brutally and prematurely dashed.[21]

Further evidence of the perceived relevance of narrative to politics and political survival concerns British Prime Minister Gordon Brown who, until October 2008, was at risk of falling from power because of the lack of a compelling story about himself. Newspapers in the first half of September 2008 hounded him for a credible tale about who he was and where he was going, and fellow party members were also demanding a more "convincing new narrative" from their leader.[22] His party political speech at the end of September 2008 and his admired and emulated initiatives in bailing out collapsed banks at the start of October cast him in the role of an experienced, trustworthy, and resourceful helmsman steering the ship of State through troubled waters. His reputation and credibility were saved by a metaphor.

Is the accusation that a government lacks a narrative a rhetorical charge, rather than a substantive one, in that it addresses what the government *says* about itself rather than assessing what a government *does* to serve its people? The answer is twofold: first, words and actions are not necessarily in complementary distribution. As Austin, Searle and speech act theory make clear, many actions are performed *through* utterances (as in "I hereby declare you man and wife"), and

---

[19] Leader in the *New Statesman,* 20 October 2008, http://www.newstatesman.com/north-america/2008/10/vote-usa-obama-american (accessed 10 October 2010).

[20] Paul Waldman, "The Triumph of Narrative," *The American Prospect*, 19 February 2008, http://www.prospect.org/cs/articles?article=the_triumph_of_narrative (accessed 10 October 2010).

[21] For an informative analysis of Clinton's Hope advertisement and Kerry's May 2004 election advertisement as stories that succeeded and failed to appeal to the gut, see Drew Westen, *The Political Brain: The role of emotion in deciding the fate of the nation* (Public Affairs, 2008).

[22] "12 Labour MPs argue that we need more than policy initiatives, we need a bold new narrative," *Progress Magazine*, 17 September 2008, http://www.progressonline.org.uk/Magazine/article.asp?a=3351 (accessed 10 October 2010).

this is especially true of politics.[23] Understanding the illocutionary and perlocutionary force of political statements is central to understanding the workings of politics. Second, for those members of the general population who are not political analysts and who are only half-listening to the cacophony of political voices, any proposed changes in policy are best understood in the context of who is proposing the change, to what end, with what means, within what time span and, above all, with what relevance to the audience. A political narrative provides a way of organising multiple loose threads of political concerns into a single, readily graspable storyline.[24]

The following definition affirms the relevance of stories to politics: "A story is a fact, wrapped in an emotion that compels us to take an action that transforms our world."[25] This definition encapsulates the four components contained in all stories.[26] These consist of an emotion, contained both in the passion with which the story is told and in the emotion it elicits in the listener; a protagonist who provides a point of view for the listener to identify with (or define himself against); a problem in the form of an antagonist or *contretemps*; and finally a change, usually in the form of a redemption. A fifth component, often overlooked because it occupies only a short space of time, is the epiphany or moment of awareness, which provides the turning point leading to change. These four or five components can be found in all prevailing political narratives. And, as George Lakoff has demonstrated, among the narratives that move us most we find that the storyline is usually drawn from myths and carried by metaphors.[27]

Aristotle identified the four rhetorical modes of discourse as exposition, argumentation, description and narration, but he deemed narrative the least relevant to politics because of its past-centredness.

---

[23] J.L. Austin, *How To Do Things With Words* (Oxford University Press, 1962); John Searle, *Speech Acts: an essay in the philosophy of language* (Cambridge University Press, 1969).

[24] David Boyle, "In search of a political narrative," *Liberator*, August 2005, http://www.david-boyle.co.uk/politics/narrative.html (accessed 10 October 2010)

[25] Richard Maxwell and Robert Dickman, *The Elements of Persuasion: use storytelling to pitch better, sell faster and win more business* (Harper Collins, 2007), p.5. Variants of this quotes exist and involve the last phrase, which can read "… an action that produces a change" and "…to take action and so transform the world about us". See

Robert Dickman, "The Four Elements of Every Successful Story," http://www.storyatwork.com/documents/4ElementsofStory_BobDickman.pdf

[26] See for instance Robert McKee, *Story: substance, structure, style and the principles of screenwriting*. (Methuen, 1998).

[27] Lakoff, "Metaphor and War".

Certainly we all respond with incredulity and/or cynicism when we see the past being re-written to accommodate a subsequent turn of events from an anachronistic perspective.[28] However, there is a valid way in which narrative *does* affect the future and that is what propagandist self-mythologisers capitalise on: narrative provides a momentum which allows past events to set the course for future ones. By appealing to emotions, singling out a protagonist, assigning a challenge for him to overcome and showing how his particular attributes and actions achieve a change in circumstances that benefits the audience, however indirectly, a narrative frames issues, directs assumptions, recommends actions, and wins allegiance.

For these reasons, public diplomats should heighten their appreciation of the power of narrative. Not only do they need to hone their own story-telling skills to persuade others to join their cause, they also need to persuade their superiors that the stories they are telling still fall within the larger narrative thrust of the government's goals (known as "policy narratives") and the nation's story. Last but not least, public diplomats need to be sensitive to the narrative background and framework within which their interlocutors are operating. The dominant narrative for one community or culture may be the all-conquering hero but for another it may be the plight of the victim. If, as one definition of public diplomacy contends, the aim is to "engage, inform and influence" other nations, the verb "inform" cuts two ways: one has to inform oneself about the other party as well as informing them about us. Without this mutual exchange of information, engagement is likely to prove sterile or violent, and influence will never be achieved.

Allegiance

Several of the expressions used in this paper testify to an equation between stories and allegiance: *to win over, to join forces, to be on-side, to buy into, to identify with*. Three factors in particular shape the understanding of allegiance: psychological, sociological and neurological.

---

[28] Virgil's machinations with time as depicted on the shield of Actium, provoked W H Auden to respond with the memorable lines: "No, Virgil, no: / Not even the first of the Romans can learn / His Roman history in the future tense, / Not even to serve your political turn; / Hindsight as foresight makes no sense." ["Secondary Epic," *Collected Poems*, ed. Edward Mendelson (Faber and Faber, 1994), pp. 598–600].

Drew Westen[29] argues that the political brain is emotional. When confronted by a conflict between data and desire, that is to say that when new information contradicts previous statements and basic beliefs, not only are partisans "likely to 'reason' to emotionally biased conclusions, but we can trace their neural footprints as they do it".[30] Westen describes an experiment in which political partisans, in a brain scanner, are exposed to three slides. In the first of these, their political leader makes a statement which is contradicted by the information provided in the second slide. The third asks for a reaction to the previous two. The experiment found that the second slide prompted neural activation patterns of distress in the circuits associated with reasoning. However, this reaction was quickly suppressed, to the extent that subjects often failed to register any contradiction or experience of distress. They had reasoned their way to false conclusions.

While we may have encountered this kind of "stubbornness" or "close-mindedness", and been perplexed by the apparent character quirk betrayed, it is revealing to find a neurological confirmation. More revealing still is the finding by Westen and his team:

> Once partisans had found a way to reason to false conclusions, not only did neural circuits involved in negative emotions turn off, but circuits involved in positive emotions turned *on*. The partisan brain didn't seem satisfied in just feeling *better*. It worked overtime to feel *good*, activating reward circuits that give partisans a jolt of positive reinforcement for their biased reasoning.[31]

Westen concludes that the political brain is an emotional brain, more subject to gut appeal than to the dispassionate power of reason and the empirical evidence of facts and information. When voters demand a change of policy (over Vietnam or Iraq for instance), their calls are not necessarily prompted by new information, but by new emotions.

Since the structure of the political brain cannot be changed, the way in which we appeal to it can and should be. The nature of that effective political appeal, described by Westen in his concluding chapter, provides a salutory checklist for the aspiring public diplomat as well. It includes the ability to "tell emotionally compelling stories about who

[29] Westen, *The Political Brain.*
[30] Westen, *The Political Brain*, p. xiii.
[31] Westen, *The Political Brain*, p. xiv.

they are and what they believe in", the recognition that "most issues … are fraught with conflicting emotions, not only between people but within people, and that the most persuasive appeals are usually those that are the most honest", and a search for networks that bridge different emotional constituencies.[32]

"Political persuasion", says Westen, "is about networks and narratives," with "networks of associations, bundles of thoughts, feelings, images, and ideas that have become connected over time".[33] Replace – or rather, expand – the scope of "networks" to include professional and social as well as neural networks, and you have a pertinent prescription for public diplomacy: it is all about networks and narratives. Once a person has chosen his allegiance, he is likely to stick to that party, ideology, religion or other belief system, regardless of appeals to reason based on contrary evidence. It takes a strong appeal to emotions to persuade him to change his views. In many cultures and ideological communities, however, a code of honour often decrees that death is preferable to disaffiliation or apostasy.

If allegiance is so powerful, how can one secure it? According to Geert Hofstede, certain basic values characterise each culture and are situated "in our guts, not in our minds".[34] Hofstede claims that values such as truth and lies, right and wrong, or good and evil are strong emotions with a minus and a plus pole and are generally, often unconsciously learned before the age of ten. This Allegiance based on Hofstede's "basic values", becomes part of a person's social identity.

Allegiance may also be acquired later in life, as demonstrated by John Turner and Henri Tajfel's Social Identity Theory.[35] In a notable experiment, subjects estimated how many dots were on a piece of paper. Since there were hundreds of dots, a correct guess was unlikely. The group was then divided into those who had overestimated and those who had underestimated the number of dots. After a small period of socialising, each group was asked to describe the attributes of their own and the other group. Invariably, there turned out to be a strong bias toward the ingroup and prejudice against the outgroup.

---

[32] Westen, *The Political Brain,* pp. 418–420.

[33] Westen, *The Political Brain,* pp. 12 and 3.

[34] Geert Hofstede, "Diplomats as Cultural Bridge Builders," in Hannah Slavik (ed.), *Intercultural Communication and Diplomacy* (DiploFoundation, 2004), p. 228.

[35] Henri Tajfel, *Social identity and intergroup behavior* (Cambridge University Press, 1982).

"We" are better than "them" with regard to looks, intelligence, humour, dress sense and other attributes with no connection to estimating the number of dots on a piece of paper.

Tajfel concludes that social identity is largely drawn from psychological factors. The tendency to categorise people into groups, the tendency to identify with a social group and derive self-esteem from this identification, the tendency to draw comparisons between social groups with bias towards the ingroup and against the outgroup, and the desire to establish one's own group as distinctive are human universals and can be assigned to "nature". The way in which they come to be articulated, however, is determined by nurture. Each individual, moreover, belongs to several socal groups, often bridging gaps and accommodating incompatabilities in the process.

What relevance do these findings, interesting though they may be, have for public diplomacy? The answer resides in Westen's claim, "We can't change the structure of the political brain, which reflects millions of years of evolution. But we can change the way we appeal to it."[36] Since the human brain is inclined to reason emotionally, it is important to recognise the value of emotional appeals, such as those founded on narratives rather than on bullet-points of dispassionate facts. Similarly, if basic values remain unquestioned (and the deeply entrenched convictions concerning the inviolability of the Truth in Western culture is a case in point), then it is important for the public diplomat either to alert his interlocutor to the nature of basic values or to find ways of presenting a position to accommodate those basic values.

Furthermore, if we divide people into "us" versus "them" categories and aggrandise the ingroup at the expense of the outgroup, the public diplomat should bear in mind that there are three avenues of appeal to a member of an outgroup: first, to engage with the person as an individual rather than a group representative; second, to capitalise on common ground to build bridges between networks or between individual interests and cultural values. Third, one can appeal to the members of an outgroup by expanding the circle of the ingroup to include the other. This is what W H Lecky recommended through his notion of the expanding circle, which begins with the individual and then embraces the family. "Soon the circle… includes first a class, then a

---

[36] Westen, *The Political Brain*, p. xv.

nation, then a coalition of nations, then all humanity, and finally, its influence is felt in the dealings of man with the animal world."[37]

I am arguing for a heightened awareness among public diplomats of how the mind works with regard to allegiance: when and why we position ourselves, whether we do so consciously, to what extent our allegiance is rationally as opposed to emotionally driven, and what makes us either change allegiances or retain them. Above all it is important to recognise that conflicts and incompatibilities of outlooks, values and allegiances need not necessarily be eradicated – after all, they often coexist within the individual – so much as *accommodated.*

The relationship between narrative and allegiance can be seen to involve (1) emotional appeal, with a stronger call to rally round the flag than reason; (2) identification, since we tend to identify with the stories of our leaders and communities, and indeed, demand that our leaders and communities should have viable stories; and (3) justification, as narratives provide a causality and momentum that justify actions through time. Allegiance is won and reinforced by all three. In the already partisan mind, desire is given precedence over data; as long as a political leader enjoys a vote of confidence, the messenger is given precedence over the message.[38] Although the analytical mind prides itself in evaluating all information "on its own merits", we are all liable to emotionally driven reasoning.

The relationship between allegiance and rhetoric is mediated primarily through a network of interrelated metaphors called "conceptual metaphors", which we rarely recognise consciously but which are instrumental in shaping our outlook. Some of these are universal, as in the case of time described as space. In English for instance, this is communicated by a *long* or *short* time (adjective), a *length* of time (noun), the years *ahead* or *behind* one (preposition), to *go* back or *move* forward (verb); I'll be with you *shortly* (adverb); to finish *off*, write *up*, talk *on*, dance *away* (aspectual verb particles drawn from prepositions indicating spatial co-ordinates).[39] The structuring of our outlook is no less true of culture-specific metaphors. In English, we often resort to

[37] W E H Lecky, *A History of European Morals*, 1869, cited in Peter Singer, "The Drowning Child and the Expanding Circle," *The New Internationalist*, April 1997, http://www.utilitarian.net/singer/by/199704--.htm

[38] Westen, *The Political Brain*.

[39] If I mention parts of speech, it is simply to illustrate how very pervasive the time/space equation is in our language.

another time metaphor, namely "time is money" (or "time is a valuable commodity"): to *spend* time, to *cost* time, to *be generous* with one's time, to *buy* or *trade* time, to *save* or *invest* time, to *lose* or *waste* time, to *steal* or *take* time, to *owe* or *repay* someone time, to put hours in the *bank*, to be a *time-rich* or *time-poor* society, to *burn* time (based not on the value of money but on the physical attribute of paper money).

It is in the structuring of morality by conceptual metaphors that the relevance of metaphor to allegiance can be appreciated. In many cultures, moral action is conceptualised in terms of financial transaction where positive moral actions are gains and negative ones are represented through loss and harm.[40] However, *where* one places the focus on these transactions (for example, on retribution as opposed to restitution), will influence one's actions, both at the level of individual behaviour and that of government policy. George Lakoff explores the clusters of moral metaphors which surround conservative as opposed to liberal outlooks and argues convincingly that the metaphors which underlie conservative paternalism (the "strict father" model) and liberal tolerance (the "nurturant parent" model) determine the political reasoning and policies of these parties respectively. He asserts that "the conservatives have carefully coined terms and images and repeated them until they have entered the popular lexicon' while the liberals" failure to do the same has cost them politically. He advises, "Liberals need to go beyond coalitions of interest groups to consciously construct a unified language and imagery to convey their worldview."[41]

Conceptual metaphors structure our worldview through the subliminal influence of a variety of linguistic expressions. Where these have to do with morality, they piggy-back on models of parenting that we were exposed to as children and are either inclined to emulate (often unconsciously or through cultural determinism), or inclined to distance ourselves from (usually more reflectively but sometimes through knee-jerk rejection). We feel "at one" with people whose values, underlying assumptions and conceptual structures we share, and this sense of solidarity tends to be deeper the more subliminally it is experienced. Since metaphors and connotations are often intuitively

[40] George Lakoff, *Moral Politics: What Conservatives Know That Liberals Don't* (University Of Chicago Press, 1997);

George Lakoff, "Metaphor, Morality, and Politics, Or, Why Conservatives Have Left Liberals In the Dust", 1995, http://www.wwcd.org/issues/Lakoff.html.

[41] Lakoff, "Metaphor, Morality, and Politics".

recognised rather than rationally analysed, a shared language of metaphors, connotations and innuendos reinforces a sense of allegiance.

Irony, which by definition involves understatement, similarly appeals to implicit understanding to create inclusion among those in the know and exclusion of those outside the loop. The use of humour and irony to create, identify, and reinforce ingroups and to distinguish them from outgroups or individual outsiders is directly connected to allegiance. The feelgood of humour and irony reinforces the positive affirmation of belonging to a group, as recognised in Social Identity Theory. At the same time, the moral condemnation present in irony demonstrates the bias against the target.

Credibility

Credibility is key to effective public diplomacy, as suggested by Nye's injunction that "credibility is the crucial resource and an important source of soft power".[42] Yet how are we to achieve credibility with an audience whose partisan inclinations make them trust the messenger more than the message? One option is to diffuse the source of the message, as suggested by Mark Leonard:

> If a message will attract distrust simply because it is perceived to be coming from a foreign government, make sure it appears to be coming from a foreign government as little as possible. Increasingly, in order for a state to have its voice heard, it must work through organisations and networks that are separate from, independent of, and even culturally suspicious toward government itself.[43]

The appeal to advocates of a similar message to speak not on your behalf, but on behalf of the same cause, may address the problem of trust and credibility.[44] Another approach is to focus on common values to create an inclusive circle or ingroup relevant to the concerns at hand.

---

[42] Joseph Nye, *Soft Power*, p.106.

[43] Mark Leonard, *Public Diplomacy*. (The Foreign Policy Centre, 2002), p. 55.

[44] An example is the case of Norman Kember, the 74 year old British peace activist kidnapped in Iraq by the Swords of Truth Brigade on 26 November 2005, where actors as diverse as his wife and family, an anti-war representative of the Muslim Association of Great Britain, an incarcerated radical Islamic cleric, an ex-Guatanamo detainee, as well as British government representatives, all pleaded for his release. See

Biljana Scott, "Whose Story Wins?", paper presented at the 47th annual International Studies Association convention, San Diego, March 2005.

This focus should appeal both to reason and to emotions, and the appeal must be sensitive to the metaphorical and narrative frameworks of all parties. This in turn involves a close attention to wording.

Persuasive speaking, according to Aristotle, involves three elements: a credible speaker (ethos), an emotional appeal (pathos), and attention to language and reason (logos). Where the messenger proves more important than the message, ethos dominates. However, pathos and logos may still be appealed to for persuasive effect; words impact on emotions which in turn impact on allegiance. The power of logos should not be underestimated, since it is through lexical choices, metaphors, connotations, entailments and other such resources that emotions are engaged. Credibility is not only related to the provenance of the speaker, his knowledge, authority, and genuineness; it is a product of a carefully modulated appeal to emotions and allegiance through words.

Conclusion

The most pressing problem facing public diplomacy is the plethora of possibly conflicting messages, likely to arise from a host of public diplomats spilling out into the world, each with a plenipotentiary mandate. In this context, the overriding skill a public diplomat should possess is a sensitivity to the role of language and narrative in influencing perception, action, and allegiance.

Although the paradox of plenty predicts that those with the most appealing story set the terms of debate and win the last word, I contest the premise that stories are necessarily in an exclusive relationship. We are capable of embracing not only diverse but conflicting stories without triggering any apparent dissonance within ourselves. This is manifest in our appeal to idioms, many of which contradict each other but all of which we keep in mind should need arise. The same holds for the contradictory lessons contained in the Bible and other religious books and for the often conflicting stories that countries, cultures and individuals tell about themselves.[45]

---

[45] Nation branding may be an exercise in telling a single coherent story about a country, yet even here, most countries either expand the strap-line with a more complex narrative which enriches the brand, or as in the case of *Britain, country of punk and pageantry*, the contradiction is presented as a virtue in the strap-line itself.

Two stories may offer an equally valid rendering. Which one we prefer is a matter of choice, whether conscious or subliminal, and is determined by emotional appeal, moral justification, provenance, and allegiance. Allegiance in turn is reinforced through cognitive and linguistic resources such as conceptual metaphors, emotional appeal, and the positive reinforcement that comes from belonging to the ingroup. In so far as the public diplomat is in the business of collaboration and accommodation rather than competition and conflict, one of his primary challenges is to recognise the respective validity and possible coexistence of contradictory stories, fine-tuning those linguistic variables which allow a winning story to be a compelling one rather than a victorious one.

PUBLIC DIPLOMACY: COURTING PUBLICS FOR SHORT-TERM ADVANTAGE OR PARTNERING PUBLICS FOR LASTING PEACE AND SUSTAINABLE PROSPERITY?

Naren Chitty

1. *Introduction*

The standard view taken by governments is that public diplomacy is a domain restricted to the public sector and that target audiences must necessarily be external publics. I begin this chapter with a discussion that seeks to broaden public diplomacy and provide a normative definition. There is public sentiment in Western democracies, including Australia, about the public's exclusion from elite discourses on foreign policy and public diplomacy. The practice of public affairs is viewed by states as a means of bringing publics on board with respect to elite constructed foreign policy projects. Educated members of the public and experts, in Australia, invariably see public affairs and public diplomacy as labels for camaflauging propaganda; they are desirous of greater participation in foreign policy construction.[1] Today, governments seek new ways to foster collective action and broaden engagement. Dialogic, rather than persuasive, forms of communication have been advocated by scholars in a variety of fields as far apart as philosophy (Habermas 1991) and public relations (Grunig 1992) as being best suited to the relatively educated publics, in contemporary mature democracies, in terms of the latter's relationship with state agencies.

Secondly, I discuss within an ethical framework drawn from western political and international relations theory and resonant elements

[1] This was evident in the submissions of the expert panel, mostly of academics Senate Foreign Affairs, Defence and Trade Committee Inquiry into the nature and conduct of Australia's public diplomacy (Chitty, 2007). There is a debate taking place on the other side of the world on public affairs and public diplomacy in the European Union that calls for greater intercultural skills in seeking citizens" support for the European Union (Valentini 2008). Again, in relation to internal communication in Europe, there have been calls for the European "ICT for all' Strategy" to aim at a more discursive democracy (Karemagioli 2008).

from Confucian philosophy,[2] the role of international and transnational actors (state, multinationals, non-government organizations and media) in the discourses on global branding of countries.[3] Theories of republicanism and democracy provide bases for discussing representative and participatory approaches to governance. International regime theory discusses the values and broad framework of international governance, providing an opportunity for comparison with governance values drawn from Chinese philosophy. The resonances, that I discovered, suggest to me a measure of empiricism in the construction of the selected values, despite their normative nature. I discuss Confucian philosophy because it is widely believed that Kevin Rudd, who was elected as Australia's Prime Minister at the end of 2007, replacing John Howard of the Liberal Party, is influenced by this philosophy – and I want to discuss, in the third section, my reading of his approach to public diplomacy during the first half year of his government. Fourthly, I will discuss fundamental values in republican governance structures, giving ear again to resonances in Chinese philosophy. The implications in terms of propriety for actors in the four sectors will be outlined and discussed. The implication for the practice of public diplomacy, is that the best public diplomacy practice is based on good governance being practiced at home.

2. *Broadening public diplomacy*

Public diplomacy (PD) may be viewed, pragmatically, as an instrument in the tool box of international public relations (IPR). Other instruments have been identified as destination branding (place branding), country branding (national branding), cultural relations/diplomacy, public diplomacy and perception management. These range

[2] My exploration of Chinese philosophy has been conducted through the English language and must necessarily therefore have its limitations. I am aware of Prime Minister Kevin Rudd's prescription of learning about other cultures through acquiring new languages and must confess to falling short of his expectations (The Australian, 20 April 2008).

[3] Gunaratne has discussed public diplomacy actors from quantum physics, philosophical (mostly Chinese) and world systemic perspectives that he treats as convergent (Gunaratne 2005). He has also discussed interdependence and a moral code that draws on common religious values, calling for a middle path of socially responsible journalism as opposed to the extremes of the libertarian and authoritarian press models (Gunaratne 2007).

from passive to active ways of managing national reputation (Szondi 2009, 292). These tools are available to professionals working in these contiguous areas in a world characterized by "mingling of media" or "multi-mediacy", and immediacy – the instant linking between media and cultural, economic, political and social domains – and the plexus of diasporic communities that are not contained by national borders (Chitty 2009a). Reflecting on the characteristics identified above it may be surmised that the traditional PD tool box has a significant omission: Public affairs (PA) or state-public relations within a country. PD and PA need to be coordinated – even in a purely strategic sense (Heller and Persson 2009, 224). PD is described by Szondi as something used "[t]o create a receptive environment for foreign policy goals; to advance these goals; to get countries to change their policies towards others; raising international profile of countries, their politicians, governments". He associates the term country branding with trade and investment and destination branding with tourism (Szondi 293). There is such a thing as a political brand, and the term nation branding captures the notion of "international profile of countries, their politicians and governments". In an audience centered approach, one would associate nation branding with the ways in which domestic and foreign audiences perceive a country. Clearly, one can distinguish between strategic and perception based approaches to nation branding. Drawn from marketing, nation branding is an important strategic instrument available to PD policy managers. It is undertaken through construction and dissemination of brand images that incorporate a handful of key national values and strengths. The branding of countries and other international and transnational actors (identified here collectively as global actors) is a process through which constructed images are mediated to publics throughout the world, often as part of broader PD strategies.

The dominant reading of the term public diplomacy is that it is a process through which one country seeks to influence publics in another country or other countries with respect to the first country's policies and image (Frederick 1993; Fortner 1993; Hachten and Scotten 2002).

Traditional diplomacy is government-to-government relations (G2G) and if one were to picture it, it would be a photo op of the Australian Minister of Foreign Affairs sitting across the table from the foreign affairs minister in another nation state. Traditional public diplomacy has been about governments talking to international publics (G2P), and includes those efforts to inform, influence, and engage such publics in support of national objectives and foreign policies. More recently, public diplomacy has grown to involve the way in which both government and private individuals and groups influence directly and indirectly those public attitudes and opinions that bear directly on another government's foreign policy decisions (P2P). (Snow 2009, 6).

P2P reflects on the fact that citizens in one country seek to influence foreign policy decisions in another. They may also contribute to the conceptualization of national image.

There can be contestation, particularly (though not exclusively) in democracies, of state or media characterization of the country, indeed about whether the state should be engaging in propaganda under the guise of branding and public diplomacy, to hide unpopular policies that contribute to a tainted national brand.

Xue examines official branding (top down strategic communication) in China by the Beijing Organising Committee for the Olympic Games (BOCOG) and public branding online by netizens, noting that:

> the assumption that Web 2.0 enables the public to actively participate in the branding process through … produsage is partially affirmed: community based production further strengthens people's engagement in evaluating current policy and suggesting solutions to problems around the general preparatory work for the Beijing Olympics and, thereby, largely unknowingly, participating in the branding of Beijing. The crucial departure is that people are no longer passive receivers of a top-down constructed brand, but are active as actors in the process of branding Beijing. This not only implies impact on the mental level, but also affects their behaviour in real life. It is particularly significant concerning the context of China, where there is no clear sense of citizenship and no tradition of active civic engagement in public affairs. Compared to the traditional mass media, Web 2.0 indeed transforms the branding mode to let site visitors virtually feel what real Beijing is and how people live in Beijing through communications on the multiple scaled spaces. Conversely, this public branding continually influences the official branding through the change of online discourse (Xue 2008).

It is worth noting, along with Xue, that it is difficult to separate place branding from nation branding in this instance. The Beijing Olympics presented an opportunity to China to use all the instruments in the IPR tool box. It also presented an opportunity to use the instruments in the PA tool box, as it is necessary for the Chinese state, to interact with China's various domestic publics as well, in relation to the Olympics. There are publics that are enthused by the Games in varying degrees.

In introducing a student interviewee, an Australian TV Anchor, George Negus, said on a "Dateline" program entitled "China's Cyber

Warriors", that "China's overwhelming Olympic pride is most evident among the so-called generation Y – the almost 250 million people born during the 1980s, like 21-year-old nationalist student Wang Tuo". Wang Tuo is shown saying: "I think, because we are from the younger generation, we should take responsibility when our country needs us". (Dateline 2 August 2008). These "cyber warriors" are concerned with protecting, from their computers at home, China's image abroad.

An alternative view of public diplomacy recognises that domestic and overseas publics can no longer be separated in a diasporic world, that public diplomacy (here incorporating relevant aspects of public affairs) needs to address both these domains and take a dialogic approach with domestic publics in the development of foreign policy and public diplomacy programs (Chitty 2007). Such an approach will have a strong participatory governance character (**P** $\leftrightarrow$ **G**, where people and government interact) and would best operate where there are educated populations. While the exercise of global branding of countries may be undertaken, through the reduction of multiple positive images, to a handful of major thematic icons that are clustered under a single icon, there are broad global discourses, such as those on global warming or the Chinese ascendancy, that take place around such themes. These discourses will include both positive and negative content. The strategic intent of branding would be that the first tier of images cascading from the national icons (country name, flag, emblem) would enhance the other tiers of economic, scientific, social and political imagery and vice versa. The national brand and sub-brands should, in the best of worlds, support each other in terms of positive valence with a robust synergy.[4]

In my view public diplomacy, in the contemporary world, consists of multiple approaches for the public sector, in engagement with second sector (businesses), third sector (Civil Society and NGOs), and fourth estate/sector (media) organizations and through nationwide participation in the development of a foreign policy that has support at home and respect and credibility abroad, while serving national interest. Normatively, I would argue, visibility in foreign policy governance cultures, structures and programmes should be promoted. The greater

[4] Valence is the term employed by Mannheim for the degree of positivity or negativity associated with an actor's image and may be differentiated from degrees of visibility (Mannheim 1994).

the commitment to and practice of transparency in diplomacy, including and particularly by leading states, the greater will be the sense and sustainability of security (Chitty 2009b, 310).

To use Habermasian parlance in relation to global branding, the global promotion of national brands is essentially strategic in nature. Habermas distinguishes between strategic and dialogical (ethical) communication (Habermas 1991). A debate on these communication types is evident in discourses about public diplomacy and national branding, Gregory employs the terms instrumental (strategic) and discourse (dialogical) communication (Gregory 2005, 9–10). But as much as the national and global discourses around a national brand may include strategic brand image dissemination by a state through different agencies, various media will frame the discourse in ways that are influenced by news values. Also, different media users will have their own mediations of the messages.

It is reasonable to suggest that national image managers would prefer that their strategic constructions will be accepted by media and publics. They would prefer that these constructions will frame discourses about their respective countries and their products and services. But, national images get caught up in wider international discourses, sometimes characterized by news turbulence, and do not always achieve expected results. We live and work within broad-gauge (global and international) and narrow-gauge (local) value systems and ethical frameworks and these shape the way in which various actors deal with global branding of countries. Contemporary image makers need to be aware that the empirical logic of reception studies suggests that the receiver does more than receive passively, dominant or preferred readings. She may negotiate readings, constructing her own counter-hegemonic preferred readings (Hall 1980). This quantum nature of reception and turbulence of discourse, explains what some have identified as boomerang effects that are experienced by national image managers (Nisbett et al 2004). Monologues from power to people do not ring with truth, even when true, because of the association of official communication with propaganda, where the term is used pejoratively.

Ellul has characterised political and sociological propaganda as having recourse to technique, or expert procedures (Ellul 1973). Undoubtedly the construction of effective strategy in a complex domain is a procedure requiring expertise. However the use of strategy does not predicate propaganda as a necessary outcome (Barber 2005). Habermasian ethical communication is dialogical rather than unidirectional and is connected intimately with the notion of the public sphere. Indeed strategy can be constructed ethically and may employ, ironically, a dialogical approach. Botan distinguishes between instrumental images (i-images) and humanitarian or ethically and dialogically constructed images (h-images), noting that organizations often prefer the former approach (Botan 2009). But the latter approach is what this chapter proposes. In terms of the current discussion, this would mean that the public sphere becomes a venue where national brands and branding strategies are discussed.

3. *Framework*

Actors & Sectors: - There are broadly four sectors that host actors who play roles in national branding. These are the conventional first (state), second (business) and third (civil society and non government) sectors; the fourth sector is the media which may co-reside in the other three sectors (Chitty 2007). There are agencies within each of these sectors contributing either directly or indirectly, formally or informally to a national brand, through the construction of brands lower down in the pyramid or through their representation or critique of any apical state-constructed national brand. Intergovernmental organizations may be added as a fifth sector.

The concept that is used widely today in relation to propriety in administering institutions in any of these sectors is "good governance". An intergovernmental definition of good governance is offered by the United Nations Economic and Social Commission for Asia and the Pacific, as "the process of decision-making and the process by which decisions are implemented (or not implemented). Governance can be used in several contexts such as corporate governance, international governance, national governance and local governance." (ESCAP). ESCAP further identifies eight characteristics of good governance: Accountability, transparency, responsiveness, equitabity and inclusivity, effectiveness and efficiency, adherence to the rule of law and degrees of participation and consensus oriention (ESCAP).

My discussion on governance will look at the contemporary western academic concepts of development republicanism (Bo Li 1999; Bray 2006; Held 1996) and international regimes (Krasner 1983) and the Confucian concept, arising from Confucian philosophy, of ren-yi, that includes the notions of establishing oneself, reciprocity, moderation, public interest and verification (Zhang 2002).

Held identifies two forms of republican government, protective and developmental, the former arising from the Roman and the latter the Greek republics. These two forms are precursors of the garrison and republican states (Chitty 2004, 42–46; Lasswell 1966 146–148; Lerner 1969 171–196;).

In terms of classical political philosophy, Lockean[5] protective republicanism employs participation instrumentally to achieve protection for citizens. Development republicanism aims at Millsian[6] moral development of citizens (Bray 2006, 4; Held 1996). The goal of moral development through democracy presupposes the existence of models of development and prescriptions of democratic propriety.

Republicanism may be essentially representative in nature, but in absorbing the values of democracy, it imbibes participation as well. George Will's commentary does not do justice to the evolution of republicanism. He writes "The central principle of republican government is representation, under which the people do not decide issues, they decide who shall decide. The second is: Elections decide not whether elites shall rule but which elites shall rule" (Wills 2008). The question is not who rules, but how ruling is conducted.

Both types of republicanism are essentially humanist. Both democracy and republicanism are based on self-government and majority rule. However republicanism has the dimension of mixed government (Bo Li 1999).

The institutionalised international system, consisting of intergovernmental agencies, has republican and therefore humanitarian values and incorporates "mixed government", with special rights and obligations being assigned to particular estates, such as, one could argue, the permanent members of the security council. These rights are protected by the "major interest" procedural norm of international regimes. International regime theory addresses intergovernmental governance of issue areas and it defines regimes "as sets of implicit or explicit principles, norms, rules, and decision-making procedures around which actors" expectations converge in a given area of international relations" (Krasner 1983). There are two types of norms, or "standards of behaviour defined in terms of general rights and obligations" (Finlayson & Zacher 1983). Substantive norms are non-discrimination, liberalization, reciprocity, safeguard and development. Procedural

[5] John Locke.

[6] John Stuart Mill.

norms are multilateralism and major-interests. (Puchala & Hopkins 1983). Multilateralism describes the democratic one-vote one-country principle at play in diplomatic forums such as the United Nations General Assembly.

International governance structures are likely to influence "organizational features of transnational actors" (Carlsnaess and Risse-Kappen 2002, 261). Transnational corporations (second sector), transnational non-government agencies (third sector) and transnational media (fourth sector) will be influenced by international discourses such as those about democracy, governance, HIV-AIDS, human rights, sustainability and terrorism. The discourse on governance is of particular interest here as it may be examined in terms of common elements from Confucian philosophy and used to comment on responsibility vis-a-vis global branding discourses.

Ren-yi is a central double barrel concept arising from a melding of two ideas in Confucian thought. Ren (the ideograph for human being and the figure two) "has been translated as "humanity", "benevolence" and "love" … and "co-humanity" (Zhang 2002, 285–310). Yi refers to correct behaviour as applied particularly to persons in authority (Zhang 2002, 286). Several steps are prescribed, for man in society, in perfecting the practice of ren-yi. The steps are as follows – with my contemporary social interpretation provided in brackets: (1) Learn the rites and about the Way [Learn about right governance within the broader social value structure]; (2) Promulgate the Way [Espouse and promote right governance and the broader social value structure]; (3) Become established with a recognised social position; (4) Share authority with other established persons (Zhang 2002, 288–289).

Does not ren-yi refer to good governance that prescribes a humanistic outlook and correct behaviour? Ren takes on an added dimension if we consider Cheng Yi's interpretation that it is a quality associated with promoting public rather than private interest (Zhang 2002, 305). In the Guangzi and the Book of Lord Shang, it is noted that acting in the public interest, rather than for private gain, will not arouse popular resentment. Collective public opinion is viewed as "sage-like" and forming coalitions between the ruler and the people is prescribed, where the ruler complies with the wishes of the people and the people reciprocate with obedience (Zhang 2002, 313).

The Confucian social prescription is one that is characterised by dyadic relationships that are based on hierarchy and complementarity of interests. Such relationships are compatible with republican government. The Mohists contribute the notion of non-discrimination or Jian Ai – "to love others as oneself" (Zhang 2002, 326–329). Moderation or Zhong Yong is another virtue extolled by Confucius (Zhang 2002, 329–337).

One may extrapolate that the governance norms of accountability, transparency, responsiveness, equitability and inclusivity, effectiveness and efficiency, following the rule of law, participation and consensus orientation, should be in the public interest rather than purely in the interest of governing elites or shareholders. Humanistic good governance is clearly compatible with ren-yi.

4. *Australian public diplomacy: The Howard and Rudd approaches*

The tensions between elite driven and popular foreign policy are seen clearly at the time of democratic transitions of power, which may be propelled by election year P><G activity. It is reasonable to suggest that the Labour Party's victory at the end of 2007 was inter alia because incoming Prime Mister Kevin Rudd's raft of policies had been crafted at least partly as a response to the electorate's dissatisfaction with his predecessor's policies. Decisions of the losing Liberal Party, related to external actors, that had grown overwhelmingly unpopular by the election of 2007, pertained to the war in Iraq, the Kyoto Treaty and refugees. Prime Minister John Howard's claim to Australia being "America's Deputy Sheriff" in the Asian neighborhood (Fickling 2004), would have generated a positive image of Australia in the minds of those at home and abroad who supported the Bush policies and a negative one in the minds of those at home and abroad who abhorred the Bush policies in relation to military intervention in Iraq and to Global Warming respectively. Domestic discomfiture with external criticism of Australia for being associated with unpopular international stances led to reflections by the government on the need for PD initiatives overseas and for launching campaigns of persuasion. Internally oriented PA dealt with unpopular policies using the format of persuasive public information campaigns. Such advertising campaigns bloated to gargantuan proportions as Prime Minister John Howard's Liberal Party-led government (1996–2007) grew older in office. Noting that the Howard Government had spent A$ 126 million between July 2006 and May 2007…*The Australian* remarked that "[i]t is a longstanding joke in the media business that the Australian Government becomes the nation's top advertiser every three years". (Sinclair and Megologenis 2007).

The common-sense observation that the longer a government remains in power, the more it loses touch with the people, has relevance here. Being in touch is to conduct a dialogue with the people. When governments drift further and further away from dialogue with the people, they are likely to construct unpopular policies, based on elite constructed logic, that have less support at home than desired, impelling them to use strategic forms of public affairs and public diplomacy practices. Rather, a constant dialogue with important publics, would be a major component of good governance and would be incorporated as practice in a new expanded public [affairs] diplomacy (*P[A]D*). *P[A]D should be based on a continuous P ↔ G*, interaction. Dialogue should not be an episodic practice, conducted only in election years when ruling parties have lost touch with the electorates after long stints in government.

The framework that was developed above, with emphasis on its western theoretic aspects, will be used in the comparison of the Kevin Rudd (Labor Party) and John Howard (Liberal Party) periods. I have written previously on the emerging approach to *PD* in Australia at the end of the Howard period and my conclusions about this period will be used here to formulate a characterization that will be used to make a contrast with the Rudd approach (Chitty 2009b). The discourse on *PD* at the Senate Hearing in 2007 had a strategic flavour, despite the critiques made by several academics (Chitty 2007). The likely reason for this was that Australians were aware that the country was viewed negatively because of the positions it had taken in relation to the War in Iraq, refugees and Global Warming. Rather than engage in a P ↔ G type preventive *P[A]D*, the Howard Government relied on a G → P approach. On the other hand Kevin Rudd's Labor Party was able to engage in dialogic communication with the electorate while in opposition, presenting itself as being internally and externally dialogic in its approach, participating in mainstream national and international liberal discourses.

All of the sectors exhibit features of "mixed government", i.e. there will be different stakeholders that contribute to policy development, under both John Howard and Kevin Rudd. Under both approaches the fundamental goals of actors in each sector need to be achieved without prejudicing the larger national and public interest, where these interests are viewed from the security and developmental needs of state and citizens respectively. Without doubt, ideological differences result in different emphases being placed by political parties on national and public interest. Under John Howard national interest was linked geopolitically to the United States as the underwriter of Australian security and public interest was linked to conservative discourses on major issues. Under Kevin Rudd and his successor, Julia Gillard, national interest continues to be linked geopolitically to the United States as the underwriter of Australian security, but public interest has become linked to centrist liberal discourses on major issues.

4.1. *The sectors*

In a democratic society, foreign policy should be debated in public. The public's articulation of its own interests should be taken into consideration in foreign policy development. Whereas reliance on public opinion polls for day-to-day management of foreign policy may not be in the best interest of a state, enjoying public support for the foreign policy of a state is a strength. This public affairs component is, in my view, within the ambit of an expanded public diplomacy. Deep and sustained public disapproval of particular policies is likely to influence policy formulation. This area, which I would like to characterise as that of foreign policy governance, will naturally be an area of political debate for political parties, second (business) and third sector (civil society/non government) organizations as well as media, which I label as the fourth sector. Table 1 shows open and closed areas for public discourse in western democracies.

Table 1. Types of Foreign Policy Context

High political arena Closed in character Example: Military intelligence
Medium political arena Open in character. Policies are debated by political parties and civil society organizations Examples: Climate, energy, immigration, military engagement
Low political arena Open in character Policies are debated by political parties and civil society organizations Examples: Commerce, culture, education, health, media, sports.

In my view public diplomacy should not merely be a therapeutic response by government to an overseas public's adverse reaction to foreign policy or a government's response to negative portrayal of a nation state overseas. Ideally it should include the growing of foreign policy in a nursery of mutual understanding, under a greenhouse of constructive transparency (Chitty 2009b, 309).

The four sectors and the public, from which they are drawn, are entangled in webs of discourse. The public mind or its multiplicity of minds may be discerned in public discourses, to be found in media texts and from behaviour emanating from various events related to the issue under consideration. Another way of investigating the public mind is through questioning experts in the area. There is a co-dependency relationship among experts, media, the public and the state (vide Table 2 below). Experts, media and the state have access to information about external events through various sources and are information rich. Experts undertake research or have access to their organization's data, media has access to field reporters and to media networks. The state has access to its diplomatic, commercial, intelligence and other information gathering networks overseas. Experts are also likely, as a collectivity, to be aware of the range of views on their subject within the larger societies and groups within which they live and with whom they engage respectively.

4.2. *First sector*

The first sector is the state sector. The first sector's domestic governance role relates to all sectors. That the ESCAP governance norms should apply in this sector comes as no surprise. In developing national images, constituents of the sector need to promote and practice ren-yi and be established as authorities that act always in the public interest. They need to select policies that are in the public interest and enjoy public support or better still, grow policies through conducting a dialogue with the public. The Howard Government's environment, refugee, Iraq and workplace relations policies did not enjoy adequate public support in Australia to win the General Election of 2007. The policies were caught up, negatively, in interwoven national and global discourses on sustainability, social inclusivity and the war in Iraq. This translated into perceptions of Australia's image in the world having suffered. The consequence was that the Howard Government spent considerable sums of money on government advertising within

Table 2. Flows between the three sectors, media & the public

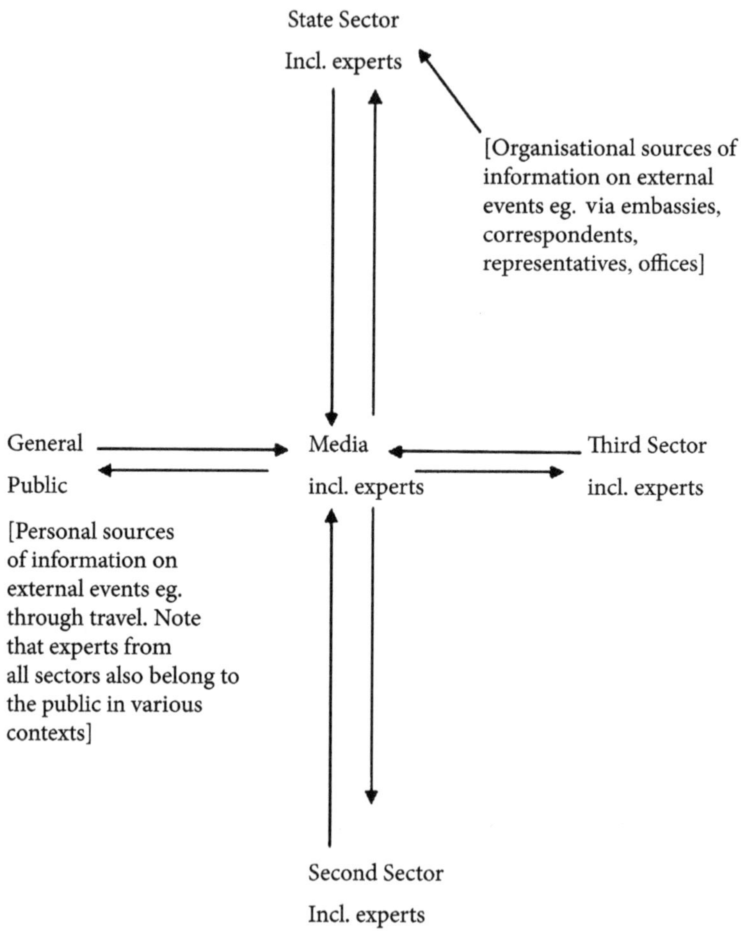

Australia and showed a particular interest in the possibilities of public diplomacy in maintaining a positive image of Australia overseas. The Australian Senate Inquiry into Public Diplomacy demonstrates this interest (Chitty 2007). On the other hand, Kevin Rudd (in the first two years of his government) adopted more popular policies in all these respects taking into account the public interest.[7] Expenditure on

[7] Interestingly in state elections in September 2008 voters have been reported to have been more interested in education, health, economic management and service delivery than national priorities on climate change and emissions trading (Shanahan, The Australian, 8 September 2008).

public diplomacy programs at Embassy level was reportedly pruned. Domestic public information advertising was slashed. At the same time there was a perception that Kevin Rudd "will clearly do much of the heavy lifting when it comes to recasting Australia's global image" (The *Daily Telegraph* 26 April 2008, 136).

There appears to have been an element of "establishing oneself" in Mr Rudd's adoption and promulgation of "correct ways" and his interest in Australia participating more fully in global governance structures, particularly the UN Security Council. Kevin Rudd's first major pronouncements on foreign policy as prime minister pointed to a return to a middle power approach to world politics, toning down from the Howard government vision of Australia as being more than a middle power – as the deputy sherriff of the United States. He said he would espouse "an active, creative middle-power diplomacy", laying out "a seemingly bold program to address climate change, security and economic issues by developing and enhancing partnerships in the region and beyond" (Pearlman 2008).

4.3. *Second Sector*

The second or business sector interests are profits and dividends for shareholders. These are private interests when juxtaposed with the larger public interest. Even so the second sector needs to take into account public interests in developing an image. Corporations can and often do emphasize public interest values such as employment, service delivery and technology development. Positive corporate image relies on values that are consonant with the public interest even if corporations must focus on the private interest of shareholders. If public interest is undermined, public opinion can result in consumer action that would have negative consequences on profits and dividends. The second sector does have to take into account the great social themes of the age such as sustainability that colour both national and corporate image. In developing a corporate image, constituents of the sector need to promote and practice ren-yi and be established as corporations that temper shareholder interests with public interest. Like states, corporations need to be accountable (to society as well as shareholders), be transparent, responsive, equitable and inclusive, effective and efficient, and follow the rule of law. Indeed Grunig's two-way symmetrical model of public relations recommends that organizations should negotiate their relationships with their publics rather than seek to transform them (Grunig and Hunt 1984; Toth 2002).

4.3. *Third sector and fourth sectors*

The third sector is about voluntarism and non-profit activity in the public interest, often around the great social themes of the age. Agencies in these two sectors play pivotal roles in mediating national image around discourses in key issue areas such as sustainability, human rights and international trade. In developing their own image or contributing to the shaping of first sector images, constituents of these two sectors also need to promote and practice ren-yi, taking particular care to be accountable, transparent, responsive, equitable and inclusive, effective and efficient, following the rule of law, and being participatory and consensus orientated.

5. *Conclusion*

I have situated PD within the tool box of IPR (along with destination and country branding, cultural diplomacy and national image perception management) and argued that it must also be combined with PA that targets the domestic public. The domestic public includes what I have called the diasporic plexus, with its international diasporic networks. The term public diplomacy, straddling the two realms as well as diasporic publics that straddle these two realms, needs to be broadened to spill into international public relations and domestic public affairs, in a manner that is characterized by partnership rather than mere courtship. The notion of sustainability needs to be drawn into our conceptualization of this broadened public diplomacy, despite our genuflection before elite constructions of realism in world politics. In this context we define sustainability as taking into account the overall security of future generations in the world at large. We need to conceptualize a world where foreign policy is constructed increasingly as a public project with sustainability as a preferred outcome.

The application of ren-yi values, or their Western equivalents, in public diplomacy practice, will contribute to an incremental construction of a preferred sustainable world politics. A sustainable world politics is not about the pursuit of power for ones own security but rather the management of power for a collective non-exclusionary security, based on principles of humanitarianism and reciprocity, principles that are contained in ren-yi.

Finally, not to put too fine a point on it, the best public diplomacy arises from measuring up, in terms of policy and practice, to the best humanitarian values of ones own civilization. As Rosalind says in the epilogue to Shakespeare's *As You Like It*, "*...good wine needs no bush*"

Bibliography

Barns, Greg and Anna Kraweo-Wheaton. "Determining a republican model". *On-line opinion: Australia's E-journal of social and political debate*. 22 April. http://www.onlineopinion.com.au/view.asp?article=7275 2008

Bo Li. "Topics in Political Theory and Practice (II) – Republicanism and Democracy". *Perspectives*. 1, 2 October 31. Available at: http://www.oycf.org/Perspectives/2_110299/Contents.htm Accessed on 23 April 2008. 1999

Botan, Carl. "A Human nature approach to image and ethics in international public relations". Journal of Public Relations. http://www.informaworld.com/smpp/title~content=t775653694 Accessed 2 October2010.

Bray, Daniel. "Models of democracy for global politics: Protecting the world and developing humanity". Paper presented to the Second Oceanic Conference on International Studies. University of Melbourne. http://209.85.173.104/search?q=cache:yEoWK9W118sJ:www.politics.unimelb.edu.au/ocis/Bray.pdf+republicanism+university+of+melbourne+david+held&hl=en&ct=clnk&cd=7 Accessed 22 April 2008. 2006.

Carlsnaess, Walter and Thomas Risse-Kappen. *Routledge Handbook of International Relations*. London: Sage. 2002.

Chitty, Naren. "Internationalizing Media Theory". In Daya Thussu (ed). "Internationalizing Media Studies". Routledge 2009a.

Chitty, Naren. "Australian Public Diplomacy". In Nancy Snow & Phil Taylor (eds) *Routledge Handbook of Public Diplomacy*. Routledge. 309–316. 2009b.

Chitty, Naren. Public Diplomacy: Developing Road Rules. Submission to the Senate Foreign Affairs, Defence and Trade Committee Inquiry into the nature and conduct of Australia's public diplomacy http://www.aph.gov.au/senate/committee/fadt_ctte/completed_inquiries/2004-07/public_diplomacy/submissions/sub15.pdf 2007.

Chitty, Naren. "Configuring the Future: Framing International Communication within World Politics in the 21st Century." *The Journal of International Communication*. 10.2 (2004.) pp. 42–66.

Ellul, Thomas. *Propaganda: The Formation of Men's Attitudes*. Trans. Konrad Kellen & Jean Lerner. New York: Knopf, 1965. New York: Random House/ Vintage. 1973.

ESCAP. United Nations Economic and Social Commission for the Asia Pacific. What is good governance. http://www.unescap.org/pdd/prs/ProjectActivities/Ongoing/gg/governance.asp Accessed on 23 April 2008.

Fortner, R. S.. *International Communication: History, Conflict, and Control of the Global Metropolis*. Belmont, CA: Wadsworth. 1993.

Frederick, H. H. Global Communication and International Relations. Belmont, CA: Wadsworth. 1993.

Finlayson, Jock A. & Mark W. Zacher:"The GATT and the regulation of trade barriers". In Stephen D. Krasner (Ed.) *International Regimes*. Ithaca: Cornell Univ. Press. 273–314. 1983. Gaensler, Bryan. "A republic would enhance the value of the Australian national identity". On-line opinion: Australia's E-journal of social and political debate. 2 July. http://www.onlineopinion.com.au/view.asp?article=7272 2008.

Grunig, J. E. and T. Hunt, *Managing Public Relations*, New York, Holt, Rinehant & Winston, 1984.

Gunaratne, S. Public diplomacy, global communication and world order: An analysis based on theory of living systems. *Current Sociology*. 53 (5), 749–772. 2005.

Gunaratne, S. Let Many Journalisms Bloom: Cosmology, Orientalism & Freedom. *China Media Research*, 3(4), 2007.
Fickling, David. "Australia seen as 'America's deputy sheriff'".
Indonesia wary of Howard's government". Guardian.co.uk. 10 September 2004. http://www.guardian.co.uk/world/2004/sep/10/indonesia.australia *Accessed 16 June 2009.*
Gregory, Bruce. Public Diplomacy and Strategic Communication:Cultures, Firewalls, and Imported Norms Paper for American Political Science Association Conference on International Communication and Conflict, August 31. 46 pp. 2005.
Grunig, L. Activism: How it limits the effectiveness of organizations and how excellent public relations departments respond. In J.E. Grunig (Ed.), Excellence in public relations and communication management. Hillsdale, NJ: Lawrence Erlbaum, 1992.
Hachten, W. A. and Scotton, J. F. *The World News Prism: Global Media in an Era of Terrorism*, 6th edn. Ames, IA: Iowa State Press. 2002.
Habermas, Jurgen. *The Structural Transformation of the Public Sphere*. Cambridge, MA: MIT Press. 1991.
Haigh, Bruce. "When the cats away". *On-line opinion: Australia's E-journal of social and political debate.* 23 April. http://www.onlineopinion.com.au/view.asp?article=7275 Accessed 23 April 2008. 2008.
Hall, Stuart. "Encoding/decoding". In Centre for Contemporary Cultural Studies (Ed.): *Culture, Media, Language: Working Papers in Cultural Studies*, 1972–1979 London: Hutchinson, pp. 128–138. [1973] 1980.
Held, David. *Models of democracy*. Second Edition. (Stanford: Stanford University Press), p. 45. 1996.
Heller, Ken and Liza M. Persson. "The distinction between public affairs and public diplomacy". In Nancy Snow and Phil Taylor (eds) *Routledge Handbook of Public Diplomacy* Routledge, 219–226. 2009.
Karemagioli, Evika. From egovernment to einclusion: assessment of the European "ECT for all" strategy. *The Journal of International Communication* 14, 2. 2008.
Krasner, Stephen D."Structural Causes and regime consequences: regimes as intervening variables". In Stephen D. Krasner (Ed.) *International Regimes*. Ithaca: Cornell Univ. Press. 1–21. 1983.
Lasswell, Harold. *The analysis of political behaviour: An empirical approach*. London: Routledge and Kegan Paul. 1966.
Lerner, Daniel. "Managing communication for modernization: A development construct", in A. Rogow (ed.) *Politics, Personality and social science in the twentieth century: essays in honour of Harold D. Lasswell*. Chicago: University of Chicago Press. 1969.
Manheim, Jarol. *Strategic Public Diplomacy and American foreign policy: The evolution of influence*. New York: OUP. 1994.
Morris, David. "Please don't come home". *On-line opinion: Australia's E-journal of social and political debate*. 23 April. http://www.onlineopinion.com.au/view.asp?article=2337 Accessed 23 April 2008. 2004.
Nisbet, E. C., Nisbet, M. C., Scheufele, D. A. and Shanahan J. E. "Public Diplomacy, Television News, and Muslim Opinion", *The Harvard International Journal of Press/Politics* 9(2): 11–37. 2004.
Pearlman, John. "Bad Time will tell whether this is a foreign policy departure". *The Sydney Morning Herald*. 28 March 2008. http://www.smh.com.au/news/national/time-will-tell-whether-this-is-a-foreign-policy-departure/2008/03/27/1206207300921.htmll Accessed 17 August 2009.
Puchala, Donald & Raymond F. Hopkins:"International regimes: Lessons from inductive analysis". In Stephen D. Krasner (Ed.) *International Regimes*. Ithaca: Cornell Univ. Press. 1983.
Risse, Thomas. "Transnational actors and world politics". In Carlsnaess, Walter and Thomas Risse-Kappen (Eds). *Handbook of International Relations*. 2002.

Shanahan, Dennis. "Bad news weekend for big parties". *The Australian*. 8 September 2008. http://www.theaustralian.news.com.au/story/0,25197,24309747-5013871,00.html Accessed 8 September 2008.
Sinclair, Lara and George Megologenis. "Propaganda overkill". *The Australian. May 2007*. http://www.theaustralian.news.com.au/story/0,20867,21785505-601,00.html Accessed 16 July 2009.
Snow, Nancy. "Rethinking public diplomacy". In Nancy Snow and Phil Taylor (eds) *Routledge Handbook of Public Diplomacy*. Routledge, 3–11. 2009.
Szondi, György. "Central and Eastern European public diplomacy: A transitional perspective on national reputation management". In Nancy Snow and Phil Taylor (eds) *Routledge Handbook of Public Diplomacy*. Routledge, 286–307. 2009.
Toth, Elizabeth L. Postmodernism for modernist public relations: the cash value and application of critical research in public relations. *Public Relations Review*. 28, 3. August 2002. 243–250.
Valentini, Chiara. Political communication in international settings: The case of the European Union. *The Journal of International Communication* 14, 2. 2008.
Will, George. "Last Word: Heepism vs Elitism". Newsweek 31 August 2008.
Xue Hui. Branding Beijing Online via the 2008 Olympics. *The Journal of International Communication* 14, 2. 2008.
Zhang Dainian. 2005. [2002]. *Key concepts in Chinese Philosophy*. Edmund Ryden, trans. Beijing: Foreign Languages Press/Yale University Press.

LOOKING AT THE MAN IN THE MIRROR: UNDERSTANDING OF POWER AND INFLUENCE IN PUBLIC DIPLOMACY

Ali Fisher

Public Diplomacy is at its core about influencing the actions and behaviour of other people, whether that is in the short, medium or long term.[1] However, rather than exerting control over behaviour absolutely, public diplomacy is about influencing the likelihood of a community adopting a behaviour, it is effectively about changing the odds of a certain outcome actually happening.

Some schools of thought and practise currently focus on using "influence" to advocate a certain image or policy. Conversely, for others "influence" is the ability to develop understanding, dialogue or relationships as a means to share power and develop collective action.[2] This results in one of the key tensions in the practise of Public Diplomacy; the division between those that seek to exert "power over" a target audience and those that intend to engage or empower a community. The divergence between the two positions is fundamentally a question of power and how that power is understood in relation to the "other". Reflecting on this power relationship highlights; how and why those "others" are selected, how priorities are identified, and ultimately how success is measured and articulated.

---

[1] Ali Fisher and Aurélie Bröckerhoff, *Options for Influence: Global campaigns of persuasion in the new worlds of public diplomacy* (Counterpoint, 2008), pp. 3–6 http://www.counterpoint-online.org/download/587/Options_for_influence_PDF_download.pdf (accessed 16 November 2008).

[2] For models based on these distinctions see R.S. Zaharna, "Mapping out a Spectrum of Public Diplomacy Initiatives: Information and Relational Frameworks," in Nancy Snow and Philip Taylor (eds.), *The Routledge Handbook of Public Diplomacy* (London, 2008), pp. 86–100;

Geoffrey Cowan and Amelia Arsenault, "Moving from Monologue to Dialogue to Collaboration: The Three Layers of Public Diplomacy," *The ANNALS of the American Academy of Political and Social Science* (March 2008), 616, pp. 10–30.

Also see Ali Fisher, "Public Diplomacy in the United Kingdom," *The Present and Future of Public Diplomacy: A European Perspective, Working Paper from The 2006 Madrid Conference on Public Diplomacy*, http://www.realinstitutoelcano.org/documentos/276.asp (accessed 16 November 2008).

Practitioners and theorists who emphasize asserting identity, perceptions, perception change or understanding, must ask themselves the question; to what end are you spending public money? What behaviour do they seek to elicit from the audience? In effect, beyond the usual that it is nice to talk about oneself, why is telling others about yourself important?

Despite the preference amongst some practitioners for focusing on perceptions, it is the *action or behaviour* which the target audience takes that gives the perception impact on the international environment.[3] Even if that behaviour is to acquiesce to certain policy goals, or at least not act to oppose that policy, success of the Public Diplomacy is rooted in behaviour rather than perception. This focus on action, however mutual, ultimately relates to the power to influence behaviour of a foreign public.

However, while all programmes seek to influence behaviour, there is a clear differentiation in emphasis between Public Diplomacy conceived as exerting "power over" a target audience and that considered empowerment. Genuine, symmetrical exchange is the point at which the two approaches meet as participants are equally open to the influence of the other while seeking to exert influence. Exchange is the point where symmetrical relationship building can take place.

The practise of Public Diplomacy to exert "power over" an audience overlaps with definition produced by Philip Taylor's of propaganda, though he notes without the associated debasement of the word. "The word "propaganda" itself implies calculated intent on the part of one person or group of people to persuade others to think or behave in certain way".[4] Empowerment in contrast provides a community with the ability to act. The statement, often attributed to Nelson Mandela, "education is the most powerful weapon, which you can use to change the world" is not referring to systematic indoctrination but the

---

[3] Mission of External Relations Directorate General, European Commission, http://ec.europa.eu/dgs/external_relations/general/mission_en.htm (accessed 16 November 2008);

Lord Carter of Coles *Public Diplomacy Review*, December 2005, http://www.britishcouncil.org/home-carter-report (accessed 16 November 2008).

Understanding and perception change are both part of British Council Corporate outcomes.

See British Council Corporate Plan 2008–2011, http://www.britishcouncil.org/home-aboutus-corporate-plan.pdf (accessed 16 November 2008).

[4] Philip M Taylor, *The Projection of Britain; British Overseas Publicity and Propaganda 1919–1939*, (Cambridge, 1981), p. 1.

possibility "through education that the daughter of a peasant can become a doctor" or "a child of farm workers can become the president".[5] As J.A.C. Brown argued, "education teaches people how to think, whereas propaganda teaches them what to think".[6]

To demonstrate the differentiation in emphasis, and subsequently the meaning of power within public diplomacy, the understanding of power within the discipline can be conceptualised in five areas. Much of current Public Diplomacy analysis focuses on the *first* aspect of power, the ability to articulate policy and the subsequent tension between message and actions. This is closely linked to the *second* meaning of power in PD; the way actions are articulated to the domestic constituency. *Third*, the nature of the power relationship with the target audience; whether that is symetrical or asymetrical in favour of the international actor or giving the participants greater ownership over the engagement. Building on the understanding of that relationship, *fourth*, is the understanding of PD and power in relation to the network; particularly understanding the type of network, an actors relationship with the networks, and the importance of certain positions in the network.

Finally, drawing on the previous meanings, the understanding of power relates to the meaning of success in public diplomacy. This highlights the assumptions upon which the identification of important people, key influencers, to be engaged and how success is measured.[7] Specifically, power within Public Diplomacy must be understood beyond a narrow masculine sense of "power over" to embrace both empowerment as an act of public diplomacy and the understandings that can come from gendered thought. As Jacqui True wrote:

> If the human world is exhaustively defined by such gendered constructions of "power-over", as in realist accounts, feminists ask, how do

---

[5] See address by H.E. Phumzile Mlambo-Ngcuka, Deputy President of the Republic of South Africa, at the Conference of Ministers of Education of the African Union (COMEDAF), 9 August 2007 http://www.thepresidency.gov.za/main.asp?include=deputy/sp/2007/sp08091312.htm (accessed 16 November 2008);

Nelson Mandela; *Long Walk to Freedom: The Autobiography of Nelson Mandela*; (Little Brown and Co., 1995).

[6] J.A.C. Brown, *Techniques of Persuasion: From Propaganda to Brainwashing*, (Harmondsworth, 1963), p. 21.

[7] For discussion of key influencers see Louise Vinter and David Knox, "Measuring the impact of Public Diplomacy: can it be done?", *Engagement: Public Diplomacy in a Globalised World* (Foreign and Commonwealth Office, 2008), p. 166.

> children get reared, collective movements mobilize and everyday life reproduced?[8]

Approaching power in this way, the analysis begins with what the actor seeks to achieve and whether that will be seen as consistent with their other actions. It then broadens to consider whether it can be justified to the domestic constituency and what form the power relationship with the foreign public should take. These practical issues provide the platform from which to consider the wider issue of conceptualising the various roles practitioners play in a networked world. In doing so this approach identifies the tensions in relation to the understanding of power as practise increasingly focuses on measurement and valorising impact.

1) *The classic power struggle; messages and actions*

The consideration of tensions in Public Diplomacy can often focus on the articulation of policy which is discussed in greater depth elsewhere in this volume. In this sense power largely revolves around the ability to engage or dictate the agenda in view of previous or contemporary acts. As recognised in 1937, "it is perfectly true…that good cultural propaganda cannot remedy the damage done by a bad foreign policy".[9] Blunders in policy or execution will inevitably undermine public diplomacy.[10] However, Public Diplomacy is not just influenced by foreign policy; it can also be undermined by a lack of commitment to policies "at home". As Geoff Miller has argued that, "National borders have become both less immutable and more porous, and the ability and inclination to see over or behind them have grown".[11] This tension between Public Diplomacy and both foreign and domestic policy creates the potential for practise to be undermined by "local" inconsistency.

---

[8] Jacqui True, "Feminism" in Scott Burchill et al. (eds.), *Theories of International Relations* (Palgrave, 2005), pp. 225–226.

[9] Eden to Simon, 22 December 1937, T 161/807, S 35581/03/38/1, quoted in Taylor, *The Projection of Britain*, p. 168.

[10] Examples of recent blunders include Birmingham City Council in the UK mistakenly using an image of Birmingham, Alabama, in its publicity material. [BBC News, 14 August 2008, http://news.bbc.co.uk/1/hi/england/west_midlands/7560392.stm (accessed 16 November 2008)].

[11] Geoff Miller, "Current and emerging challenges to the practice of Australian diplomacy," -*Australian Journal of International Affairs* (2002), 56:2, pp. 197–206.

The tension caused by local inconsistency was particularly evident during oral evidence given by *Asialink* to the Australian Senate hearings on Public Diplomacy.[12] However, Australia are not alone in facing the tension caused by inconsistency. The "'interconnected' realities of global relationships" creates advantages for those seeking to conduct PD[13] but the ability to look behind the national boarder to see the realities which exist also exacerbates the tension created by the local inconsistencies.[14]

The Public Diplomacy associated with climate change, while it receives less attention from academic public diplomacy analysis, highlights many of the tensions over "local" inconsistency. While arguments over the specifics of the science are important, much of the engagement with the population will not be an analysis of the detail but will deal in images presented to them by various advocacy campaigns. As such, "local" inconsistency will create an area of tension for Public Diplomacy.[15]

This tension between message and action severely curtails the ability to exert "power-over" an audience as it will be clear the behaviour promoted by the Public Diplomacy programme has not been adopted by actor promoting it. This ultimately influences the options available to practitioners as their actions at home limit their power to shape the agenda overseas. However, the relationship with their own actions is only the first tension; before they can act they must also consider their relationship with the domestic constituency and foreign publics.

---

[12] At the hearing *Asialink* questioned the commitment of New South Wales to public diplomacy spending. When challenged about this lack of commitment, the Senator from New South Wales conducting hearings into Public Diplomacy said "It is not my government," demonstrating the inconsistency in commitment between local and senatorial representatives from the same state. See Senate Standing Committee on Foreign Affairs, Defence and Trade, *Nature and conduct of Australia's diplomacy*, 15 March 2007.

[13] Jan Melissen, "Wielding Soft Power: The New Public Diplomacy", *Clingendael Diplomacy Papers* No. 2, p. 9.

[14] Jan Melissen, "The New Public Diplomacy: Between Theory and Practise," in Jan Melissen (ed.), *The New Public Diplomacy* (Palgrave Macmillan, 2005), pp. 13 and 16.

[15] See Philip M Taylor, "Public Diplomacy and Strategic Communications," in Snow and Taylor (eds.), *The Routledge Handbook of Public Diplomacy,* p. 16. For further examples of local inconsistency, including cases of climate change and human rights, see.

Ali Fisher, "Clear and Present Tensions in PD," *Trials of Public Diplomacy Conference*, London, April 2007.

2) *Power and the domestic audience*

Many understandings of the discipline, in theory and practise, have a tendency to conflate the meaning of Soft Power and public diplomacy. This conflation does not acknowledge the broader understandings of public diplomacy; however, it does demonstrate the uneasy relationship between the understandings of power and public diplomacy, particularly when the message is being articulated for consumption by a domestic audience. Soft Power may sound dynamic to the domestic constituency, but it ultimately limits the power of Public Diplomacy practitioners to engage in the full range of possibilities.

Arguing that a country is using soft power has become increasingly popular in both political and practitioner discussion. Faced with a threat, "an unprecedented challenge from the dark side of globalization", as Nye described it, the desire to create a dynamic narrative in response is understandable. The War against Terror, War on terror, and other articulations provide an appearance of a strong response. The response for Nye, is to draw a parallel with previous challenges; "Like the challenge of the cold war, this one cannot be met by military power alone. That is why it is so essential that Americans - and others - better understand and apply soft power."[16]

Following similar logic, UK Foreign Secretary, David Miliband in his first speech at Chatham House argued that "we need to think how we can deploy Britain's assets—both the soft power of ideas and influence, and the harder power of our economic and military incentives and interventions".[17] Equally a 2005 report for the State Department argued "for an enduring commitment to soft power, to winning hearts and minds in the cultural arena".[18]

However, just as Joseph Nye argues for an application of soft power, he also notes, soft power "is an analytical term, not a political slogan" and as such has a specific meaning:[19]

---

[16] Joseph Nye, *Soft Power: The means to Success in World Politics* (Public Affairs, 2004), p. xiii.

[17] David Miliband speech, "New Diplomacy: Challenges for Foreign Policy," Chatham House, London, 19 July 2007, http://www.chathamhouse.org.uk/news/view/-/id/392/ (accessed 16 November 2008).

[18] US Department of State, Report of the Advisory Committee on Cultural Diplomacy, *Cultural Diplomacy The Linchpin of Public Diplomacy*, September 2005.

[19] Joseph S. Nye, "Our Impoverished Discourse," *The Huffington Post*, 1 November 2006.

> Soft power is the ability to get what you want by attracting and persuading others to adopt your goals. It differs from hard power, the ability to use the carrots and sticks of economic and military might to make others follow your will.[20]

In this expression of soft power, Nye demonstrates his understanding of influence as "power-over"; to make individuals to "adopt your goals". The goals are created and then means are used to persuade others to enter into action in support of those goals.

Many practitioners who must publicly account for their budget do so by making dynamic claims of "power over" the audience, which narrows Public Diplomacy to only a few possible approaches. This exposes the classic tension within Public Diplomacy theory and practise, the relationship between the language of dialogue, mutuality or two-way communication, and the development of many strategies and programmes which maintain a realist, state-based author-audience power relationship that demonstrates a very different approach to power.

Listening in the soft power context "requires understanding how they are hearing your messages, and fine-tuning it accordingly".[21] This significantly limits the field of public diplomacy, reducing "the two way street" of dialogue and genuine exchange to one of message refinement.[22] This is problematic, while being the target of soft power is likely to be preferable to influence down the barrel of a gun, "No one likes being used for target practice, whatever the munitions", as Daryl Copeland wrote recently.[23] As a result, "merely shooting messages rather than bullets will not do the trick".[24]

However, those who have to justify their budgets or actions to a domestic public have a pressing and immediate need for clear statements of action. This creates the need for a dynamic narrative for domestic consumption, through which to gain support for future actions. Such dynamic narratives focus on exerting "power-over" the audience for a predefined goal, rarely leaving space for genuine dialogue and empowerment.

---

[20] Joseph S. Nye, "Propaganda Isn't the Way: Soft Power," *International Herald Tribune*, 10 January 2003. Also see Nye, *Soft Power*.

[21] Nye, *Soft Power*.

[22] Melissen, "Wielding Soft Power"; Melissen, "The New Public Diplomacy".

[23] Daryl Copeland, "Military public diplomacy meets political counter-insurgency: Two sides of the same COIN?", International Studies Association conference, 2008.

[24] Copeland, "Military public diplomacy".

Domestic pressure also leads to a focus on "representation" and self-centred language rather than genuine engagement in which the domestic constituency is expected to move its position. *The Future Embassy Report* produced by CSIS demonstrated the need within the domestic constituency for representation. The report argued "(t)he truest test of the value to our nation of the U.S. diplomatic presence abroad is whether the people we ask to represent us effectively promote American values and interests".[25] Considering the response to 9/11 Matt Armstrong highlighted "the struggle for minds and wills has returned to the open battleground over perceptions and support".[26] His argument that "we must stop telling foreign publics what we want our own people to hear" clearly exposes the tension created by pressure from the domestic constituency for "representation".[27]

In the informational framework or monologue conception of communication, the domestic pressure to frame a particular message creates tension with the framing for the external audience.[28] This tension escalates rapidly when considered in relational, dialogue or collaborative conceptions, cutting to a fundamental meaning of power in relation to the domestic audience. For genuine dialogue to occur there must be an element in which both sides are prepared to shift their position, yet public diplomacy practitioners rarely risk suggesting to their political masters that the domestic audience must shift their position or identity rather than just the foreign audience.

The tension between representation and building links is nothing new and was demonstrated in an article in the Daily Express from November 1944. It complained that Frank Wallace had been sent by the British Council to "advise the Spaniards on game preservation". At issue was not the development of a closer relationship with General Franco, it was that "this kind of "projection" of Britain was utterly misleading and most damaging … scrutiny of the British Council will lead inevitably to the conclusion that it is unfitted to the

[25] George L. Argyros et al., *The Future Embassy Report*, (Center for Strategic and International Studies, 2007), p. vi.

[26] Matt Armstrong, "Operationalizing Public Diplomacy," in Snow and Taylor (eds.), *The Routledge Handbook of Public Diplomacy*, p. 67.

[27] Armstrong, "Operationalizing Public Diplomacy," p. 70.

[28] Zaharna, "Mapping out a Spectrum";
Cowan and Arsenault, "Moving from Monologue to Dialogue to Collaboration".

great task of presenting Britain to the world".[29] For the *Daily Express*, building relationships, or dialogue, was secondary to the projection of an image.

Similarly, in recent years the domestic articulation of Public Diplomacy is particularly assertive, in terms of "Finding America's Voice" or looking at "influencing foreign publics – not with arms, not even with arm-twisting, but with the softer power of ideas".[30] If this domestic pressure for representation is successful, it limits the power of Public Diplomacy to genuinely *engage* with populations overseas, or at the very least, to admit domestically the full extent of what is being attempted. As a result, practitioners rarely articulate the argument to the domestic constituency that "Public Diplomacy is not always about you" as Nick Cull succinctly described it.[31]

This relationship with the domestic audience has a major impact on the power to frame Public Diplomacy programmes. The desire to be represented abroad in a positive way forces the domestic consciousness into the framing of overseas initiatives rather than allowing Public Diplomacy to be seen as a means of achieving policy goals through influencing behaviour. This is not to deny the impact of country of origin effects, yet it demonstrates the tensions created by the necessity to negotiate a power relationship with the domestic constituency in framing a PD initiative.[32]

This tension with the domestic constituency can be seen in American practise. It is evident in what James Glassman termed the "war of ideas" but stretches back into earlier responses to 9/11. As Nancy Snow described the approach;

> The effort to share values ended up showing a harsh contrast between the daily life realities of Muslim people living in the United States and

[29] *Daily Express*, 30 November 1944, quoted in Frances Donaldson, *The British Council: The First Fifty Years* (London, 1984), p. 131.

[30] Miliband, "New Diplomacy"; *Finding America's Voice: A Strategy for Reinvigorating U.S. Public Diplomacy*, (Council on Foreign Relations, 2003);

James Glassman speech, Council on Foreign Relations, 2 July 2008, "Public Diplomacy in the 21st Century", http://www.america.gov/st/texttrans-english/2008/July/20080702123054xjsnommis0.3188745.html

[31] Nick Cull, "Public Diplomacy: Seven lessons for its future from its past," *Engagement: Public Diplomacy in a Globalised World* (Foreign and Commonwealth Office, 2008), p. 16.

[32] K.I Al-Sulaiti and M.J Baker, "Country of origin effects: a literature review," *Marketing Intelligence & Planning* (1998), 16:3, pp. 150–199.

> those living under much harsher regimes. Instead of a hoped for message that "our success is your success" it was "our success isn't your success" and here are the images that prove it.[33]

This was due to the "shared" approach being framed in asymmetric terms, influenced by the domestic pressure for representation rather than genuine collective identification of values. This was exacerbated by the corrosive "with us or against us" narrative which while popular within some domestic constituencies, limited the opportunity of individuals to engage if they were resistant to being subordinate to an American narrative.

While this point has equal relevance to the discussion of power relationships with the target audience, its relevance here is the way such lines are designed in relation to the domestic rather than foreign audience. Such rhetoric may garner support for the initiative at home, but actions designed with the domestic audience can damage the delivery of the initiative abroad.

The necessity to negotiate any potential tensions with the domestic constituency leads many Public Diplomacy practitioners and analysts alike to either overlook, or deliberately underplay, the possibility identified by Nick Cull recently; "(s)ometimes the most credible voice in public diplomacy is not one's own".[34]

3) *Power relationship with the foreign public*

Understanding the nature of the power relationship aids the differentiation of messaging or Soft Power from facilitative, niche, diplomacy and the collaborative or co-developer approach of the open source methodology.[35] It demonstrates succinctly whether the actor is seeking to exert power over the foreign public or work collectively with them.

Nye's recent explanation of exerting soft power presents a position based on producer and recipient; the message is fine-tuned, tested and honed as it is conceived of as projected onto an audience.[36] The power

[33] Nancy Snow, "Rethinking Public Diplomacy," in Snow and Philip Taylor (eds.), *The Routledge Handbook of Public Diplomacy*, p. 8.

[34] Cull, "Public Diplomacy," p. 16.

[35] Nye, *Soft Power;* Alan Henrikson, "Niche Diplomacy in the Public Arena: Canada and Norway,", in Melissen (ed.), *The New Public Diplomacy;*

Ali Fisher, "Music for the Jilted Generation; Open Source Public Diplomacy," *The Hague Journal of Diplomacy* (2008), 3:2.

[36] Nye, *Soft Power,* p. 111.

relationship is one of a producer and a passive audience to whom Public Diplomacy is done in line with a predetermined agenda of an international actor.

The assumptions of this approach characterise it as neither mutual nor based on a reciprocal relationship. It excludes the development of common goals through dialogue, nor provides support to empower others to realise their goals. It is neither compromise nor negotiation. It is a belief in one's own perspective over another. It is an asymmetric power relationship in favour of the actor over the foreign public.[37]

Juxtaposed with the asymmetry of soft power is the facilitative approach of niche diplomacy where the benefit comes from helping others to achieve their goals.[38] These facilitative approaches invert the asymmetry of the relationship between the international actor and the target of the initiative. This can be seen in initiatives run by Norway or Singapore and, while it was not articulated in these terms, the 1967 Malta initiative with regard to the seabed beyond national jurisdiction.[39] These initiatives are focused predominantly on other nations. They realise national goals by engaging with other states to facilitate collective action.

Rather than exert power to drive people to a position, these initiatives influence by providing a mechanism that facilitates the creation of certain initiatives. As Alan Henrikson put it, "[i]f a country carries out measures for the international good, even what might be deemed the "global public good", then it is seeking something that is "universalizable", extending well beyond national selfinterest".[40] Whether or not the goal is "universalizable" is a question of scale, the vital part of

---

[37] The Green Day Problem demonstrates the understanding of power. See Fisher and Bröckerhoff, *Options for Influence*, pp. 22–23.

[38] Henrikson, "Niche Diplomacy in the Public Arena";
Kishan S. Rana, "Singapore's Diplomacy: Vulnerability into Strength," *The Hague Journal of Diplomacy* (2006), 1, pp. 81–106.

[39] Henrikson, "Niche Diplomacy in the Public Arena"; Rana, "Singapore's Diplomacy";
Tommy Koh, "Size is not density", in Arun Mahizhnan and Lee Tsao Yuan (eds), *Singapore: Re-engineering Success,* (Singapore Institute of Policy Studies, 1999);
Jamie Metzl, "Network Diplomacy," Georgetown Journal of International Affairs (Winter/Spring 2001), http://www.carnegieendowment.org/publications/index.cfm?fa=view&id=681&prog=zgp (accessed 16 November 2008);
Arvid Pardo, "The Origins of the 1967 Malta Initiative," *International Insights* (Fall 1993), 9:2, pp. 65–69.

[40] Henrikson, "Niche Diplomacy in the Public Arena," p. 68.
Also see Inge Kaul et al. (eds), *Providing Global Public Goods: Managing the Globalization* (Oxford University Press, 2003).

niche diplomacy is that is can be presented as "beyond national self-interest" subsuming the national into the collective effort. It is this which inverts the asymmetric power relationship from that evident from those pursing Soft Power. Soft power may be easier to articulate to the domestic constituency, but empowerment has greater potential to attract engagement from the foreign population as it relies not on honing attractive things for their consumption but in engaging through actions in which they are already interested.

The tensions caused by the power relationship with the foreign publics can be seen through the analysis of recent US actions, and particularly the "War of ideas" as outlined by James Glassman. The discussion of US military an action in Iraq, by Matt Armstrong, has presented a credible argument about the role of information based Public Diplomacy. However, the tendency to give primacy to a particular nation within a collective effort highlights a potential tension in both the narrative and academic analysis. He argues "unless the people think the U.S. is winning, the insurgent narrative will continue to gain traction".[41] Yet did Thai, Italian, Bulgarian, British, and Spanish coalition members, along with the many thousands of Iraqis die so the US could win? It is the blurring of the national with collective ambitions, particularly within a domestic "American" narrative that creates tension with foreign publics. If there is to be collective engagement, the narrative must also be collective; not merely an assertion of American power.

If people are to be "liberated", the articulation of the Public Diplomacy must maintain the appropriate collective or empowering power relationship rather than focused on US pre-eminence. If action is to be collective, the aspirations of the foreign public must be central, not a by-product of US goals. Otherwise Public Diplomacy will seek "power-over" the audience, an audience the US claims to seek to work with or liberate. Whilst this is perhaps an unfortunate turn of phrase in Armstrong's piece, it is the clearly stated way in which, Assistant Secretary of State for Public Diplomacy, James Glassman understands of his role.

James Glassman has argued that "war of ideas as we are leading it today" built on that of Karen Hughes, who sought to "isolate or marginalize violent extremists who threaten freedom and peace".[42] Whilst

---

[41] Armstrong, "Operationalizing Public Diplomacy," p. 70.
[42] Glassman, Public Diplomacy in the 21st Century".

framed as a collective effort for common benefit, there is a clear invocation of leadership. The problem is not with that goal per se but with the blurring of the national and global interest amidst the assertion of leadership. If the strategy to which Glassman refers was to be based on partnership, this was undermined by the American perception of primacy confirmed by the repetition of Senator Joe Lieberman's comment that James Glassman was "the supreme allied commander in the war of ideas". Such an attitude, even in jest, is ill-suited to the development of partnership as it contains asymmetric assumptions about the power relationship.

The tension such an asymmetrical power relationship creates can be shown within the specific example Glassman sights in his speech at CFR, specifically isolating those he terms "violent extremists".[43] To do so he must work collectively, yet the narrative has an asymetry, focusing on American leadership, values and action. Ultimately it is a projection of US terms despite the recognition in the speech, that the most "credible voices are Muslim voices".[44] The foreign publics are not given space to negotiate or engage in dialogue. They are effectively subordinate to the US approach whether they are potential allies or violent extremists. The tension this creates amongst formal allies stems from the desire to be recognised as partners rather than subordinates. For those with common goals of isolating violent extremists, but who do not wish to be subordinate to or explicitly aligned to the national interests of the United States this narrative is alienating. Many potential allies will not take too kindly to the idea that they ultimately work for America and in many contexts it will even be used against them by the very violent extremists the US also seeks to oppose; a classic PD own goal due to failure to manage power relationship with the foreign publics.

It is clear the that the power relationship with the domestic constituency and foreign public can individually cause tensions for the practitioner to negotiate. When domestic and foreign tensions combine it can produce Public Diplomacy that has the opposite impact to that intended.

While harder to sell to a domestic audience, because of the less dynamic narrative, creating an asymmetric power relationship on the terms of the foreign public, rather than Public Diplomacy actor, can

[43] Ibid.
[44] Ibid.

help reduce the potential tension with that public. For example, in the 1960s the British Council noted experience had "shown that the Council's best work is done in close co-operation with the relevant authorities, especially the educational authorities, of other countries". It became the "cardinal principle of the Council to aim at mutual benefit both to Britain and to the other country".[45] Equally, in 1947 the British Council Monthly Review noted;

> The longer one is engaged in cultural relations work the clearer becomes the essentially reciprocal nature of the operation, and the clearer the wisdom of the maxim that each party should give the other what the other wants, rather than what the giver thinks is good for him.[46]

These older perspective has many parallels with today. The increasing contemporary emphasis on multilateral initiatives, identifying collective initiatives based on common interest, particularly through an Open Source approach, envisages a power relationship which is based on a peer-2-peer environment.[47] Power, respect and authority have to be earned rather than asserted and an actor cannot merely assume it has a superior position over subordinates over which it seeks to exert power.[48] Once this approach is adopted, alternative short term desires to appear powerful, for domestic consumption, will damage that approach and relationship with the foreign public. For example, a listening exercise will create resentment if it is used merely as an opportunity for policy promotion.[49] Just as the relationship with the domestic audience influences the engagement with the foreign public, so the decision to adopt a collective, facilitative or empowering approach is likely to cause tension with the domestic constituency, as it is unlikely to be sufficiently representational.

To further analyse the meaning of power within contemporary Public Diplomacy the relationship must not be seen as merely a question of the actor, constituency and foreign public, but the relationship and role within a network of actors.

---

[45] "What is the British Council?", *British Council Annual Report*, 1965–1966. p. 10.

[46] "Commentary", *Monthly Review of the British Council*, 1:1, June 1947.

[47] Fisher, "Music for the Jilted Generation".

[48] For an extended discussion of the importance of power within the relationship, see R.S. Zaharna, "An Associative Approach to Intercultural Communication Competence in the Arab World," in Darla Deardorff (ed.), *SAGE Handbook on Intercultural Communication Competence* (Sage, 2009).

[49] See Ilana Ozernoy, "Ears Wide Shut", *The Atlantic Monthly*, November 2006; Fisher and Bröckerhoff, *Options for Influence*, p. 23.

4) *Power relationships in a network*

Forming networks has become an increasing part of Public Diplomacy narratives and study in recent years.[50] The growth of multilateral initiatives, including EUNIC, along with the rise of international issue focused NGO, and technology breaking down the barriers between foreign and domestic, has created a context comprised of numerous hubs engaging as part of a network. As such, the understanding of power relationships in a network; recognising different types of network, and understanding how operating within networks poses challenges to many of the assumptions about power and influence and particularly the importance of core and periphery. This can be shown both through the practical analysis of Glassman's recent speeches and consideration of the concepts on which engagement within a network would be based.

Despite his focus on American leadership, James Glassman explicitly referenced a networked engagement when he highlighted the work of Daniel Kimmage. Glassman argued "Web 2.0, with emphasis on social networking, holds the key to public diplomacy communications, at least for the start of the 21st century". However, while both Glassman and Kimmage, in his article *Fight Terror with YouTube*, were focusing on online networks they had very different conceptions of the power relationship with the network members.[51] Glassman, as discussed earlier, was focused on asserting a leadership position. Kimmage, by contrast, argued;

> The most damaging disruptions to the [Al Qaeda media] nexus, however, will come from millions of ordinary users in the communities that Al Qaeda aims for with its propaganda. We should do everything we can to *empower* them.[52]

---

[50] See, for example, R.S. Zaharna, "The soft power differential: Network communication and mass communication in public diplomacy," *The Hague Journal of Diplomacy* (2007), 2:3, pp. 213–228;

R.S. Zaharna, "The Network Paradigm of Strategic Public Diplomacy," Policy Brief, *Foreign Policy in Focus* (April 2005), 10:1, http://www.fpif.org/briefs/vol10/v10n01pubdip.html (accessed 16 November 2008);

Brian Hocking, "Rethinking the "New" Public Diplomacy," in Melissen (ed.), *The New Public Diplomacy;* Fisher, "Music for the Jilted Generation".

[51] Daniel Kimmage, "Fight Terror with YouTube", *New York Times*, 26 June 2008, http://www.nytimes.com/2008/06/26/opinion/26kimmage.html (accessed 16 November 2008).

[52] Ibid. (emphasis added).

Leadership and empowerment require two fundamentally different relationships. The failure to recognise the different network types and resultant power relationships can lead to tensions in the conduct, and ultimately limit the effectiveness, of Public Diplomacy initiatives.

Leadership of a network is recognised in many forms, Brian Hocking has identified a hierarchical conception in which; "the foreign ministry and the national diplomatic system over which it presides act as gatekeepers, monitoring interactions between domestic and international policy environments and funnelling information between them".[53] It equally could envisaged as a centralised network. Contrasted by Paul Baran, with decentralised and distributed systems, the centralised network has "the hierarchical structure of a set of stars connected in the form of a larger star".[54] John Arquilla and David Ronfeldt later highlighted this centralised system as

> The hub, star, or wheel network, as in a franchise or a cartel where a set of actors are tied to a central (but not hierarchical) node or actor, and must go through that node to communicated and coordinate with each other.[55]

While emphasis differs slightly the classic "hub and spoke" image is recognisable as in most descriptions of the centralised network.

Whether funnelling information in the hierarchical conception, or providing a channel through which other nodes can link and coordinate, as RS Zaharna argues;

> the hub effectively controls the exchange of information. It provides the central leadership and develops governing structures to plan and coordinate work, recruit and manage members, solicit funds, and channel resources.[56]

Whatever the role US representatives may seek to project to a domestic audience, a centralised hub role is not the one which Kimmage envisaged when suggesting empowerment.

---

[53] Hocking, "Rethinking the "New" Public Diplomacy," pp. 35–36.
Also see James Moody and Douglas R. White, "Structural Cohesion and Embeddedness: A Hierarchical Concept of Social Groups," *American Sociological Review* (2003), 68, pp. 103–127.

[54] Paul Baran, "Introduction to Distributed Communications Networks," *On Distributed Communication* (RAND, 1964), p. 1.

[55] John Arquilla and David Ronfeldt, *Networks and Netwars*, (RAND, 2001), p. 7.

[56] Zaharna, "The soft power differential".

In the contemporary context Public Diplomacy practitioners must recognise, not just the centralised but the dispersed peer-2-peer environment to which Kimmage referred.[57] Numerous populations around the world face common challenges. This argues for a collective approach, the conceptualisation of dispersed networks and the adoption of an open source approach to Public Diplomacy. The power of a genuinely dispersed networked approach is that each actor is independent, each engages on the basis of being a peer, and each makes his/her own arguments. The power of this approach is fundamentally undermined if one group claims that they are leading all the other groups. While it is useful to claim that everyone works for you, there are times when "they" can only work toward the same goals if you can subsume the national into the collective, rather than branding the collective as, in this example, "American".

The misrepresenting the role of an international actor in a network creates a tension within public diplomacy practise. The need to accurately recognise the type of network goes beyond centralised and dispersed, to include for example long chains, but the importance of recognition remains the same. The actor must adopt behaviour appropriate to the type of network in which they operate. RS Zaharna along with David Ronfeldt and John Arquilla have discussed options of using networks and networked communications which further demonstrate the practical benefits from effectively negotiating these tensions and power relationships.[58]

Public Diplomacy practitioners are increasingly emphasising collaboration, multilateral initiatives, a networked model of engagement or even an open source methodology.[59] This has the potential to break down the hierarchical producer and recipient relationship, and creates

---

[57] Ravi Kumar et al., "Structure and Evolution of Online Social Networks," http://www.tomkinshome.com/andrew/papers/starpower/starpower.pdf (accessed 16 November 2008).

[58] Arquilla and David Ronfeldt, *Networks and Netwars*;
Zaharna, "The soft power differential";
Zaharna, "The Network Paradigm of Strategic Public Diplomacy";
Fisher, "Music for the Jilted Generation";
Michelle Shumate et al., "Storytelling and globalization: The complex narratives of netwar," *E:CO* (2005), 7:3–4, pp. 74–84 http://www-rcf.usc.edu/~monge/pdf/Storytelling_Netwar_ECO_2005.pdf The practical use of networks is also a focal point of *The Dispersed Networks Project* and has been featured on *Wandren PD*.

[59] Zaharna, "The soft power differential"; Fisher, "Music for the Jilted Generation"; Miliband, "New Diplomacy".

a means for collective action.[60] Communication "is not all about warfare, about winning "hearts and minds" for the sake of achieving military victory. It is, as Karl Deutsch long ago emphasized, the method of *community*".[61] While it can at times be useful to conceptualise the network as one with the Public Diplomacy actor in the centre, there are times when the power relationship is somewhat different. The misunderstanding of this relationship can create significant tensions within the practise of public diplomacy.

In addition to the understanding of networked communication, the practical insights borne by network analysis has much to offer which is yet to be fully embraced by the practitioner community. In particular it provides an insight into the understanding of power as it relates to positions in a network and Public Diplomacy, by challenging the traditional understandings of the importance of the centre, or core, and periphery of a network.

The classic understanding of central and periphery tends to equate greater power or importance to the centre. Were one issue to be described as central and the other peripheral, the comparative importance intended would be clearly conveyed. However, this is not necessarily the case in a network; both core and periphery have vital roles. The importance, as Thomas Valente emphasised, of marginals, those at the periphery, is that they "act as bridges in diffusion".[62] Indeed "as many studies … have shown, it is not opinion leaders who are early adopters, but instead marginals or individuals who are bridges to other networks who first adopt an innovation".[63] As a result, the periphery is "where inflows and outflows of knowledge and innovations occur".[64] This gives the periphery huge importance and influence.

---

[60] Fisher, "Music for the Jilted Generation".

[61] Alan Henrikson, "What can Public Diplomacy Achieve?", *Discussion Papers on Diplomacy*, 2006, p. 2.

[62] Thomas Valente, "The Diffusion Network Game," *Connections* (1996), 19:2, p. 35.

[63] Valente and Davis, "Accelerating the Diffusion of Innovations Using Opinion Leaders," *Annals of the American Academy of Political and Social Science* (Nov., 1999), 566, pp. 62–63.

See also Marshall H. Becker, "Sociometric Location and Innovativeness: Reformulation and Extension of the Diffusion Model," *American Sociological Review* (1970), 35, pp. 267–282;

Everett M. Rogers, *Diffusion of Innovations* (Free Press, 1995).

[64] Valdis Kreb and June Holley, "Building Sustainable Communities through Network Building," 2002, http://www.orgnet.com/BuildingNetworks.pdf —. I would like to thank RS Zaharna for drawing this article to my attention. See Zaharna, "The soft power differential".

Those that are in these positions, as RS Zaharna has highlighted, have become known as boundary spanners.[65] "Boundary spanners are well-positioned to be innovators, since they have access to ideas and information flowing in other clusters. They are in a position to combine different ideas and knowledge, found in various places."[66] This, as RS Zaharna argued, creates the "ability to break through cultural walls, in an era of heightened cultural identity" which "gives network communication the edge over mass communication".[67] The potential to adopt or facilitate this boundary spanner function largely requires a peripheral position, yet authority and success are traditionally articulated in ration to a centralised position. The tension between the power to control and the power to influence is fundamental to the understanding of Public Diplomacy.

This tension between in the understanding of power between core and periphery is important in conceptualising not just the position of the actor, but the communities the organisation seeks to engage. Specifically this tension relates to the work on the diffusion of innovation through networks. The speed of diffusion through the network depends on the position of the individual in the network that first adopts it, be that technology, understanding or policy.[68] Early adopters are more likely to be at the periphery of a network, yet faster diffusion speed depends on core members adopting the technology or policy.[69]

The modelling run by Thomas Valente and Rebecca Davis, highlighted the significant difference in adoption speeds between scenarios where the early adopters were central parts of the network and those where the early adopters were on the periphery.[70] They concluded "if the first adopters are those individuals who are on the margins ... the rate of diffusion is slowest".[71] As a result, "when diffusion starts with these individuals, the innovation must percolate through the network

---

[65] Zaharna, "The soft power differential".

[66] See Valdis Krebs, "Social Network Analysis, A Brief Introduction", http://www.orgnet.com/sna.html (accessed 16 November 2008).

[67] Zaharna, "The soft power differential".

[68] Valente, "The Diffusion Network Game,"

[69] Valente and Davis, "Accelerating the Diffusion of Innovations Using Opinion Leaders," pp. 62–63.

[70] Valente and Davis, "Accelerating the Diffusion of Innovations Using Opinion Leaders," pp. 62–64.

[71] Valente and Davis, "Accelerating the Diffusion of Innovations Using Opinion Leaders," p. 62.

before it reaches opinion leaders who are in the position to set the agenda for change".[72] This argument is supported by Barbara Wejnert;

> The predictive power of an individual actor's status on adoption of an innovation varies positively with the prominence of the actor's position in a network.[73]

While other factors including "structural equivalence of individual and collective actors" also influence diffusion, the targeting of well connected individuals may appear to be the way to rapidly spread information through a network. However, this assertion creates a problem for Public Diplomacy. As noted earlier "it is not opinion leaders who are early adopters, but instead marginals ...who first adopt an innovation".[74] Therefore, the tension exists between targeting those most likely to allow rapid diffusion, due to their connections, and those most likely to adopt the innovation due to their marginal position.

A centralised narrative would focus on the actors with more connections, yet if they are unlikely to adopt the innovation, the quantity of connections through which to disseminate that innovation becomes virtually irrelevant. Focusing on the periphery finds those most likely to adopt innovation, but when they do, diffusion through out the network will be a slower process. Each Public Diplomacy actor must negotiate this tension, though many currently only focus on the core of well connected individuals who has a traditionally important role, such as politician or journalist.[75] In some instances these may be the people to focus on, in others circumstances however, likelihood of adoption will trump ability to facilitate diffusion if the core is resistant to the innovation.

The articulation of the role adopted by the PD organisation is equally influenced by this understanding of power. Many currently focus on centralised networks through which to project messages, placing themselves at the core. However, in many instances an alternative

---

[72] Ibid.

[73] Barbara Wejnert, "Integrating Models of Diffusion of Innovations: A Conceptual Framework," *Annual Review of Sociology* (2002), 28, pp. 297–326;

C. Baerveldt and T. Snijders, "Influence on and from the segmentation of networks: hypotheses and tests," *Social Networks* (1994), 16, pp. 213–232;

J.S. Coleman et al., *Medical Innovations: A Diffusion Study* (Bobbs-Merrill, 1966).

[74] Valente and Davis, "Accelerating the Diffusion of Innovations Using Opinion Leaders," p. 62.

[75] Vinter and Knox, "Measuring the impact of Public Diplomacy".

understanding would be to act as "boundary spanner" through which innovation can diffuse from one network to another. The first option provides a means to exert power over an audience, the second empowers a network.

Conceptualisation of power and influence, therefore, depends on the identification of different positions in the network, and the relative importance placed on those positions for a particular innovation, understanding or policy. In doing so, the understanding of success toward which the international actor works becomes increasingly important.

5) *Success – Who to target and what is success?*

The four preceding considerations of power within Public Diplomacy all focus on the tension between different ways of thinking about influence. Linking these tensions together is a key issue which is at the heart of James Glassman's misinterpretation of the concept proposed by Daniel Kimmage. While Glassman talked of leadership, Kimmage talked of *empowerment*, the key issues at stake were who is important and what is success?

Empowerment, while receiving limited attention in Public Diplomacy, has received significant coverage in development activities and from groups working to close the inequality gap between men and women, such as the Fawcett Society.[76] The marginalisation of empowerment highlights a wider issue; feminist and gendered thought have received very little attention in both Public Diplomacy writing and practise.[77] This is troubling because, "gender analysis of international relations can no longer be considered new. In both history and

---

[76] See, for example, Bridget Byrne, *Gender, Conflict and Development, Volume I, Overview*, Netherlands Special Programme on WID, Ministry of Foreign Affairs;

Bridget Byrne et al. *Gender, Conflict and Development, Volume II, Case studies: Cambodia; Rwanda; Kosovo; Algeria; Somalia; Guatemala and Eritrea*, December 1995 (revised July 1996);

Donna Pankhurst, *Women, gender and peace building* (University of Bradford, Department of Peace, 2000) Fawcett Society is the UK's leading campaign for equality between women and men. They trace their roots back to 1866, when Millicent Garrett Fawcett began her lifetime's work leading the peaceful campaign for women's votes.

[77] No attempt is made here to construct a fully formed gendered perspective of public diplomacy in theory and practise. The issue is to understand meanings of power which create points of tension in the field, one of which is presented by feminist understandings of international relations.

political science, scholars of women or gender and foreign relations have carved out what are now robust sub-fields" yet there is much work to be done before gender in Public Diplomacy, both in theory and practise, becomes one of those sub-fields.[78]

Ann Tickner argued "theoretical divides evidence socially constructed gender differences. Understanding them as such may be a useful entry point for overcoming silences and miscommunications, thus beginning more constructive dialogues".[79] This is an important point for understanding Public Diplomacy in theory and practise. Just as Tickner recognised in her commentary on Hans Morgenthau "the need for control has been an important motivating force for modern realism" so the tension between exerting "power over" and empowerment is evident in Public Diplomacy.[80]

The identification of a target audience is an important part of understanding power within the practise of Public Diplomacy. Two particular tensions have to be negotiated, first, on what assumptions does a public diplomacy organisation consider individuals to be important within their society? Second, what is success; are resistant individuals to be broken down or potential supporters empowered?

The first question of assumptions relates to the understanding of importance and influence which different socially constructed roles can exert within a society. The choice by an international actor to focus on for example, employment status or public role over roles considered family or private may reflect certain gendered assumptions. Similarly, emphasis on formal and rather than informal roles are also reveal important gendered assumptions.[81] Much of this work builds on the "powerful feminist critique of ideas of rationality as they have developed in Western Culture" and poses questions about the assumptions upon which Public Diplomacy practitioners identify the target audience or "key influencers".[82] In addition, gendered understandings of

[78] Philip Nash, "Review of J. Ann Tickner, *Gendering World Politics*", *H-Diplo* (May 2002).

[79] J. Ann Tickner, "You Just Don't Understand: Troubled Engagements between Feminists and IR Theorists," *International Studies Quarterly* (1997), 41:4.

[80] J. Ann Tickner, "Hans Morgenthau's Political Principles of Political Realism: A Feminist Reformulation," *Millennium* (1988), 17:3, p. 432.

[81] See, for example; Elisabeth Prügl, *The Global Construction of Gender: Home-based Work in the Political Economy of the 20th Century* (Columbia University Press, 1999);

Jean Bethke Elshtain, *Public Man, Private Woman: Woman in Social and Political Thought*, (Princeton University Press, 1981).

[82] Carol Cohn, "Sex and Death in the Rational World of Defense Intellectuals," *Signs* (Summer 1987), 12:4, pp. 687–718.

security challenge assumptions about the key issues of a foreign public, a perspective further demonstrated, for example, by African Feminist thought.[83] A far reaching analysis on the specific impact of applying "gendered lenses" to Public Diplomacy in theory and practise is long overdue.[84] Each of these elements profoundly influences the identification of a potential audience or community which must be considered as creating a potential tension within Public diplomacy.

In addition to the assumptions and tensions involved in identifying key individuals within a foreign public, the measurement of impact is another area of practise in which the tensions in Public Diplomacy are played out.[85] This leads directly to the question of success. The ability to show whether Public diplomacy has impact requires a clear measurement system. Furthermore, the identification of positions within a network requires an ability to measure that network and engage in the appropriate way with the members of it. While useful these systems may contain conscious or unconscious assumptions about power influence and success, which unless articulated cannot be understood alongside the data the measurement system produces.

Each of the above understandings of power, along with the consideration of gendered thought, force actors engaged in Public Diplomacy to consider what success means. The question of success must not be applied just to the international actor, but an understanding of what success means to all those involved, collaborators, partners, or the target audience. The failure to understand these different meanings of success will negatively impact on the ability to conduct and measure Public Diplomacy.

The comparison by Ann Tickner of the writing by men and women about power highlights Nancy Hartsock's argument that "power as domination has always been associated with masculinity" while by contrast "when women write about power they stress energy, capacity and potential". This engages with David McClelland's portrayal of

---

[83] See, for example, Cynthia Enloe, *Maneuvers; The international politics of militarising women's lives* (University of California Press, 2000);

Gwendolyn Mikell, *African Feminism: The Politics of Survival in Sub-Saharan Africa* (University of Pennsylvania Press, 1997).

[84] V. Spike Peterson and Anne Sisson Runyan, *Global Gender Issues*, (Westview, 1999).

[85] Discussions of measurement include Pierre Pahlavi, "Evaluating Public Diplomacy Programmes," *The Hague Journal of Diplomacy* (October 2007), 2:3, pp. 255–281;

Vinter and Knox, "Measuring the Impact of Public Diplomacy.

"female power … as shared rather than assertive".[86] Juxtaposed with the current debates and tensions within the Public Diplomacy, the common language highlights the potential which gendered analysis has for the understanding of power in both articulating success and identifying the tensions within the discipline.

Conclusion

In Public Diplomacy, the actor must weigh a perceived need for control and a centralised understanding of influence against the case for engagement and empowerment. Partnerships are becoming an increasing part of public diplomacy practise. How much the partnerships are on the terms defined by the Public Diplomacy organisation or genuinely associative in their approach, focusing on shared power and goals will demonstrate the understandings of power upon which they are developed.[87] How success is articulated to the domestic constituency and foreign public, and in relation to previous actions by the organisation, provides a key point at which the power within public diplomacy must be considered.

An emphasis only on control, a centralised understanding of a network, and exerting "power-over" ultimately narrows the field of possibilities. These may be effective in certain situations. However at other times, alternative understandings of power within the five areas discussed, will yield different possibilities, create the potential for novel perspectives and the development of new means for exerting influence through Public Diplomacy. Power must be a key consideration in the development of future public diplomacy strategy as the navigation of the understanding of power, by the actor, audience and domestic constituency, will be fundamental to ongoing innovation of the discipline.

Ultimately the approach will begin with the question, what does the organisation want to achieve; an assertive approach which exerts "power over" a target audience to influence their behaviour as the organisation wants, or a collective approach that empowers those

---

[86] Tickner, "Hans Morgenthau's Political Principles," p. 434;
Nancy Hartsock, *Money, Sex and Power: Toward a Feminist Historical Materialism* (Northeastern University Press, 1983);
David McClelland, "Power and the Feminine Role" in David McClelland (ed.), *Power, The Inner Experience* (Wiley, 1975).

[87] Zaharna, "Mapping out a Spectrum of Public Diplomacy Initiatives".

better positioned within communities and networks, to achieve the goals they identify, where they overlap with those of the PD organisation. Is Public Diplomacy purely a tool to support the extension of an organisation's power or a means to engage and participate in the development of a genuinely shared future?

CONCLUSION

The US National Security Strategy, May 2010, sets out the strategy to make "America stronger and more secure" through "global leadership". While the strategy recognises the importance of international cooperation, it envisages a modernisation of US diplomatic capabilities to ensure America is "steering" rather than participating in that cooperation.[1]

In March 2010 Judith McHale, the US Assistant Secretary of State for Public Diplomacy and Public Affairs, declared, "To meet the challenges and seize the opportunities of the 21st century, we need a foreign policy that uses tools and approaches to match a changing global landscape of engagement".[2]

The essays in the volume raise the issue of whether the dilemmas facing Public Diplomacy can be alleviated by the succession of an Administration which features "engagement" in its political rhetoric. As Philip Seib wrote in response to the plan for Public Diplomacy unveiled by the Obama White House:

> U.S. public diplomacy has remained in the doldrums even with Barack Obama at the helm. That doesn't appear to be changing. The "strategic imperatives" laid out in this plan are tired bromides: "shape the narrative; expand and strengthen people-to-people relationships; combat violent extremism; better inform policy-making; deploy resources in line with current priorities". Wow.
>
> The document says this framework "is the first phase of a process for developing a detailed strategic plan for Public Diplomacy". But if the detailed plan is to be based on this framework, why bother?[3]

If there is an "opportunity to redefine Public Diplomacy in a way that will have a lasting impact in this new century", those involved will have to change mindset, approach, organisational structure, and skills.

---

[1] US National Security Strategy, May 2010, http://www.whitehouse.gov/sites/default/files/rss_viewer/national_security_strategy.pdf

[2] Judith McHale, Public Diplomacy: Strengthening U.S. Engagement with the World, March 2010 http://uscpublicdiplomacy.org/pdfs/PD_US_World_Engagement.pdf

[3] Philip Seib, "US Public Diplomacy's Flimsy New Framework", USC CPD blog, 8 March 2010 http://uscpublicdiplomacy.org/index.php/newswire/cpdblog_detail/us_public_diplomacys_flimsy_new_framework/

McHale was correct to highlight, "The global challenges we face today require a complex, multi-dimensional approach to public diplomacy"; however, this multi-dimensional approach means working within a network of exchange rather than an ego-sphere of influence. In her speech, given to State Department officials, McHale used "audience" repeatedly, but did not mention cooperation, collaboration or collective goals.[4]

The tension is highlighted by McHale's observation, "We have a chance to remake American leadership, establishing a new paradigm of strength in partnership for the common good." This will only be "new" if the focus is on how America can work *with* others. This requires asking the right questions and searching for genuine collaboration, rather than asserting that the US is *bound* or has the *power to lead*; in the 21st Century, as power is dispersed, others are not bound to follow.

Collaboration for the Public Diplomacy of tomorrow

Organisation

The difficulty of creating a coherent organisation, in which bureaucratic structure reflects the rhetorical approach, is of particular importance. The Public Diplomat can be advisor rather than subordinate advocate only if he/she is seen as a conduit through which the perspective of others can pass to identify shared challenges and collective goals. Advice cannot be limited to how a message will "play" with an audience, and there is no point being in on "takeoffs" if the advice focuses on making the takeoff look nice rather than providing input into the flight path. To adopt the Public Diplomacy of the future, the US will have to organise the bureaucracy in a way which shows genuine commitment to working in collaboration.

Language

The forms of language individuals adopt provide insight into their conception of the world. In the case of contemporary US public diplomacy, this language often reflects an underlying (though occasionally explicit) assumption that initiatives will work best if America is

[4] Judith McHale, *PUBLIC DIPLOMACY TODAY, 2009 Global PAO Conference.*

leading. Often these perspectives are of a world where American goals are presented as those for the common good and thus universal. This may work well for an audience at home; however, while those in the overseas "audience" may well agree with elements of the argument, assertion of American leadership may well undermine their willingness or ability to engage.

The Public Diplomacy of tomorrow is more than adopting a listening posture to ensure you know how others hear you, allowing a further refinement of your message. This is fundamentally different from asking the right questions, listening for an answer, and assessing the opportunity to collaborate on the basis of the response.

Personnel

A new public diplomacy requires the ability to work in partnership and places the emphasis on different skills, perhaps even different personnel, from those associated with image or message projection. To use Daryl Copeland's phrase, 21st century diplomacy cannot be conducted by those who flap like a fish out of water as soon as they step outside the embassy.

Stakeholders and Local Knowledge

The ability to identify the right people with whom to engage requires an approach which recognises the importance of different stakeholders. Initially it may not appear efficient to consult widely when an organisation already knows what it wants to achieve. That, however, is an assertive approach which ignores the benefit of access to local knowledge and nuance. Many initiatives have failed due to a lack of such knowledge, either from missing specific information or from framing the "other" merely as an "audience".

Even terms such as "trust" are culturally contingent. As such, public diplomacy needs to engage stakeholders in participative planning and evaluation rather than projecting itself onto recipients.

A Public Project

Given the redistribution of power in the 21st Century, the ability to engage with communities and networks of influence is likely to rest on a mindset which recognises the development of an initiative as a public project. This means planning "in the open" rather than developing an initiative or strategy within Government offices and then presenting it in a nice-looking PowerPoint. In the US this is likely to require at the very least modification of the Smith-Mundt Act if American Public Diplomacy is to genuinely embrace the future of engagement.[5]

Constructing a strategy, narrative, or identity and then trying to persuade others to adopt it depends on external motivation rather than more successful intrinsic motivation; the sense of involvement in the development of an initiative has been shown to lead to greater levels and longevity of adherence. Effective public diplomacy requires a change of approach which focuses on means to increase the likelihood of cooperation rather than the identification new tools to herd an audience into a cathedral you have already built. As RS Zaharna says, "impressive numbers in reaching international audiences have not translated into any measurable support for U.S. policies"..."Yesterday, the communicator with the most information won. Today, the one with the most extensive and strongest network wins."[6]

Power of the Network

The way that "power" is understood will influence whether public diplomats can move to a collaborative approach. If power is constructed as the ability to decide the answer and making others follow, then Public Diplomacy, through an ego-sphere of influence, will make all others subordinate to a set of aims. Those others will experience external pressure to think or act in a particular way—however attractive the presentation of the idea—rather than an appeal to a more sustainable intrinsic motivation.

This view of Public Diplomacy understands the international environment of a network of interconnected communities and interests. To engage effectively, public diplomats will have to shed the idea of a network centred around them and recognise that they are only one group in a network of influence.

This emphasis on collaboration is not a blinding of the public diplomat to objectives for the sake of developing relationships; it is a blend of the relationship-building approach with the realisation of key

[5] Matt Armstrong has been one of the most vocal critics of the Smith-Mundt Act through MountainRunner.us.

[6] RS Zaharna, "The Network Paradigm of Strategic Public Diplomacy", *Foreign Policy In Focus*, September 2005.

goals. Laurie Wilson highlights the distinction between relationships and action;

> It is important for practitioners to devote some time to identifying and building relationships, or they will forever be caught in the reactive mode of addressing immediate problems with no long-term vision or coordination of strategic efforts. It is like being trapped in a leaky boat: If you spend all your time bailing and none of it rowing, you will never get to shore.[7]

In a cooperative-based initiative, all those in the boat organise so they can pool their efforts and row together. The identification and development of relationships is an important part of the process of agreement not only on who is bailing and who is rowing but also to which shore everyone rowing. All may want to be captain, but if each shouts that he/she knows the answer and everyone else should paddle at his/her command, the voices and water level will most likely continue to rise. The most efficient way forward is to find a method for all to cooperate on getting to shore rather than being in command.

However, amidst growth evidence of a "wealth of networks", this is just the start.[8] Public Diplomacy will require "a substantial degree of interconnectedness" and emphasis on "openness and transnational cooperation".[9] Its future rests upon multi- and interdisciplinary research to find the most effective strategies for developing cooperation. This in itself will be a collaborative endeavour; it is time to practice rather than preach.

---

[7] Laurie J Wilson, "Strategic Cooperative Communities: A synthesis of Strategic, Issue-Management, and Relationship-Building Approaches in Public Relations", in Hugh M Culbertson and Ni Chen (eds), International Public Relations: A Comparative Analysis (Mahwah NJ: Lawrence Erlbaum, 1996) p. 78.

[8] Yockai Benkler, *Wealth of networks*, (Yale 2006).

[9] Robert Cooper, *The Breaking of Nations: Order and Chaos in the Twenty-First Century* (London: Atlantic Books, 2003) p. 76.

INDEX